The
PARIS
we love

THE WORLD IN COLOR SERIES

FRANCE : Paris and the Provinces
SWITZERLAND
GREAT BRITAIN : England, Scotland, and Wales
ITALY
THE UNITED STATES
BELGIUM AND LUXEMBURG
THE NETHERLANDS

THE WORLD IN COLOR

THE
PARIS
WE LOVE

edited by
DORÉ OGRIZEK

Introduction by
Jean Cocteau

McGRAW-HILL BOOK COMPANY, INC.
New York   London   Toronto

THE PARIS WE LOVE

Printed in France

CONTENTS

INTRODUCTION by Jean Cocteau.   7

ART IN PARIS by Jean Desternes.   9

PARIS IN FORMER TIMES, by René Héron de Villefosse,
illustrated by G. Annenkov.   59

THE ISLANDS, by Maurice Garçon, *of the Académie Française*,
illustrated by R. Joël.   97

FROM THE HALLES TO THE MARAIS, by Jacques Perret,
illustrated by Beuville.   117

THE PALAIS-ROYAL, THE LOUVRE AND THE TUILERIES,
by Jacques Wilhelm and Yvan Christ, illustrated by I. Arnstam and Galanis *of the Institute*.   137

THE FAUBOURG SAINT-GERMAIN, by Jules Romains *of
the Académie Française*, illustrated by André Beaurepaire.   169

SAINT-GERMAIN-DES-PRÉS, by André Salmon, illustrated by
Denise de Bravura.   183

THE LATIN QUARTER, by Léo Larguier *of the Académie Goncourt*, illustrated by Marc Doelnitz.   201

MONTPARNASSE, by André Warnod, illustrated by Cyril.   221

THE OPERA AND THE CENTRE, by Louis Chéronnet, illustrat-
ed by Bernard Villemot.   241

UNDER THE SIGN OF SAINT MARTIN, by André Beucler,
illustrated by Grau-Sala.   265

THE DOMAIN OF THE PARISIENNE, by Lucien François,
illustrated by Monica.   287

THE BALLAD OF THE CHAMPS-ÉLYSÉES, by Paul Gilson,
illustrated by Brenet.   313

THE INVALIDES AND THE CHAMP-DE-MARS, by Marcel
Brion, illustrated by Guillaume Gillet.   329

CHAILLOT, PASSY, AUTEUIL, by Francis de Miomandre, illustrated by Bernard Milleret.   345

THE BOIS DE BOULOGNE AND NEUILLY, by André Maurois *of the Académie Française*, illustrated by Michel Ciry.   363

THE PLAINE MONCEAU, by Jean-Louis Vaudoyer, *of the Académie Française,* illustrated by Philippe Jullian.   379

MONTMARTRE, by Pierre Lestringuez, illustrated by Touchagues.   397

FROM BELLEVILLE TO GRENELLE, by Philippe Lefrançois, B. Nabonne and Yves Gandon, illustrated by Fontanarosa, R. de Villepreux and Chancel.   417

THE QUAYS AND THE BRIDGES, by Pierre Mac Orlan, *of the Académie Goncourt*, illustrated by Dignimont.   463

PARIS, THE HOME OF THE EPICURE, by Jean Oberlé, illustrated by himself.   483

PARIS NIGHTS, by A.-M. Max, illustrated by R. de La¥ererie; with a list of the theatres.   497

Plates by : de Berroetta, D. Bouchène, R. Chapelain-Midy, Delaunay, Othon Friesz, Monique Jorgensen, Kisling, Berthe Morisot, Pissarro, Quizet, Renoir, Rousseau, Signac, J. Thévenet, Utrillo, Van Dongen, et H. de Waroquier.

End-Papers by A. Serebriakoff, from a 17th century Gobelin tapestry. Title pages designed by E. M. Perot.

Maps by Lucien Boucher, I. Arnstam and A. Serebriakoff.

CHERISH THE SPECTRES
OF THE PAST

*P*aris is a city of seven hills, and even more. *Montmartre, Montsouris, Montparnasse, Mont Valérien, les Buttes-Chaumont, Montagne Saint-Geneviève... there are more besides.*

On and among these hills are the towns which together make the City herself. Towns and villages. For instance, the Palais-Royal, where I live, is a small town surrounded by walls. To return to the real city you have to climb stairways; you must push open gates of iron; you must make your way through vaulted corridors.

In my film Orpheus *I created an imaginary city, using the districts of Paris taken out of their true setting. In doing so, I discovered towns and villages previously unknown.*

Foreigners know Paris better than we do. They look at her with different eyes, and in their case familiarity has not dimmed the scene. It is not unusual for a foreigner to enlighten us about the secrets which surround our daily lives.

It is just the same when we visit them in their own countries. They think that we form fanciful pictures of their cities; in fact, we see them only as they should see them.

Paris, however—because of her purely fortuitous beauty, because of the old things which have become a part of her, because of her entanglement of buildings and tenements—Paris yields herself to discovery as an attic beloved in our childhood gave up its secrets. The meanest street offers glimpses of paddock and farms. Vast expanses of waste land, peopled only by gipsy caravans, surmount a troubled sea of mist and stone, where in the hubbub of the city, steep stairways plunge downwards into tiny gardens. Balzac, cast in bronze clings to the wreck. Waves of stone and light menace him. He resists; and my heart is wrung each time a plank is loosened and torn away from his raft.

We love the remains of this raft which they are determined to destroy. The public authorities who carry out this destruction do not understand that they are squandering a treasure, and that new things need the relief of contrast with the old.

The ruins of various quarters fill us with wonder, but only beauty ages well. As with the ruins of the Marais, so with those of St. Cyr; we are amazed by the majesty of their outline.

That Paris should spread, that new districts should be built is right and proper. But it is a tragedy to destroy places that witnessed famous deeds, events and pageants, from whose ghosts the very atmosphere of a city is created.

It is true that the pick-axe can never quite vanquish these ghosts, for, if their haunts disappear, they will still seek them, and will enwrap our own spirits in an enchanted mist.

Jean Cocteau

ART
IN PARIS

JEAN FOUQUET. — *St. Margaret and Olibrius.*

THE MIDDLE AGES

UITE naturally it is to Paris that we turn for a general view of French Art. We can follow its course from the Cluny Museum and Notre-Dame to the Museum of Modern Art—six centuries of artistic endeavour.

At the Louvre, surmounted by grinning gargoyles, are the stiff, recumbent effigies of the priest, the noble lady in her wimple, the warrior in coat of mail, beneath his battle-shield. Illustrious kings are there—the elegant Childebert with his trim beard, pulling nonchalantly at the girdle of his red mantle, and the good-natured Charles V whose somewhat sly benevolence contrasts with the haughty imperiousness of his tightly-corseted spouse. There is also the procession of saints—the elegant Valerie amid her seraphs, holding her severed head against her arched bodice, the hair trailing down her immaculate robe. Saint James appears as a pilgrim on his way to Compostella, his pouch by his side, his hat bedecked with a shell. Saint John of the Calvary of Loché in Touraine, stylised in pure lines carved from light wood, is a miracle of faith and serenity in face of sorrow. The Seneschal of Burgundy, Philip Pot, stretched out in stiff black armour, sleeps his last, his head resting on a pink cushion flecked with gold, his feet propped against his faithful dog, in the midst of eight mourners in sombre hoods.

The whole of medieval sculpture had its place in the sanctuary and we can still read on the portals of Notre-Dame the long story of the Bible in the form of images. The stonework reveals the fate meted out to the good and to the wicked—hell's fumes or the paradise of the elect. Episodes from the life of Christ and the Virgin, miracles, galleries of saints, but also scenes from the lives of scholars of the University, and the sufferings of the strumpet caught up on a ladder. We see the reaper sharpening his scythe, and the other tasks of the seasons, punctuated by the signs of the Zodiac. It is the " wonder of the world " among the cathedrals of France. We can go to the Palais de Chaillot to see the panels of Moissac and Vézelay reconstructed in the Museum of French Monuments, as well as the finest examples of Romanesque frescoes : the blues and ochres of Saint Julien de Brioude, the delicate pink of Saint-Savin, the grass, the gold, the outpoured blood, on the vaults of country churches.

Saint Jean de Loché.

Student Life (Notre-Dame de Paris).

In the Parisian tapestries we discover other harmonies, other ladies in 15th century head-dresses, woven against a background of blue meadows where fresh waters flow, where the ladies' mantles and the tunics of their cavaliers have scarcely faded, in their dream landscape.

The craftsmen in stained glass who made the Sainte Chapelle a shrine of light glowing with azure, fire and sunshine, and those who gave its glory to the great rose-window of Notre-Dame, bear comparison with the craftsmen of Chartres and Bourges. And the oldest stained glass of all is in the Basilica of Saint-Denis, dating from the days of the builder-bishop, Suger. In their sphere, too, the Parisian illuminators embellished the margins of their manuscripts with azure fields, jewels and flowers. As the prerogative of the clergy, illumination was at first hieratic; later it became an increasingly dainty pastime; little scenes came to life, illustrating the customs of the times. With Fouquet and Bourdichon it reached the heights of perfection : the artist inscribed his vision of the world in miniature form, just as he might depict it in an easel painting.

Very often medieval painters were also "miniaturists;" we discover the delicate style of the Breviary of Belleville, of Jean Pucelle, in the *Parement de Narbonne* which describes the scenes of the Passion in neutral tints, on silk. Another great work of illumination is the Martyrdom of Saint Denis which Jean Malouel carried out by commission of the Duke of Burgundy at the end of the 14th century. Against a backcloth of gold, between two saints of Montmartre—Rusticus, already beheaded, and Eleutherus—the great, bearded executioner raises his menacing axe to cleave the block; fair, smiling angels circle round the dark trickle of blood flowing from the crucified martyr.

The Louvre possesses the first known French portrait, that of King John the Good, on a wooden panel overlaid with plaster. It may have been done by Girard d'Orléans at the time when his royal model was a captive in London—at the beginning of the Hundred Years' War.

A contemporary of Jeanne d'Arc, Jean Fouquet, has left us a speaking

Fragment of a stained-glass window in the Sainte Chapelle.

JEAN FOUQUET. — *Charles VII.*

likeness of Charles VII. Huddled into his wadding of red velvet, his blasé air emphasised by the thick under-lip, the tired eyes, the long red nose, he nevertheless wears with dignity his heavy hat, zigzagged with golden braid. Fouquet also worked for two influential personages, the Chancellor Juvénal des Ursins, puffed up by his own vanity; for Etienne Chevalier, his second patron, he undertook to illustrate one of the finest books in the world, the " Book of the Hours," which was torn to pieces. Forty of its pages are preserved in the Museum of Chantilly—while, near the *Battle*

MAITRE DE MOULINS. — *St. Mary Magdalene.*

of Cannes and the *Coronation of Alexander*, the Louvre exhibits " Saint Martin sharing his cloak with a beggar on the Pont-au-Change," and, in a placid Touraine landscape, St. Margaret at her distaff while General Olibrius rides up on his white horse.

At the Louvre again, near the *Pietà* of Villeneuve—depicting in stylised form a sorrowing group against a golden background—we find works of the " Northern School " such as the *Miracle of the True Cross*, revealing a slender nude; and, by the Maître de Moulins, a charming *Magdalene*— the lady donor at her side—showing us how frank the artists of that time could be.

The Diana of Anet.

THE RENAISSANCE

AFTER the mad escapade of Charles VIII and Louis XII's repulse by the warrior pope, Julius II, France had to pay dearly enough for the bellicose whims of those empire-dreamers. But the disappointed army that returned from Italy, considerably reduced in numbers, brought back in their waggons the artistic seeds of the century, and manners and fashions, arts and letters, became Italianised. It was Francis I who transplanted the Florentine and Venetian cuttings into French gardens.

Between the reigns of Louis XI and Henry IV French Art changed profoundly. In place of the scowling dungeons of Plessis-lès-Tours there arose richly ornamented façades, set against a background of arti-

16

ficial lakes, staircases, like that at Blois, or that architectural extravagance, that royal caprice, Chambord. The entire Italian colony brought in by Francis I displayed on the walls and ceilings at Fontainebleau the iridescent grandeur of its mythology.

Every step forward marks a tendency towards over-refinement—in sculpture above all.

The Huguenot, Jean Goujon, succeeded in being the most Greek of sculptors, and yet remained the most French of them all. In his nymphs on the Fountain of the Innocents, he gave a liquid quality to marble veins, and attained the mere suggestion of a breeze caressing the long arms of those beautiful maidens. Whether he was arranging his allegories to decorate a façade or to support a cornice (as he did with his Caryatides at the Louvre), within the narrow confines of architecture his chisel achieves a maximum of grace. But where he excels is in the cool, slender freshness of his nudes. His Diana and the Stag, sculptured for Henry II in the court of the castle of Anet, shows her languishing beneath cascades of water flowing from the horns of the stag and the mouths of the hounds. " That's Greek ! Greek, not Italian ! " exclaimed David of Angers.

Two of his contemporaries were to achieve fame through two works, both funereal but in different ways—Ligier Richier of Lorraine by his skeleton on the tomb of René de Chalon, that coy, emaciated

JEAN GOUJON.

The Fountain of the Innocents.

17

The Duke of Alençon.

figure who offers his bleeding heart to heaven—and Roger Bontemps, who strove to depict everything " according to historical truth "— following the terms of his contract. To that end he conjured up both the pikemen of Marignan and the engaging serving-maids with their sprightly mien. About 1560, at a time when it was not healthy to be a Protestant, they became, like Jean Goujon, " religious fugitives " and went into exile. It was then that an artist of 25 appeared—Germain Pilon. Through him the renown of French sculpture lasted until the end of the century. At Saint-Denis he executed a magnificent effigy of Henry II and of his young widow, Catherine de Médicis, naked, but lifelike—with the royal pair enthroned above in coronation robes. The king's heart is borne by three charming graces. On the tomb of the Chancellor, René de Birague, he firmly set an image of the old man, kneeling, and was as meticulous in portraying his model's arthritis as in displaying on his frail shoulders the heavy folds of the ceremonial mantle.

This desire to perceive and depict the individuality of the model as exactly as possible is found in the painting of this period. It was the age of subtle portraiture. The 16th century chronicles are the more alive to us because—to a fine degree of accuracy—we are familiarized with the features of the great men of the day, portrayed at times with malicious candour. This is certainly true of the kings : Francis I with his long nose and lively face, the toque with the ostrich feather cocked over his perfumed hair, a necklace streaking the black and white satin of his low-necked doublet. François Clouet also portrayed the disquieting Henry II : his shapely leg, fist on hip, glowering eye, and scornful sulk above his short goatee. " Eyebrow daunting the

Elizabeth of Austria.

boldest, eyebrown brown e'en in the blackest darkness," sang the poet Maurice Scève. And then there is Charles IX with his pearl-decked hat and earrings dangling on his well-fluted ruff—the same frothy collar as was worn by the handsomest Columbines of the period, and such as graced the neck of his gentle wife, Elizabeth, daughter of the Emperor Maximilian—a very good and wise woman, Brantôme tells us, who talked very little, and then only in her native Spanish. Portraits of royalty and all the princes of the blood are there; fair damsels, duped husbands, rough captains and warriors in lace, courtesans and favourites, and even that worthy Pierre Quthe, the apothecary of the Rue Sainte Avoie who had such a fine garden. Cup-bearers, comptrollers, commanders, the master of the wardrobe or the country squire, each is portrayed there "true to life."

THE
17TH CENTVRY

THE phrase " The Great Century " at once conjures up the memory of Versailles and the brilliance of Louis XIV. But it was only in the mid-17th century that the celebrated Academy of Louis XIV was founded, which was to become the most elaborate enterprise of State publicity. The fertile elements of classical art can be discovered much earlier and the greatest painters of the century are almost all " Louis XIII ": Poussin, Claude, Georges de la Tour, Philippe de Champaigne and the Le Nain. So also are the two engravers, Jacques Callot and Abraham Bosse; Callot, the champion of beggars, gypsies and troopers who gave such a detailed record of the horrors of war, the showmen of the Pont Neuf and the mummers of the Italian comedy; Bosse, who scrupulously noted the studied gestures and well-bred gallantry shown by his "Bourgeois," either at home or out walking beneath the "*Galerie du Palais.*"

"I have neglected nothing," Poussin proudly affirmed. And the best example this exile set was in his professional conscience and integrity. Most of his work was painted in Rome, in his little house on the Pincio; he only returned to Paris when recalled by the king, staying at the Louvre for a brief period of a year and nine months. In his severe self-portrait in the Louvre, the knitted brows appear from beneath long hair parted in the centre; his dark eyes, set between reddened lids, fix their dreamy gaze beyond this world. From the black satin emerges a ringed hand, clutching a pink-ribboned portfolio, whilst in the background arises the smiling figure of a fair attendant of Flora...

For he applied his scrupulous talent to illustrate the great myths of antiquity. He loved to set in contrast the wild dances of the Dryads to the peaceful groups of people reclining in the quiet repose of a drowsy countryside at the approach of twilight. We see a leaping Bacchus in his leopard-skin, and Narcissus asleep beside the fountain. He depicted all kinds of religious subjects too, which people liked to say were insufficiently Christian : perhaps because he refused to paint Christ, as he used to say, "wry-necked, or looking like a mollycoddled priest." However, his two masterpieces in the Louvre, which alone were almost sufficient to establish his reputation, are the two perfect compositions, *The Poet's Inspiration* and *Arcadian Shepherds*, which are summed up in one word—harmony.

COYSEVOX. — *The Great Condé.*

Claude Gelée, known as "Le Lorrain," also spent a long period of his life in Rome. Like the Norman Poussin, he yielded to the antiquarian illusion. But he lacked Poussin's culture ; he meditated less, relying more on his native instinct— and this made him the greatest

NICOLAS POUSSIN. — *The Poet's Inspiration.*

French landscape painter prior to Corot. Son of a peasant family of the Moselle, he went to Italy with one of his relatives silk merchants. He experienced poverty and was often a vagrant before he settled down in Rome. There he painted countless pictures of the magic of the setting sun against the rigging of outward bound sailing ships, and blue valleys with murmuring cascades.

Before the advent of the court painters, who arrayed in tender hues the lords and nobles of Louis XIV's reign, there appeared that astonishing portrait painter, Philippe de Champaigne, who depicted Louis XII in his black breastplate, and the great " Scarlet Man, " Richelieu, with his emaciated triangle of a face posed upon the large inverted triangle of his cardinal's purple. He also left us less official portraits, notably those of the Jansenists of Port-Royal : the two nuns, for instance, with large red crosses on their white robes—a scene illustrating a solemn episode in his own life and in that of the Jansenist movement. The young woman who has just taken the veil is his own daughter, miraculously saved by the good graces of Mother Agnès Arnauld, who is portrayed by her side. She had, by her prayers, healed the young girl of paralysis, and so the picture in the Louvre is the happiest of votive offerings.

One of the most remarkable painters of that epoch was totally unknown until a short time ago. Like Vermeer, he rose from the shadow of oblivion to the front rank. Was he at any time in Italy ? Georges de la Tour certainly hardly moved from Lunéville, but he must have known something of the work of Caravaggio, and perhaps of Zurbaran. He too shut his windows to paint in an enclosed room, shifting the position of the torch to find new and thrilling lighting effects. But he makes a restrained use of these sources of light, to enhance a scene or to simplify the lines—as if it were for him but a way of getting behind his subject, to probe its very essence. His only setting was light against bare shadows. His *Nativity* consists of five psychological studies of faces turned towards the Child, who seems to be the very source of light of the whole Vigil, and in whom converge all the lines, attentions, emotions — offerings, prayers, amazement, smiles, loving care. Like Vermeer in his

G. DE LA TOUR
St. Jerome

treatment of humble folk, he immobilises them in silence and makes a calm face radiate intense life. More silently still, he brings out of the night an oval face or the curve of a shoulder, dense shadow lending fulness to the forms. Streaks of vermilion red amid browns and violets emphasize a gesture—the conscious hesitation of an arm before it falls—skilful shading forming the relief of a brow—fingers joined in prayer, outstretched in affliction. A painter of silence, concentrating on the essential, forgetting the inessential, La Tour sometimes imparts to us the magic charms by which he has made eternal a moment of inspiration.

In 1629 the three Le Nain brothers were living together in Paris in the St. Sulpice district. In 1648, just after Le Brun had founded the Royal Academy, Louis and Antoine died within two days of each other in their studio, while Mathieu survived them by 29 years. These three brothers lived during the age of preciosity, at the time of *Julie's Garland* and Arthénice's *Blue Room*. Unlike their contemporaries, they proved themselves to be sincere painters of reality, and their canvases—called "daubings" by the people of that age— provide racy commentaries on country folk, taken from life, and are for us infinitely more captivating legacies than the allegories of the adroit decorators of Versailles. Painting in somewhat pallid tones, relieved here and there by a yellow shawl, by the blue serge of a tunic or the pink of a young rogue's smock,—or again, by the ruby-red of claret sparkling in the Sunday glass of wine; here we are introduced as friends into a rustic interior, received by the whole family—the day-labourers settle round the hearth, the imp-faced child continues to play on his pipe... There is also the blacksmith at his forge, and the farmyard where the haycrop has just been stacked.

These three bachelors, who worked in such close partnership that they adopted the same signature without their Christian names, remained outside official art circles—which were to be so richly orchestrated—for the greater

LE NAIN. — *A Peasant Family.*

glory of the " Roi Soleil " around whom Versailles grew to grandeur.
Le Brun returned from Rome with nostalgia for the ceilings of the Farnese
Palace. He swelled all the sails of mythology in glorification of Louis XIV.
We have to admire his genius for inspiring others rather than the ingenuity of his own allegories—for those magnificent tapestries on which
the Gobelins' workshops were for long years to be kept busy—and for
the part he played in embellishing Versailles. For despite the fact that
work was done to commission, artists succeeded in imposing their
personal ideas.

THE 18TH CENTVRY

CLODION. — *Young Girl Asleep.*

Louis XV, confronted with the gigantic suites of Versailles, had small drawing-rooms and comfortable boudoirs arranged there for himself. Mme. de Pompadour installed her sheep-folds in the parks of the Trianon. In the same way 18th century art embedded itself in the flounces of Louis XIV's day: a little more powder on the wigs, a more marked coquetry in the ladies' frills and furbelows, and much less restraint in manners. Seen from afar, and especially in contrast to the gory upheaval of 1789, it was a perpetual festival; grand parties and concerts in the gardens, scandalous conversations where idle prattle was seasoned by the mandoline.

Boucher and Fragonard disclose the secrets of the alcove. La Tour and Perronneau sketch the mocking smile of the wags of the day, and Greuze imparts a seductive naivety to his young ladies of fashion. But there is also Watteau's melancholy, Houdon's graceful sense of balance, and Chardin's calm integrity. Sculpture developed in the direction of the " rococo " style from the moment that Guillaume Coustou sent his " Horses of Marly " bounding into the sky, and Robert Le Lorrain unleashed even more fiery steeds, rearing and prancing in the sun above the stable door of the Hôtel de Rohan. If the painted or sculptured portraits sometimes betray feverishness, and if the eye is questioning, the mouth smiles. It is the smile that we find in all the heads of J. B. Lemoyne; at the Louvre : Réaumur and the architect of the Place de la Concorde, Ange Gabriel; at the Comédie Française, Mlle. Clairon— all the nuances of the smile, from the naive to the sardonic. Similarly Clodion, who was a " genre " sculptor, knew how to express all the shades of youthful charm in his fresh young subjects, as delightful in their roguish postures as in their slumber. Under the Regency and Louis XV, the position of artists changed. Thus La Tour was able to take liberties with grandees that would have been unthinkable in the preceding reign. He allowed himself to be impertinent even with the king, and had to be entreated to go to Versailles ("I don't go to town to paint"). Two years after the first sketches were done, he returned to finish the portrait of La Pompadour : he had just taken off his wig,

G. COUSTOU. — *Marie Leczinska.*

WATTEAU. — " *L'Indifférent* ".

his garters and the buckles of his shoes to be more at ease, when the king came in—"You promised, Madame, that your door would remain closed." The king apologised and promised to keep quiet. But La Tour put on his wig and his garters again—"I find it impossible to obey your Majesty. I will return when Madame is alone. I don't at all like being interrupted."

Things had changed, and even Largillière, after a time, deserted the court to paint the wealthy bourgeois. Twenty-five years earlier Watteau would have been employed to decorate the ceilings at Versailles. Now when he arrived from Valenciennes at the age of 17 and established contact with the Flemish colony in the Faubourg Saint-Germain, Watteau was engaged to paint theatrical scenery. Later he worked for the wealthy financier Croizat, an experienced collector with whom he learnt to love Titian, Veronese and Rubens. In 1715 the young man, then 28, was accepted by the Academy, with his sketch for *The Embarkation for Cytherea*, which he finished only five years later. He died at 37, having given new trends to French art. For twelve years his feverish hand resolutely pursued an unattainable dream : for, to his eyes, his finest masterpieces were mere sketches. To his mind, reality should be taken apart and re-moulded into lyrical ballets, on the lines of those *"amours déguisées"* which gave the evenings at the Palais Royal their charm.

Unremittingly he sought the poetic element in reality; he filled his notebooks with quick sketches for later use in his compositions, where fantasy creates a world of its own—and a very real one—in which sturdy trees appear out of an almost imperceptible haze, and where music seems to vibrate in the dank leaves—such as roused the admiration of the youthful Renoir.

All his short life he fought against illness and melancholy; his cough prevented him from sleeping; he constantly moved house in search of a spot where he could forget himself, sometimes escaping for months at a time in quest of solitude—all this to create works of art that were supreme and smiling in spite of all. While the frivolous world gave itself up to festivities, and couples prompted each other to journey to the Island of Love, the virtuous Watteau remained aloof, soothing his melancholy with music from afar. He is so sure of himself as he arrays his clusters of maidens, dainty as flowers, and his amorous tight-rope walkers, so dear to him throughout his work, and through whom he was able to

F. BOUCHER. — *Diana at the Bathing Pool.*

immortalise his own dream personality. We see Gilles with his arms
dangling—a weakling, whose listlessness might well turn to cynicism,
but of whom we know very little, beyond the fact that he is withdrawn
into his dream. And then, in very subdued tones, gliding across the
scene towards little Finette with her mandoline, is the carefree boy, neither
insolent nor indolent, yet at the same time a little of both.

Boucher, a born decorator, could equally well adorn a carriage door or
a screen in a boudoir, remount a sky on a ceiling, peopling it with hordes
of chubby cupids, or strew a trinket-box with roses. A decorator,
certainly, but David uttered a loud exclamation when some one made a
show of disparaging Boucher in his presence : " Steady, sir ! It's not
everyone who can be a Boucher !". He brings us Chinese festivals,
Venetian and Parisian festivals too, for he knows how to give a bronze
glow to the unveiled body of the waiting-maid, or to reveal the voluptuous

radiance of Diana, her shivering foot brushing the edge of the lake in which she is to bathe.

Chardin is the observant admirer of everyday things—stone, porcelain, hare's fur, the flesh of skate, (" That's flesh, that is—that's blood ! " exclaimed Diderot), the lemon beside the oysters, the spectacle-case and the wool of a skirt. Like Cézanne, he is capable of being moved by an apple, and it was the latter who, at table, making a glass sparkle, growled : " What a cunning devil that Chardin was, with his eye-shade. " For one always imagines him as he portrayed himself at the age of 76, in his night-cap, a green eye-shade protecting those eyes that peered so mali-

CHARDIN. — *The Spinning Top*.

FRAGONARD. — *Inspiration.*

ciously through thick spectacles. But the young carpenter's son achieved enviable renown with his *La Raie* and *Le Buffet*, two still life compositions which he exhibited in the Salon in the Place Dauphine. They say it was as the result of a challenge from his friend Aved that he began figure painting. The former, who painted portraits, one day hurled at him: " You imagine that it is as easy as painting stuffed tongue or saveloy ! ". Chardin, piqued by this, began *The Servant drawing water at a fountain.* Thus came into being the series, so excellent in their genial simplicity, painted in his little apartment in the Rue Princesse. In those tranquil interiors we see the *Pourvoyeuse*, back from the market, cleaning her vegetables. The little girl, who has to say grace before beginning her meal, is already a coquette. Chardin loved children, providing they were not too noisy, and he depicted them busy playing "goose," in front of a house of cards, or, like the son of Geoffroy the jeweller, enthralled by the spinning of an ivory top.

Greuze almost brought to the point of perversion the unlaced bodices of his round-shouldered, weeping maidens, and the lifted petticoats of his conventional dairy-maids. But Fragonard seems the more typical painter of the 18th century. He blends Watteau's grace with Boucher's gallantry, the alertness of La Tour and Perronneau, masters of pastel colouring, with the mannerisms of the fashionable painters like the Tocqués and the Nattiers—so clever in the art of stiffening the bodice. In a word, he portrays the peculiarities of the "precious" age. This son of a comely glove-maker of Grasse died in 1806, struck by lightning while eating an ice—a symbolic end, indeed ! After a short period with Chardin, he found his real master in Boucher. On his return from Rome, a baron commissioned him to portray his mistress from a roguish angle. He painted his celebrated *Escarpolette*, which brought him into vogue. There followed an increasing number of gallant scenes : pursuits, affectionate tussles and gentle caresses. He makes his greens and pinks shimmer, as if impetuously daubed at random—and yet each stroke is made with careful attention to the harmony of the whole. The sculptor Houdon delved deep into nature in the dissecting rooms, and his exacting demand for truth was coupled with a desire for simplicity which gave him style. " Don't go near, he bites ! " used to be said of his bust of the Abbé Aubert. He brings out with equal skill the languorous coquetry of countesses and the podgy good-naturedness of Franklin, Mirabeau's small-pox, or the " hideous smile " of Voltaire.

HOUDON. — *Voltaire.*

RUDE. — *The Marseillaise.*

THE
19TH
CENTVRY

J ACQUES-Louis David was 41 at the time the Bastille was stormed
and it was with half-hearted enthusiasm that he accepted the realiz-
ation of those theories " à la Rousseau " which he had so often
discussed with his Encyclopaedist friends. After the night of August
4th, Mme. David, dressed in white, offered her jewels on the altar of the
motherland. In 1790 the Constituant Assembly entrusted David with
the task of immortalising the " Oath of the Tennis Court," and gave him
the former church of the Feuillants as his studio. In 1793 he painted
Marat assassinated in his bath by Charlotte Corday and, by refusing all
grandiloquence, produced the masterpiece of revolutionary art that
merited the title of " the first civic *pietà.* " He suffered a short
term of imprisonment in the Luxembourg where he painted the only
landscape of his career, while, from the prison window, watching his
children coming up the avenues of the park. It seems that he wanted

to escape from himself, to forget Greeks and Romans, in his two portraits of the smiling Sériziat couple : the smart cavalier with his white-powdered hair, whip in hand, wearing fawn-coloured boots, and his wife, the sister of Mme. David, in a white dress and large straw hat, holding in her arms the wild flowers gathered during her walk.

Nowadays we prefer the David of the portraits—his vigorous sketch of the First Consul, the *Three Ladies of Ghent* whose simpering smiles greet us from the wall of the Louvre, the Courtrai magistrate's wife in her white dowager's cap, and her two ugly, drooping daughters, painted during his exile in Brussels.

For David the regicide—who successively repudiated his aristocratic and then his Robespierreian friends and threw in his lot with Napoleon —refused Louis XVIII's tempting offers—perhaps for reasons of discretion. His grandiose fresco of *The Coronation of Napoleon* established him as a painter of the Empire period, along with his pupil Gros, who, in his *Pestiférés de Jaffa*, was the precursor of Delacroix. Napoleon removing a glove to touch a pestiferous tumour on one of the dying men in the oriental hospital, or shown with pallid features riding his bay horse over the blood-stained snow, surrounded by rotting corpses, is, in Gros' conception, already the legendary prince who capers at the head of the glorious illusions of Romanticism.

Next to the fine works of Prud'hon, who continued the 18th century tradition even after the Revolution, the Louvre

L. DAVID. — *Bonaparte*.

GÉRICAULT. — *The Epsom Derby.*

possesses three portraits of women by Baron Gérard. None of them has the sparkle of his Récamier, languid in her white muslin gown. David, hearing that this seductive personality was being painted by a rival, left his brilliant sketch unfinished. It nevertheless reveals the charm of the young lady who, even at 23, was already famed for her wit and her caprice.

David's influence was beginning to wreak havoc. But at the dawn of the century a young man from Rouen grew tired of the work of his masters and his fellow-students. It was Géricault—" I didn't understand that 'painting by the yard' at all—it just made me shudder." Sensitive and restless by nature, he would have " traced the outlines with a wire ", if it were possible. Wishing to sing the praises of the Napoleonic epic, and at the same time a passionate horse-lover, he exhibited his two paintings of horsemen in the salons of 1812 and 1814 : first, the victorious officer of the guard, revealing his pent ardour; second, the wounded trooper beneath a leaden sky, expressing the tragedy of the fall of France. In his

large canvas, *The Raft of the Medusa*—a scene of a contemporary ship-
wreck—his desire for realism was so strong that he roamed the hospitals
to sketch the dead and the dying. He has also left us startling faces
of the insane, showing to what lengths his curiosity in the human race
could lead him.

One of the major disputes of 19th century French painting centred
round the great names of Ingres and Delacroix, each taken as a symbol,
waved as a banner : the former by the partisans of form, the latter by
the champions of colour. Not that Ingres despised colour; but, for

INGRES. — *The Turkish Bath.*

him, it was a mere " servant ", while form held first place as " art pure." Nor that Delacroix was a poor draughtsman : but for him the essential was harmony of tone, and, as one of his contemporaries said : " he interlaces shades of colour, breaking them up and, using his brush like a shuttle, seeks to create a fabric wherein multicoloured threads intertwine and break off continuously." While Delacroix's nudes writhe round the bed of Sardanapallos, Ingres' figures are heaped together in the warmth of his *Turkish Bath*. The line of the back is sleeker, the breasts like globes of porcelain. Ingres' sensuousness finds ready scope in the harem, as he moulds that " ideal clay " into the marmoreal hips of the " Source " or the nude of Angélique tied to her rock. Ingres remains for us the master of portraiture, from his study of M. Cordier

to that of Bertin the elder. He gives us the perfect picture of the bourgeois of the revolutionary government, as in his pencil sketch of the Forestier family—in which the young lady standing by the clavicord would have become Mme. Ingres, had he not stayed so long in Italy (eighteen years). In the Louvre again, is the portrait of Monsieur, Madame and Mademoiselle Rivière : the father seated in his study, his hand tucked in his waistcoat (it was the year of the battle of Austerlitz), with chamois garters on his crossed legs; his wife spreading out her large white shawl in

CHASSERIAU
The Two Sisters.

studied disorder against the turquoise blue of the softly-cushioned sofa; and the daughter, all innocence in her organdie dress.

Chassériau, whose drawing had the graceful outlines of Ingres', achieved the glow of Delacroix's colour in his painting. His short career was marked by a real flash of genius. He died at 37 after showing extraordinary precocity. He was a native of Saint-Dominique, and there was always something of " back yonder " in his

DELACROIX. — *Self-Portrait.*

work. Rome was for him a sepulchre. However, it was there that he painted the great preacher, Lacordaire, in reclusion at Saint Sabine. After painting the *Two Sisters*—in which Adèle interested him more particularly, with her more dream-like face and a rose in her bodice— he devoted the better part of his last years to the East, and in the salon of 1845 his *Caliph of Constantine* ranks beside Delacroix's *Sultan of Morocco.*

Delacroix was only 21 when the *Raft of the Medusa* was painted. Soon a storm broke over his head also. His *Dante and Virgil*, a scene in which the boat advances over the sulphurous waters of Hell, spelt " genius " to Thiers but " daubing " to Delécluse. At 26 Delacroix slowly worked out *The Massacre of Scio.* At the very time his canvas was being exhibited, the work of Constable—the English landscape painter—came as a revelation to him. He returned at once to the Salon, to change the character of his colours then and there—making them much brighter, and giving

his shadows a mottled clarity. Haunted by Hamlet, Faust and Don Juan, he became the real painter of Romanticism. His *Sardanapallos*, in 1827, marks the pinnacle of his fame. " Delacroix, a lake of blood haunted by evil spirits." In 1830, his *Liberty Guiding the People*, which was displayed on the barricades, was his salute to the July revolution. Two years later he jubilantly discovered " the East," whilst accompanying the embassy to the Sultan of Morocco. He brought back wonderful memories which were to provide material for a series of richly coloured works such as the *Women of Algiers*. At the age of 39 he painted his own portrait, the stocky, somewhat sallow face, the line broken by a short moustache, the eyes proud beneath rebellious locks which remained black until his death. Already he was experiencing those attacks of laryngitis that were to torture his last years. He made painting his sole mistress, as his faithful friend Baudelaire tells us. In his later work we catch a glimpse of the tremor that ran through him, and of his hankering after the outrageous; he admitted that " there was something black in his heart that had to be satisfied." He decorated the library of the National

Assembly—" a terrible hymn composed in honour of fate and of inconsolable grief." In the *Entry of the Crusaders into Jerusalem*, he gave the world one of his most powerful works, in which a beautiful captive, her hair falling in coils, bows her bronze back beneath the horses' hoofs. After his death in the little studio in the Place de Furstemberg—nowadays such a picturesque Delacroix museum—the last sentence that he wrote in his notebook was : " The first merit of a picture is to be a feast to the eye...."

Corot's artlessness—often mixed with malice—has frequently led him to be compared to La Fontaine. He certainly has the latter's freshness and spontaneous mastery. The son of a milliner in the Rue du Bac, he worked for eight years at the " Caliph of Baghdad," a draper's shop in the Rue St. Honoré. However, he succeeded in winning over his parents, and the day he was allowed to go and sketch on the banks of the Seine, all the shop-girls came to watch him in his ecstasy of meditation. Whilst in Rome, he painted several rustic masterpieces, and discovered his

DAUMIER. — *Crispin and Scapin.*

CARPEAUX. — *The Dance.*

own style and idiom for expressing the light of dawn, noon and twilight. " There is hardly any daylight left, Corot, by which to see your modest name inscribed in a dark corner. " Then he undertook a great *Tableau of France*, setting out for Auvergne, Normandy, and Avignon with his materials on his back. Later on, a haze came over his palette and the luminous clarity of his earlier work is often preferred to the diaphanous greys of the damp glades in his Ville d'Avray. It is only recently that. Corot has been placed among the great painters of women. It was he who said : " Every day I pray God to make me a child again, by which I mean that I want to see and depict nature as a child does, without bias." His friend, Daumier, a native of Marseilles who conquered Paris with the point of his pencil, was much more than an entertainer. If Gavarni gives us some amusing Parisian figures, he never aspired to the fiery vision of the creator of Robert Macaire. " You would think they were Daumiers ! " exclaimed Daubigny of the Michael Angelo frescoes in the Sistine Chapel. *La Rue Transnonain*, for example, is a great work, equal to Callot's engravings, a work that anticipates the romantic illustrations of Gustave Doré. Daumier, that *enfant terrible* of lithography, was also a painter of importance. In a scene such as a third-class carriage, or a masquerade, or a washerwoman by her window in the Ile Saint-Louis, or in the legend of Don Quixote, he recaptures something of Rembrandt's tones. It is also known that he modelled his victims in clay, and the collection of his caricatures in relief is not unworthy of the master sculptors of that time.

The latter endeavoured to follow the great tradition of Houdon, who lived long enough to do a very fine bust of Napoleon. Rude is especially renowned for his allegory of the Arc de Triomphe, his *Departure of the Volunteers of 92* to which the name of *The Marseillaise* was given because of its strident figure of " Victory. " On his return from Brussels in 1827, where his Bonapartist opinions had exiled him, this son of a Dijon blacksmith held back from Romanticism. This was not the case for David of Angers, who chiselled the medallions of all the literary and artistic glories of his time, and also—over the portico of the Pantheon—images of the Motherland, Freedom and History.

G. COURBET. — *The Model.*

Barye, who began as a goldsmith, became the best animal painter of his age. Carpeaux, the greatest sculptor of the century before Rodin, had a hard struggle against poverty. While in Rome, he began his famous little *Pêcheur à la Coquille* and, on his return, won renown as a portraitist; he executed the bust of Princess Matilda and of the architect; Garnier. But his group representing *The Dance*, over the portico of the Opera House, created a scandal. This bevy of lithe, soaring bodies seemed too bacchanalian for the Second Empire. It was not until after the war of 1870 that he was able to carry out his *Four Parts of the World*, for the fountain in the Observatory Gardens.

Gustave Courbet lines up all the principal elements of his painting to incorporate them in his large demonstration canvas, *The Painter's Studio* :

an allegory based on his work over a period of seven years. By his side is a nude, as stocky in form as his *Baigneuses*; on his easel is a landscape of Franche-Comté with its dense woods and rocky soil, opening up a view as from a window; on the left, social life— those who are exploited, and those who make their living from the death of others : an Irish girl in tatters, and a huntsman filling his pipe; on the right, behind a lady in a shawl, is Baudelaire reading the newspaper; finally, in the centre, the broad shoulders of the master, brush in hand. This generous-natured man preached the gospel of realism—putting the artist at the service of truth in however humble a form. " If you want me to paint goddesses, then show me some," he used to say.

Meanwhile he painted whatever came his way, upsetting theories and authoritatively imposing his direct and healthy temperament. Before taking part in the 1848 revolution, he equalled Giorgione in his self-portrait, *The Man with the Leather Belt.* For his gigantic *Burial at Ornans* he painted life-size characters on a canvas 23 feet wide, in his grandfather's granary, using the whole family as models. The parish priest, with his curate, arrived in his heavy cope, and the two choristers who insisted on " having their portraits done." This ambitious and crowded work, which Marquet, and later Paul Claudel, considered *the* picture of the century, caused a scandal. So also did the *Demoiselles de la Seine*, and the *Cerfs*—painted as if with a trowel—not to mention his subversive theories and his boastful but effective actions. Under the Commune, he took part in the overthrowing of the Vendôme Column, and as a result spent six months in prison, a military court awarding him the maximum penalty. So he died in exile in Switzerland, having carried out to the letter his grandfather's good advice at the time of his birth : " Shout loud and keep straight." If Millet followed Courbet in peasant themes, can we speak of realism in regard to Degas and Manet ? They certainly took their subjects from all around them. But what alchemy they made of reality !

Degas, maturing by a slow, secret process behind locked doors : Manet in the open courtyard, fluttering his brush impulsively but unerringly, finding a harmony of colour with simulated ease : the one full of sarcasm, the other with a touch of vain egoism, but both of them so richly versatile, and both revolutionaries without knowing it.

Degas was an admirable draughtsman even in his earliest work, deriving useful lessons from Holbein and Ingres. His first portraits (including one of himself) show an uncompromising search for precision which soon led him to discard historical subjects (his young Spartans have been criti-

E. MANET. — *The Fife-Player.*

cised as too " Montmartrian ") to illustrate modern life in all its facets.
He chose the most uninspiring of subjects—a chiropodist extracting a
corn from a foot—to make a masterpiece of it. He took stock of events
from a distance, often taking an oblique view and apparently foreseeing
what cinema producers call *depth of field*. There are in his pictures musicians, laundresses, two bohemians slouching in front of a glass of absinthe
sticking to the marble-topped café table. He depicted the quiver of prancing horses on the racecourse and the motley crowd of jockeys and fops.
He left us vivid images of back-stage life at the ballet, of the young dancers
scratching and contorting themselves, or suddenly taking wings in their
gossamer ballet dresses.

Under the apparent severity, the studied classicism of his art, one
detects an extreme sensitivity, that " cold-fever " of which Huysmans
speaks. Manet, on the other hand, seems more superficial, with a light-

CAMILLE PISSARO. — *The Approach to the Village.*

CLAUDE MONET. — *The Argenteuil Boat-Races.*

ness of touch that makes him the real father of impressionism—an instantaneous art that exploits the keen sensation of the moment. The son of a Parisian magistrate, Edouard Manet, as a cabin-boy on the *Guadeloupe*, had once to repaint in red the rinds of Dutch cheeses. This was his first pictorial attempt. It was mainly in his honour that in 1863 Napoleon III founded the " Salon des Refusés," and his *Déjeuner sur l'herbe* provoked the most violent attacks. At that time Manet was considered the apostle of ugliness, and his *Olympia*, " with a washerwoman's body " was refused the following year, as was the *Fife-player* in 1864. " Penny-coloured print " they called it, but Zola exclaimed : " I do not believe it would be possible to obtain a more powerful effect by less complicated means." Towards the end of his life, he turned to " open air " painting, but he always stood apart from the impressionist movement—except in the opinion of the gossips of the Café Guerbois. This period is recalled to us by Fantin-Latour's groups, in which we recognise Baudelaire,

Verlaine and Rimbaud in the *Coin de Table* and *L'Hommage à Delacroix*. The label " impressionist " was attached derisively to the friends of Claude Monet who, in 1874, exhibited a picture entitled *Impression*. Artists of different temperaments, from the Dutchman Jongkind to the English Sisley, united their efforts in kindred researches. Delacroix had already turned his attention to problems of colour : shadows which were never quite black and contrasted colour values. By the division of tones, the pursuit of real shades of colour in the atmosphere, the patient analysis of light, the impressionists were to upset traditional ways and open large horizons to modern art. Encouraged by Boudin and Jongkind on their way through Normandy, young Monet came to Paris and soon became the head of a little group, whose artistic integrity and good faith was beset by insuperable difficulties before being taken seriously : the public shook with laughter on seeing this " painting of madmen." Fleeing from their creditors, continually exposed to the jeers of the journalists, these anarchists of the brush quietly went on with their luminous land-scapes, untiringly seeking to capture on canvas the reflection of sailing ships in the Argenteuil basin, or the summer haze on a hill dotted with red poppies. We see Claude Monet under the glass roof of the Gare Saint-Lazare, or in front of his haystacks, in a series of canvases in which he noted the variations of light and shadow all the day long. In his *Cathedrals* (of Rouen), and then on his property at Giverny, in the *Nymphéas*, beneath grey skies and bright skies, morning, noon and evening, he studied the grey harmonies, the pink harmonies, the green harmonies...

Renoir had also to wage a bitter struggle, but this is non-apparent in his work, which is a hymn to the joy of living. Earning sixpence a dozen for painting roses on porcelain, Renoir, the tailor's son, frequented suburban dances to find the theme for his " *Fêtes galantes.*" His *Rendez-vous des Canotiers* expresses the same happiness and youthfulness as his shadowy *Balançoire* or his celebrated *Moulin de la Galette*, a charming and magical effect giving the Montmartre dance-hall the freshness of verdant nature, depicting young, smooth-cheeked girls jesting with unruly youths between two polkas. Renoir passed his youth in the district which, until 1870, was to be found in the Cour du Carrousel, and he profited from the proximity of the Louvre. Boucher's *La Diane au Bain*, which made such a strong impression on him at that time, is, in short, the source of all those *Baigneuses* that made him famous : those rosy, long-haired

RENOIR. — *Young Girl.*

CÉZANNE. — *Card Players.*

maidens, full of feline grace, whose small, triangular faces reappear in his interiors and his scenes of Parisian life. Renoir was the painter of women, and at the end of his life, at Cagnes, the old man, crippled and seated in his bath-chair, had the paint brush tied to his wrist, in order, even with his last breath, to give expression to that rounded flesh which for him was only finished when " he felt a desire to give them a whack on the buttocks. " He never sought to theorise, and his artistry is summed up in this sally : " For me a picture ought to be something likeable, joyous and pretty—yes, pretty ! There are quite enough trying things in life without our making others."

Cézanne, at the time of the first impressionist exhibitors, had the honour of being considered the most grotesque of the group, and even when he returned to his native Aix in 1897, he was still lampooned. In his retreat, he pursued with dogged perseverance the work that was to be the inspiration of the present Parisian school. It would be impossible to overestimate his contribution to modern painting, for, wishing to "make impressionism something as solid and enduring as the art of the Museums ", he achieved this by turning his back on all formulae and painting as if he were the first to do so. While Sisley walked in Monet's shadow, and the aged Pissaro allowed himself to be influenced by young Seurat, Cézanne departed from the method of coloured dots and, by painting " on a broad scale," discovered a new technique. He was obsessed by the fear of " being clapped into irons ", and it was as difficult to get him to change his mind, in the words of Zola, " as to persuade the towers of Notre-Dame to dance a quadrille." His peevish grousing contributed to the building up of the legend that now surrounds this idol of painting whom one can liken to Van Gogh, the bright archangel of expression with his astonishing mystic quest. Like the son of the Dutch clergyman, the heir of the hatter-banker of Aix trod a sorrowful road. His material life, commonplace enough in itself, conceals the

GAUGUIN. — *Women of Tahiti.*

anguish of his inner life which found no relief in " bleeding sacrifices " like those of " L'Homme à l'oreille coupée."

" When colour is richest, form has reached full measure ", said Cézanne, and Van Gogh : " I use colour in strong measure to express myself arbitrarily." Gauguin used an arbitrary play of colour to achieve a more decorative form of work, without the fitful agitation of Van Gogh, nor the depth of Cézanne, who doggedly sought the structure of the eternal in the passing clouds of reality.

Gauguin passed a troubled youth; four years in Peru, the country of his grandmother, Flora

TOULOUSE-LAUTREC
Jane Avril.

Tristan. On leaving the seminary at Orleans he joined the merchant navy and travelled between Rio and Greenland, settling down after the war as a bank-clerk. He made money and was able to buy a number of canvases by wretched painters. He then gave up business, wife and children. Living in poverty, he de-

VLAMINCK. — Marly-le-Roi.

veloped his frenzied personality, and his final style was determined by his meeting with the young Emile Bernard in Brittany. In this Pont-Aven milieu was born the "symbolist" school that Sérusier and Maurice Denis continued after him. A synthetic stylisation found its outcome in the divided tones of his Breton heads against a background of violent orange and red. Then he sold all that he had to pay the price of a voyage to Tahiti, from whence he brought back, after two years, 42 canvases and the realisation of his own genius. Going from one adventure to another, such as a leg broken in a sailor's brawl, he returned to Oceania, where he died. He has left us that variegated work in which, among the hibiscus and the bougainvillea, exotic maidens offer us " all the gold of their bodies" in gardens full of symbolic meaning.

Impressionism had an aftermath in Seurat who perfected "chromo-luminarism" in scientific form. Aided by his personality, this stippled art resulted in great works—*La Baignade, La Promenade à la Grande Jatte,* and his *Cirque* in the Jeu de Paume Gallery. An independent, Toulouse-Lautrec, was the witty narrator of life in the nineties, particularly in Montmartre. A dwarf of princely birth, he used to sit at the tables of the Moulin Rouge, or at the races, and sketch with a certain cruelty the contortions of the celebrities of his day. Drunkard as he was, a draftsman of genius, and a scapegrace, he found among women and on the racecourse the subjects that he rendered immortal, by means of lithographs, posters and canvases. He continued the style of Degas while bringing to it a " new thrill "—that of the century which was dawning.

This century of modern art, so rich with its Fauvism, Cubism and the School of Paris—and, after the titanic figure of Rodin, great sculptors such as Bourdelle, Despiau, Maillol. In painting, a froth of new theories followed in the wake of various movements, all claiming to liberate painting. Let us note a few landmarks. Bonnard, Vuillard, Maurice Denis and the Nabis set up as the apostles of the gospel preached by Gauguin in the Bois d'Amour at Pont-Aven. At the time when Bonnard and Vuilllard were trying out fleecy harmonies and muted tones, Rouault discovered a style of his own. It was the period of the first Fauvist manifestations—about 1905. With Vlaminck and his friends, the " shock-palette " came on the scene. Colours, according to Derain, must be cartridges of dynamite. Raoul Dufy reclad nature in Harlequin's cloak : " Nature ? It's only an hypothesis ! " a saying that Matisse might have adopted as he pursued his distortion of the world, light-hearted amid his birds and under the patronage of Brother Sun.

It was about 1910 that the strange polyhedrons of the Cubist painters began to spring up like mushrooms in the dew, in the wake of Braque and Picasso who, with his *Ladies of Avignon* added negro art to the fray. In these laboratories where mathematicians rubbed shoulders with magicians, chemists with alchemists, the world was transformed. Even stranger transformations were accomplished by that versatile ace of the paint-brush, Pablo Picasso, who arrived in Paris at the turn of the century and fostered a revolutionary climate in art life at the very time when artists from all the world over had met together in the School of Paris.

Modern painting—from Fernand Léger to Dunoyer de Segonzac and from the Douanier Rousseau to André Lhote—with the present controversy between abstract painters and the defenders of figurative art, marks—polemics aside—a fertile stage, proving, if proof be needed, that Paris remains the capital of Living Art.

Jean DESTERNES.

THE PARIS MUSEUMS. *It depends upon him who passes here whether I remain tomb or treasure... Friend, enter not unwillingly...* These lyrical words of counsel by Paul Valéry, on the front of the Palais de Chaillot, serve for all museums. There are a thousand and one ways of visiting the Louvre, whether we start with the winged horses of Assyria or the 29 rooms of ancient statuary. Near by, the MUSEUM OF DECORATIVE ARTS exhibits suites of furniture, and at the Jeu de Paume, are the impressionists. For the history of Paris, go to the CARNAVALET MUSEUM in the Marais district. There you will see the evolution of the capital from its origin : Louis XVII's school task, the spectacles of Béranger, the stones of the Bastille and Charlemagne on his horse. At the CABINET DES MÉDAILLES you will find Dagobert's throne and near by, the sword of Boabdil, last king of Granada. If you are a numismatist, have a look at the coins—in their thousands—in the Museum of the Quai Conti. At the Légion d'Honneur are collected all the decorations of the world, as well as souvenirs of Napoleon. This latter visit should be supplemented by a look at the ARMY MUSEUM in the Invalides which preserves military trophies starting with the Stone Age, the Constable's sword, and valiant armies of toy soldiers.

Among the more scientific collections, you can begin with the fossils at THE MUSEUM and end with Blériot's flying-machine at the ARTS ET MÉTIERS and the atomic wonders of the PALAIS DE LA DÉCOUVERTE. At the MUSÉE DE L'HOMME a survey is made of the whole world—Eskimo kayaks, Soudanese tom-toms, not to mention Descartes' skull. In the other wing of the Palais, Popular Arts and Traditions hold the place of honour ; the MONUMENTS FRANÇAIS have been faithfully reconstructed and also Romanesque frescoes. At the MUSÉE DE CLUNY you will find the Middle Ages, at the MUSÉE GUIMET, the East. There are the museums of the great collectors (Cognacq-Jay, Jacquemart-André), those devoted to illustrious men, Rodin, Delacroix, Clemenceau, Victor Hugo; there are souvenirs of the Opera and the waxworks of the MUSÉE GRÉVIN—there are even museums devoted to fishing, law and hygiène—not to mention temporary exhibitions, such as those held at the MUSEUM OF MODERN ART. Whether it be at the ORANGERIE or the PETIT PALAIS, or in the private galleries, whether the attention of the moment be riveted on the ceramics of Picasso or " The horse throughout the ages," artistic activity is always remarkably alive in Paris.

MONTMARTRE

VILLETTE

L'OPERA
ET LE CENTRE

X^e ARR^t

BELLEVILLE

LES HALLES

LES ÎLES

LE MARAIS

MÉNILMONTANT

BERCY

ATIN

GLACIÈRE

LA SEINE

LUCIEN BOUCHER

There is no olace on earth, I thought where language has a faster beat, more resonance and less constraint than in this city of Paris where literature, science, the arts and the public life of a great country are jealously concentrated. The French have gathered all their ideas within walls. We live there in our own fire.

Paul VALÉRY.

The Louvre in the 16th century.

T IS CON-

siderably more than two thousand years since Paris was founded, for we find, in Caesar's commentaries, mention of the passage of Roman troops through the village of Lutetia-on-the-Seine. Long before 53 B. C., the Ile de la Cité must have been a settlement of boatmen and fishermen where, perhaps, there was already a welcoming inn, where travellers could rest on their way from Orleans to Amiens or from Sens to Rouen. In the heart of the Parisian basin, this spot was to become a network of communications to the north, south, east and west; this site, between the calmly flowing rivers Marne and Oise that link up with the majestic current of the Seine, soon chosen for a garrison by the officers of the occupying legions, was to become a market and eventually a small capital.

The Island spread to the Left Bank, rather than to the marshy Right Bank. Thermal baths, temples and arenas were erected on the flank of the Montagne Sainte-Geneviève. An aqueduct brought pure water from the Rungis and Wissous springs, ten miles from Lutetia. The boatmen built an altar to Tiberius, the emperor god; wheat, wine, timber and apples were brought to the banks by boat; the boat, the first to give an impulse to its growth, has remained the emblem of the city.

Tradition relates that Saint Denis, who was converted in Athens by Saint Paul, was sent from Rome to convert the Parisians at the end of the first century. He founded the first church in a crypt of the ancient monastery of the Carmelites in the Rue Denfert-Rochereau. Arrested by order of the Prefect of Rome, he was thrown into jail with his companions, Rusticus and Eleutherus, on the very spot where the Ile de la Cité flower market is now held. On a cold, misty October morning, he was taken to the Butte Montmartre, where the temple of Mercury stood, a few antique columns of which can be seen in the venerable chapel of Saint Peter. The Rue des Martyrs commemorates that tragic ascent.

On a level with the Rue Antoinette is the spot where Denis and his two companions were beheaded by the sword. To the amazement of the crowd, the devout bishop seized his white bearded head in both hands, washed it in the Fountain of the But, and then walked about six thousand paces northwards. Catulla, the devout, inspired woman, awaited him and buried him at the spot where stands today the Basilica of Saint Denis. Good King Dagobert ordered his tomb to be erected in the same place, and the Capetian Kings in turn were put to rest beside the first Bishop of the Capital. The martyr's blood was perpetuated in the colour of the

coat-of-arms, that crimson background to the silver boat. With the blue of France, and the white of the plume of Henry IV, it later made up the tricolour flag.

We have very few texts to hand from which to study the development of Lutetia. We must be content with the excavations which have enabled us to discover small thermal baths in the Rue Gay-Lussac, a large building in the Rue Soufflot, and a theatre in the Rue Racine. The Arena in the Rue Monge has been considerably restored and it is almost certain that Emperor Julian, who was crowned in his beloved Lutetia in 359, inhabited a palace on the Island and not that building, whose thick walls can still be seen in the Boulevard Saint-Michel. A sarcophagus, hewn out of an antique milestone, shows us that, in 307, the name Lutetia was no longer officially used. The name of the population alone still survived, as in many other places, and the etymology of the name Paris has been sought in vain.

Anxiety reigned in the little town faced with the danger of barbarian invasions, the aftermath of the ever-declining Roman Empire and the pressure of tribes from the East. The Left Bank became a desert of thistles and brambles. The Parisians withdrew into the Cité and hastily erected ramparts with the stones of deserted monuments. Traces of fire bear witness to disasters and catastrophes but most contemporary accounts are so coloured by miracles that it is hard to know what to believe. Fortunatus tells the story of the life of Saint Marcel who was bishop in the year 400. It appears that Marcel rid the town of a monster called a *Tarasque*, whose lair was the tomb of a lady of easy virtue. He advanced fearlessly towards the monster, struck him on the head three times with his crosier, wrapped his stole around the monster's neck and said : "Either go thou to the desert, or throw thyself into the sea." For a long while, on Rogation days, a wicker dragon was paraded, and children threw pastries into it for the sick people of the Hôtel-Dieu hospital, to commemorate this event.

It was to Marcel that Geneviève, the young shepherdess, was introduced, her name meaning in Celtic " daughter of Heaven." Because of her serious demeanour, her gentleness and her surprising reputation, the Bishop agreed to accept her religious vows, although she was only nine years old, Never had things looked so black, for the Huns, whose misdeeds were passed from mouth to mouth, were about to cross the Rhine after having martyred the eleven thousand virgins of Cologne.

While streams of refugees from the east and the north overwhelmed the streets of Paris, Geneviève, through Divine inspiration, succeeded in persuading the people that the Huns would not enter the town and also persuaded the chariot drivers to turn back and go peacefully home.

Attila's hordes, repelled by the fervour of her prayers, turned away from the valley of the Seine and were crushed near Châlons-sur-Marne. In Paris, Geneviève was universally regarded as a saint. More and more miracles occurred wherever she set foot. Clovis, king of the Franks, who was baptised in Rheims, acceded to her slightest desire, and his wife Clothilde loved her so dearly that she caused her to be buried, in 512,

beside her husband in the Basilica of the Holy Apostles at the summit of the hill which henceforth bore the name of Montagne Sainte-Geneviève.

Till the year 1000, religious impulse governed the development of Paris, the spot chosen by God and sanctified by Denis and Geneviève. Childebert erected the Basilica of Saint-Vincent, which later became Saint-Germain-des-Prés. Later, on the northern plain along the ancient Roman road, rose Saint-Merry, Saint-Martin-des-Champs, Saint-

Laurent. Saint-Médard stands on the banks of the small river Bièvre. On the spot where used to stand the cell of the hermit Saint Severin, rose a chapel that bears his name. On the Mother Island, beside the palace which was to become the Palais de Justice, the forge of Saint Eloi, good King Dagobert's friend, was dedicated to God, under his name.

It was about the year 650 that Saint Landri, Bishop of Paris, decided to found the church of Saint-Germain-l'Auxerrois and built the Hôtel-Dieu beside his residence and church. His spiritual functions made him the real head of the town, the one to whom all supplications were made in times of famine or danger. After the Huns, it was the Normans who coveted Paris, and she again lived through years of anguish and suffering.

Along the swan's route, strong forces of Scandinavians devastated the provinces. They sailed up the rivers, pillaging abbeys and carrying their booty back to Denmark. In 845 they tore the gilded copper plates from the roof of Saint-Germain-des-Prés. After the alarm, Paris prepared her defences. Wooden towers were erected at the entrance of the two bridges and were called the great and small Châtelets. Frightened provincials took refuge in the Cité, monks from the neighbourhood brought their treasures and relics there for protection. In November 885, a fleet of seven hundred Norman ships was observed on the Seine and King Siegfried requested free passage; his request was not granted. He then besieged Paris. The defendants were spared nothing : arrows and bolts, were showered down upon them, the Châtelets on the bridges were burnt down, and famine ensued. The Normans set up their camp in the neighbourhood of Saint-Germain-l'Auxerrois and constructed movable towers.

After a year of siege, the Emperor Charles the Fat came at last with a powerful army. He wished to negotiate, but the Parisians held fast and compelled the Normans to drag their ships through the fields, out of their reach. The hearts of the people went out to the defender of Paris, Count Eudes, and they offered the crown to him and to his descendants, the Capetians. The latter devoted themselves to establishing peace in the Ile-de-France. Paris, delivered from outside peril, grew and prospered. By the year 1000, the old tower of Saint-Germain-des-Prés, first bell-tower of the capital, had already arisen in the midst of blossoming orchards.

The monks from the surrounding monasteries, which formed an exterior ring around the urban centre, began to reclaim the land, and cultivated vines and acres of corn. Woodcutters got to work in the forest of Rouvre to the west—what remained is today the Bois de Boulogne—and also in the forest of Bondy to the east, which today is the Bois de Vincennes. Boats moored at the Grève, the present-day Place de l'Hôtel de Ville; later, streets branched out from there, each of them specialising in a particular craft. Bakers settled near the mills by the riverside. The butchers also settled close to the water's edge, a natural sewer in which to throw their refuse. All round the primitive Notre-Dame Cathedral were canonical schools. Robert the Pious rebuilt the Palais de la Cité, where Louis VI died on a bed of ashes with arms stretched crosswise, so grieved was he at the death of his son Philip, thrown from his horse by a herd of pigs. From that day, only the pigs from the Saint Antony monastery were allowed to ramble in the streets, providing they wore a bell.

The scholars of Notre-Dame inhabited the Left Bank, amidst the Roman ruins. Toward 1115 Professor Abelard crossed the Petit Pont and gave his lectures on the Montagne Sainte-Geneviève. He met with great success. Cheap boarding houses, the first colleges, were established on the

slopes which climb to the Abbey where rests the Patron Saint of Paris. The capital had assumed its present-day geography: the spiritual and temporal powers on the Island, markets and trade on the Right Bank, clerks and foreign intellectuals on the Left Bank.

One King of France gave all his affection to the town, and made it a capital: he was Philip Augustus, who was baptised in Saint-Michel's chapel in the Palace by the Bishop of Paris, Maurice de Sully, in 1165. The latter was the son of a poor woman who gathered dead twigs at Sully-sur-Loire; his obscure origin had awakened in him the ambition to become famous. As soon as he was elected Bishop of Paris in 1160, he decided to give the young city an incomparable cathedral. Following the example of Suger, who shortly before had erected the Basilica of Saint-Denis, he combined two churches of the Cité into the choir of the new Notre-Dame, the high altar of which was consecrated by a papal legate in 1182. Only the main portal and the towers remained to be built.

Philip Augustus was only twenty-five when he decided to protect Paris from invasion by surrounding it with a belt of stone ramparts, with gates and towers (the most famous of these towers was the Tower of Nesle which used to stand on the site of the present Bibliothèque Mazarine). This enclosure was in the shape of a heart pointing downwards, beginning on the Right Bank near the Pont des Arts, passing by Saint-Eustache and Saint-Paul, and ending at the Quai des Celestins. On the Left Bank it started from the Tower of Nesle, reached as far as Rue Soufflot and to the end of the Rue du Cardinal Lemoine, at the Tournelle bridge. To this vast system of defence, a keep had to be added, as in London. It was decided to build it at the most vulnerable spot, the spot where the Normans had established their camp ; this was the Louvre Tower, from the site of which can now be seen that wonderful view of the Tuileries and Champs-Élysées, " where passed all the seignories of France."

The King, who resided in the Palais de la Cité, kept in the great tower only his records, his gold coins and his cross-bows. Philip Augustus was a great friend of the Parisians, and he gave the bourgeoisie a share in the government before leaving for the crusades. He entrusted them with the treasure and the Royal Seal. He showered privileges on the water tradesmen and gave orders for the main streets to be paved with stone for they were constantly turned to muddy streams by the rain. He

Ferrand de Flandre as a prisoner at the Louvre.

had the water from the Belleville and Pré-Saint-Gervais springs brought to the Champeaux market.

The fame of Paris University, to which Philip Augustus granted many privileges in 1200, had spread all over Europe. The Emperor of Constantinople called for teachers from it, the Pope took an interest in it. There was such an influx of students to the Left Bank that rents had to be controlled and colleges founded. The orchards disappeared and Dominicans and Franciscans settled in the Rue Saint-Jacques and the Rue de l'Ecole de Médecine. The former were nicknamed Jacobins because of the site they had chosen; the latter were nicknamed Cordeliers because of their attire. When later the revolutionary clubs held their meetings in these secularized monasteries, Robespierre was a Jacobin and Marat a Cordelier, odd irrelevancies both.

The Templars' Keep then stood beyond the ramparts, a rival of the Louvre Tower; in its last years it served as prison for the unfortunate King Louis XVI. It was destroyed by order of Napoleon to avoid any subversive meetings.

When Saint Louis ascended the throne, he found a prosperous town, endowed with large public buildings. His virtuous soul inspired him to erect a wonderful shrine, a miracle of daring and grace, in order to offer our Lord a purely spiritual gift. To house the invaluable relics of the Passion of Our Lord which he had acquired, he ordered Pierre de Montereau to build beside his palace the graceful and enchanting Sainte Chapelle. In two years, the glass shrine sprang into being. Joinville has related that he saw the King, wearing a white peacock bonnet,

supervising the work. Meanwhile, Robert of Sorbon, the King's chaplain, founded a college in the Rue Coupe-Gueule, for sixteen Masters of Arts, called the Sorbonne. There were haunted ruins on the site of the present alleys of the Observatoire; they were said to be those of the castle of Vauvert. Evil spirits often came out to torment the late passers-by, and the nearest street was called Hell Street. The Chartreux monks from Gentilly, utterly weary of this state of affairs, proposed to Saint Louis that they should inhabit these baleful ruins. The King agreed and the exorcism lasted three days and three nights, during which time the Parisians saw an infernal smoke rising into the sky and heard the rumbling of thunder. The Chartreux were victorious and they settled on the spot. It became a habit among the Parisians to send whoever disturbed them to the " diable vert " (green devil) meaning " diable Vauvert " (Vauvert devil) or more explicitly, " so far, that one knew not where."

Two very important records enlighten us as to the life of the Parisians in the 13th century: the first is the Book of Crafts, in which Etienne Boileau had inscribed the customs and statutes of the Guilds in 1255. Later, under Philip the Fair, in 1292, the first " Who's Who " of the capital was compiled, it was the poll-tax roster of all the tax-payers, their names, professions and addresses. This book is a most valuable source of information for the Registry Office.

Philip the Fair considered it necessary to augment the judicial machinery. At Montfaucon, close to what is today the Buttes-Chaumont, were erected large gallows where criminals were hanged, sometimes even after their execution. It was from his orchard, situated practically on the site of the present day Place Dauphine, that the King of France watched the sufferings of the Masters of the Order of the Templars, who were accused of being too rich and who were burnt alive on one of the small islands that became attached to the Ile de la Cité, by the building of the bridge called the Pont-Neuf. In 1304 the first popular uprising, caused by the devaluation of the currency, set the small craftsmen against the monarchy, but the hanging of twenty-eight of the leaders on the four elms at each of the main entrances to the town soon quietened the people's passions.

The bourgeois aristocracy was wealthy at the dawn of the 14th century. Financiers, usurers, notaries and merchants owned both town and country houses. The milliner of greatest renown, Isabelle la Commanderesse, could not satisfy the demand for hats. In the Rue des Jongleurs the poor wretches did not pay taxes any more than monkeys did when crossing the Petit Pont, for they merely had to pay with "monkey money," that is to say with imitations of monkey faces. Beyond the Porte Saint-Honoré, the street bearing the same name led up to the Quinze-Vingt, the hospital for the blind that Saint Louis had founded, where today is the Rue de l'Echelle. Beyond the Porte Saint-Antoine, the street that bears the same name led to the monastery of Saint-Antoine, a branch of the Cistercian order; today it is the Saint Antoine hospital; in those days, all along the way, windmills turned while vegetable gardens prospered and grapes ripened in the vineyards of la Villette, la Chapelle, and Montmartre. If peace had continued, prosperity, its obvious outcome, would have embellished this town, for its one desire was to make the best of its exceptional situation, and its reputation, which was already world-wide. Paris had one thought only, to increase her prestige. But

tension was growing between France and England. The troops of Edward III advanced as far as the bridge of Poissy in 1346. After the disastrous battle of Crecy, the black plague decimated the city. The time-worn ramparts of Philip Augustus crumbled away. The curtain rose on a century of nightmare.

At the meeting of the States General in 1355, in the great hall of the palace of the Cité, gesticulating speakers demanded money. Among them Etienne Marcel set himself against Charles, the young Dauphin, whose father, John the Good, was later taken prisoner by the English. The working class, driven on by Marcel, went " on strike " and proceeded fully armed to the "House of Pillars," which the town had just purchased and which was the ancestor of the present-day Hotel de Ville. Three hundred men dug a ditch on the Right Bank in front of the old ramparts. Weapons of war were placed at the gates of the city. The Provost of the Merchants, Marcel, went as far as having two of the Dauphin's counsellors, the Marshal of Champagne and the Marshal of Normandy, assassinated before his eyes. He then forced the Dauphin to wear the red and blue hood. This led to civil war, just when the enemy was in sight. The surroundings of Paris were devastated by large companies of rebels and by the Jacquerie, encouraged by Marcel, whose treason reached its peak when he set the English prisoners free. The people of Paris then recovered their senses, Etienne Marcel was killed near the Porte Saint-Antoine, and the Dauphin returned amid general rejoicing.

Other cities are towns; Paris is a world.

Charles V - 1539

He became Charles V, " the Wise," and devoted his reign, only too short, to peace and the beautifying of Paris. He completed the new surrounding wall, and built the Bastille to protect the town on the east as the Louvre protected it on the west. The police force was re-organised under the Knight of the Watch and his men on horseback and on foot. Traffic became intense. The King, who had unpleasant memories of the Palais, decided to have the Louvre restored by Raymond du Temple, and also a "hostel for pleasant pastimes" built near Saint Paul.

However, the outlook became darker with the untimely death of Charles V. The Regents wished to levy new taxes and this brought about the riot of the Maillotins. In 1392 the High Constable Olivier de Clisson was attacked at the break of day while on his way home. The King wished to pursue the aggressors right into Brittany. He caught sun-stroke in the forest of Le Mans and went completely insane after the episode of the ball of the " ardents " at the Hôtel Saint-Paul, where five of his companions as well as himself, masked and disguised as savages, caught fire. The government split into two factions : the people on the side of the Duke of Orleans, and those on the side of his cousin, the Duke of Burgundy.

It was then that the struggle between the Armagnacs and the Burgundians began. Meanwhile the war between France and England flared up again. These are the darkest days of the history of Paris.

The tyranny of the Cabochiens, murderous hirelings who were allies of the Duke of Burgundy, weighed heavily on the town. They executed with the axe, and set fire to the houses. After the treaty of Troyes in 1420, the English armies peacefully occupied the town and settled in the Bastille and at Vincennes. In 1429 Joan of Arc was rebuffed at the Porte Saint-Honoré, the Place du Théâtre Français of today. She was wounded in the leg and gave up her attempt, but the tide of battle was to turn once again, for on April 4th, 1436, the High Constable de Richemont attacked the Porte Saint-Jacques at the head of the liberating army. He was acclaimed by the population, and a procession in honour of Sainte-Geneviève took place to thank her for liberating the capital once again.

Little by little the suffering town regained her former appearance. In

hard winters, wolves still devoured children in the streets. François Villon, the great poet, who was brought up close to the Sorbonne, sang of the gay parties of students, those " lovers of taverns and girls." At the Pré-aux-Clercs, near Saint-Germain-des-Prés, the students played bowls, practised archery and, under the leadership of

the poet, formed expeditions to tear down the amusing tavern signs of wrought iron, which decorated their houses. On the Right Bank, around the charnel house of the Innocents under the arcade in which was painted the Danse Macchabée or Macabre, were situated the fine lingerie shops. The gardens spread along the built-up areas which, little by little, were developed and became new townships "fors la ville," forsbourgs (suburbs). In the reign of Louis XI, rich dwelling places and large churches arose with that exuberance of ornamentation which even the Italian Renaissance hardly ventured to change.

Guillaume Fichet, Rector of the University, sent for Gering, Krantz and Freiburger, who installed their printing presses first at the Sorbonne and then in the Rue Saint-Jacques. The new-born printing industry had to fight against the clamorous copyists, who feared for their livelihood. Progress caused the disappearance of the fortress-like aspect of private houses such as the Conciergerie and led to the erection of that delightful pair of residences, the Hôtel de Sens and the Hôtel de Cluny (today a museum).

Francis I decided to rearrange the old Louvre and Pierre Lescot began for him, at the corner of the Salle des Cariatides, the magnificent Palace that we now know. His principal collaborator, Jean Goujon, began to work on that jewel of the Parisian Renaissance style, the Fountain of the Innocents, which was completed by the sculptor Pajou. In 1540, the Emperor Charles V came to visit Paris and was sumptuously entertained there. It is said that he was astonished to hear Francis I state that the largest town in his kingdom was Rouen. " What about Paris then ? " he asked, " A country ! " replied the King. The Fountain of the Innocents was inaugurated by the most beautiful festival that had ever been seen, the solemn entry of King Henry II on the 16th June, 1549. The crowds gathered in streets decked with tapestries and decorated with flowers, to watch an amazing procession pass by; the Mendicant friars, the University scholars, the crafts, the watchmen, the lawyers, the municipality, the parliament, preceded the Chancellor of France, who rode a white charger, the knights and pages of honour, the marshals of France, the Constable de Montmorency and the King in his golden armour, followed by his equerries and halberdiers.

They passed through gateways and triumphal arches. Lutetia dressed as a Nymph, at the Châtelet, and the loveliest Parisian women, perched beside the Naiads of Jean Goujon, bore witness to the prestige of Mythology. Obelisks and rhinoceroses gave evidence of the discovery of distant lands.

The Renaissance was at its height and was embodied in four lovely churches, the last creations of the Gothic tradition : Saint-Gervais with its stained glass windows by Jean Cousin, Saint-Merry where a charming 18th century decoration adorns the choir, Saint-Etienne-du-Mont with its keystones and its rood-screen, unique in Paris, and lastly Saint-Eustache, the most astonishing nave in the Cité after Notre-Dame. One must also pay tribute to the proud tower of Saint-Jacques-de-la-Boucherie, still very medieval in its appearance though constructed between 1520 and 1530.

Communications having by this time become easier, as the roads were safer and in better condition, the shops became filled with pomegranates and exotic fruits, and the fish markets with salmon and herring from the Low Countries. Inns were licensed; numerous foreigners, especially Italian artists and bankers, who had come with Catherine

A cabaret in the time of Francis I.

St. Bartholemew's Eve.

de Médicis, settled in, but kept their customs and fashions. Benvenuto Cellini had a studio at the foot of the tower of Nesle; Scipio Sardini had his house built on the banks of the Bièvre where today stands the central bakery of the Hospitals. Nicolas Houel in 1579 founded a rest house under the name of Christian Charity, from which the School of Pharmacy originated. Doctors and barristers rode about on mules, for the narrowness of the streets did not allow large coaches to pass. Tournaments had become obsolete since the tragic death of Henry II in the Rue Saint-Antoine, close to the Palais des Tournelles. Tennis took their place; two hundred and fifty tennis courts already existed at the end of the 16th century, where young Parisians took exercise before lawn-tennis came into fashion. For mental recreation, the first literary salons opened their doors to the poets of the Pleiade. In the Rue Seguier, the Morel ladies entertained Joachim du Bellay, Ronsard and Erasmus, and typographic masterpieces were printed by Simon de Colines, the Estiennes and the Langeliers.

The wars of religion, still latent since the first skirmishes during the reign of Francis I, checked the march of progress. As long as they were limited to decapitating statues of the Blessed Virgin, or singing psalms at the Pré-aux-Clercs, they were not alarming, but the execution of Etienne Dolet, who was burnt in the Place Maubert, that of Anne du Bourg, who was strangled in the Place de Grève for having, at the meeting of the council, compared Henry II to the wicked Ahab, stirred peoples' minds intensely. The looting of Saint-Médard, the burning of the temple of the Partriarch close by, were trivial events compared with Saint Bartholomew's Day. This massacre lasted three days. Streams of blood flowed in the streets and the Seine was overflowing with corpses.

The result was a division into two factions, both set on revenge and inflamed by false information.

To avoid being separated from her sons, the Queen Mother, Catherine de Médicis, undertook, with the help of Philibert Delorme, the building of the Tuileries with gardens checkered with flower-beds and ornamented with a grotto adorned with ceramics made by Bernard Palissy. The stones for the construction of the Tuileries were brought by ferry-boat just above the Pont-Royal. The name of Bac (Ferry) was given to the street which took the place of the green track where the drays used to pass. A new line of bastions enclosed the Butte des Moulins, where today the Avenue de l'Opéra opens out, the Faubourg Saint-Honoré, where new communities, Feuillants and Capuchins installed themselves, and the Tuileries. In 1578 Henry III laid the foundation stone of the Pont-Neuf, the only bridge without houses built on it. The King was so grieved by the death of his favourites Quelus and Maugiron that the name of " bridge of tears " was almost given to this daring passage over the river.

A few years of turmoil — in which the League drove Paris into open revolt against Henry III, and then, after his murder, against his successor, Henry de Navarre— plunged the unhappy capital into a misery

The Favourites' Ball.

she had never yet known. The people devoured horses, donkeys and three thousand cats that were boiled in enormous cauldrons. They ate grass, slate pounded into powder, and flour made with the bones of skeletons. Mothers preserved their babies in salt to feed on them, while fanatical priests preached war to the knife.

Henry IV decided to end all this, and became a Catholic, saying that Paris was well worth a Mass. On March 22nd, 1594, as the result of a well prepared plot, he entered the town at dawn by the Porte Neuve, between the Louvre and the Seine. A few snipers on the housetops were soon reduced to silence. The friends of the Spanish intruders left the town with the alien troops. King Henry permitted no reprisals and was satisfied with watching the defeated armies pass the Porte Saint-Denis while he exclaimed vehemently: "Give my regards to your master, but don't come back." It was the dawn of two centuries of peace in which the tormented city was to reach the height of its fame.

This most popular of French kings escaped seventeen attempts upon his life and fell victim to the eighteenth. His statue on the Pont-Neuf, the best known and the best situated in Paris, overlooks a construction which was successfully terminated during his reign and which remained for many years a major centre of attraction for Parisians—the Pont-Neuf, as admirable when seen from the Cité as from up-stream. The Flemish painters who were the first to depict the Parisian landscape have left us portrayals of life on the bridge: the booths where quack medicine was sold with any amount of parading and buffoonery; the song-writers, flower and orange vendors; the dentists and performing dogs, who made it a meeting place unparalleled in the world. Beside it was a pump, named the Samaritan after its bas-relief of Jesus at Jacob's well. The pump, which disappeared in 1813, gave its name to a bathing establishment with a palm-shaped chimney ; this establishment gave Ernest Cognacq the idea of calling his neighbouring store by the same name, and it is known today as " Samar " to the public at large.

It appeared, said the chroniclers, " that

never before had so many bricklayers been seen at work in Paris. " The Place Dauphine took on its triangular shape, with its apex leaning on the Pont-Neuf and its base on the Palais, where the ladies and their cavaliers besieged the shops of the Galerie Marchande, in which trinkets, books, knick-knacks, fineries and dainties abounded. On the site of the Tournelles ruins, the King, on the advice of Sully, visualised the founding of a silk-weaving industry, similar to that of Milan. He thought that a beautiful square would be appreciated by the Parisians and would form the centre of the symmetrical buildings, at the very heart of the Marais district, haunted by the dandies and the great men of the day. The engineer Chatillon designed the plans of this Place Royale, the Place des Vosges of today, which fell into disuse when the duellists and *précieuses*— de Montmorency-Bouteville and Marion Delorme—vanished.

When a violent epidemic or a plague devastated the town, the sick, who were packed together several in the same bed at the Hôtel-Dieu, rapidly succumbed. In 1607 the King gave the order to build the Saint-Louis Hospital, outside the town, close to the Montfaucon gibbet. The buildings intended for contagious cases were separated by courtyards planted with trees; we can still admire their harmonious designs and their French-style roofs. On the Left Bank, the Maison de la Charité was erected, facing the convent of the Petits Augustins who had been invited to settle in the domain of Queen Margot, where today stands the Ecole des Beaux-Arts. The Carmelites in 1605 took up their abode in the Rue d'Enfer and the Capuchin nuns, the following year, settled close to the Capuchin monks. Their convent gave its name to the famous boulevard.

Beyond Saint-Victor, an enclosure was made by Vespasian Robin, the King's herbalist, for the cultivation of medicinal herbs—the present-day Jardin des Plantes. The fashion for bathing in the Seine brought coaches, bathers, and spectators in crowds. Down-stream at the foot of the Chaillot hill was the Savonnerie carpet factory. The Provost of Merchants, François Miron, finished the building of the Town Hall, which had been interrupted by the wars of religion. The quays, streets, fountains and watering places were restored and enhanced. The Great Gallery along the water's edge was hastily built to connect the Louvre with the Tuileries. Rue Dauphine was opened up in a bee-line from the bridgehead of the Pont-Neuf; and Paris was preparing to celebrate the

coronation of the King's second wife, Marie de Médicis, when suddenly
Ravaillac's pointless act put an end to a reign of peace and order.

The Florentine regent gave a Tuscan character to her two creations :
the Luxembourg, built by Salomon de Brosse, after the style of the Pitti
Palace, with a park imitating the Boboli gardens and a Medici fountain,
surrounded with groves and rockeries, and the Cours-la-Reine, between the Tuileries and the Savonnerie, designed to imitate the walks
along the Arno. From the outset the Cours-la-Reine was a great
success, a popular rendezvous for coaches like the Avenue du Bois
de Boulogne at the end of the nineteenth century—the great outdoor
reception-room. There was the Pont-Neuf for the people, and the
Cours-la-Reine for the beautiful ladies and their courtiers.

New monasteries again abounded. In imitation of Saint Peter's at Rome,
a blossoming of domes sprang up all over Paris, starting with that of
the Carmelite convent in the Rue de Vaugirard, the Catholic Institute which
dates from 1625. That of the Order of the Visitation was larger and
appeared shortly before the Val-de-Grace which was built by François
Mansart and dedicated to Our Lord as a votive offering for the unexpected
birth of the Dauphin (the future Louis XIV) in 1638. Saint Vincent
de Paul surpassed the crowd of saints of the time with his foundations
of Saint-Lazare, the Filles de la Charité, and Enfants Trouvés.

Paris overflowed with vitality as the work of the great builders became more and more apparent. Michel Villedo, a mason from Limousin,
levelled out the Butte des Moulins. Claude Charlot was building all
around the enclosure of the Temple. Christophe Marie and his collab-
orators plotted out the Ile Saint-Louis. Barbier laid out the park of

Queen Margot that extended from the Rue de Seine to the Rue de Belle-chasse, and lined the Rue du Bac with houses. In 1624 Jacques Le Mercier undertook, at the request of Cardinal Richelieu, the building of the Palais-Cardinal. The same architect built the chapel of the Sorbonne and surveyed the complicated reconstructions at the Louvre. In the new great gallery were installed the Royal printing presses and studios for painting, for engraving and for die-sinking.

Théophraste Renaudot carried out amazing schemes. He gave free consultations to the needy, created an advertising agency, a centre for sales information, a pawnbroker's office and the first printed periodical. The founder of poor-law administration, of auction marts, of pawnshops and of the press, he died while wrestling with all sorts of difficulties, for his protector, the Cardinal, had died before him in 1642. However, the French Academy had been founded and the comedians of the Pont-Neuf were about to inspire young Molière. On Saint John's feast day the whole of Paris crowded into the Place de Grève to applaud the fireworks and dance, while cask after cask of wine was emptied.

The unhappy recollections of the wars of the Fronde caused Louis XIV to live away from his capital. However, Colbert maintained the link between Paris and Versailles and the main city continued to grow in grace and beauty. The solemn entry of the King started in 1660, contrary to custom, from the Place du Trône through the Faubourg Saint-Antoine. Queen Anne of Austria watched, with Mazarin and Turenne, from the balcony of the Hôtel de Beauvais. In 1662, a great equestrian pageant took place, the *carrousel*, which left its name to the area where the festival took place, with parades of Romans, Persians, Turks, Indians and Red Indians on horseback. On the other side of the Louvre a handsome façade was needed. Claude Perrault, the brother of the author of "The Fairy Tales" was entrusted with this work; he designed the colonnade. Shortly afterwards he was entrusted with the building of the Observatoire. The most populous kingdom of Europe had no reason to fear attack. The moats around Paris were filled in. The ramparts were made into boulevards lined with trees and embellished with gates. Of all the gates, only the Porte Saint-Denis and Saint-Martin remain today with their bas-reliefs where the latest victories were celebrated.

The tower of Nesle, in ruins, was demolished to fulfil the desire of the dying Mazarin that a college of the four nations should be built—the Institute of today. Colbert encouraged the Gobelins craftsmen and the workshops of the Faubourg Saint-Antoine. The Police Lieutenant, Nicolas de la Reynie, undertook to rid the capital of blackguards and of the felonies which found their source in the Courts of Miracles. His men chased away the beggars and false cripples. The women and children were parked in the buildings of the Salpêtrière, the gun-powder warehouses; the men were sent to the castle of Bicêtre, and Paris was cleaned up.

Bruant, the architect, designed the new " Hôpital Général des Pauvres " which kept its former name of Salpêtrière. Close by, the Royal Botanical Gardens presented rare vegetables and exotic plants to admiring amateurs. By order of Colbert, Le Nôtre laid out anew the gardens of the Tuileries and gave them the appearance of formal and geometrical gardens. The large avenue that divided them in two became, as it climbed up the opposite hill, a beautiful avenue lined with trees which continued the vista as at Versailles. The overgrown land through which it passed was already called the Champs-Elysées. All around the town, country houses surrounded with gardens made a green and flowery belt. Auteuil, Chaillot, Clignancourt, Reuilly, Bercy, Montrouge were among the most attractive.

Colbert's death did not put a stop to these undertakings. They became even more ostentatious as the " Grand Siècle " drew to its close. Marshal de la Feuillade was the creator of the Place des Victoires; he entrusted the building of it to Jules Hardouin, nephew of François Mansart. This gave the latter, who was as good a speculator as an architect, the idea of purchasing the Vendôme estate situated around their mansion, and of creating the magnificent square, then called Place Louis-le-Grand and today Place Vendôme. It was a wonderful setting for the equestrian statue of Louis XIV by Girardon. However, the great aristocrats despised these magnificent façades and it was the newly-rich who were the first to dwell there.

In 1685, the Pont Royal took the place of the Tuileries ferry. All along the Seine, facing the gardens, fine houses on the Quai d'Orsay reached to the Grenouillère. At the entrance of the Plaine de Grenelle, hard work was being undertaken to achieve the finest and most monumental of edifices, the Invalides. The royal mansion of the Invalides, a sumptuous pendant to the Salpêtrière, has preserved to this day its incomparable majesty. The miracle of Paris made possible the building of this cupola by Jules Hardouin-Mansart—this inverted golden chalice, with its outline always perfect and majestic against the ever moving sky, which changes from grey to blue and from darkness to flaming brilliance.

So long as Paris exists, there will be gaiety in the world.

Nostradamus - 155

The famous Persian of Montesquieu came to Paris at that time and wrote: "Paris is as large as Ispahan; the houses are so high that one would swear they were inhabited by astrologers." Everyone looked round as the Persian went by, yet the streets of the Capital were not devoid of entertainment—be it the crowd pressing into the Rue Quincampoix to buy from Law the bank shares of the India Company ; or the Grand Thomas on the Pont-Neuf, in his red costume with peacock feathers, and his three-cornered hat, selling, at sixpence a phial, his solar balm, claiming that it cured all diseases; or in 1730, the tomb of the saintly deacon, Pâris, adjoining the church of Saint-Médard, which became the centre of strange convulsions and amazing miracles, and was the cause of such queer disturbances that the police had to intervene.

The Regent resided in the Palais Royal, and rebelled against the pious austerity of the court at Versailles by giving elegant supper parties. Paris relaxed to its heart's content. The Faubourgs Saint-Honoré and Saint-Germain extended towards the west, while the Duke of Antin arranged the lay-out of the Champs-Elysées, made a road which became the axis of a new district, later called the Chaussée d'Antin, and designed the Avenue of Widows which became the Avenue Montaigne of today. The Count of Evreux requested Mollet to build him a beautiful residence in this new district. The Marquise de Pompadour bought it in 1753, had it decorated by Boucher and Van Loo, and bequeathed it to the King. Beaujon, the banker, owned it later, then the Duchess of Bourbon who gave it the name of Elysée-Bourbon. It welcomed Murat, Bonaparte, the Duke of Berry, Louis-Napoléon, and all the Presidents of the Republic down to this very day. On either side of it, the best architects erected throughout the whole century, mansions for the Charost, the Duras, the Beauveau families; these mansions met with a diversity of fates, the least unpleasant of which was to become a ministry or an embassy.

On the other side of the river, the same good taste was displayed in erecting mansions for the financiers and high officials. The Matignon and Biron mansions have kept their former gardens and we must admire, in the Rue de Grenelle, the fountain by Bouchardon set up for the purpose of providing water to a district without springs. There were no more Solemn Entries of Kings, but there were numerous occasions for popular rejoicings: the arrival of the Turkish Ambassador, Mehemet Effendi, in 1731; the great fireworks on the Seine in 1739, with illuminated barges between the Pont Royal and the Pont Neuf; and the six hundred weddings that were celebrated the same day in 1751, in honour of the birth of a Prince, with a dowry of three hundred pounds to each young bride.

The Ecole Militaire was built by Jacques-Ange Gabriel, and its parade ground, the Champ de Mars, was established between the years 1750 and 1760 in the centre of the plain of Grenelle. The neighbouring district, the Gros Caillou, so-called because of a milestone, saw the appearance of pleasure gardens where drinks were sold, and military hospitals in the midst of its vegetable gardens. The architect of the Ecole Militaire had the good fortune to win a competition for the planning of a square intended for the equestrian statue of Louis XV, which had been offered to the King by the municipality, and it is to him that we owe the Place de la Concorde, perhaps the most beautiful open space in the world, a wonderful link between the Tuileries and the Champs-Elysées.

Coaches, numbering three in the 16th century, by this time numbered twelve thousand. Fiacres and sedan chairs did not help to simplify the traffic problem. In 1760 Bourgeois de Château-Blanc succeeded in enforcing the establishment of street oil lamps with reflectors that dazzled the coachmen and horses. The Cartouchians—the disciples of Louis-

Dominique Bourguignon, alias Cartouche, the famous Robber Chief—
were compelled to give up some of their misdeeds because of such street
lighting. Although, however, at night the streets were still unsafe, in
the daytime they were crowded, in addition to strollers, by itinerant dealers,
whose characters have been preserved in the amusing selections of the
Cris de Paris. It was a deafening concert: " Cry little 'uns, you will
be given windmills !... Here comes the watercress, giving health to your
body... Feast yourselves, fair dames, here comes pleasure." The knife-
grinder offered to sharpen the knives, the little Savoyard with his
marmot offered to sweep the chimneys, the magic-lantern operator
climbed to the heights from whence people beckoned to him, and there
were many others. It was an entertaining sight, constantly changing.
It was no longer a mystical age; even the churches reflected this in their
outward appearance which was influenced by the Gesù church in Rome.
The great Saint-Sulpice remains strange and theatrical. Soufflot, inspired
by his travels in Italy, found it hard to complete the new Sainte-Geneviève
church, which became the austere Panthéon and is not very much like a
sanctuary. The love for antiquity gave predominance, towards the end of
the century, to the Basilican or Neo-classic style. Saint-Louis d'Antin,

Saint-Philippe-du-Roule, and that great square house, the Church of the Madeleine, bear witness to this cold trend so different from Chartres and Rheims.

The century of critics and wit, in its finest sense, could not but give the theatre a preponderant place. The French comedians acted in the Rue de l'Ancienne-Comédie, then the Luxembourg hall of today was built for them and called the Odéon. For the first time, in the new surrounding district, the names of men of letters were given to the streets: Racine, Corneille, Rotrou. The Italians moved from the unpleasant Rue Mauconseil to the theatre which had been built on the Choiseul estate, to which they gave their name, hence the Boulevard des Italiens. Harlequin, Punch and Pierrot now belong to the Boulevards, and the Opéra-Comique has kept its place since 1793. The Opéra, which had, with Lulli, replaced Molière at the Palais-Royal, was destroyed by a great fire in 1763. Moreau rebuilt it and a second similar catastrophe reduced it to nothing once again in 1781, while Gluck's *Orpheus* was being played. Then it, too, was moved to the Boulevards where it remained. The theatre of the Porte Saint-Martin was built for the ballet dancers. The Boulevards were by now the most attractive promenades of Paris. On the way to the Capucines was nothing but flowered terraces and newly built villas. The side-streets were alive with girls who sold flowers, fans, pin-trays—charming friends of Rétif de la Bretonne. At the Boulevard du Temple the entertainments began; the tight-rope dancers and Nicolet the jester were side by side with Audinot's marionnettes. Turco the monkey was the rage of Paris. Each day could be seen le Grimacier, Fanchon la Vielleuse, Curtius' waxworks—forerunner of the Grévin Museum.

The people of wit attracted to their houses the aristocracy of letters.

In the Rue Saint-Honoré, Madame Jeoffrin, in the Rue Saint-Dominique, Madame du Deffand, in the Rue de Bellechasse, Julie de Lespinasse, held literary salons. Jean-Jacques Rousseau used to play chess at the Café de la Régence and young Danton flirted with the cashier of the Café du Parnasse. Crowds were already queuing up at the Civette to buy the best

Rose Bertin

tobacco. Smoking, illusions, make-believes, hoaxes, all found favour. In the Champs-Elysées, the Colisée was the first music-hall; it met with short-lived success. In 1779, the Duke of Chartres had just laid out and planted a garden of solitude, with grottoes, pagodas, temples, groves, ruins and rocks; it was later called the Parc Monceau.

English-style jockeys raced in the Sablons plain near the Porte Maillot. Audacious adventurers entrusted their lives to a globe of silk, inflated with hydrogen, and to the amazement of an enormous crowd, Charles and Robert Montgolfier flew from the Tuileries in December, 1783. The fashion for air-balloons was astounding, the hats from the famous milliner to the Queen, Rose Bertin, were inspired by them, and there was not a trinket that was not " à la Montgolfière ". Fashion played an important part. While Nicolas Ledoux surrounded Paris with rotundas and little doric temples, along the exterior boulevards, the enclosure of the Farmers-General, fashion took up its headquarters in the new Palais-Royal which had just been transformed by the young Duke of Orleans, the future Philippe-Egalité. Eager for novelty and for news, the crowd hustled there under the arcades where the most frequented shops stood side by side, as well as on the paths of the garden near the small cannon that was fired at noon.

Deadlier cannon sounded later when the French Revolution took place in Paris, following its well-known course. It shattered the capital with its six hundred thousand inhabitants just at the peak of a constructive era. Industry had come to life in the outskirts of the city. " New France " had been built, the present-day Faubourg Poissonnière, as well as " New London " between Saint-Philippe and the Etoile. Mansions were deco-

Camille Desmoulins at the Palais Royal.

rated with delicate china, soft carpets and sparkling mirrors. Small Gothic churches fell into ruin and were finished off with the pick-axe. The pestilential charnel-houses were done away with and the bones of ancient Parisians were moved to the galleries of the old quarries, which were named Catacombs. Fire-engines brought the water up from the Seine to Chaillot and to the Gros Caillou.

The Louvre, encumbered by shacks and undesirable dwellings, was cleared of all these and became a Museum surrounded with lawns. Around the city wealthy financiers built sumptuous residences. The storm broke at the Palais-Royal, where Camille Desmoulins harangued his fellow citizens, and two days later the Bastille was stormed.

Palloy, the patriot, directed the work of the thousand workmen who demolished the old fortress. In its place they planted a signpost inscribed with the words " Dancing here ". Designations changed. The Champ-de-Mars became the theatre of popular manifestations, the most grandiose of which remains the festival of the Federation or July 14th, 1790. Soon after that famous day, August 10th, 1792, the royal statues were pulled down and shortly afterwards, on the Place de la Concorde, then called the Place de la Révolution, the guillotine operated close to the statue of Liberty, towards which, Madame Roland, while stepping to her death, stretched out her arms, saying: "Freedom ! What crimes are committed in thy name !" However, David embellished the entrance to the Champs-Elysées with the horses that Guillaume Coustou had sculptured for the Marly watering place; they are the most animated and conspicuous statues in Paris.

Bonaparte fired on Saint-Roch on Vendémiaire 13, 1795, and saved the Convention from the reactionary factions. The Directory prevented the communists of Babeuf from taking possession of the Grenelle camp. Soon the churches timorously opened their doors again, while the number of public balls, six hundred and forty of them, was a sign that

The Storming of the Bastille.

passions were calming down. During the storm many plans were made, which resulted mainly in changes in street names and the demolition of many religious houses to provide new space. Saint-Victor became the Halle-aux-Vins. The Chartreux monastery enlarged the Luxembourg; the Jacobin club of the Right Bank became the Saint-Honoré market.

One Parisian watched over the statues and tombs that were in danger of disappearing in the whirlwind. Sometimes at the risk of his life, he protected them from harm, by creating at the Petits-Augustins the Museum of French Monuments, the contents of which now form the basis of the sculpture section of the Louvre Museum; his name was Alexandre Lenoir and he deserves our praise.

In fact, the Paris that Napoleon inherited was very similar to that of Louis XVI and still contained many winding medieval alleys, with steeply gabled houses. Much remained to be done to give it its modern appearance and to rid it of its foul gutters and noxious odours. Between the Gare Saint-Lazare and the Place Saint-Augustin of today, stood the Petite-Pologne with its hovels teaming with ruffians, where the " Courts of Miracles " had come to life again. Warrens and wasteland in those days penetrated deep into what seems to us the centre of Paris today. It was not long since the wolves had departed ; while at Montmartre and Montrouge, windmills were still turning.

Frochot, the Prefect of the Seine, endeavoured to make Paris in appearance a worthy Capital of Europe, to satisfy the Emperor's wish. There was a utilitarian plan and an ornamental plan. The first concerned the bridges, the quays and, generally speaking, the waterways and streets. The Rue de Rivoli was opened first, and the Ourcq canal was constructed with the Villette basin, a vast stretch of water at that time covered with sailing ships and framed with Italian poplars. Fountains sprang up : that of the Palmier, in the Square of the Châtelet in 1870, l'Egyptienne in the Rue de Sèvres, the Dieu-Mars in the Rue Saint-Dominique. The Pont des Arts was built, facing the Institute, the first to be built of iron ; the bridges of Austerlitz and Iéna followed next. Frochot decided to turn Montlouis, property of the Jesuits near Charonne, into a necropolis; it was wooded, vast and picturesque. It retained the name of Père Lachaise in memory of the father confessor of Louis XVI.

In 1806 Napoleon signed a number of decrees intending to give Paris

The Statue of Henry IV reinstated on the Pont-Neuf.

the character of ancient Rome. Arches, columns, fountains, temples—nothing was lacking. He was then at the height of his power. The Madeleine became the Temple of Glory in honour of the armies. Percier and Fontaine erected in the Place Vendôme a Trajan column surmounted by a statue of the Emperor, with spiral-shaped decorations, depicting the battle of Austerlitz, chiselled in the bronze of twelve hundred cannons taken from the Russians and Austrians. In front of the Tuileries, at the Carrousel, an arch was erected, a pleasing imitation of those of Constantine and Septimus Severus, as a gate of honour to the palace; the building was finished in 1808. At the Etoile de Chaillot at the top of the Champs-Elysées incline, on an ideal spot, Chalgrin started to build a gigantic arch dedicated to the armies of the Empire. Louis XVIII continued it in honour of the Duke of Angoulême and the Spanish expedition. Louis-Philippe finished it with Blouet in 1836. The astonishing fact is that each of these regimes spent the same sum of money on the Arc de Triomphe.

After the French campaign a short one day battle ensued under the walls of Paris. The armistice once signed, at la Villette, the allies entered the town on the 31st of March, 1814, and marched right up to the Champs-Elysées where the horses of the Cossacks were said to have nibbled the bark of the young trees. Rue Napoléon became the Rue de la Paix. Louis XVIII entered Paris in his barouche drawn by eight white horses; the Hundred Days passed without any noticeable changes.

The statue of Henry IV was restored on the Pont Neuf; a white flag flew on the Vendôme column; everywhere the bee was replaced by the fleur de lys. The construction of the markets, slaughterhouses and canals was continued. The *Chapelle Expiatoire* consecrated the cemetery of the Madeleine where the remains of Louis XVI were found; that is almost the only monument left by the Restoration. Galleries were the fashion. The Passage des Panoramas was an agreable place to visit. The " fashionables " shopped at the " Fille mal gardée ", at the " Singe Violet ", at the " Lampe merveilleuse " or at the " Masque de fer ". Gas lighting was welcomed enthusiastically. The New Athens was being built on the slopes of Montmartre. This became the " Quartier de l'Europe ", with streets bearing the names of capitals—after that, the Francis I district. Grenelle and Batignolles were divided into lots beyond the enclosure, by speculators. Capitalists, such as Violet, Cardinet and others, are honoured by streets that bear their names. Yellow stage-coaches left each day for distant journeys in all directions. As early as 1828, popular omnibuses shortened the distances in the great city. The bus lines were given pretty names : Dames Blanches, Béarnaises, Carolines, Sylphides, Gazelles ; they linked together the essential centres described by Balzac.

The new churches were more and more barren and devoid of life. Notre-Dame - de - Lorette, and Saint-Vincent-de-Paul are alike in meticulous care and mediocrity. Tottering regimes were chased away one after the other by popular anger. Three days of street fighting in 1830 brought back the tricolour flag. The July Column was erected in the Place de la Bastille in

A Street Battle in 1830.

memory of the victims, and the Count de Rambuteau, the new Prefect—
a hardworking and simple man—directed municipal works conscientiously and thriftily. He increased the number of primary schools, organised savings banks, and built the prison of La Roquette; he also extended
the pavements and set up gas street-lamps. He continued the construction
of sewers but did not indulge in any adventurous undertakings. Apart
from the paltry street that bears his name and the Louis-Philippe and
Saints-Pères bridges, a few quays, and the connection of the Louvier Isle
to the Right Bank, no works of great scope can be attributed to him.

Louis-Philippe, however, was anxious that the Place de la Concorde
should be worthy of its name. He would not have
in its centre either the statue of Louis XVI or a statue
of Liberty. The Luxor obelisk was approved by the
moderates and prevented any outburst of political
passions. Hittorf prepared the rest of the ornamentation with fountains of the sea gods and the heavy
statues depicting the towns of France; on the 25th October, 1836, " to
the cheering of a great crowd " the final plan of the most beautiful
square in the world was officially sanctioned. For an expanding city
(for little by little its immediate surroundings were covered with houses:
Les Ternes, Vaugirard, la Courtille), it was necessary to have a larger
Town Hall than that of the 16th century. The old houses that surrounded Saint-Gervais were pulled down. In spite of the barricades,
and in spite of attempts to kill the peace-loving king, the spirit of Paris
changed but slowly. The first warnings of impending change sounded
unrecognised in the hearts of Parisians on that solemn morning of
December 15th, 1840 when weeping Veterans of the Imperial Armies
escorted the ashes of the Little Corporal to the Dome of the Invalides.

The minister, Thiers, dug moats to make the last fortifications, those
that gave Paris the shape shown on the plans of the Métro. He prepared
for invasion, but did not pay enough attention to the expansion of the
railways and allowed their stations to grow up haphazardly in spaces that
were too narrow. In 1843 a Paris citizen could go and lunch at Rouen
and return to Paris to sleep. What a revolution ! From Julius Caesar to
Louis Philippe, the speed of transport had not increased ! The stations were
too inconvenient and had to be rebuilt. The men who worked there suffered
from deplorable social conditions to which the authorities paid no attention

When Paris takes
snuff, the whole of
France sneezes.

Gogol

and which were partly the cause of the 1848 revolution. Under the menace of a popular uprising, the King and Queen took a cab at the Place de la Concorde, drove through Passy, then to Saint-Cloud. After that to England, and from then on no more descendants of Philip Augustus sat on the throne of France. The personalities changed, the setting altered. To guarantee employment for workmen, the Second Republic opened national workshops; however, certain unpopular decrees caused barricades of stones and casks to appear once again in the old streets. Shooting took place in the Faubourg Saint-Antoine. The victorious armies grouped together, and Louis-Napoleon Bonaparte gathered partisans around him to prepare his *coup d'état*. Twenty years of peace furthered the striking alterations planned by the head of the State and put into effect by the most famous of Prefects of the Seine, capable of the best and of the worst, Baron Haussmann.

It was a strategic plan that brought about the opening of the new, straight wide streets and boulevards, to permit the army to take action against riots. Napoleon III caused the old part of Paris to be opened up, under the pretence of modernising it, but mainly to isolate the groups of old narrow streets, so easy to barricade with bits of furniture and a few cobble stones. The Rue de Rivoli was completed; the Boulevard de Strasbourg and the Rue des Ecoles were opened up. Baltard was entrusted with the building of metal pavilions which are " Les Halles " of today, and the engineer Alphand, knowing the affectionate recollections the new Emperor had of Hyde Park, exerted himself to design a new Bois de Boulogne in the English style, with a landscape as unexpected as it was varied, with lakes and chalets.

The Avenue leading to the Bois de Boulogne was bordered with lawns and flowerbeds; on each side of this elegant thoroughfare, mansions were built similar to the Trianon and to Chenonceaux. It was the era of imitations. In the heart of the city, under the pretence of disencumbering the Gare du Nord and the Gare de l'Est, the thrust of the Boulevard Sebastopol created havoc in the old Châtelet district, passed over the Ile de la Cité, and climbed the Montagne Sainte-Geneviève under the name of Boulevard Saint-Michel. In its turn, the Boulevard Saint-Germain ripped open François Villon's old quarters. During the Crimean War, the district of the Gros-Caillou was laid out, with the Avenue de l'Alma and the Avenue Bosquet.

From 1858 to 1868 the great crime of razing the Cité was committed. The building of the Hôtel-Dieu and the Préfecture de Police were no excuse for that massacre of revered antiquities.

Notre-Dame now stands dismally at the end of the dead sea of asphalt that is its present day Parvis. It was also the age of squares, those postage stamps of greenery, not as large as those of London but made in their image.

The Bois de Vincennes also became anglicised. The Place de l'Etoile was successfully transformed; the star was given new rays, and a ring of small symmetrical mansions. The Place de la Nation became its pendant in the east. The Boulevard Malesherbes was launched towards distant Clichy, skirting the Parc Monceau on its way. In this still very undefined district, Emile Péreire built up such a large fortune that a wide boulevard was given his name.

The year 1860 promised new alterations, but certainly not the wave of the wand that was to join to Paris the ring of villages enclosed in M. Thiers' fortifications, that gave Paris pretty well the shape and size it has today. Five hundred thousand more inhabitants were added by signing a decree. The railway with its tentacles served the suburbs. Chalkpits stood bare in the new Paris. They became the Buttes-Chaumont—with much ingenuity and taste, we must admit. In the south, the Montsouris park concealed the great reservoirs. Around Garnier's new Opera house, a whole set of new streets intertwined and were given the names of musicians. The Avenue Napoléon started from the Palais-Royal and became the Avenue de l'Opéra as soon as carriages began to pass along it in 1879.

The international exhibition of 1855 took place in the Champs-Elysées where English-style garden paths were laid out, bordered with châlets and kiosks—quite a village of large edifices, Marigny, the Palais de Glace, the Cirque d'Eté; in the surroundings were erected beautiful mansions for the celebrities of the day: Rothschild, Pillet-Will, Schneider, La Païva, Morny. Haussmann was not only a juggler with property; thanks to his assistant, Belgrand, he improved the water system by making the pure water of the rivers Marne and Aisne flow into the houses. The buses increased in numbers; 32,000 gas lamps illuminated the lively city now covering fourteen thousand one hundred and sixteen acres. The 1867 exhibition

Paris will never *taken, save wh* *Parisians will it.*

Camulogenus - 53 B.

was opened on the Champ-de-Mars; it marked the zenith of the regime. Sovereigns from all over the world, from the Tzar to the Sultan of Turkey, from the Viceroy of Egypt to the Emperor of Japan were guests. Parades, festivals, banquets and the awarding of prizes took place unceasingly. From the Mabille Ball in the Avenue Montaigne to the Variétés where *La Belle Hélène* was played, Paris danced, smiled, amused herself and put all her hope in the future, while watching the prize ox go by which it nicknamed : " L' Pied qui r'mue. "

The collapse of 1870 proved once more how close together are the Tarpeian rock and the Capitol. In October the Prussians were already at Choisy-le-Roi, at Bougival and Epinay. The forts held fast and balloons were flown to carry dispatches. Notwithstanding the glorious engagements at Le Bourget, Champigny, Buzenval, the city could not rid itself of the enemy around it ; German shells began to rain down ; the cold became intense and food supplies scarce. The responsible generals signed the armistice, causing many Parisians to rise against them and proclaim the Commune. Dreadful weeks of fratricide ensued which ended with the burning down of the Tuileries, the Hôtel de Ville, the Cour des Comptes, the Palais de Justice and a number of other buildings. At the Père Lachaise there was savage fighting to the end, followed by ferocious repression. On both sides atrocities were perpetrated, one leading to another. It was a nightmare in black and red.

Slowly the ruins were restored or demolished. The architect Abadie crested the summit of Montmartre with the white Sacré-Cœur. The Third Republic slowly continued Haussmann's work with the boulevard

that bears his name, the Boulevard Raspail and others. It enlarged the stations, set up Ministries, built townhalls, barracks, schools, post-offices, hospitals and the offices necessary for the two and a half million inhabitants. Private concerns proceeded with the building of the great stores that came into being under the Second Empire, as well as gigantic hotels, theatres, cinemas, cycle-racing tracks and stadiums.

Unattractive statues sprang up at each crossroad. The 1878 exhibition left behind the Trocadero, with its slender minarets still alive in many memories; the following one, that of 1889, left us the most popular monument in the world, the Eiffel Tower, that amazing masterpiece of a daring engineer who wished to achieve a vertical metal construction. We have grown accustomed to it so that we find in it a certain schematic beauty. It was the final tribute to the apotheosis of metal-work.

The 1900 exhibition opened under the sign of the fairy Electricity. It left in particular the two palaces of the Champs-Elysées bloated and bristling with baroque sculptures, and the Pont Alexandre III decorated with lions, garlands and winged spirits blowing trumpets. It was in honour of these last days of the nineteenth century that the first Métro was opened.

The 1937 exhibition, organised, alas! while storm clouds were gathering, showed to millions of visitors a Paris that seemed to defy the threat of death. It gave us the Modern Art Museum and the Palais de Chaillot which present from the Right Bank an unequalled view over the levels of the Left Bank, where, in days gone by, the Gauls of Camulogenus dared to oppose the legions of Labienus.

We remember from our early days the last horsedrawn buses and, a little later, the last *bateaux-mouches*, the river-steamers that carried people so slowly from Charenton to Suresnes. Today, the traffic that pollutes the air and fills the streets with noise, is regulated by red and green traffic lights which would have horrified our grandfathers. The new church towers were conceived by excellent pupils cognizant of the trends of all the schools of architecture but lacking in that unaccountable spark of genius. We can moan at certain unfortunate buildings; the macaroni style of 1900 makes us smile; the Palais Berlitz makes us rightfully angry, for it has not understood the eternal moderation of Paris, welcoming all trends and knowing how to reconcile them under her golden rule of delicacy and harmony.

Notwithstanding the last two wars—the one, scarring the capital with bombs and shells, the other, sombre beneath a lengthy occupation — Paris, faithful to her motto, has shown our generation that, although lashed by the waters, nothing could sink her. She has acquired long experience; many museums cradled behind her walls are proof that she is conscious of her past and wishes to preserve its memory to teach future manhood that she is still the radiant centre, the heiress of Athens, open to the hapless, to the artists; refuge of intellectuals whose freedom of thought it encourages. After the terrible blows that have shaken our planet, it is good to be within the shelter of her spiritual walls, stronger than steel, and to repeat the line of the poet while we contemplate her treasures with delight:

" *Nothing can compare with Paris.* "

René-Héron DE VILLEFOSSE.

the Islands

E. M. PEROT

KISLING. — *Notre-Dame*.

ARIS RISES

from the banks of a river whose tide runs slowly and indolently. The Seine has, without much effort, traced itself out a sinuous route, seeming to have chosen the " primrose path of dalliance " so as to linger as long as possible in a mild region.

Its harmonious curve is dominated, to the north, by an amphitheatre of hills. The river passes Belleville, Montmartre and Chaillot, as if in review. To the south it waters the foot of the Montagne Sainte-Geneviève, then settles down in the plain before winding round Boulogne. Large trees shadow its quays, although as far as the eye can see, to the distant horizon, there are buildings along its banks, as it passes between a double row of monuments from which spring forth clock towers, domes, slender spires, façades and bell-towers. It is like a splendid boulevard which crosses, from east to west, an ever changing city, full of unexpected vistas, always beautiful, and from which emerge, at the actual centre, two islands, like two ships at anchor that are keeping guard.

Other capitals exist in the world, and some of them are larger. There are some that draw their grandeur from some great natural feature, but none that unites, to such an extent, both grace and variety. Whether the traveller passes from one bank to another, whether his dazzled gaze wanders from the Etoile to the Louvre, whether he takes in the vast panorama that spreads out from the foot of Montmartre, or whether he surveys harmoniously laid out gardens, he is always brought back to the river and its " Iles " from which the city arose. One must first contemplate from afar the Cité and the Ile Saint-Louis and then, only, approach them with respect. Early morning is the ideal time to stroll towards the Quai de la Tournelle, once the embarkation point for Melun, Sens and Auxerre. The rising sun enables one to see the wonderful picture formed by Notre-Dame, the Sainte-Chapelle and the points of the towers of the Palais, framed by Saint-Gervais, the Hôtel de Ville, the

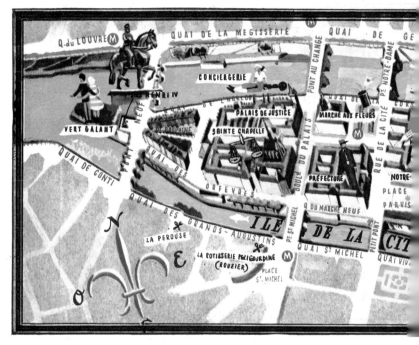

Tour Saint-Jacques and Saint-Germain-l'Auxerrois on the right, and on the left by the Mint and the dome of the Institute.

The Cité is the very heart of Paris. Isolated between the arms of the river, as proud as her motto, she surveys around herself a tentacled city spreading out, having grown like a cancer, having scaled the hills, reached the plain, absorbed the scattered villages, and which, having burst out of three enclosures, has extended seemingly beyond limits.

The dimensions of the Cité have remained practically the same as they were in the time when its first dwellers took refuge behind the reeds that lined its banks. Everything began from her. Formerly composed of a handful of islets, she became one, thought herself impregnable, fought everything to maintain her independence, and has protected even her riverside residents, without reward. She is the mother, but her offspring have closed her in. She can no longer survey the horizon. Along the quays and on the side of the hills a million windows spy

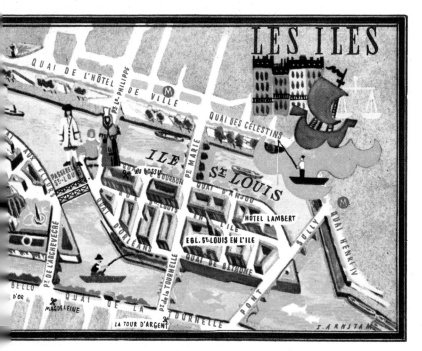

LES ILES

on her. Her profile conjures up a dead past. If one goes too deeply into her streets and squares, one will come out disabused. But observed from afar, her outline at least evokes the memory of what she once was. The Ile de la Cité, the largest, was neighbour to the Ile Gourdaine, the Ile-aux-Juifs, the Ile-aux-Treilles, and the Ile-au-Moulin-Buci. The Cité early formed a refuge when enemy incursions endangered the state. Monasteries were installed round about; to the south, Sainte-Geneviève; to the west, Saint-Germain-des-Prés; to the north Saint-Germain l'Auxerrois, with Saint-Laurent to the east.

Early on two bridges were built. The Grand Pont which in 1141 became the Pont-au-Change facing the Saint-Denis route, and the Petit Pont which gave access to the Rue Saint-Jacques. The Parisians were aware that in opening their island, they were piercing the breach and at the head of each bridge they established two forts on dry land : the greater and the smaller Châtelet—vain protection that could not assure that isolation without which the integrity of the city could not be preserved.

It does not pay for parents to be too familiar with their children. Familiarity breeds contempt. Nobody gains by it, and even politeness disappears. So it was for the Cité, whose children, encumbering the banks, were unable to maintain the respect due to her.

Warnings, however, were not lacking. It might be said that Providence took it upon itself, during the centuries, to fill the gap left open by the indulgent weakness of which the real Parisians, those of the island, continuously showed the symptoms.

Protectress of those who lived around her, the Cité gathered in neighbours who asked for asylum in the hours of danger. In 837, for the first time, the Normans appeared. They turned back on seeing the proud village ready to defend itself. They returned in 845, pillaging the surrounding country, but did not set foot on the island whose banks were defended against the future by ramparts. Higher towers were set up on the bridges and when, in 885, a new armada of seven hundred ships approached, Paris was able to defend herself against the assault. The relics, preserved in neighbouring convents and removed in haste, escaped desecration. The attacks against the Grand and the Petit Ponts failed at first, but the Châtelet caught fire. The assailants redoubled their efforts. It was then that a sudden flood carried away the bridges. The defenders of the Châtelet, remaining on the banks, perished, but the island, once again isolated, remained inviolate. One year of siege did not overcome their resistance, and the Normans had to retire. In the 16th century, the canons still sang in church : " From the fury of the Normans, deliver us, O Lord ".

Scarcely was the danger passed when the bridges were rebuilt. Later, others were thrown over the water. Often, admonitions from heaven warned the Parisians that they were opposing destiny. The Pont-au-Change, at first built of wood, was burnt down several times. It was also carried away by the waters. In 1296 it collapsed. It was rebuilt in stone. The houses which bordered it were burnt down in 1621. It was rebuilt in 1647, embellished by Louis XVI, and enlarged by Napoleon III.

The Petit Pont was carried away by the flood in 1196, rebuilt, destroyed again in 1205, fell in 1405, and again in 1409. In 1618 it was burnt down. A century later, a woman making a vow put a lighted torch in a small

wooden bowl on the water, and left the lighted float to drift. The torch
set fire to a hay barge. The sailors, terrified, cut the cables and the
flaming barge ended up against the bridge, whose houses it set on fire.
Before taking its present shape, the Petit Pont was destroyed sixteen
times.

A similar fate befell all attempts to join the Cité to the banks of
the river. Tremendous fortitude, however, was shown in the struggle
against the elements, whose very destructiveness was its protection. When
the Notre-Dame bridge was carried away on the 25th of October, 1499, the
Aldermen were accused of negligence. They were arrested and
Parliament fined them a considerable sum. They died in prison,
since they had not enough possessions to pay their fine. Fortunate
days, when civil servants were personally responsible for their
errors, and had to treat public matters with as much solicitude as
their own.

Stronger and stronger bridges were built — as the result of experience. Even the composition of the water of the Seine was changed to prevent freezing and to prevent the iceflows from smashing the piles at the time of the thaw. It is seldom remarked that the Seine no longer freezes. In the old stories the frozen river is often mentioned. Sometimes, during winter, it could be crossed on foot. At all events, ice flows drifted down each year. This is no longer so. The residual products of industry that poured into the river seem to have modified even the chemical qualities of the liquid, which remains insensible to the greatest cold. One might even ask if it is water that now flows in the Seine.

Through paying no attention to so many providential warnings, and by defying nature, the Cité found itself open on all sides. Nine indestructible bridges today give access to every kind of harmful element. The Cité, the " Sacred Ark " of the great city, has become a corridor. Everything has been done to rob it of a charm which, however, it discreetly preserves, to the delight of an ardent few who can ignore the mutilations and sacrileges and trust to their own imagination.

The construction of Notre-Dame was undertaken in 1160 on the site of a pagan temple that had been succeeded by two chapels, dedicated to Saint Etienne and Saint Marie, which had fallen into ruins. The edifice was built with a pious fervour without departing from the primitive plan. It attained perfection by the unity of its style and remains, perhaps the most complete, the most harmonious and the most elegant, of Gothic cathedrals.

When one studies its apse, its beautiful flying buttresses stir one by their audacious daring, which makes them lightly straddle space to support

DAUMIER. — *The Counsel's Speech.*

a structure pierced with immense stained-glass windows. The towers of the façade are perfectly symmetrical and their grandeur is in no way burdensome. Their lines are straight. Only by the handling of space and mass are they graced with light and shade, and, therefore, relief. Inside, its massive pillars preserve a mysterious chiaroscuro. For him who takes refuge under its arches, memories come crowding in to recall the great days of the history of France: royal marriages, Te Deums of joy in the days of victory, processions of flags, solemn and sacred vows, supplications in times of distress, deeds of grace, and extravagant celebrations to the Goddess of Reason: for eight centuries the cathedral has housed the joys and sorrows of a people.

At the other end of the Cité arose the Palais: old dwelling place of the Emperor Julian, castle of the Merovingian kings, abode of the first Capetians; a towered fortress whose base was watered by the river. Saint Louis established justice there, and built, to receive the Crown of

Thorns, the most magnificent shrine of all times, a pearl of medieval art. Built in three years, the Sainte-Chapelle with its two superimposed sanctuaries, seems, by its fragile elegance, to defy the laws of construction. The supporting walls are so thin that from inside one can only see the stained-glass windows mounted in a delicate stone frame. These windows are so clear and sparkling that it used to be said of wine: " It is the colour of the windows of the Sainte-Chapelle. "

The Palais, reconstructed by Philip the Fair, abandoned to the lawyers by Charles V, was altered and enlarged. Beyond the Palais were gardens. Between the Palais and Notre-Dame, there was a maze of narrow streets bounded by houses which overlapped and ran into each other to the point of encroaching upon in the side of the cathedral; a multitude of churches, ten parishes, two hospitals, the Bishop's Palace, market squares, and monasteries with their cloisters.

Then the Cité widened out, filling up the loop of the Seine which separated it from the Gourdaine and other islets. In 1707 Harlay obtained permission to build on the newly acquired territory. He erected uniform structures of brick and stone around a triangular space. The Pont-Neuf was built across the extremity of the Isle, and a statue of Henry IV was erected on the central platform. A strange work, which has since disappeared, it had known quite a few changes before its completion. The horse had been ordered from Jean de Bologne to bear the effigy of Ferdinand of Tuscany. The sculptor and his prince both died before completion. Cosmo II had the horse finished by Pietro Tacca, and not knowing what to do with it, sent it to Marie de Médicis. The ship sank, and the bronze stayed for one year at the bottom of the sea. It was recovered and finally arrived in Paris in 1614. The rider was missing. Dupré, a mediocre sculptor, was commissioned to do a statue of Henry IV. He did not make it to scale, and the King seemed to be mounted on Gargantua's mare. The strange destiny of effigies ! It was in front of this image of Henry IV that Mancini's body was burnt, and that passers-by were made to kneel. Three years later, they tore down this tyrant's statue. Another statue, the present one, was erected under the Restoration. Fernand Fleuret, that delightful poet, told me one day that his grandfather had assisted at the casting, and that the bronze contained a secret: in the monarch's right fist, a golden statuette was enclosed—a legend, possibly born in the mind of an imaginative poet, but nevertheless worth repeating.

The island was now completely furnished. Through the piling up of rubble in the course of the centuries, the banks had been raised. The quays sheltered the Cité from floods. The primitive barque had become a high-decked ship. The chimes of the clock of the Samaritaine tolled out the hours. Under the entablature of the bridge appeared the grimacing gargoyles of Germain Pilon. All the crafts were represented there—from the "swallower of ships" who sat at the Pont-au-Change, not like a devouring giant but as a ferryman, downstream of the arch—to the artisans, the traders, and the thousand small money-makers, who cluttered up the Pont-Neuf—acrobats, drawers of teeth, quack doctors, buffoons, Tabarin,

The Tour de l'Horloge and the Flower Market.

Mondor and Brioché, the showman of marionettes. The gamesters offered illusory fortunes and, in the semi-circular openings on the bridge, privileged stall-keepers had their booths.

The Palais itself was full of bookshops and trinket shops. While solemn members of Parliament drew up decrees, people came for the news in the lobbies, where the "Gazette of Holland" was secretly sold. Birds were freed on the king's path to remind him to show favour to the prisoners. Flowers were sold on the quays. Racine, Boileau, La Fontaine, Lulli and Mignard met at the tavern of the *Pomme de Pin*.

The Cité remained the soul of the Capital, ardent and animated. Part of the story of the Revolution took place between the Conciergerie, the lower part of the Palais, and the old Hall of the Grand'Chambre, with its gold coffering, which became the revolutionary Tribunal. Already Louis XVI, following a fire, had rebuilt a façade, little in harmony with

the medieval bastions which, to the north, lined the Seine. One should not be too biased against this edifice, which, after all, is elegant in its way: a public monument cannot be rebuilt. Each age adds something in accordance with contemporary fashion. The important thing is that it be in good taste.

Meanwhile, up to the nineteenth century the Cité had kept its own character. Eugène Süe, in one of his book was, with good reason, able to imagine in the Rue aux Fèves, the existence of the Cabaret du Lapin Blanc, an ill-famed tavern where Prince Rudolphe protected Fleur de Marie against the persecutions of La Chouette and l'Ogresse. A merchant whose store still existed in 1847, under the name of the *Gerbe d'Or*, had proudly written over his door: *Founded in* 410, *idem in* 1600.

Alas ! the ship had opened its hatchways too wide.

The town-planners came in. Haussmann, who had enough space, from the Gare de l'Est to the Seine, from the Grands Boulevards to the Etoile, from the Louvre to the Opéra, from the Place Saint-Michel to the Barrière d'Enfer, from the Halle-aux-Vins to the Chambre des Députés, came in as an iconoclast, scornful of traditions and without regard for a sacred past, to exercise his administrative virtues and love of the straight line. Under the pick-axes of his demolishers, everything between Notre-Dame and the Palais was razed to the ground. All the old and charming houses disappeared. Gone were the Hôtel-Dieu, the Archbishop's house, the churches of Saint-Pierre-aux-Bœufs, Sainte-Marie-la-Madeleine, Saint-Landry, Saint-Denis-de-la-Chartre, Saint-Barthélémy, Saint-Pierre-des-Arcis, and Saint-Eloi; ruined were the ancient houses where wood married stone; torn down the house of Abelard and Heloise and the Hôtel des Ursins and also that of the Councillor Broussel, and the shops of the Rue des Marmousets, where dwelt the barber who cut the throats of his clients and sent the bodies to his neighbour, the sausage-maker; the Marché Neuf disappeared too.

When the Cité was reduced to the state of waste-land, filled with débris and plaster, a new Hôtel-Dieu was built, as sinister as a prison, less attractive than a morgue, and also a Police Station along with a Prefecture—an immense rectangle, so heavily grim that it seems to menace public freedom rather than protect it. On the southern bank, facing the interminable boulevard which leads to the Gare de l'Est, a ludicrous Chamber of Commerce was constructed in a heavy, overloaded architectural style, inconvenient, narrow in spite of its shape, and surmounted by an absurd dome, copied to flatter the Emperor from the model of the *Municipio* at Brescia.

The Seine beats like an artery that carries green blood to an island that might well be its heart.

Henri Calet

The Place Dauphine was broken up and the base of the triangle fell in. Fortunately the Prefect fell into disfavour at the moment when he was contemplating joining the Gare Montparnasse to the Gare du Nord. Perhaps he was even thinking of having a bridge on the tip of the Vert Galant !

They took the soul out of Notre-Dame and reduced it to a mere exhibition piece. Instead of towering protectively above the surrounding groups of buildings, it was isolated, restored by Viollet-le-Duc and now stands alone in a square, as cold as if it were in a show-case. On the site of the Archbishop's house was planted a public garden. The façade is nothing more than an architectural curiosity in front of which sufficient space has been left to allow a tourist's camera to capture the whole on a single plate.

Recently they have had the absurd idea of flood-lighting it on festive nights with powerful projectors, thus reversing the shadows. The edifice, whose hollows and salients were designed for sunlight, finds itself lit up inside out, and seems, at night, with its inverted shadows, to be a large construction of millboard without colour or relief.

The Palais did not escape the fury of the ravagers. The momentum had been given and for fifty years they enlarged it without taste. Although, along the Seine, they respected the Tour d'Argent, the Tour Bonbec and the Tour César, the Tour de l'Horloge was deprived of its old bell, which used to sound the alarm in days gone by. The beautiful clock of Henri de Vic, ordered by Charles V, decorated in the reign of Henry III, was repainted, regilded and renewed. Then they spread out towards the Place Dauphine. They had scarcely started when the revolutionaries of the 1871 Commune set fire to the Palais. It was a heaven-sent opportunity to disfigure while repairing. On the site of the Place Dauphine they set up an enormous façade without any conformity with the rest of the building and without caring that they had used, for the monumental entrance stairway, a different type of stone that was at odds with the patina and which, because of its whiteness, seems to be always new. Then they continued demolition alongside the Quai des Orfèvres. There they built walls decorated with false bastard turrets and stuck ridiculous statues into them.

Not least, they had succeeded in enclosing the Sainte-Chapelle in a deadly dull courtyard. The unhappy building raises its spire in vain to heaven as if to show its presence to the outside world and call down curses on the heads of those who condemned it to perpetual imprisonment.

Thus the Palais, patched up and enlarged, has become an inextricable and useless labyrinth where all the services are muddled together. The antechamber of the Conciergerie where in 1793 the roll-call of the condemned was heard, a sacred place peopled by tragic shadows, has become an ugly station restaurant.

The north is Gothic, the east Louis XVI, the west Napoleon III and the south a hybrid nothingness. The rapid advance of administration deeply modified the life of the Cité. Merchants and artisans disappeared and only civil servants and tourists are now to be seen. It is no longer a place where people want to stroll. The flower-market, the last survivor, is very severely regulated and at the bird-market, permitted once a week, a licence is required before you can sell a canary.

Still, the mutilated island retains its pride. For him who sees it from afar the nave remains triumphant, with its towers, its clocks, and its spires. From the Pont des Arts, its profile still gives an illusory effect. If one goes into the island, one may still venture into the small, ancient part that exists beside the Rue Chanoinesse, Rue des Chartres, or Rue des Ursins where Racine lived. Occasionally, in a fleeting glance, one notices some part of Notre-Dame which resumes its symbolic value and once again becomes the protecting mother around whom everything gathers and throngs. Towards the side of the Place Dauphine, amidst a baseless triangle of houses, one may find again the mellow, contemplative air of a provincial city, in the hours when the Palais is still and the square no longer a car park. It remains in the shade, and when approaching the apex which opens out on the Pont-Neuf, one may still cast a reverent glance at the house of Madame Roland. At the

The Pont Marie.

angle of the Vert-Galant, slightly raised above the level of the river, a garden gives us a little solitude, where we can marvel at the magnificent view of the Louvre, and rediscover some of the poetry which administrative ravages did everything to dispel.

There are silently gathered the last enthusiasts, philosophical anglers whom no misfortunes can touch and who, indifferent to world revolutions, survey the bobbing of a cork whilst watching the river run lazily by.

The shiplike city has, since time immemorial, towed, like lighters, two little barges, the Ile de Notre-Dame and the Ile-aux-Vaches.

Until the days of Henry IV the Ile de Notre-Dame was covered with meadowland where the washerwomen hung out their lines. People also used to celebrate feasts and to amuse themselves there. It is there that Saint Louis armed the knight, Philip the Bold, and took the cross before embarking for Tunis.

There official duels and jousts took place. Archers came to practice and law students feasted. The Ile-aux-Vaches served as a wood store and as a dockyard for ship-building.

One bridge, the Pont-Rouge, used to join the foreland of the Cité to the Ile de Notre-Dame. It was burnt down and carried away several times.

At the beginning of the reign of Louis XIII,

The Quai des Orfèvres.

a master tiler lived there and built a small chapel. It was at a time when it had been decided to let out the island. On April 19th, 1614, Marie, the master builder, made a contract. He undertook to fill up the canal which separated the Ile de Notre-Dame from the Ile-aux-Vaches, to surround the island, now made one, with quays and stone parapets, to open up roads and build two bridges. As a reward for his labours, Marie reserved to himself the right to build and exploit on his own account a tennis court, twelve butcher's shops, a steam bath-house, to own washing ships and a water pump, and to collect for sixty years an annual tax of twelve *deniers* on each house built.

Associated with Le Regratier, treasurer of the Cent Suisses, and Poulletier, the war minister, Marie frantically went to work and fulfilled his obligations. In 1650 the quays were built. Intelligent town planning for once had led to the building of streets in harmonious proportion. The church of Saint-Louis had been built. Fine mansions were rising: most of them remain and bear witness to the good taste of the times. Noblemen and members of Parliament established their dwellings there. On the Quai Bourbon at number 3, was the tavern of the " Franc Pinot ", owned during the Revolution by Renault, whose daughter, Cecile, wished to assassinate Robespierre and so was responsible for the guillotining of her entire family; behind it at number 15, stood the town house of Claude Le Charron, Lord of Ville Maréchal. At number 19, one can still see the town house of Maupas; at number 31 the Boisgelon mansion; at number 43 the Martroy mansion. On the Quai d'Anjou, which is a continuation of the Quai Bourbon, stands at number 1 the magnificent Lambert mansion, decorated by Le Sueur and Lebrun, preserving a provincial and old-fashioned appearance with its rather gloomy garden and melancholy tower. At number 5 one may still see the mansion of the Marquess Poisson de Marigny, brother of the Pompadour. At number 17 the superb mansion of Lauzun remains one of the jewels of the capital. Roger de Beauvais and Baudelaire lived there. It is there that the poet wrote :

> " *The shimmering dawn, in robe of red and green,*
> *Slow moving, on the lonely Seine was seen.* "

It is there that Théophile Gauthier had his first taste of hashish. On the Quai de Béthune, the lovely house of Bretonvilliers with its French garden and its little lake has been destroyed, but there is still a fine arcade to evoke the past. Further on, the Maréchal de Richelieu lived, at number 16.

All the streets of the island are no less rich in associations and relics. Since it was first inhabited, the Ile Saint-Louis served as shelter for those who, fleeing the crowds, sought a quiet retreat.

Towards the end of the 18th century Rétif, the nocturnal visitor, wandered silently like a black shadow along the quays, engraving on the walls the dates whose memory he wished to keep alive.

" The tour of this island has become a delight to me. All the days are inscribed on the stones : a word, a letter, expresses the mood of my spirit. Three years ago, at the same moment, on the same day, I was thus ! and today ! " Later on the romantics took refuge there.

Restif de la Bretonne.

Here Arvers composed the sonnet to the unknown lady whom indiscreet scholars recognised as Marie Nodier.

The inhabitants defend their island. More heed is paid to them now than in the bad days of Haussmann, and heaven protects them. A dreadful cast-iron bridge, which joined Notre-Dame to the Rue Saint - Louis - en - l'Ile, collapsed in 1940, as if to show that only isolation could protect this happy place. Notwithstanding this warning, a similar but temporary monstrosity was erected. Let us beg Providence that this one may collapse in its turn.

The Quai d'Anjou.

The Métro has never passed this way. Buses make a detour. There is not even a taxi rank. Peace reigns. Jean-Jacques Brousson, a fine scholar and a noble craftsman in words, sustains his literary transports in tranquillity. Francis Carco pens his stories of violent love, for which his travels and excursions into the outer world have given him the material. Dignimont, looking out over the river from his windows in the Rue Boutarel, sometimes leaves his delicate water-colours and watches with an astrologer's glass, to make sure that no invasion is menacing the ship.

Ile de la Cité, Ile Saint-Louis, heart of Paris, predestined spots where breathes the spirit, great ships at anchor that no tempest has been able to sink, and which, although mutilated, live on as jewels miraculously preserved, may heaven grant that you may be revered and remain truly isolated in the middle of the great river which loves you, and which inspired Racine to write :

> *I am the Nymph of the Seine.*
> *It is I whose famous banks hold treasures*
> *That outrival Spain in her glory.*
> *This is the happy abode of the greatest kings ;*
> *The scene of their pleasures and their hearts' delights.*
> *Here you will breathe the gentlest air on earth.*
> *I receive the tribute of a myriad nations*
> *But to flow beneath your rule is greater far*
> *Than to rule the Empire of the seas.*

Maurice GARÇON,
of the Académie Française.

FROM THE HALLES TO THE MARAIS

a·M.·PÉROT

PISSARO. — *The Pont-Neuf.*

AN WE DE-

termine the centre of what is called "Parisian life?" Has it not changed from district to district about once every hundred years? But as far as food is concerned, Parisians have never wanted to desert the Halles. There is no reason for feeling sentimental about this tenacity; much had to be destroyed to make way for the growth of this superabundant larder, and the ravages are not ended yet. The site was once called the *Champeaux;* the Carolingian gardener, who used to grow his lettuces on the good soil of Aubervilliers, brought his produce hither, and we can imagine the butcher, in the time of the Gauls, chopping his ribs of beef from wild oxen at the corner of the Rue Montorgueil. Philip Augustus built the first market worthy of the name and Napoleon III the vast iron shelters that the Parisians oddly call "pavilions." In the meantime much has happened there: fires, riots, festivals, tortures, processions, variations in the prices of cheese and pork, all kinds of pranks and brawls, movements of people and ideas, amid the piles of cabbages, the baskets of eggs, and the carts of offal.

One of the best ways of approaching the Halles is by the Métro that brings you up to street-level beside the church of St. Eustache. You find yourself at a venerable cross-roads, almost as turbulent as in the time of the Wars of the Fronde. St. Eustache is the finest church in Paris after Notre-Dame; we are glad to see it here, in preference to a bank, giving its blessing night and day to the kindly fruits of the earth, mingling the notes of its famous organ with tomato auctions, and lending the support of its ancient walls to the piles of cabbages. When its sanctuary door is opened, real fair-ground noises spread into the nave and a whiff of fresh fish and squashed garlic adds a little body to the incense at High Mass.

The Halles are never quite asleep, but they really wake up with a start at two in the morning, when the market-gardeners arrive. They

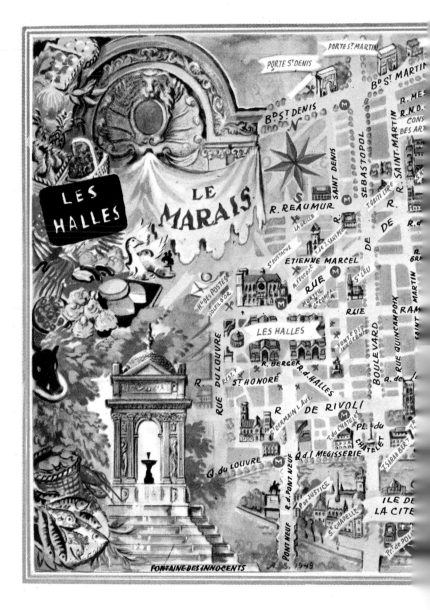

LES HALLES

LE MARAIS

come in from every corner of the near and outlying suburbs, from the
north and the south by the thousand-year-old routes of St. Jacques,
St. Martin and St. Denis, from the east by St. Antoine, from the west
by St. Honoré—carts, lorries and strange vehicles of all kinds—and
meet at the thousand-year-old assembly point. Everything is unloaded
on the pavement—known here as the *carreau*. Then the nocturnal population of market folk again begins to set up among the barrows, baskets,
panniers, bundles and crates, that ephemeral and leguminous city with its
avenues of salads and neat pyramids of vegetables. This is the time when
people come from afar, from Auteuil and Chicago, to eat onion soup in
one of those little eating-houses that cater for real or imaginary rogues
under the quaint tavern signs, inherited from the age of the Musketeers
or the days when peacocks were roasted. I strongly recommend a bag
of chips fried in horse or donkey fat, at about seven or eight in the
morning. While munching them, listen to the strange noises—the wild
music of bones being sawn, the lumbering of barrows over cabbage-
leaves; learn some Parisian blunt speaking, notice the smart repartee.
Go from one pavilion to another, from one world to another. In the
fish-market you will roam over a gluey ocean-bed and imagine that a great
trawler has just berthed beside St. Eustache's. Then, shaking the fish-
scales off your soles, you enter the cheese pavilion where the air smells
mellow. Farther on the sickening odour of red meat will tempt you to
discover the thrills of prehistoric ages; thousands and thousands of
disembowelled bullocks form long narrow corridors where the well-
informed buyer walks slowly, with bended head, assessing and criticising,
like a connoisseur of good painting. A daughter of a dozen quarterings
of Parisian butchers, in her bloodstained array, is gracefully leaning her
elbows on a basket dripping with soft entrails, and the meat porter with
his pink cap is swathed in an overall knotted at the shoulder, an old style
going back to the days of the Burgundians. On the butter-cheese-eggs
side, the blue blouse is the rule—if your heart is really in your profession,
and among the florists there can still be seen the little black skirt with a
thousand pleats which gives the flower girls their spruce and sprightly
line. Slender remains of past glory ! The throng has lost its colour,
its finery, its distinctive marks; it has become grey with time—except
for the little Sister who trots along in the same habit as in the 10th century,
in search of cut-price spinach.

Traditions die—others are born. The pedlars on bicycles have adopted the custom of parking their machines, complete with trailer, around the Fountain of the Innocents—there where Paris was accustomed to bury its dead from the time of the Merovingians. We know that Villon loitered, meditated and picnicked in front of the famous *danse macabre* that decorated the most celebrated charnel-house in Christendom. He liked to frequent this district, so rich in windfalls, and when you are a real poet and somewhat wretched withal, it is good to eat a saveloy you have not paid for, in company with the dead. Now the dead have gone; their bones have been carried off to the catacombs and all that remains is the dust, scattered in the corners of the square. For this place is now called the Square of the Innocents—ever since 1858, at the time when the first squares made their appearance. In the middle of the square rises the famous fountain of Pierre Lescot and Jean Goujon : four nymphs draped in their limpid marble, defying drought. And yet they have not always been lucky with their flowing water. As early as the time of Charles IX, there were complaints of trafficking with fraudulent pipes and filching the king's water from the nymphs. But these nymphs have nevertheless wonderful reminiscences—to begin with, that day (the 16th of June, 1549) which saw the solemn entry of Henry II into Paris. The opportunity was taken to inaugurate this beautiful fountain. I beg you to forget for a moment the baskets of salads and the cycling porters, just to let a delegation pass : there are 350 printers dressed in black with white plumes, goldsmiths in crimson velvet, and 120 men-at-arms, their weapons in hand.

For Henry IV, on the other hand, the district recalls unhappy memories. He was assassinated quite near here, in the Rue de la Ferronnerie, opposite No. 11, by Ravaillac—as even the most ignorant schoolboy knows. It happened just the day before the queen's solemn entry into Paris. The King was in an open carriage, his beard flowing in the wind; his purpose was to make a surprise visit to the Innocents to see how the preparations for the festival were proceeding.

" To the Trahoir Cross," Henry IV had said to the coachman. It was still one of the most famous centres of Parisian life since the days of St. Louis. The cross has now been replaced by a fountain, and the fountain has dried up. It was at the corner of the Arbre Sec and the Rue St. Honoré. The latter, a populous adjunct of the Halles, has not greatly changed since January 16th, 1622, when Molière first saw the light of day at the corner of the rue Sauval. The house has been demolished and the devotees of Molière still lament it. Child of the Halles, Molière saw the façades of numbers 70, 97 and 99 built, as well as the first houses with uneven numbers. The chemist at No. 113 was, perhaps, M. Purgon: at any event the house was already in existence at the time of Louis XVI and it seems that Ferson came here to buy his invisible ink to write to the queen.

Let us return once more to St. Eustache. Stand in front of the classical façade which faces the narrow Rue du Jour. Go into the courtyard of No. 25 and you will discover a little Renaissance mansion, hemmed in and stifled by the encroachments of commerce. The whole of its ground floor is lined with cold storage rooms. Frozen ghosts of the past assure themselves that, after all, it is better to survive in the butcher's shop than

to surrender to the town-planners. Farther on we cross the Rue Montmartre which leads to the boulevards. It begins in the larder and ends in the newspaper world. On the way are little eating-houses, their fronts marked by wrought-iron grills ending in pine-cone designs. Before the war one used to meet, at the lower end of the street, a large grey goose called Juliette, a native of the Halles, who made a habit of feeding in the most crowded part of the pavement and who sometimes bawled in a drunken voice that loudly proclaimed her upbringing. Not far from here is the tower of Jean-sans-Peur, still

standing like a Bastille that has not yet been stormed. It bears a fine name, redolent of halberds and conspiracies, of the horns of the unicorn and long swords trailed down damp stairways. It stands there with delightful insolence, in a street completely indifferent to that kind of thing. The Boulevard Sébastopol has nothing to compare to it, being what used to be called at the end of the 19th century "a great modern artery." It is the businessman's street in daytime and loses caste (just a little) at night—reminiscent of its lively origins and associations with *apaches* and ladies of easy virtue. It has become bourgeois and engrossed in the wholesale silk business and nobody now would ever dream of calling it "the Sebasto." Haussmann's genius was responsible for this boulevard. It was meant to discourage the building of barricades and to relieve the traffic on those two great highways, so aged and cramped, the Rues St. Denis and St. Martin. If you try to look at all the wrought-iron balconies in the Rue St. Denis, you will have to walk with your nose in the air for a couple of hours. Be sure to make a few excursions into some of the numerous little passages that lead off both sides of the street. Some are full of twists and turns bringing an aromatic whiff of the age of Louis XIII, others call to mind the spacious 19th century railway station—which has a certain charm. Footsteps resound eerily and the booths shed the same dismal light as that from dirty window-panes. If you have not the time to go into the church of St. Leu, at least you ought to know that it houses the shrine of Sainte Clothilde, the first queen of France. Then, from a slight distance, cast a glance at its two towers : close one eye and look at them as they appear one behind the other, and you will have a little glimpse of the Middle Ages. Perchance a lady of the streets may take this opportunity to extend a discreet invitation to you, in a pure northern accent. She has been waiting for you there—at one of those street-corners leading to the Boulevard Sébastopol—since the days of Philip the Fair. And no-one would stop you from seeking out the lovely Haulmière.

On the other side of the boulevard is the Rue St. Martin, an even more ancient highway : the chariots of the Roman army passed this way and ten centuries of pilgrims have trodden this route to Compostella. But today it is the travellers selling babyclothes and the roundsmen of ready-made suits that we meet. The dressmakers, tailors, and shirtmakers whom we see plying the needle behind the antique windows, are rarely disturbed by processions. In the year 384 Saint Martin, already well-known through the story of the mantle shared with a beggar, kissed the face of a horrible leper who was healed instantaneously—on the spot where stands the old abbey of Saint-Martin-des-Champs, better known as the Conservatoire des Arts-et-Métiers. The site of this miracle is now dedicated to technical education. We might find a connecting link between the kissing of the leper and the Museum of Industrial Hygiene. The library is installed in the large refectory, a masterpiece of the 13th century. In the church you can admire Foucault's pendulum, set up in place of the high altar; Cugnot's machine is in the apse and Blériot's aeroplane in the nave, along with a hundred other very instructive exhibits that, willy-nilly, become impregnated with the religious atmosphere and take on the appearance of votive offerings. Of the numerous churches that lined this pilgrim's way, there still remain Saint - Nicolas - des - Champs and—pre-eminent-ly— Saint - Merri, the old parish church packed with history, renowned for its canons and its tocsin. It is one of the few churches in Paris that have remained completely true to their own

century, in its setting of narrow streets and ancient roofs. Of course, the town-planners are threatening to make a clean sweep of all this; they love to " disencumber " ancient monuments—by putting them in quarantine in a barren area where they have no right to exist. The maniacs with the pick-axe have already made some savage onslaughts in this district under the pretext of hygiene, in the name of the straight line and the square that is said to rejuvenate ageing cities. It must be admitted that there were in these part some antique remains of a rather squalid kind; they could have been carefully weeded out, but the civic boors preferred the pick. There still remain touching little fragments, such as the end of the famous rue de Venise which leads into the rue Quincampoix. Here modern finance was born, and the French Revolution cradled. The street has not changed since the time of Mr. Law. From those same iron balconies, powdered-wigged bankers and velvet-clad accountants watched a swirling, frenzied crowd. The quill-pens fluttered in the perruques, the famous hunchback was making his pile. Many a time he would come to cadge a pint in the tavern of the Epée de Bois, where the other day I drank an indifferent *pelure d'oignon* to his health.

At the Châtelet we cannot talk history, for it has none; the people we see there are always in a hurry. They leave the Métro only to get into the bus. It is the most important centre of communications in all Paris. The Châtelet Métro station is renowned for its innumerable bifurcations, and the accordion players greatly appreciate the flattering echoes of its long, vaulted corridors. As to the buses, very few Parisians could name all the lines that circulate round a kind of large fountain that nobody ever looks at. On both east and west sides are theatres, and then, further to the east, the tower of St. Jacques-la-Boucherie, which only dates from the time of Francis I. From the top of its 160 feet, Pascal invented the barometer. Later on, an individual installed a small lead-shot factory there; he projected molten metal from the top of the tower into a trough of water. To put an end to these pranks, the city bought up the tower and enclosed it in a square.

The Place de Grève has not been transformed into a square but it has been stripped of all historical associations. It requires a little effort of imagination to picture the spectacular executions and the festivals with their smoking bonfires and casks flowing with wine. There stood the ancient Maison des Piliers and later the amazing Hôtel de Ville, the work

The Tour St. Jacques.

of Boccador, an immense *pastiche*, lumpish and flashy. However, the pigeons which fly over the square lend a certain charm, and there is always a certain bustle due to its nearness to the Bazaar—much more important in the eyes of the Parisians than the Hôtel de Ville. From the Rue de Rivoli onwards we again strike the riotous quarters —the Rue Beaubourg, for example, which is the former rue Transnonain. In the side streets you will see many fine old mansions, among them the Hôtel d'Halwyll in the Rue Michel Lecomte where nowadays mustard is made. The Rue des Vertus, formerly so named from its street-walkers, has always appeared to me singularly honest. If you are thirsty I can recommend the little grilled café under the sign of the Lion at the corner of the Rue de Gravilliers, after which you must go and pay your respects to the oldest house in Paris—3 Rue Volta. It has not yet a square of its own. At the Rue du Temple we have reached the Marais. Under this name we include the districts of Saint-Gervais, Saint-Paul and the Temple. For more than a century the Marais was the capital of the civilised world. There are real proofs. In spite of the transformer's pick-axe there are still more than a hundred mansions in this little plot that will provide you with lessons in the art of building. Nowhere else will you find such good taste and such aptitude for producing masterpieces. The castles and royal residences have disappeared; the 19th century upstarts went off to build in other districts, leaving to the Marais the privilege of revealing the life of the 17th century city. Most of the mansions have now lost their role as such. No longer are concerts and little supper parties held there; neither is history, national or local, made there now; in fact, you could hardly find a respectable night's lodging. Mignard's ceillings suffer from damp. But somehow they all succeed in surviving; some, bleak and stately, as museums; others are given over to the anonymous personnel of the public services, but the greater number are abandoned to the perils of commerce or—decrepit and crippled—await the barbarous onslaught of the pick-axe on their balustrades and the lorries that will load their broken plaster, in dust peopled with ghosts. However, these doorways with their pediments, these courtyards with their porticos, these embossed façades and pilastered fountains are not slumbering in a desert region. Life goes on in the Marais, intense and arduous, perhaps a little beggarly here and there. There are no more princely residents, the bloods are no longer intriguing in drawing-rooms, there are no more illustrious love affairs nor cabals, no historic assassinations, nor poets' alcoves. Only the artisans remain. Since the time of Henry IV the best workmen of Paris have brought their tools to this quarter, where " work well done " was sought after, honoured and discussed, by all the connoisseurs of Europe. The sumptuous days are past, the fine gentlemen have left and the famous coquettes prefer their spacious terraced apartments; but the workmen stay on. When it is said : " He is a workman of the Marais," well-bred people have a tendency to raise their hats.

We have arrived at the Rue du Temple, as I said. We are approaching the Marais, and I will no longer act as your guide and lead you into this historical labyrinth, swarming with charming spectres and gallowbirds who watch for you beneath the arches and beckon to you from the balconies, ready to relate a thousand tales and to present you with one of those archaeological pageants where Anne of Austria, Augustus Comte, Louis XVI, Victor Hugo, Montgomery and Rachel are jumbled together in a hullabaloo of halberds, carriages, cheering crowds, musicians in ruffles, duels in broad day light, daggers in the moonlight, wedding bells and prison bolts. I should lose you at the first turning. Stroll about at your own risk and peril, and if you lose your way and forget the number of your bus and even the year when you were stranded in that insignificant little hotel in the Rue François Miron, thinking that you would pass an uneventful night there, and if you go to the end of the passage and discover with amazement a small court with wood-carved walls, and you stay there, prisoner of a lute-player attired in her

Louis XII finery—then so much the better for you.

All the same, I will give you a few clues, and I will mention first of all some famous places of which no trace exists at the present day, and which are endowed with an occult power as keywords in Parisian history. On the west is the Temple and the shade of its tower, built in 1270 by the knights of the red-cross who made this famous enclosure the centre of their Order. For a long time it was a much frequented place of refuge and immunity; the old-clothes-men of the Carreau du Temple are dubious heirs to this privilege. After the drama of the Revolution, the old Tower was in turn a barracks, a monastery, a cheese-store, a public baths; it was then pulled down and replaced by a square. When the soil is saturated with history the city-fathers plant privet there —it is a principle of municipal rotation of crops. To the south are memories of the Hôtel Saint-Pol, a collection of rustic residences planned for Charles V. The Rue des Lions still conjures up memories of the royal menagerie; to-day it is full of North Africans. The Rue de la Ceriseraie reminds us of "hennins" fluttering in flowery orchards. In No. 7 Rue Beautreillis, at the far end of the courtyard, near an old oak staircase, you will see a noble creeper, clearly an off-shoot of the very illustrious vines whose grapes Charles VI loved to pick. The firemen have settled down here in force, beside the conventual grapes. To the east, the Tournelles—of which there remains only the name and the association with Henry II, who came to die here after the tournament of the Rue Saint-Antoine. Such was the grief of his loving wife that the house of mourning was razed to the ground. Thus it was that the Place Royale came into being on the vacant plot. You can see it there today, almost unspoilt: thirty eight pavilions built over arcades and arranged in a square measuring 450 feet a side, each different, but in complete harmony. Wise Parisians go from time to time to take a " Place Royale cure ": it is an excellent way of raising one's spirits and ridding oneself of complexes. In this edifying setting, a square has been built, where one can meditate at ease. It is swarming with grubby children, who caper and frolic on the gravel which once resounded to the gallop of horses' feet and the tread of swashbucklers in their lace-trimmed coats. Louis XIII on his marble horse now lends his shadow to knitting mothers. This resort is today called the Place des Vosges in honour of the department which, in 1799, was the first to pay its taxes—a record that has never been disputed. The finest pavilion is No. 14; in recent years it has been, in turn, town-

The Place des Vosges in the time of Louis XIII.

hall, synagogue and school, but it was, like the others, designed as a dwelling for man. Victor Hugo has his museum at No. 6 and Mme. de Sévigné was born at No. 1. Her passage through the Marais is marked by a dozen or so mansions; she finally settled at Carnavalet, which is today the museum of Paris. You will find there the marchioness's bed, the bones of a few prehistoric Parisians, tavern signs, the order to the Swiss to cease fire, signed " Louis " and Marie-Antoinette's last scent bottle. Mme. de Soubise, who lived close by, left her house to the Archives of France, which are the most important in the world. The arms factory built for Sully has become the Arsenal library; it also houses interesting souvenirs such as the psalter of St. Louis, the committal order of " The Man in the Iron Mask " and the picture of Charles Nodier listening to the verses of De Musset. Not far away, the scholars of the Lycée Charlemagne go to school in the old mother-house of the Jesuits, but the Servites' convent in the Rue des Francs-Bourgeois was less fortunate: it has become a bank. The very fine and well-restored villas in the precincts of St. Gervais now house the police offices. I have not the heart to show you all the mutilation that the Marais has undergone since the time of Napoleon III, the misuses of money as well as the wanton absurdities. We should even thank the town-planners for not having replaced all the classical façades by hygienic monstrosities and tenement buildings. I will point out two examples—the elegant post-office, a delightfully ramshackle building which in 1934 took the place of the Hôtel d'Argenson, a banal masterpiece of the 17th century; and the fancy biscuit architecture of the balconied Basque chalet, the municipal annex, that blends so happily with the medieval silhouette of the Hôtel de Sens. You will find at the Hôtel de Sens, among other things, associations with Queen Margot and d'Annunzio — it is worth a visit. On the east side, a cannon ball has been driven into the stonework and remained there since 1830 like a nut in a pudding; the old wall withstood the shock unflinchingly. I think that in a very little while the 15th century masonry will have completely absorbed the democratic cannon-ball.

Then again, I should tell you of the half-a-hundred buildings overladen with good references, such as the Hôtel Lamoignon, the Hôtel de Rohan with its astounding horses of Apollo, and that very seductive Hôtel de Beauvais in the Rue François-Miron, built for Cathau, the shrewd, one-

BEUVILLE

eyed chambermaid who taught Louis XIV a thing or two. A little later, the king made his entry into Paris with Marie Thérèse and, from a balcony, his mother, Anne, watched the procession, seated between Turenne and Mazarin. Look at this balcony and the narrow street, and picture the procession forcing its way through the crowds, the trumpets at point-blank range, the family atmosphere. From the same windows, a hundred years later, the passers-by could hear a youngster of seven playing the clavicord surprisingly well : it was the young Mozart. Talking of music, do not forget to go and see the organ on which Couperin played, in the church of St. Gervais, a flamboyant and classical building where

Mme. de Sévigné was married. I must also draw your attention to a very large number of pianos in the magnificent apartments of Sully. It is not a piano museum; the pianos are for sale and the saleswoman who accumulates them alongside the tarnished woodwork is unassailable. Almost opposite, in the Hôtel de Mayenne, the " den " of the " Ligueurs," the handsome Quélus came to die after the duel of the king's favourites. The front of this mansion is a grocer's shop, the back a school. Never forget, as you pass through the Rue St. Antoine, that it was once a Roman road. It is a great transversal artery that runs from the smart districts of the west, by way of the Rue de Rivoli; it becomes somewhat dusty and commonplace from the Rue du Louvre onwards, and the part we have now reached is pleasantly disorderly.

We must not forget that the Marais is steeped in the drama of the Revolution. The bloodshed, the echo of the cries of horror and the shouting, the head of Mme. de Lamballe among the 117 victims of the Rue du Roi de Sicile, and the nightmares of the Prison de la Force were evil obsessions that lasted long, and fashionable Paris, having experienced serene and sumptuous years there, decided to change its abode. The district of the Temple with its sinister memories has, however, grown wiser; nowadays it manufactures, without the slightest touch of cynicism, paper streamers, kazoos and practical jokes. If that is not enough to dispel your gloomy imaginings, then go to the Rue des Jardins St. Paul, to seek out the merry, laughing Pantagruel or traces of the perfume of Ninon de Lenclos in the Rue des Tournelles and of Marion Delorme in the Rue Thorigny. After which, you can go and steep yourself in the Middle Ages in the Cloître des Billettes, in the Rue des Archives, the oldest close in

Paris, built on the site that witnessed the miracle known as the " Dieu Bouilli " when Jonathan the Jew, to his damnation, boiled the eucharistic host after impaling it on a dagger—one of the most sensational happenings of the year 1290. The Jews are still in these parts, in the Rue des Rosiers, for instance, where everything is Hebrew—the notices, the pastry-shops, the meat, the secret meeting-places, the sounds and smells : archaic and impecunious Jews who are preparing the conquest of the Elysian fields with formulas from the Old Testament. Some of them wear the traditional gown and are bearded like prophets, and as they stand against the classical façades, with their black velour hats and cabalistic silhouettes, one would imagine that they are in league with all tradition.

This voluntarily accepted ghetto stretches to the west as far as the Hôtel Bisseuil with its Medusa heads, where Beaumarchais wrote the *Marriage of Figaro*, and northwards to the Hôtel d'Albret, Rue des Francs-Bourgeois. Have I awakened enough ghosts ? After so many turnings and counter-turnings in the recesses of history and a few half-pints of old *Beaujolais*, drawn off in the cellars of the Reine Isabeau, towards evening you will see lorry-drivers in puce-coloured livery with silver brocade, the baker's wife in a Chardon petticoat, and the firemen in tournament array. But do not trouble to venture into the Marais if you do not wish, however little, to transport yourself back to the days of Jean-sans-Peur and if you cannot imagine the desperate gallop of the assassins of the Duke of Orléans in the Rue Vieille-du-Temple, and if you will not quicken your steps down the Rue des Archives to lend a hand to Molière in dispute with his candle-lighters; if, last of all, you do not clink glasses with the joiner in the green overall, who today is making a divan but yesterday was plying his plane on a shutter of the Hotel Montmor.

THE
PALAIS ROYAL
THE LOUVRE AND
THE TUILERIES

E. M. PÉROT

PAUL SIGNAC. — *The Pont Royal* (*detail*).

T THE heart of the most lively district in Paris, the Palais-Royal is a tiny island of verdant peace. Once within its walls, calm follows upon the bustle of the neighbouring streets and the ceaseless stream of traffic that pours down the Avenue de l'Opéra and the Rue de Rivoli towards the new districts. The animation has departed from the galleries, which today are lined with moribund and unused shops, where of old there was flourishing trade. But the houses that have flanked the garden since the reign of Louis XVI are all alike and have become the enviable abode of men of letters and of wealthy admirers of old Paris.

The successive transformations that the palace has undergone since the death of Richelieu have meant that practically nothing of the 17th century buildings remains, except the broad outline of the plan of the palace and of its garden. Such as it is, however, the Palais-Royal is still one of the most important blocks of buildings on the Right Bank, and one of the richest in historical associations.

Despite its name, it was a royal residence only between 1643 and 1652, during the minority of Louis XIV. Moreover, during this short period it was commonly known as the Palais-Cardinal, the name it bore when Richelieu resided there. The " Domain of my Lord Cardinal " formed a long, large rectangle, and was—according to the principles of classical town-planning—the nucleus of the new district which came into being once the city's boundary had, between 1634 and 1647, been extended westward. It was bordered by the Rue de Richelieu, at the end of which, between the new bastions, stood the gateway of the same name. The regular outline of the surrounding district, made up of roads at right-angles parallel to the Seine, was broken in the 19th century by the construction of the Avenue de l'Opéra. But the general lines of the Cardinal's domain are still intact today.

In 1624, Richelieu acquired a mansion alongside the Rue St. Honoré.

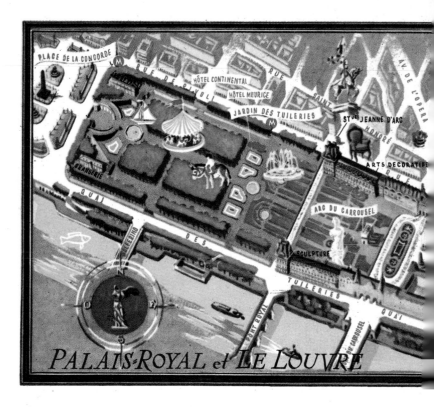

PALAIS·ROYAL et LE LOUVRE

Then, as his ambition grew with his fortune, he purchased large tracts of land around it. The king made him a gift of the old rampart that crossed the present garden obliquely from north-east to south-west. In 1632, Guy Patin wrote : " the Cardinal is leaving his house in the Rue St. Honoré where they are now beginning to build exceedingly. " Le Mercier began the new building in 1635, and Desgost, the king's gardener, designed the avenues and flower-beds.

The following year, doubtless with the object of thwarting the slander of the envious, the minister bequeathed his future palace to Louis XIII. In 1639, the principal buildings were completed.

The panoramic engraving of La Boissière, that appeared in 1665, shows the finished palace. The entrance court, opening on to the Rue St. Honoré, occupied the site of the present first court; the second

court was bordered by two wings—one of which still exists. Their ends were joined by a portico, which has now been replaced by a peristyle opening onto the garden. To the east and west of the actual palace there stretched the offices and outhouses.

Of this group of buildings, all that remains today is the ground floor of the east wing of the second court, decorated—between the windows—with large ships' prows, symbolising one of Richelieu's offices—that of Grand Master of Navigation.

Much has been written in description of the splendour of the rooms and the magnificence of the furniture and the art collections. In this quasi-royal setting, the great minister would take his walks. He suffered from chronic headaches and slept barely three or four hours. In the middle of the night, he would dictate to his secretary, and then sleep again until six o'clock. He would rise at eight and attend mass, then walk in the garden. He dined sparingly, then immersed himself in audiences and despatches, passing the evening in " honourable distractions. " Modern historians have exploded the absurd legends built up, without any foundation on fact, by Dumas and Hugo, and the picture of the great servant of the State has happily replaced that of " The Scarlet Man " and the cynical seducer. What alone is true, is the opulence of his household, which numbered scarcely less than twelve hundred persons. A revenue of 1,400,000 pounds—more than six hundred million French francs or 1,800,000 dollars—was expended, largely on entertaining. All this wealth was bestowed on him by royal favour, but the Cardinal made intelligent use of it. However, his passion for buildings and works of art would have ruined a King Midas.

Richelieu died on December 4th, 1642, and so, six months later, did the king. The Regent, finding the Louvre lugubrious, chose the

Palais Cardinal in its stead. Young Louis XIV must then have played in its gardens and, according to the not very reliable account of Saint Simon, was so badly supervised that he fell into the water. He even chased an unleashed boar on horseback in the little wood. Anne of Austria demolished several mansions to free the site of the future Place du Palais-Royal. She was also responsible for some interior alterations— Madame de Motteville described her " grey room ", while engravings preserve the memory of her bathroom, decorated with flowers and landscapes on a golden background. The civil war of the Fronde took the palace by surprise. The royal family had barely time to escape with Mazarin. On their return, they were almost held prisoners. When peace was restored, the court was set up again in the Louvre. The Palace, now empty, was assigned as a residence to Queen Henrietta of France, widow of Charles of England. The marriage of her daughter brought it into the Orléans family, who held it until the advent of the Second Republic. The young couple had the garden replanned by Le Nôtre. Life continued sumptuously and the festivals were resplendent. But this brilliance was short-lived. From the pulpit of Notre-Dame arose the cry of Bossuet: " Madame is dying, Madame is dead... " Monsieur, the brother of Louis XIV, nevertheless remarried the following year. His new wife was the Princess Palatine; this large German woman, ugly and hoydenish, was to be the mother of the future Regent. She longed for her native land, and heartily detested her palace where Monsieur held a sumptuous but informal court that has been depicted at great length by Saint-Simon. A less select, but persistent crowd was in regular attendance in the garden, which, ever since its inception, was open to all comers.

The reputation of the Regent, the son of Monsieur, is similar to that of Richelieu. The famous suppers of the Palais-Royal that the prince gave to his intimates, in a wing with a separate entrance opening on to the Rue de Richelieu, were not the orgies that rumour made them out to be, but only rather unconstrained parties, especially free in language, in the company of those he called his " *roués.* " The Regent was a patron of artists; he loved Paris, considering himself its master in the absence of the monarchy, and heartily detested Versailles. He was also an amateur chemist—Saint-Simon said of him that " he wanted to see the devil ." In any case, he largely contributed to the creation of a new style which

marks a felicitous transition between the majestic Louis XIV art and the grace of the Louis XV style.

His son, the Duke of Chartres, who, in 1724, became Duke of Orleans, was a strange man. The melancholy that overcame him on the death of his wife, in 1726, caused him to abandon his palace and settle down with the monks of the Abbey of St. Geneviève. The new Duke of Chartres, nicknamed Louis the Fat, reacted against his father's tastes and led a brilliant life in the residence that had been left to him. He made many changes there, and d'Argenson wrote in 1752 that he " almost entirely rebuilt the Palais-Royal. " The fire at the old Opera-House in 1763 was, at least, to give him the opportunity of building a new one on the same site, and at the expense of the city of Paris. It was cited as an example of good planning since the stage could be seen from every seat in the house. A new fire destroyed it in 1781.

The changes made in the Palace itself, from 1763 onwards, gave it practically the same appearance as it has today. The lower part of the façade facing the square, which up to that time was very massive, was pierced by nine bays, flanked by Tuscan columns. The principal

façade, at the far end of the first court, was surmounted by an upper storey, and Pajou adorned it with a pediment bearing the Orléans coat-of-arms. The architect Constant d'Ivry also completely rebuilt the side facing the Court of Honour. Louis and Fontaine completed it according to his plans but unfortunately added a storey that was not in harmony. Pajou had placed there—in 1766—the four statues that can still be seen. At the centre of the eastern wing, on the side facing the Fountain Court, Constant d'Ivry built a very gracious projecting salon that now looks out on to the Rue de Valois. A new staircase was also built, used today by the Council of State, and surmounted by an oval cupola. It has lost the wrought-iron bannisters designed by Jacques Caffiéri, and Defernex' groups of children supporting the candelabra, but otherwise still remains almost in its original state, with Demachy's false perspective, and the three high doors on the first floor that used to give access to the different apartments. On the death of his wife, the Duke left the palace for his country-house in the Ile-de-France, and in 1776 transferred it to his son, the future Philippe-Egalité.

It was only in 1792 that Philip III of Orleans, in obedience to the law concerning the nobility, chose as his family name " Egalité. " By the same decree the garden was renamed " Jardin de la Révolution "—a title that it well merited.

While still Duke of Chartres, the prince had made himself conspicuous, under the old regime, as the prototype of those curious characters, so numerous in the 18th century, who loved novelty fraught with danger. His great mistake was wanting to play a political role and to enter into conflict with the monarchy. He was one of the chief artisans of the Revolution, until this cost him his head. His wildly expensive tastes soon frittered away his immense fortune. His passion for building first accentuated—then served as an attempt to remedy—the disaster. The work he initiated gave his Parisian domain its astonishing political and fashionable role. The second fire at the Opera-House, on June 8th, 1781, was to lead to radical changes. The city was unwilling to pay for its reconstruction, and the king commanded that the new Opera-House be built near the Tuileries. Thus the principal theatre of Paris was lost by the house of Orleans.

The Duke, in need of money, decided to divide up a strip of land surrounding his garden and to build there a row of houses to let, facing on to the garden. Three streets were to be constructed behind these houses and were to receive the names of the Duke's sons—Beaujolais, Montpensier and Valois. The Rue de Beaujolais could only be built in a straight line by removing the ruins of the Opera-House and cutting through the Fountain Court. At the same time, the new theatre was to be built further to the east, on the corner of the Rue de Richelieu, and the projecting apartments that occupied this ground were

DE MACHY. — *The Palais-Royal at Night.*

to be demolished. To replace them, Philip decided to join the two wings of the Court of Honour by means of a large block of buildings facing the garden, which would replace the Cardinal's original portico. The architect Louis was entrusted with the work. The theatre—the present-day Comédie Française—was built, as well as the 60 houses. Practically one third of the area of the garden was sacrificed, but it was embellished by the superb arrangement of those identical façades, with the symmetrical repetition of monumental pillars framing arcades and opening into a covered way that forms a delightful promenade.

But money was lacking for the main part of the Palace. The foundations were begun, and on these the Duke constructed vast temporary galleries of wood and glass; beside them were stalls let out to merchants and occupying the whole of the square formed by the galleries.

The reconstruction of the building begun by Constant d'Ivry, between the first Court and the Court of Honour, was not to be completed until the 19th century. Interest centres henceforth on the houses and the galleries that lined the garden; their development was a prodigious success. The thronging traffic of the Rue St. Honoré broke abruptly into this enclosure. The Duke had taken pains, when installing tradesmen alongside his garden, to see that its elegance was preserved. The shops were reserved for luxury trades and very strict terms of maintenance were demanded of the tenants. Jewellers (there were 59 in 1786), booksellers, cafés, were set up in the stalls; on the upper stories were at first very select clubs, but after the Revolution came the shady gambling dens and the women.

The reputation of " Parisianism " was so well established in this place from the outset, that foreigners hastened there immediately they arrived in Paris. The pleasures of life and the means of squandering a fortune were abundant, and it was possible to live there without ever needing to leave. Until 1789, it had a certain tone. In that year everybody had access to it. The Almanack of 1786 cites an unbelievable number of restaurants, cafés and hotels : the restaurants—Labarrière (the smartest) Vanvilliers, the Taverne Anglaise and the Grotte Flamande; the hôtels—Milan, Beaujolais, Valois, Saint-James, de Penthièvre and d'Orléans; the cafés—de Foy, du Caveau, de Chartres, des Variétés and the "mechanical" café, where the dishes arrived from the basement straight on to the table. To these must be added the shows—from Seraphin's " Chinese Shadows " to the " Little Comedians of My Lord the Count of Beaujolais " that occupied the present-day small hall in the Theatre of the Palais-Royal ; from the " Fantoccini" to the " Variétés," housed in a temporary hall beside the wooden galleries. Finally the museum (so-called), containing Curtius' wax figures, which were later transferred to " Madame Tussaud's " in London. In the centre of the garden itself, hollowed out of the centre of its southern end, was the vast circus ring, covered by a rounded roof. The Café de Foy alone had the privilege of placing its chairs in the garden, where it likewise had a pavilion. Later on, the rotunda of the café of that name was established.

A motley crowd thronged this enclosure. Fops and elegant women, foreigners, officers, and above all, the incorrigible idlers. At the " Arbre de Cracovie", on the terraces, and in the cafés, the " *Nouvellistes*" gathered. This welter of ideas and intrigues was carefully fostered by a demagogic prince, and Chamfort, speaking of the Palais-Royal, rightly called it "the Forum of the Parisian people."

The rainy summer of 1789 favoured the famous " Café de Foy palavers " and the partisans of the new ideas also gathered at the Café du Caveau and the Café Corazza. Extempore orators prevailed upon the crowd to adopt the famous " motions " that gave their name to the " *motionnaires* " of the Palais-Royal. They generally excelled in their stupid sectarianism.

On June 30th, 1789, at the news of the arrest of eleven French guards for " refusing to fire on the people " the habitués of the Café de Foy arose and swept the crowd along with them to the Prison de l'Abbaye, to free the soldiers. On the 12th of July, at the same spot, Desmoulins climbed on to a table and unleashed the passions of his audience against the dismissal of Necker. There was a stampede to the Curtius Museum, and the wax effigy of the minister—in default of his person—was borne in triumph, along with that of the Duke of Orleans. But on the 22nd of July it was a real head, torn from a living body, that of Foullon, that the populace was brandishing on the end of a pike. Only in such a spot

" *Incroyables* " *and* " *Merveilleuses* ".

The Palais-Royal Cannon.

could an event such as this have taken place. Bonfires were made there of royalist newspapers, and an effigy of the Pope was solemnly burned.

But, after 1793, reaction began to set in, and the Palais-Royal was justly accused of having become a den of royalists. Lepeletier de Saint-Fargeau was assassinated in the basement of the Café Février. Already the Muscadins were brandishing their large walking-sticks, and after the 9th Thermidor they gave chase to the terrorists under the admiring eyes of the " *Merveilleuses* " who were, in all weathers, attired in transparent gauze. It was now the Jacobins' turn. A picturesque multitude, with an affected accent, found its painters in Carle Vernet, Opiz and Debucourt. Barras was conspiring in the apartment he let to " la Montansier " whose theatre was packed since she admitted courtesans to the foyer. The new fortunes of the Directory quickly crumbled. A general sense of relief marked the end of so many crimes and found free expression in debauchery.

During this time, the Palais, already emptied of its splendid art collections by Philippe-Egalité's sales, and conscientiously pillaged by the

" patriots ", was like a great deserted house. The Tribunal was housed there, and then, in 1809, the Stock Exchange and the Trade Council. In 1804 life was still in full swing: fifteen restaurants, twenty-nine cafés, seventeen billiard saloons and eighteen gaming-houses shared the favours of the Parisians, and at the mezzanine windows, as well as in the avenues of the garden, a bevy of maidens was on the watch. There was feverish speculation on the Stock Exchange. The gambling-dens, which the ancient regime had prohibited, were flourishing in larger numbers than ever, and parties went on until dawn.

The arrival of the Allies in Paris after the fall of the Empire, brought new life to the galleries. The Cossacks were shocked at the loose morals of the Parisian women—and on good grounds. Well received in most cafés, the Allies ran many a risk—at *Mont Saint-Bernard* or *chez Lemblin*—of incurring a duel, whilst Blücher in a first-floor gambling-den, lost all his estates in a very few days. Soon soldiers on half-pay were unsheathing their swords and crossing them with those of the old body-guard.

The return of the Orléans dealt a rough blow to this wild ardour. The son of Philippe-Egalité settled down in his ancestral home. Little by little, he made a clean sweep. In 1828, the notorious wooden galleries were sacrificed, and with them the thousand of rats that haunted them. The Orleans Gallery replaced this " Tartar encampment "—a phrase that well described the motley clientele. The new gallery was built of solid material and—height of luxury !—illuminated with " hydrogen gas ". In 1837, the courtesans were finally expelled from the extensive promenade—where, more than anywhere else, they deserved their name of " peripatetics ".

Louis-Philippe was proclaimed " King of the French " and for once the Palais-Royal escaped the usual revolutionary bonfire. The royal family settled, however, in the Tuileries; but it was only a postponement of the evil day. On February 24th, 1848, inevitably, the rebels set fire to the Palais-Royal. The flames devoured the suites and Louis-Philippe's picture gallery. When the republic was proclaimed, the Palace became state property.

Under the Second Empire, it became the residence of King Jerome of Westphalia and his son. They set up sumptuous apartments there, some of which still exist. Scarcely had Haussmann completed the new

The Courtyard of the Palais-Royal.

fittings of the Theâtre Français, by the building of the staircase and the two foyers, as well as the addition of a square, than the old palace was once more ablaze. The fire was carefully planned by the revolutionaries of the 1871 " Commune ": paraffin cans had been placed in different parts of the palace. But the destruction was incomplete. The Valois pavilion and a part of the principal building alone were sacked. Among the few rooms that were spared were those that Louis Philippe and, later, King Jerome, had restored and which, at the present time, are occupied by the Council of State and the Directorate of Fine Arts. The restoration undertaken in 1872 did not include the ruined interiors. Only the great 18th century structure, with certain more recent adjuncts, remains. The sole restoration of the 20th century has been a happy one. The Orleans Gallery has been pulled down, but the four rows of columns have been saved. Facing on to the garden, they form a most harmonious peristyle.

Since the time of Louis-Philippe, the Palais-Royal has slowly lost its vitality. The suppression of gaming and the banishment of the women of pleasure under the last French king, dealt the death blow. Until about 1880, however, luxury trades never ceased to prosper in an increasingly calm enclave; Balzac, like so many fashionable people, did his shopping there. The growth of Paris westward meant the transformation of the galleries into an almost deserted spot, where sellers of military medals took the place of antique shops selling rare and exotic objects and moribund booksellers; the cafés closed their doors. The delightful " Hôtel de Beaujolais " alone survives, and the restaurant Véfour, after a long slumber, has reopened in a luxurious way.

When evening comes, the galleries are only peopled with shadows. A few wretched, famine-haunted creatures hail the passer-by. These distant descendents of the resplendent daughters of the Palais-Royal have only the

The Rue de Beaujolais.

attraction of decrepit relics. They pass away their days in those little, one-eyed hotels of the Rue de Montpensier, which may also be reached from the Rue de Richelieu by passages and steps lined with very dubious trades.

However, a new population that delights to nestle in old buildings or to open its windows, in the very heart of Paris, on a park that is alive with the shouts of children and the song of the birds, has settled there in the last twenty years. Colette lives in a house with its entrance in the Rue de Beaujolais—she has only to bend her head to see Cocteau at his mezzanine window. Paul Reboux, Mireille, Jean Marais and his dog are their neighbours. Between the Bibliothèque Nationale and the Théâtre Français, the Palais-Royal is a miniature literary province. One must read Colette's delightful work "*Paris de ma fenêtre*" to capture its day-to-day charm. Near by, is the Café de la Régence, where Diderot watched chess being played on rainy days, and the Univers, where—if they are lucky—the young playgoers of the Théâtre Français can admire their favourite stars.

The district has an added charm; it is the one that can boast the largest number of galleries, passages and arcades in Paris.

Those of the Rue de Rivoli form a circular way round the Place du Palais-Royal and link up with the arches that give access to the garden. There is thus an attractive covered walk, with shelter from rain or sun, stretching all the way from the Place de la Concorde to the far end of the Louvre and the tiny Place Saint-Germain-l'Auxerrois. There are not many such delightful thoroughfares for a stroll as this long gallery, with its reminiscences of Milan and Turin, which has existed since the time of Napoleon.

Thus the quarter has a soul of its own, compounded of history, of nobility, of artistic creations—for its frontiers are limited—and the Avenue de l'Opéra, a few yards away, is already another world.

Jacques WILHELM,
Curator of the Carnavalet Musenm.

the Louvre, we realise the dual nature of this palace. This is as it should be, because thus can we understand it better and love its complex and engaging character, first of all musing over its forgotten outlines and sites—walls, towers and pavilions, that have long disappeared.

To the east, in a corner of the stiff and opulent Square Court, the first thing that we recall—with considerable emotion and even tenderness—is an early, almost fabulous, feudal abode. For this marks the original site of the dazzling fortune of the Capetians, and in a way, of France itself. On the very soil of this Court, begun by the Valois and completed by the Bourbons, the general outline of the keep and surrounding towers of the Gothic fortress tells the story of the beginning of that great future.

To the west we have to imagine the two long arms of the immense palace joined by a large group of classical buildings, a majestic dome dominating them. A few old Parisians can still remember this, since only seventy years separate us from the destruction of what constituted the Château of the Tuileries, the residence of kings and emperors, the objective of riots and revolutions.

The original contours of this monumental collection of buildings—where today only the trees and flower-beds of a garden are a reminder of a defunct and forgotten castle—had to be embellished or dismantled before it gradually attained its present appearance.

Philip Augustus built the first château of the Louvre towards the end of the 12th century, at the same time as he constructed a solidly fortified wall round a rapidly growing Paris. He was reluctant, however, as were his successors, to live in the new castle since the interior fittings were still very rudimentary. Charles V, a learned and artistic king, left no stone unturned to repair Philip Augustus' fortress and to increase its height; and it was in a newly adorned castle that the king of France was to entertain the emperor Charles IV and his son Wenceslas, king of the Romans.

During the Hundred Years' War and the tragic English occupation of Paris which lasted sixteen years, from 1420 to 1436, the Louvre became the residence of Henry V of England, then of the Duke of Bedford, the regent of the unhappy " kingdom of the lilies, " while the young Henry VI of Windsor, at the age of ten, was crowned king of France and England.

When the occupation ended, the legitimate kings of France took less interest in the Louvre than in their Parisian mansion of the Tournelles and their castles on the Loire. But with Francis I everything changed ; the court returned to Paris, the ponderous medieval keep was pulled down and the resplendent monarch entertained Charles V in the grim fortress that had been swiftly and superficially beautified. Then in 1546 the king ordered the architect Pierre Lescot to draw up plans for a palace in the Italian style to replace the outmoded feudal residence. The castle of Philip Augustus and Charles V was condemned, but up till the time of Louis XIV remains of the Gothic fortress still existed side by side with the new wings that were progressively built.

Henry II continued the work initiated by his father. There had never been so harsh a break with tradition; adjoining the military and mediæval walls of the old Louvre there arose on the west side a resolutely Greco-Roman Renaissance palace—one might almost say " provocatively ". Jean Goujon set about the decoration of the exterior as well as the interior according to the same audacious and revolutionary canons. And the sons of Henry II, in their turn, continued the work on the new palace by building the southern half of the Square Court in an identical style. Catherine de Médicis, widow of Henry II, had in 1564 entrusted Philibert de l'Orme with the building of an independent residence, west of the Louvre : this was the château of the Tuileries. A central pavilion, soon to be surmounted by one of the first cupolas ever seen under the Paris sky, housed a remarkable oval staircase of which the steps were " no higher than the four fingers ", as the Venetian ambassador at Paris wrote, "and were miraculously held by a light marble needle."

At about the same time the queen-mother undertook, this time at the Louvre, the Little Gallery, decorated with beautiful Florentine reliefs that Henry IV completed at the beginning of his reign. And

with the building of this little Gallery in 1565, Catherine intended to join, by means of a Great Gallery, the new Tuileries and the Louvre.

Towards the end of the century and during the wars of religion, the Louvre remained one of the most important political centres of the kingdom. With the return of peace and under the impetus of that good and fair king Henry IV, it passed through one of the most luxurious periods of its history. The Great Gallery, dreamt of by Catherine de Médicis, was launched along the bank of the Seine, between the brilliantly decorated Little Gallery of the Louvre and the newly-enlarged Tuileries on the south, reaching to the new Pavillon de Flore. Plans for the unification of the double palace began to exercise peoples' minds— an extraordinary " grand design " to which every sovereign and every artist in turn attempted to attach his name—and which was only achieved two hundred years later by Napoleon III. The Great Gallery, 1,470 feet long, is one of the largest in the world and remains an excellent example of the latter Renaissance style, at least in the part nearest to the Louvre. The part that adjoins the Tuileries, conceived in a more " classical " spirit, was unfortunately recast under the Second Empire. On the

Cour Carrée.

ground-floor and the mezzanine floor of this immense block the gracious and far-seeing king set up a real " nursery " of painters, engravers, goldsmiths, carpenters and, above all, tapestry-workers, all summoned to renew the decorative art of France.

After the assassination of Henry IV and after that of Concini, perpetrated by order of the young Louis XIII, in front of the drawbridge of the palace, the energetic and methodical reorganisation of the kingdom by Richelieu resulted—as far as the Louvre was concerned—in a full resumption of the work. It was decided to quadruple the Square Court. The Pavillon de l'Horloge and its solemn dome was built; the west wing was extended, the north wing was begun. More fragments of the medieval Louvre disappeared, notably an amazing openwork staircase of the time of Charles V, which was destroyed without a shadow of regret. Finally Richelieu installed, in the Great Gallery, the Mint as well as the Royal Printing Press which he had just founded, and Théophraste Renaudot's " Gazette de France. " Thus were the press and the coinage in the Cardinal's powerful grasp.

After the death of Richelieu and Louis XIII and the return of Louis XIV and Anne of Austria to the Louvre, which they had left during the wars of the Fronde for the Palais-Royal, the double residence of the kings was again to benefit by the re-establishment of peace. Thus the queen-mother set up on the ground-floor of the Little Gallery a luxurious summer suite; only the allegorical paintings on the ceilings have been preserved.

In 1661 men were at work in the Little Gallery on a stage where the " Ballet de l'Impatience " was to be performed in honour of the young queen Maria Theresa, whose approaching maternity had just been announced at court. One of the men dropped off to sleep and forgot a lighted torch that set fire to the beautiful gallery, which was complete-ly destroyed. The following year, Louis Le Vau, the new architect, replaced it by the Apollo Gallery which Le Brun and the great decorators of the century wonderfully adorned and where Louis XIV thought of placing his most precious art collections. Le Vau then demolished the last vestiges of the feudal castle, completed the Square Court according to Pierre Lescot's original plans, and built on the Seine side, at the centre of the southern wing, a pavilion crowned with a dome. All that remained was to construct a monumental façade on the east side. Bernini was summoned and he submitted the most Italianized plan in the world. There were several months' hesitation, even after Bernini had laid the first stones of the façade. But, faced with critics who did their best to humble his pride, he returned to Rome. It was then that the great king chose a plan for the façade drawn up by Le Vau, Perrault and Le Brun conjointly, that was

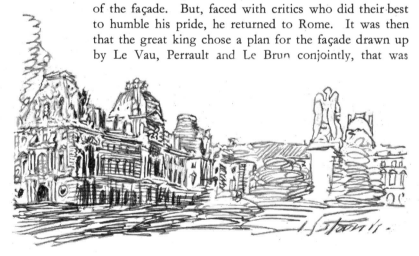

carried out between 1667 and 1670. The front facing St. Germain l'Auxerrois, so bold and austere, is quite illogical in relation to the interior façades of the palace; it is, none the less, an undoubted masterpiece of rhythm and harmony, the most perfect piece of architecture in the whole palace and a most striking manifestation of the art of the Great Century.

The court of the young king was becoming, at the same time, one of the most brilliant in Europe, and Etiquette was to rule the life of Louis XIV with the same symbolic solemnity as it later did at Versailles. Nevertheless the king wrote: " Access is free and within the reach of all the prince's subjects, with the exception of lackeys and other liveried persons. " Everybody found his way into the palace, even to the room where the king dined and the queen dressed. While Molière was reading his comedies in the Salle des Cariatides in the Louvre, Cardinal Mazarin was building in the northen extension of the Tuileries a theatre " for the relaxation of the young king and the entertainment of his people " which, with its thousands seats, was the largest in Europe. The Salle des Machines (as it was called) was inaugurated in 1662 with the ballet of the Italian tragedy " Amorous Hercules ". The same year a memorable tournament was held on the space between the two palaces; it was led by Louis XIV at the head of his court and in the presence of fifteen thousand spectators who had come to celebrate with the king the birth of the great dauphin. This tournament (*carrousel*), held with such an extraordinary display of pomp and luxury, was to leave its name to the Square. The very aristocratic quarter that had been allowed to grow up since the 16th century between the Louvre and the Tuileries reached its zenith at that time, owing to the illustrious Hôtel

The Château des Tuileries.

de Rambouillet, " an academy of good manners, virtue and knowledge. "

Between 1664 and 1666 the Château of the Tuileries, until then unfinished and uncomfortable, was completed on the north side by the Pavillon de Marsan and had its interior fitted out for the king, upon the orders of Colbert, who was charged with the duty of preparing Louis XIV's residence in Paris. As to the exterior, Le Vau and d'Orbay had replaced the charming Pavilion of Philibert de l'Orme with a more extensive building surmounted by a massive dome, corresponding to that of the Pavillon de l'Horloge at the Louvre. Sumptuous apartments—where the names of artists employed at the Louvre reappear—were likewise fitted out (with no little ability) in the Château, whose height had been raised. Finally the garden was entirely redesigned by Le Nôtre who extended the view of the Tuileries to the Rond Point de l'Etoile across a road that marks the origin of the present-day Champs-Elysées. So the progress of Paris westward was accentuated.

About 1674 all the work both at the Louvre and at the Tuileries was interrupted. In 1682 Louis XIV finally settled at Versailles with his government. Moreover artists, whom Henry IV had been the first

to house under his roof, came little by little to occupy the Louvre, in association with men of letters and science, while the palace itself, left incomplete, was abandoned by its legitimate owners. This very unusual situation was to last until the time of Napoleon.

Louis XIV had already installed the French Academy in the palace; from 1679 onwards the Academy of Architecture, that of Painting and of Sculpture, and that of the Sciences, came to join the former. That same year, Le Brun organised a "Cabinet of the King's Pictures" which he opened to the public and which is, in consequence, the predecessor of the present museum, dating back to the end of the 17th century. The Great Gallery, from 1679 onwards, housed the periodical exhibition of painting which about 1725 was installed in the Salon Carré—whence its name of Salon. "Crowds are thronging it," wrote Sébastien Mercier, " people have been streaming there during the whole six weeks, without a break from morning to night; there are times when one is suffocated." To this must especially be added the progressive invasion of the Louvre by the artists who had elected to live in the Great Gallery, even the Apollo Gallery, and up as far the terrace of the Colonnade, daringly building staircases or temporary partitions in the stately wings of the ill-fated palace. Finally a real " pavement artists' exhibition " was held under the entrance gallery of the Colonnade. This attractive but dangerous anarchy in the palace of the monarchy is rather bewildering to the imagination.

The middle of the 18th century, however, saw a certain amount of order return to the palace, thanks to the intervention of the Marquis of Marigny, brother of Madame de Pompadour—nominated by favour of the latter to the post of Director-General of the King's Buildings. The Square Court was cleared and the Colonnade freed of the old buildings that screened it. Soufflot and Gabriel built the attics that the excessive height of the Colonnade required. But the artists and men of letters were only in the slightest degree put out by this; and foreigners, beginning with the Emperor Joseph II, came to visit this paradoxical palace as one of the most piquant curiosities of Paris.

At the same period, Count d'Angiviller, Marigny's successor, envisaged the founding of a museum in the Great Gallery. Projects for a museum were under discussion from the reign of Louis XV, when a public picture gallery had been organised in the Luxembourg Palace. Numerous plans were drawn up to establish by law what had already existed in fact since the time of Louis XIV; the Cabinet of the King's Pictures was unfortunately too often disorganised and dispersed. The Ancient Régime had not the time·to carry out d'Angiviller's very reasonable plan; the Revolution took it up in 1791 and brought it to a successful issue.

The château of the Tuileries, also deserted by the royal family was, however, Louis XV's abode during his minority. In 1725 sacred concerts were held in the vast central *salon*, which were very well attended; Goldoni never ceased to extol their " magnificence ". In 1764, after the Opera House at the Palais-Royal had been burnt down, a new one was set up in a hall fitted out in the former Théâtre des Machines, and Rameau's " *Castor et Pollux* " was presented for its inauguration. Six years later the Comédie-Française took its place and it was here that Voltaire received the famous " Apotheosis ", when the whole of Paris became delirious over the cunning old rascal, almost stifling him with flowers and crowns; it was three months before his death.

On October 6th, 1789, Louis XVI and the royal family settled in the Tuileries; they had been brought back from Versailles by a multitude brandishing pikes and branches of poplar. " A civic and saturnalian festival, " decorously wrote the *Moniteur*. And Barrère eloquently proclaimed to the Assembly : " The King of the French will henceforth make his habitual abode in the capital of the Empire" ; the Assembly itself chose the Couvent des Feuillants, situated a few steps away from the Tuileries.

An astonishing medley of events, warlike and peaceful, revolutionary and cultural, was the continuous lot of the "double" palace throughout the Revolution. On June 20, 1791, the royal family attempted to escape; they were recognised at Varennes and brought back to Paris; from April 1792 to 1793 the guillotine was permanently set up in the Place du Carrousel. On the 10th of August, 1792, the Tuileries were taken and

pilaged in the course of a bloody insurrection; the same year the Convention decided on the organisation of the " Museum ", setting up a commission that was to be presided over by David. On January 21st, 1793, the King of the French was guillotined in the Place Louis XV; on August 10th, the Great Gallery, transformed into a museum, was at last opened. During this time the National Convention was installed in a hall that had been rapidly fitted up for their meetings in the Salle des Machines. To record the history of the Tuileries of the Revolution is to record the history of the Revolution itself—which Napoleon Bonaparte was to crown by settling, on February 19th, 1800, in the palace, that still bore the scars of the Revolution.

The " infernal machine " from which Bonaparte escaped to the north of the present Place du Carrousel amid the maze of streets and houses that still divided the double palace, decided the First Consul to begin the partial destruction of this inconvenient quarter. A road was then made between 1802 and 1808. It joined the Tuileries directly with the Louvre and was the prelude to a plan of Napoleon's—which he was never able to carry out—of joining the two buildings. It was at that time that Percier and Fontaine, the new architects appointed by the First Consul on his return from Egypt, completed the decoration of the façades of the Square Court, indulging in an infinite number of regrettable alterations and heightening of the buildings, insisted upon by the Emperor despite the advice of a commission of artists. The same two architects built the small triumphal arch of the Carrousel, at that time surmounted by the horses of St. Mark's, Venice, and restored the interior of the Tuileries. Lastly, north of the Carrousel a gallery was begun, between the Pavillon de Marsan and the Tuileries; this was the Napoleon wing. But the events of 1814 prevented the carrying out of the final plans of a whole group of galleries and courts that would have ruined the original proportions of the double palace, as the Emperor himself realised. In 1806, he had, in order to reinstate the Louvre in all its dignity and unity, harshly expelled the artists, the last heirs of the over-benevolent hospitality of the ancient régime. And it was in the newly fitted out Great Gallery that the wedding procession of Napoleon and Marie Louise took place in the midst of masterpieces won by the armies of the Republic and the Empire.

On January 28th, 1814, the Emperor bade farewell to his guards at the Tuileries; on May 3rd, Louis XVIII settled in the " Château " which he left on March 20th of the following year to give place to the Napoleon of the Hundred Days. On June 23rd, Louis XVIII was again at the Tuileries after this tragically ironical "general post." The Restoration

only produced work of a minor importance in the double palace. Louis XVIII and Charles X resided at the Tuileries and the museum of the Louvre continued to grow. In 1830 the Louvre and the Tuileries were taken by the insurgents and Alexandre Dumas, who was in the fighting, relates how "the nuptials of the common people with freedom" were consummated on the king's

bed! A little later the victorious Louis-Philippe, in his turn, settled in the Tuileries, which were subjected to some unfortunate alterations.

On February 24th, 1848, Louis-Philippe abdicated and fled from the Tuileries, which was invaded and sacked by the mob. "Cristi, how you sink down in it!" exclaimed the urchin Daumier, flopping down with satisfaction into the abandoned throne. Three months later, the Second Republic decreed the completion of the Louvre, the "People's Palace", which had assembled under its roof the Museum, the National Library, and rooms containing industrial exhibitions—which Victor Hugo grandly called "A Mecca of intelligence". The east side of the Great Gallery was then injudiciously restored, as was the Apollo Gallery, Delacroix finishing the decorations that Le Brun had begun. But it was only after the *coup d'état* of Louis-Napoléon Bonaparte—who installed himself in the Louvre in 1852—that the "great design", which had waited since the end of the 16th century, was carried out.

Between 1852 and 1857, the decayed quarter (nowadays it would be called "insanitary") dividing the double palace was completely demolished by Haussmann. Visconti, and after him Irfuel, built the wings of the present Carrousel Court (then called Place Napoléon) which they joined up with the Great Gallery, and on the north, opposite the Palais-Royal, with new buildings. It was an immense task, based on quite a logical plan; but the style, a heavy Renaissance *pastiche*, is often execrably turgid, especially in the high pavilions surmounted by voluminous roofs with a great deal of superfluous ornament. The western part of the Great Gallery and the Pavillon de Flore were later unfortunately destroyed and rebuilt in a very dubious style. The triple entrance of the Carrousel dates from this period, i. e. 1861 to 1870. Despite the incessant work which was to disturb the daily life of the inmates of the Château, the court of the Tuileries witnessed the brilliant scenes of the civil marriage of Napoléon III with Eugénie de Montijo in the Salle des Maréchaux, and the great official balls right up to the famous " Sovereigns' dinner-party " at the time of the 1867 exhibition, when there were assembled at the Tuileries, around the Emperor of the French, the emperors of Austria and Russia and the kings of Italy, Sweden and Prussia. The triumph of the Second Empire took place in the heart of the Louvre and the Tuileries, now united—but for how short a time ! On September 3rd, 1870, the Empress heard the news of the disaster of Sedan. On the following day, the Third Republic was proclaimed; Eugénie fled, passing through the entire length of the Great Gallery, and leaving the Louvre by the entrance gate of the Colonnade, escaping from the crowd in a cab. Thus did this gallery, conceived by Catherine de Médicis and executed by Henry IV with a view to aiding a possible flight in case of insurrection, serve the purpose of a fallen sovereign three centuries after its foundation.

The effective union of the two palaces was to last less than fifteen years : during the night of 23-24 May, 1871, the revolutionaries of the Commune, tracked down by the Versailles army that had entered Paris, drenched the Tuileries in paraffin and then set fire to the palace. The fire almost completely ravaged the interior of the château of Catherine de Médicis, Louis XIV and Napoléon, leaving only the walls standing. The Louvre was only just saved in time. Eleven years later, supposedly aesthetic considerations condemned the pitiable but admirable walls of the Tuileries, still almost intact. They were sold for disposal at a sum of thirty three thousand francs. The stones that survived this cruel auto-da-fé are to be found to-day throughout France from the Tuileries garden to the Château de la Punta at Ajaccio, and even abroad from Hungary to the United States. Some paper-weights were cut out of the marble and distributed among subscribers to a serious-minded newspaper.

The life of the newly-restored Louvre (the Pavillon de Marsan and the Museum of Decorative Arts date from the beginning of the Third

The Louvre Museum in the 19th Century.

Republic) was indistinguishable, from then onwards, from that of the Museum, which continued to grow and become more complete.

THE LOUVRE MUSEUM

The ancient and royal collections, enriched by the conquests of the Republic and the Empire, the purchases and gifts that have multiplied down to our own time, make this museum one of the most undoubted masterpieces of international art.

From the immense Great Gallery of Henry IV, recently restored according to the plans of Hubert Robert, where are grouped round the Gioconda masterpieces of Italian painting from Titian to Raphael and Tiepolo, to the Salon Carré where are now collected, with El Greco and Goya, the works of the Spanish school, one passes through the Flemish and Dutch rooms, marked by outstanding works of Van Dyck, Rubens and Franz Hals. It is a suite of dazzling wonders—now completed by a new room of French painters, from the Primitives to the 19th century. To this collection must be added the incomparable Apollo Gallery of Louis XIV—where are preserved the Treasure of St.

Denis and the Crown Jewels, and the very beautiful rooms of the Colonnade which contain the carvings of the royal apartments as well as tapestries and works of art, ceramics and enamels. Such a setting has conferred upon the first museum of France a charm and a prestige that one rarely finds elsewhere in so marked a degree.

The sculpture rooms containing examples of Egyptian, Oriental, Greek and Roman civilisations, as well as medieval, Renaissance and classical examples, are ranged on the ground floor of this palace in what were formerly some of the most luxurious apartments. It is quite moving to realise that the most important works of art of the French Middle Ages, or of the Italian Renaissance, from the tomb of Philippe Pot to the slaves of Michael Angelo, are exhibited in that part of the Great Gallery which was rebuilt by Napoleon III.

The rehabilitation of the museum has now been going on methodically for some years. The task of the 20th century will be the embellishment of this palace. Our century must fulfil a work of infinite delicacy and complexity, the conversion of a palace into a museum that is wholly devoted to the Fine Arts. That is the new " great design " that must from henceforth be emphasised. Its realisation will perpetuate the achievements of three centuries of French endeavour.

Yvan CHRIST.

THE
FAUBOURG
SAINT-GERMAIN

E·M·PEROT

MONIQUE JÖRGENSEN. — *Hôtel Clérambault*
(*from " Les Hôtels Historiques" pubd. by Marcel Daubin*).

be surprised to find my signature appended to an essay which has as its subject—among all the " villages " that go to make up Paris—the Faubourg Saint-Germain. I have never systematically avoided or voluntarily ignored this *faubourg*. The numerous and often cordial pages which I have consecrated to the Saint-Papouls should be sufficient to prove this. Also I who have taken my dog, called Macaire, from Rue Vaneau to the corner of the Rue du Bac and the Boulevard, can hardly be suspected of having ignored the flavours and smells of this part of the world. However it is true that I would have been more at ease, more carried away at the outset by a wave of lyrical emotion, had I to invoke a more intense or a commoner Paris, with tightly packed crowds, with inextricable confusions of streets and houses; or, even that melancholy and liveliness that strike one, each in its turn, on the highways of Montmartre, Menilmontant or Picpus.

But I did not wish to escape from a difficulty which fate seemed to impose upon me. For it was either the wanderings of fate or the caprices of fortune that arranged that I should be born in the womb of Montmartre (I arrived there at the age of three weeks), which made me live from then on, in heaven knows how many districts, and which finally deposited me, in 1946, like Moses's cradle, in an eminently respectable little backwater of the Faubourg Saint-Germain.

I was faced by an incontestable fact. At the moment when I was asked to write, in a book dedicated to Paris, about one of the " villages " of Paris, the " village " in which I was living was the famous Faubourg. Why deny it ? I had already, for more than two years, learnt to live there. Had I not, at the same time, without looking for it or being fully aware of it, acquired certain traits, certain pulsations from it ?

And should I not profit from my completely spontaneous apprent-

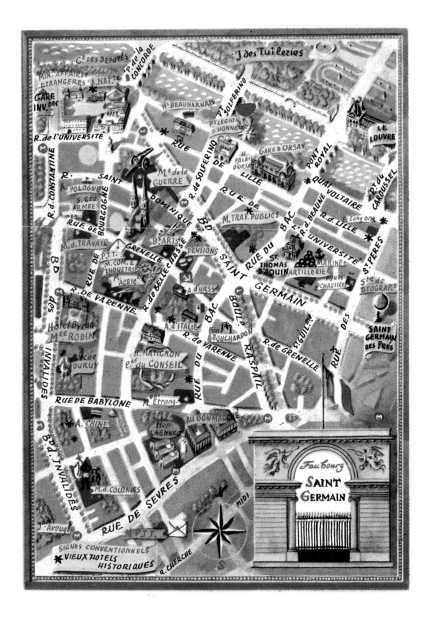

iceship as an inhabitant to try to explain, ever so little, to people, and above all to myself, one of the districts whose originality—however profound—has most chance of passing unnoticed, or of being reduced simply to a list of curiosities for the learned ? That would be a pity. For town-lovers well know that the investigation of strange places in a town, or a part of a town, is certainly well worthwhile and often indispensable. However, it does not in any way take the place of a completely different kind of knowledge, more interior and more intuitive; in the same way as the delineation of personal traits has nothing to do with dreaming, or reflectively contemplating a face.

Here then is a district which, in its actual form, resembles no other. It is unique in Paris, and there is scarcely anywhere in the world to compare with it. But, to notice this, to appreciate the charm which it emanates—which is a medley, and easy to ignore because it does not at once affect the senses—it is best to look at it close at hand, and then to reflect.

This district is the result of a very curious historical operation : a sort of invasion, followed by occupation. The invader, in installing himself in what he had conquered, did not deliberately destroy it. Certainly, he was heavy-handed. He demolished all that annoyed him, and rebuilt, thinking to improve it. He made large clearings, which he thought useful, and constructed around them coldly commonplace buildings, without so much as asking himself whether the age-long aspects that he was supplanting and the town that he was disfiguring were not worthy of special treatment. But, more often still, he tried, in the manner of all invaders, to alter completely that which already existed He, as one says now, "requisitioned" the buildings and the homes. Since his sole consideration was to acquire large edifices, his choice usually fell on the most magnificent. He changed their character to make them serve his needs or his dreams of grandeur. As his needs were often prosaïc, and his ideas of grandeur a little big, he proceeded without malice to a complete form of vandalism from within. A mean passageway, where a fat and badly dressed man is drowsing at a white wood table stained with ink, has replaced a sumptous gallery. A large drawing-room, with its mirrors, its panels, its decorated ceiling, has been changed into four disjointed rooms, separated by partitions, the colour of a barracks or a hospital. Pipes of all sorts, whether for stoves or hot water, wires in

173

loose bundles wander wherever they please. Even in the halls, which aim at a certain amount of dignity, new ornaments, vases, allegorical females, bear witness to the sad moments that decorative art has suffered.

Similar adventures have occurred in widely different places. But here their importance was derived from the outstanding character of the parties concerned. The invader was no less than the French government. The territory invaded, and then occupied, was not any little village, but one of the most exceptional formations which a very mature civilisation could achieve; a city, as closed in its way as the city of Carcassonne, a little enclosed town, where for two centuries the greatest families of the Kingdom, little by little, had gathered together, establishing side by side, their mansions or, for want of anything better, their apartments, creating among themselves a neighbourliness, an intimacy, a feeling of being among themselves which only the Marais had known in a previous epoch of Parisian history. Governmental France, the France of the Powers, had installed itself in the old City of the Nobles.

An 18th Century Interior.

It is here that I would like the reader to reflect a while, so that nothing of the flavour may pass him by. Ask a Parisian point blank, even one with experience; talk to him of this district. That his thoughts will turn first of all to the Palais Bourbon and its immediate surroundings, is only natural. In the same way he will recall, without difficulty, the Ministry of Foreign Affairs, and the War Ministry. (Let us leave on one side the Invalides, which are practically on the border.) But you will see that it will take him several minutes, perhaps a good quarter of an

The Seine and the Palais Bourbon.

hour, to convince himself that practically all the Ministries, about twenty big Public Administrations or Offices and many Embassies are gathered together in this zone, practically without one's noticing it; that within the limits of a large village, a capital has been formed, within a capital, the equivalent for France of a condensed Washington.

How did this amazing situation arise? Because, not being seen by the eyes, it did not impose itself on the mind. There were none of those ostensible groupings, those symmetrical official palaces, those Government squares that one sees elsewhere. The invader without making any fuss, and almost stealthily, went to lodge with the inhabitant.

On the other hand, put to the test one of these absent-minded wanderers, who can only see straight ahead, who can cross the same part of a city twenty times without even delving to the right or the left. He will be mistaken in the other sense. What will remain in his memory is having walked along wide and pleasant streets of a very modest and conventional picturesqueness, which go to or from the river. He is oblivious of the existence of a " Faubourg Saint-Germain " which is as shut out from the outside world as is possible, though lacerated and distressed by internal devastations. On top of this, if our absent-minded passer-by tried to explore the side streets, as far as the Rue de Poitiers or the Rue de Chanaleilles, nothing in the façades or in the enclosing walls would tell him much. He would have to penetrate even further, before he could suddenly discover some majestic courtyard or a garden whose beauty and silence would seem to him unbelievable; he would have to set foot in the suites of drawing-rooms with their high windows, where neither the decorations nor the furniture seem to have changed since the times when the " City of the Nobles " was entertaining. He would even have, for a few hours, to associate himself with a mode of life out of the ordinary, even today, but oddly persistent.

For one must, in all fairness to the invader, say this : he has

The Parliament (from an old print).

The Place du Palais Bourbon.

certainly not destroyed or driven everything away. At times he even took precautions when he installed himself, and showed both delight and respect—he himself and those who were attracted to him. In this way, Ministries even preserved precious fragments. In this way also, the town hall of the district, behind a guise of promising nothing, now preserves for you the surprise of its pomp and pageant. In this way, the idea of making use of the luxuries they inherited, without spoiling them, came more naturally to the Embassies.

And in the streets themselves, what evidence of this historic invasion do we find ?

First of all, there are the occupants. By that I mean to say the army of bureaucrats who share amongst themselves the Ministries and their offices. It is a daily and fleeting population, since it lives elsewhere. The streets ought not to be affected by its presence, except during certain limited times of the day. But the difference from working-class suburbs is that it is not strictly bound to a time-table of arrivals and departures. One could say without any malice that there is at all times throughout the day some civil servant who is arriving at, or leaving his work. The more one approaches the senior grades, the less the time-table seems

to coincide with the activity. One of the results is that, except during the early hours of the morning or the late evening hours, the street is never emptied of this element, which although respectable is not exactly indigenous. At certain times, however, these comings and goings coincide and swell into a veritable torrent. I can recall, when I began living here, being suddenly struck with alarm. Under my eyes, a street, normally rather quiet, would fill out with men and women by the hundreds, more or less well dressed, who neither shouted nor smashed windows, but did not hesitate to invade the pavements, and who hurried off, all in the same direction. I thought of a riot of the middle classes. (How would that work out?) But it was simply the normal hour (or almost) for closing down all the offices, and which for many—the subordinates at least —practically corresponded to the time when work should stop.

At other times or in other streets, or thanks to a certain amount of discernment, one can learn to recognise a totally different type, the

really indigenous,—the rest of
the conquered people. And the
most noticeable among them
are the old maids, or ladies
of a certain age, sometimes widows.
Everything about this type is
odd; and particularly the physique.
These ladies often have horsy
faces, or if you prefer it, harshly
masculine faces : a visible bone
structure; long and pronounced
features; noses and jaws which seem
to ask for respect rather than a kiss.
They are tall. Their step is firm and
long. Do not expect the voluptuous
gait and the traits which writers of
American detective stories give to
their heroines. Their dress is
severe : mostly black—with a gleam
of white. Often a white ribbon
around the throat. (How does it
happen that this bit of white ribbon,
so easy to copy, seems to give forth
such an air of distinction ?) Fashion
has never been fully accepted, or if
it has, it has been rigorously controlled. Long before the time of
long dresses, the skirts always
avoided being too short. Certainly, on some occasions, hard
times added a touch of poverty to
their outward appearance. But
when one thinks of women of the
same age, who flourished in other
districts, with their skirts of knee-
length, sometimes even higher, their
exhibition of fat legs and their

bloated thighs, which seem to ask for a chance of being shown, one has to admit that the atmosphere of Rue Las Cases, or of Rue de Varenne, if slightly obsolete, has, nevertheless, its virtues.

The other elements of the fixed population have fewer peculiarities. By associating with them, however, one grasps what the French Government and the Old City of the Nobles altered in their ways of life. For example, the little shopkeepers resemble, in a general way, those of anywhere else. Only here we observe the results of their aping of these two sets which tends to keep them in their respective spheres of influence. So there is the hairdresser for the civil servants—where the minor secrets

and worries of State find a favourable audience—and there is the hairdresser for the well-born, and even for the high-born. (One cannot always call him to one's house.) I found out that here, also, there was an outpouring of confidences, but of a different kind, although at times free enough; and that the reserve natural to such distinguished clients gave way to the magic of their surroundings. In between these two—and this

A Reception at the Embassy.

difference is not always affected by the prices—there is the hairdresser for the servants of the great houses.

Let us not be simple enough to think that the conversations here are especially loose or scandalous. Possibly it is the opposite. Where for their masters it is an occasion to relax, for them it is an occasion to show that they do not belong to a badly brought up world of ill-gained riches. Another virtue of the Faubourg Saint-Germain is that of seeming to inspire amongst the servants a lively sense of differences which makes them at times sacrifice their own interests to pride. One must say that, without exception, they are wont to receive from those who employ them, consideration, and an equable courtesy—even real affection. This is something that those small women covered with jewels who have fits of rage which hurt their servants—only to make it up an hour later with a large tip—cannot in the least understand.

It would only be right to give a separate place to the trade and crafts-manship which is also to be found in these parts, with special reasons for their being there : antiques, repairs of old furniture, restoration of pict-

The Palace of the Légion d'Honneur.

ures, objects of art and tapestries. Without doubt it is far from being a privilege exclusive to this district. The sixth *arrondissement*, to mention only one, can boast of even more antiquaries. But in this district the wandering client and the lover of the unexpected are rarer.

The repairers, above all, work for people they know and who are loyal to them. This is reflected in their ways.

Lastly one should not forget the position and the surroundings. If one goes to the heart of the district, there is nothing very remarkable, nothing outstanding. The value of the streets is in their detail and what they make you feel rather than the overall picture they form. The charm of the best preserved corners does not offer to the eye a more picturesque poetry than one finds in a distant provincial town or in a cathedral city, at Bourges, at Moulins, at Dijon... But there is the river bank; the quay of the Seine which Parisian municipal grace makes us now call the Quai Anatole-France. It is one of the most majestic walks which Paris can offer that born patrician, the Parisian, with the view looking directly over the Tuileries and the Louvre and the Palace of the Légion d'Honneur on the right. Between the two, the vista stretching out over this great river to the most famous sights of all. One has only to start crossing the Solferino bridge to notice the prow of the Cité, Notre-Dame and the Institute. One may even forgive the Gare d'Orsay, for only a thousand years will be enough to make it resemble an engraving of Piranesi. By that I mean a thousand years of peacefully growing old. For one's heart tightens at the thought of what might have happened, only recently, to all this, in the course of a few days.

Jules ROMAINS,
of the *Académie Française.*

ST GERMAIN DES PRÉS

E. M. PÉROT

JACQUES THÉVENET. — *The Institute.*

T IS NOT

very easy to define the boundaries of a district whose distinctive features are Art and Letters.

J. H. Rosny senior, a former inhabitant of the upper Rue de Rennes, situated between Saint-Sulpice and Saint-Germain-des-Prés, remained faithful to the end to an illusion whereby he claimed that he belonged to Montparnasse, because he could just see its railway station when leaning over his balcony. In wishing to be a citizen of the neighbouring district, then in its heyday, he was not so much attracted by smart cafés—flashing *Coupoles* and shimmering *Dômes*—as by the populous corners where he could find, both in their misery and their joy, the daughters of those whom J. K. Huymans has pinned up like butterflies and described so brilliantly for us.

One wonders whether Léo Larguier, while enjoying with him a drink of the whitest of white wines in the Place Gaillon, undertook to explain to his venerable colleague and President of the Goncourt Academy that, by merely dreaming he was a citizen of Montparnasse, he was shirking his duties towards the small country of his choice—that lovely spot, that he, Larguier, had named " Saint-Germain-des-Prés, my village ".

On the other hand, the poet-author of *Isolements*, also sinned in his own way by quite arbitrarily extending his village to the banks of the Seine, on the delightful pretext afforded by Théodore de Banville, who lived in the Rue de l'Eperon and who confided to us in a poem :

I go to see, when it is noon,
The etchings on the quai Voltaire.

This charming Parisian district of Saint-Germain-des-Prés was for a long time no more than the lobby of the Faubourg Saint-Germain —that " *Côté de Guermantes* " described by Marcel Proust—and the mere vestibule of Saint-Sulpice, where, changed into fountains, the

four   stone   bishops   survey   the   shadows   of   Manon   and   Renan.

No one could foresee that one day Saint-Germain-des-Prés would triumph over Montparnasse.

Let us admit right away that Saint-Germain-des-Prés owes everything to its cafés.   Fortune favoured it the day a store bearing the sign of the " Deux-Magots " closed its doors and was shortly re-opened by a bartender, who only retained from the old draper's the two Chinese figures made of painted and gilded wood.   Then came Lipp, the brewer from the banks of the Rhine, who has since been succeeded by Marcellin

Cazes. And was it not under the sign of *Flore* that Charles Maurras recounted his tales of the royalist league, he, the habitué of the café which is at the corner of the boulevard and the rue Saint-Benoît, where Rémy de Gourmont, the thinker, the Sage, the " big brain " of the literary periodical " *Mercure de France*," also had his headquarters ?

There were no signs predicting existentialism. If the prosperity of Saint-Germain-des-Prés had begun before the advent of those great physical as well as spiritual disturbances which have given the world the colour it has to-day; if we must, to keep close to true facts that are hard to define, trace the coming into vogue of this district back to the eve of the First World War, when Jacques Copeau opened the theatre of the *Vieux Colombier*, still called by wicked minds the *Folies-Calvin*; if we must conjure up those dress-rehearsal nights, when, after the curtain had dropped, the people known to be amongst the most intelligent in Paris—including a fair sprinkling of pretty women—found it necessary to refresh themselves with beer and sustain their precious reflections with cold chicken, or a morsel of choucroute—it is an obvious fact that Saint-Germain-des-Prés owed its tremendous boom to the magisterial apparition of J. P. Sartre and Simone de Beauvoir.

They can no longer be seen, writing, writing, writing again, with fountain-pens that never seemed to run dry, from the opening of the cafés till closing time.

They have fled, for fear of being smothered by the crowd of disciples whose genuineness too often might leave them in doubt. They have fled, but the existentialist crowd has increased in numbers; furthermore, people come from all over the world to gaze at existentialists at large.

It is worth while taking a long journey to admire the youth of Saint-

Germain-des-Prés. It has style, and it is real youth. The boys and girls are generally good-looking. Thick is the hair, worn flat and low on the brows of the boys whose Tartar-like moustaches have put out of countenance the ugly, monkeylike beards of the students of the Beaux-Arts, who have remained faithful to the café terraces of the district, so close to their impressive school in the Rue Bonaparte. As for the girls we can but comment on, while not too severely criticising, their peculiar hair style. These young girls, so up-to-the-minute, remind us of Ophelia and even of that *Inconnue de la Seine*—a plaster cast of a drowned girl of twenty—which we can see in the numerous art shops of the district.

The friendly foreigner from Oslo or Cincinnati would be mistaken if he thought that so many boys and girls were wearing themselves out covering pages for publishers, when they were not at the cafés.

Existentialism is a type, a fashion, a mood. In Saint-Germain-des-Prés one is existentialist as, fifty years ago, one was "decadent," from

Saint-Sulpice.

the *bistros* that neighbour the Rue de l'Echaudé, made famous by the Père Ubu (that humorous individual described by Jarry) to the Cabaret of the "Divan Japonais" on the slopes of Montmartre. The "decadent" girls wore their hair in the "empty tummy" fashion (for, the French proverb says, "an empty tummy has no ears")— with the same compliance, the same artlessness, as does Simone de Beauvoir's distracted flock, which now puts on the pathetic look of the *Inconnue de la Seine*. One evening I found myself, by chance, on the first floor of the Café de Flore. It was existentialist to the hilt. The *Inconnue de la Seine* was letting the son of Gengis Khan gently squeeze

The Court yard of the Ecole des Beaux-Arts.

her waist. One of my companions was greeted by one of the most handsome juvenile leads in the place, the most authentic existentialist in the room, judging by his appearance. To my great surprise, someone asked him whether he was satisfied with " business. " He replied that things were not too bad considering the times. Would you like to know what kind of business it was ? This fine young fellow sold house-boats to the rich and fashionable.

You can get one for three million francs, the price of a good car—not expensive, according to him—compared with everything else. This is to show you that, just like the Café de Flore, existentialism has its various levels.

There was a time, mercifully short, when a minority of existentialists indulged in certain forms of eccentricity, somewhat pitiful perhaps, and bordering on cynicism. It was the time of deliberately shabby clothes, with shirts hanging out of the trousers and flapping in the wind. More decent apparel is now the rule. The last devotees of a form of existentialism that imitates the "daubers" of former days, in certain ways, have motorised Bohemia by going everywhere in a car, an amazing old bus painted all over in yellow and black checks.

One is not at all existentialist at the Brasserie Lipp with Marcellin Cazes, the founder of the literary prize that bears his name. The habitués of the old place still miss seeing Léon-Paul Fargue drinking his glass of Vichy water there. That great writer and hero of the sky, Saint-Exupéry, who was here known as "Saint-Ex," used to come and join him. The beautiful Valentine Tessier, another faithful customer, really seemed to descend from the *Carrosse du Saint-Sacrement*, the title of the play being shown at the Vieux Colombier.

It is a fine day indeed, when spring is born and the Cazes prize awarded. The candidates for the four figure cheque are scattered about and have spread into other cafés as far as the *Rhumerie Martiniquaise*, without going quite so far as the *Café de Cluny*, the outpost of the Latin Quarter.

There are as many journalists and radio reporters with what they call their sound truck, as assemble for the Goncourt prize. Then follows the feast, in honour of which Cazes takes the trouble of travelling to his native Rouergue, in quest of the choicest ingredients.

May those who seek in this book useful, accurate information for travellers, bear in mind that, since May 1949, the cafés of Saint-Germain-des Prés have returned to their prewar customs. They remain open until two o'clock in the morning. It is therefore enough that a great Prima Donna should perform one night, or that a thrilling verdict should be pronounced at the Palais de Justice, or a violent debate should take place at the Palais-Bourbon, for the cohorts of existentialists—or so-called—to be overwhelmed by those who represent, as in the past, the "Tout-Paris," from the great barrister Moro-Giafferi to Francis Carco, from Henri Torrès to Suzy Delair.

It is at the Deux-Magots that André Breton holds sway, he who has remained surrealist in this age of existentialism, when most of his comrades and disciples have more or less betrayed that which was defined as obscurism in the days of Paul Souday, the critic—then famous, now

The Terrace of the Deux-Magots.

forgotten. His former friends upbraid him for I know not what in the political line—reminiscent of the differences between the Turks and the Moors, and between Stalin and Trotsky. And Breton does not care—more archangel-like than ever—now that his beautiful ash-blond hair has turned to blond ash. Opposite him sits his faithful friend, Benjamin Péret, author of *Il était une Boulangère* (There was once a baker's wife) and of *Je ne mange pas de ce pain-là* (I don't eat that kind of bread)—this second book not being a sequel to the first.

Distinguished dissidents soon appear. From time to time, just to make sure of what can and must be preserved in obscurism and automatism and all that, Breton and Péret cross the Boulevard and go off alone to Lipp to "throw a small one behind their tie." This is the expression used in the narrow bar of the *Reine Blanche*, the little spot in this great metropolis where it is fashionable, or at least the custom, to queue up in order to make your way into the cramped passage, if you are one of those valiant exponents of the " self-sufficient being " convinced of the necessity of keeping going till the hour when the bashful stars close their weary eyes. It is also at Saint-Germain-des-Prés—usually in charmingly old-fashioned hotels—that we find those Americans who have come to seek, in the old world, the emotions of a less highly organised life than the one they live on the other side of the Atlantic—that old ocean dear to Lautréamont, of whom the young existentialist girls speak so well, although they have no more read his books than those of Kierkegaard, their other intellectual passion. Some of these uprooted " *amerloques* " are newspaper correspondents, others bravely hold down obscure jobs; many have cheque books. We can be sure that from their group will rise to-morrow some new Miller.

Future diplomats, future statesmen, the students of the School of Political Science in the Rue Saint-Guillaume will, let us hope, conceive some plan for eternal peace, while sitting in one of the cafés dominated by the antique steeple, drinking mild drinks, and observing the demeanour of these cosmopolitans and their enchanted guests.

The St-Germain-des-Prés Club.

We must note, in passing, that in former days these young gentlemen from " *Sciences Po* "— so called in school slang—looked extremely formal, as if already absorbed by the Quai d'Orsay. The spirit of the School has altered a great deal since it was nationalised. For a number of students it is no longer fashionable to shine by the stiffness of one's collar. On the contrary, a certain slovenliness is now tolerated, as indicative of daring opinions. Is it a nursery of proletarian ambassadors ? In any case, it sometimes happens that these young men, who are stuffed with international law, and will one day be called upon to direct the different branches of Foreign Affairs—excepting the Protocol, of course— turn completely existentialist.

Shall I mention the " dives " ? Of course I must. What shall I say about them ? The first one—too noisy, according to the vehemently expressed opinion of the bourgeois inhabitants of the old Rue Dauphine— was the renowed " *Tabou* ." It could be adequately described in a few words, by stating that the whole of the Café de Flore might have dropped a few feet lower, with part of Harlem and the whole of Greenwich Village of New York thrown in on top. A spicy detail : the manageress of the Tabou made her début in the intellectual world by carrying off, with hardly any effort, the first Paul Valéry prize, a posthumous bequest of the author of " *Charmes* ". Perhaps, after all, the *Tabou* was not the first dive in Saint-Germain-des-Prés. I remember a literary prize night when, led by a publisher who was swelling with gratitude, the jury descended into a secret dive. Now, to enter, one passes beneath a neon sign.

There is the *Rose Rouge* in the Rue de Rennes. Then there is, in the Rue Saint-Benoît, the Saint-Germain-des-Prés Club : Léo Larguier, who lives nearby, pretends to hate its hubbub—he who sleeps the sleep of the just, through yesterday's alarms and the eternal storm.

The dives are considered to be novelties by those who are not well acquainted with the history of literary life. In the intellectual districts there had always been dives. Those of Saint-Germain-des-Prés perpetuate the dives of the Latin Quarter, that of the *Soleil d'Or* where the periodical *La Plume* entertained, that of the *Hydropathes* where Rodolphe Salis found inspiration for his *Chat Noir*.

I have shown from the very start that Saint-Germain-des-Prés is not a district that is either square or round. If old Rosny went astray by turning his back to it, to make out that he was in Montparnasse once he had reached the boundaries of the Plaisance district, dear Léo Larguier was right: Saint-Germain-des-Prés is a star whose beams radiate afar; it includes, of course, the Rue des Saints-Pères—where Petit Pierre, who became the great Anatole France, used to stand in awe; the Rue de Seine, the Rue Bonaparte, the Rue du Dragon that leads to the Croix-Rouge cross-roads. It also comprises the Buci cross-roads where, in 1848, Baudelaire, tormented by Freudism before its day, was heard to propose the summary execution of his father-in-law, General Aupick. This caused consternation among the revolutionaries, who greatly respected the former director of the Polytechnic School, which was considered to be the nursery of republicans from whose ranks, whether at the top or bottom of the class, would spring so many taskmasters.

Dear Buci of my youth! Buci of my *Tendres Canailles*, full of picturesque daubers—not always honest—including even counterfeiters such as those who inspired André Gide in his novel *Les Faux Monnayeurs*; daubers in cloaks and pointed hats, with thick walking-sticks and clay pipes with bowls in the form of skulls whose place has been taken by the wearers of loud check shirts, with hair tumbling over their brows and tartar moustaches.

Before the existentialist era, the only youths who indulged in rowdiness around Saint-Germain-des-Prés were those of the School of the Fine Arts. In those days, Derain, the famous painter, had his studio in the Rue Bonaparte, right opposite the main quadrangle of this seminary of aesthetics from where emanate the winners of the Prix de Rome and future members of the Institute; also obscure drawing masters and quite a number of strong-minded artists, weary of academic studies, who will be the future glory of independent art.

Derain had already sown his wild oats, and now enjoyed nothing better than the folly of his juniors. He never failed to lean over his balcony every time a burlesque procession started out from the great courtyard on the quasi-solemn occasion of the *Quat'z' Arts* ball, when mock Egyptian Pharaohs, comic Babylonians or dreamlike Atlantiades carry away, in a crazy round, beautiful girls—so scantily clad that soon the words of a former celebrated old inhabitant of the district become true: "Nature's dress is the skin." Another occasion was the end of the yearly *Rougevin* competition, when the students,

Saint-Germain-des-Prés.

harnessed to carts decorated with Venetian lanterns, go with much shouting to the Place du Panthéon, where they burn the works which cost them such noble efforts.

" It's wonderful ! ", the master would exclaim, he whose heart and soul were still so young—" They look as if they were pouring into my studio... " We must admit it, the youngsters of the School of Fine Arts are not as gay as they used to be—especially the painters and the sculptors. The last happy lads are the students of Architecture; there are so many today—including foreigners—that new studios had to be opened for them in an annex at the corner of the Rue Mazarine and the Rue Jacques Callot. If in those parts you happen to hear the sound of a hunting horn or a bugle, you can be sure it is one of those apprentice builders who is sounding the brass. Perhaps one of these good fellows will build for us the modern Parthenon. The main body of these determined visionaries will perpetuate the blessed corporation of estate agents.

May heaven prevent them from causing too much destruction under the pretext of town-planning! Demolitions and reconstructions have often done even more harm to this fine old district, this village, than the construction of the Rue Jacques Callot, which added modern art galleries to those of the Rue de Seine. We are apprehensive that other streets may be ripped open and suffer the fate of the Rue des Saints-Pères, where the pick-axe abolished all the exquisite memories of wanderings around the second-hand book-shops—and even that Wonderland shop, that vast garrison of toy soldiers, where we recall, not without emotion, having heard retired colonels holding an academic discussion with boy scouts over the particular detail of a uniform. Everything has been torn down. It is enough to make Anatole France turn in his grave. And why? To insult the Sequanian soil with the frightful cement carcass of the still unfinished Medical School.

Town planners, please spare at least the other side of the street, where exciting shops still survive, including many fine booksellers. Do not touch the Rue Visconti. It is narrow, and few of its houses could stand up to the installation of modern conveniences, it is true. But gentle Racine lived there, Gérard de Nerval day-dreamed there. In this same street Balzac's printing venture ran him heavily into debt. Eugène Delacroix had his studio there before settling in the Place Furstemberg. It was in the Rue Visconti that he entertained George Sand and Chopin. On certain nights, the wanderer who takes pleasure in evoking the past can imagine that the evening mist is made of the smoke of George Sand's cigar, while the breeze carries with it incomparable minor chords from one of Chopin's sonatas.

Place Furstemberg.

Have pity on the old village streets ! Have pity, you planners of a Rue de Rennes that will lead from the Gare Montparnasse to the Seine over which will stretch an X bridge ! Have pity on the dear old streets with such pretty names : Rue Dauphine, Rue Mazarine, Rue du Pré-aux-Clercs, Rue du Jardinet, Rue de l'Eperon, Rue des Ciseaux, Rue du Sabot, Rue Princesse, Rue de l'Echaudé, Rue Cardinale, Rue de l'Abbaye, Rue Bourbon-le-Château—where the curator of the Carnavalet Museum, led by a poet, discovered some paintings of Hubert Robert in an attic; Rue du Dragon, still untouched in its pure Louis XV grace— and, thanks to the Académie Jullian, still full of the fragrant memory of Marie Bashkirtseff and the lovely slav charm she disclosed; lastly, the Rue des Canettes, where a crumbling house bears a stirring memorial with the name of one who lived there before the 1914 war and who gave his life " For France, for Paris and for his Rue des Canettes."

Saint-Germain-des-Prés had other martyrs in the dark days of the second world war, as well as during the moving days of the liberation of Paris. Its monuments did not suffer over much. The invaders, collectors of bronze, picked on the unfortunate Broca—who was famous for his " circumvolutions, " if I dare express it so—and who well deserved the twofold honour of standing as the idol of the " saw-bones, " on the threshold of the Medical Faculty, and firm on his pedestal at the boundary of the village of pure intellectuality, on the frontier of the country of endless debates, having given the best of his genius to the study of grey matter.

The bronze collectors did not dare touch Danton, nor the symbolic figures that surround him opposite the cinema that bears his name. They also respected Diderot, possibly overawed by the prestige of the word " Encyclopedia." There remains a bust of Laënnec, and they are looking for a verdant spot for Apollinaire, who lived at No. 202 in the Boulevard. Will the poet who wrote " *Alcools* " be set up beside the inventor of auscultation, or the fanatic ceramist, Palissy, who, in order to heat his oven, only left his family the straw of their chairs ?

Because the district is now one of the most popular in Paris, its reputation having become world-wide, the international cinema has chosen it as background. If you find the Boulevard closed at the top of the Rue de Rennes, do not think there is a riot. The Parisian police, called out for the purpose from their station in the Rue de l'Abbaye, are merely clearing the field for the actors and film operators who are taking pictures of a choice exterior. Come closer. Perhaps you will be lucky enough to find yourself there on the very day that Charles Laughton has arrived from London especially for the occasion, with a thick moustache stuck to his upper-lip, to be filmed in some episode of the eventful life of Inspector Maigret, the hero of Simenon's books.

They are shooting a film at Saint-Germain-des-Prés : that gives the excuse for much philosophising, and a certain amount of food for thought. Young men, the juniors of these hard times, who call themselves producers when they have no other social position, feel they must indulge in comments. Awaiting their turn, perched on the high stools

The Old Curiosity Shop.

of the Deux-Magots, with their legs crossed high— often shapely limbs at that — a cheap cigarette between their small lips, extras try to pose as stars —not without envying two or three Ophelias or *Inconnues de la Seine*, who enjoy the privilege of living at the café without working. Yet how wide that Ophelia from the Flore opens her eyes when a fellow with a green eyeshade, and with a leather bag strapped round his waist, issues envelopes, in exchange for their signatures on a receipt, to those extras who leapt from their stools. André Billy, the sole Goncourt habitué of the Saint-Germain-des-Prés cafés, is right in advocating that a "Bohemian life throughout the Ages" should be done.

Saint-Germain-des-Prés is all that. All the past and all the future, tinged with all the vivid colour of the present. And yet Léo Larguier himself, who was the first to honour his beloved "village" in his rhythmic prose, can still rove about in peace from the least literary café, which I have not named, to another café that bears the name of a Métro station which is still temporarily closed. He has fled from the Flore— after due deliberation—and for no reason. He would be at leisure to meditate there in peace—just as Rémy de Gourmont, if he returned amongst us, after reading the plate affixed to his house in the Rue des Saints-Pères, close to a famous publisher's, could comfortably, in the midst of the existentialist mob—loud rather than noisy—glance through all the morning papers, as was his habit, at an hour when serious-minded people of his day would be reading the only respectable evening paper "Le Temps."

And what is there so very novel that would prevent us from wandering in the bookshops from the Rue des Saints-Pères to the Rue de Seine, the Rue Jacques Callot, the Rue des Beaux-Arts; and from lingering in the Rue de Seine with the merchants and brokers at the bar of *La Palette* which has become a small, modern painting Exchange; or from having a drink *Chez Constant*, knowing what a crowd there is on varnishing days, even if in the neighbouring picture gallery the tiniest cocktail is offered to the critics? In the Rue Jacob, you will find the most modern of bars, including Riquette's, run by that admirable girl who offers her walls, free of charge, to the painters of to-morrow.

Ancient and modern are happily married here. Believe me, from shop window to shop window one learns more about style than at the Ecole du Louvre. I would not go as far as to maintain that cousin Pons, that touching character from Balzac, could unearth an inexpensive find every day in the portfolios of the art dealers of the district; on the other hand, one sees plenty of booksellers from the Right Bank browsing profitably among the shelves of their innumerable colleagues of the Left Bank.

The discovery, in the Rue de Seine, of a painter who, in order to set his " Realism in Courbet's manner " in violent contrast to " Abstraction in Picabia's manner, " painted a damsel in scanty underwear; the finding of a first edition in the bookshop with the pretty name of Anacréon; a call at Riquette's to clink glasses with a follower of Sartre; the " one for the road" at the Deux-Magots or the Flore before dining at Lipp's—all that goes to make a fine day in Saint-Germain-des-Prés. You are welcome to crown it with a tour of the smart bars, from the *Montana* to its anonymous neighbour that takes pride in displaying as many up-to-date books as surprising drinks—if you so desire.

André SALMON.

the latin quarter

E. M. PÉROT

H. DE WAROQUIER. — *St. Etienne-du-Mont (detail)*.

OOKING

back to the days when you were a student in the Latin Quarter half-a-century ago, and now that chance leads you back there again, you ask the mirrors in the shop-windows of the Boulevard Saint-Michel or the Rue des Ecoles to show you the slender silhouette that you had in 1900. But the windows of the cafés, the hatters, the outfitters, and the booksellers only reveal to you a white-haired old gentleman, who bears no resemblance to the young man of twenty that once walked these streets. I wanted to make a pilgrimage there before writing these few pages.

The area is a large one and eludes the administrative divisions of the municipality of Paris. It is entirely an imaginary quarter, and yet we can assign boundaries to it, as did Théodore de Banville who lived and died near the Boulevard Saint-Michel.

" The Latin Quarter," he said, in a Paris guide published in 1867, " comprises practically the whole of the 5th and 6th *arrondissements*. It is bounded on the north by the Seine, the Quai des Grands-Augustins, the Quai Saint-Michel, the Quai Saint-Bernard; on the south, by the Boulevard du Montparnasse; on the west by the Rue Bonaparte; on the east by the Halle-aux-Vins. It includes the Ecole des Beaux-Arts, the Institute, the Mint, Saint-Germain-des-Prés, Saint-Sulpice, the Charité, the Luxembourg, the Palais du Sénat, the Hôtel de Cluny, Saint-Séverin, Saint-Julien-le-Pauvre, Saint-Etienne-du-Mont, the School of Medicine, the Lycée Saint-Louis, the Sorbonne, the Collège de France, the Sainte-Geneviève and Mazarin libraries, the Law School, the Panthéon, the Pitié, the Jardin des Plantes, the Ecole Normale and the Ecole Polytechnique."

The poet of our days would add the Ecole des Mines, the Ecole Coloniale, the Schools of Pharmacy, of Physics and Chemistry, and behind the Panthéon, in new streets and ancient alleys, all those laboratories and institutes conserving a form of witchcraft which did not exist in his time.

Radium, for example, he would have taken for a flash from some mysterious heavenly body.

The Latin Country has always been that of Bohemia, youth and fantasy. The clientèle of wine merchants used to consist of ineffectual visionaries, ladies of easy virtue, students up from the provinces in process of becoming academicians, dramatic authors, statesmen, all of whom were, in a word, out to conquer Paris.

I am speaking of those who saw themselves as the ambitious heroes of Balzac; but most of them were satisfied with being assiduous at the lecture courses of their Faculty, with frequenting the cafés, the Source, the Vachette, the Harcourt, the Taverne du Panthéon and with dancing at the Bal Bullier on Thursdays and Saturdays. Those who are still living are probably doctors, lawyers, retired civil servants; some will no doubt

have been chairmen of their local Councils, looking back to the sublime days when, after having drunk many beers at 20 centimes, they bawled on the way from the Rue Gay-Lussac to the Châtelet:

In the Boulevard Saint-Michel
There's many a naughty gel
Casting a merry eye
At the students passing by.

Those who come back to Paris on business from time to time find very little of what they left behind there. The café where they used to go is replaced by a loan-society. Time respects nothing: he is an old alchemist who changes the tavern into a shop or a bank. For them, as for me, the Latin Quarter is a Paradise Lost.

The aspect of a town, if not its very form, " changes alas !

The Boul' Mich'.

more quickly than the heart of a mortal'', as Baudelaire said. At the corner of the Boulevard Saint-Michel and the Rue des Ecoles, a bank has taken the place of the café Vachette where I used to see the poet Jean Moréas every day between 1903 and 1910. He would stop on the threshold. His monocle gleamed and with an unfriendly eye he took stock of the scene. He then came and sat down at his table, at which I was already seated. He announced to the world in general that everything was *sinister* and that he would never set foot in the place again. The cigar he was smoking was worthless... You let him ramble on... Isidore, the waiter, served him with a little glass of *marc* which provoked unflattering reflections on café proprietors and Burgundian distillers... One heard the muffled hum of an incantation : Moréas had declared peace with his heart and the world, and was murmuring one of his " Stanzas " !

The Rue des Ecoles, full of the most pleasant ghosts, has scarcely changed, and I rested on a seat in the garden that lies behind the Hôtel de Cluny. A few ruins, a few stones reverently assembled, are all that remains of Julian the Apostate's baths.   Here you can descend the very steps of history to the oldest Paris of all.

We must not forget that the Boulevard Saint-Germain reaches to the Halle aux Vins and that the Jardin des Plantes is only a few steps away. The latter is rather like an earthly paradise whose upkeep was too costly and which had to be handed over to a pedlar, turned nursery-gardener. It is possible to travel a long way here without moving.   Light a cigarette, lean against the iron bars behind which camels are passing, and you are in the East.

In the neighbourhood of hospitals, barracks, factories and railway stations, the former " Royal Garden of Medicinal Plants " is a deserted Eden.   All the species are jumbled up here; the Japanese copper-beech grows beside the French plane-tree, the catalpas are side by side with the maples and the Chinese peachtrees blossom beside magnolias and firs.

A lion, who does not condescend to look at the passer-by, whose great yellow eyes are heedless to all around, hears with indifference the sound of a siren on the Seine; the condors and the bald vultures raise their white-flecked eyelids and spread the vast span of their wings in a way that calls for the icy solitudes of the Cordilleras, and the visitor strolling by senses the wild nostalgias and savage desires of these captive beasts.

Behind the tall glass-cases of the Museum we see the chalky carcases of prehistoric monsters and we can imagine them alive—at the time when the iguanodon, enormous and awkward, with its flaccid skin and horny snout, its claws armed with immense nails, waddled along, terrifying and grotesque, hopping over the marshes, drinking their waters dry—in the moist twilight of the Secondary Period...

Here is the house of Buffon.   A host of associations arise in our minds in front of this façade which seems to be asleep under the branches.   We picture the lovely end of a peaceful day that has eluded the calendar...

A valet dressed like a figure in classical repertory opens the door, and by the dim light from the window-panes we notice, in the middle of the room, a man of incomparable nobility.   He is wearing silver-buckled shoes, white stockings and breeches of russet silk, while his wig, tied with a large black ribbon, flows on to his plum-coloured coat.   Lace cuffs frame his beautiful hands, a diamond badge sparkles at his side,

The Hôtel de Cluny.

and round his neck he wears the pale blue ribbon of the Order of the Holy Spirit; it is the Comte de Buffon. He is surrounded by a group of people—entomologists, palaeontologists, celebrated historians... In one corner Monsieur de Jussieu is deep in conversation with Cuvier who has donned his frock-coat embroidered with green palm. Buffon is smiling at a story told by Bernardin de Saint-Pierre, and now he rises deferentially to greet Jules Michelet who arrives, pale in his black tail coat, his snow-white hair brushing his clean-shaven cheek... Without worrying about the dates when these celebrities were born, we can picture them all in this old-world setting...

Dominating the Jardin des Plantes, the cedar of the Labyrinth seems to be stretching out its horizontal branches in benediction, like the arms of the patriarch. Monsieur de Jussieu brought it back from Lebanon when it was quite young, in his large hat. At school we were all thrilled with the story. This giant of a tree stayed comfortably in the good naturalist's topper, like a geranium in a flower-pot ! Water ran short in the ship and Monsieur de Jussieu heroically gave his ration to the cutting. The sacrifice was not in vain, and if Jussieu's hat still lies in some cupboard, it ought to be hung on a branch of the great tree on his birthday...

The longest streets and the boulevards of Paris change their appearance as they pass through different districts of the capital. The Boulevard Saint-Germain, for instance, in the neighbourhood of the War Office, is a staff colonel; at the top of the Rue des Saints-Pères, it becomes a respectable shareholder of the 6th *arrondissement;* and if it is a professor near the School of Medicine, and a student at Cluny, it resembles a tramp on reaching the Place Maubert. This is where the Latin Quarter turns into an Arab quarter by virtue of all the " sidis " that one finds on leaving the Place Saint-Michel and taking the narrow streets that still have a touch of the Middle Ages—the Rues Galande, de la Huchette, or Saint-Séverin. In passing I drank a glass of Anjou wine at the Bar of the Dodecaneses. I had never before seen this word in the plural but the landlord of this tavern was right, for the twelve Sporades islands in the Aegean Sea were known under this name. Round the counter were youths so dark and curly-haired that they must have come from Tunis or Lemnos or Missolonghi...

Is it in memory of dear François Villon and of the bad boys and fallen girls whose company he liked, that there are still vagrants in these parts ?

There must still be in Chicago or New York, in Sweden or Brazil, comfortable old gentlemen and serious white-haired ladies, convinced that it was at the peril of their lives that they took cherries-in-brandy in the thieves' kitchens of the capital, at the *Guillotine* or *Chez le Père Lunette*. A guide led them in a party into those dangerous lairs, where the clientèle consisted mainly of harmless tramps. The tourists were told that " the army of crime "was recruited from their ranks. The police never ventured into those cellars ; the chill of danger and evil was felt on entering. Some real " bad lots " passed by; the drinkers of woodspirit had knives in their pockets ; the girls who accompanied them were formidable jades... But it was all faked !

That excellent artist, Joseph Hémard, who knows the quarter better than anyone else, has told us : " One of the cellars was specially renowned for the noise of heavy blows that came from it; not an evening passed without there being a 'man knocked out'. In the midst of the tumult that followed the victim's fall, the sound of a whistle was heard followed by a cry of alarm : 'The coppers !' The landlord turned out the light; the spectators were led out by a guide and found themselves in the street, glad of having escaped the consequences of a nasty incident, otherwise delighted with their evening's entertainment and with the luck of having a never-to-be-forgotten memory. Meanwhile, however, the lights went up again, the ' knocked out man ' quietly got up and awaited the next session... "

All that is no longer amusing; there are no more grand dukes, no

more " making the rounds of the cabarets; " " Titine " and the " Escalope " of the " Sébasto " have gone, the louts and the touts and the pimps have hung their knives up on the wall— perhaps they even have respectable banking accounts now.

Near the church of St. Julienle-Pauvre some harmless " cellars " still exist. Over the door of one of them entitled " *Maison historique de la Vieille Chanson Française* " we read : " Open from 9 till midnight. Visit of the three floors and the vaults, dungeons, oubliettes, and the underground river; then upstairs, a museum of old Paris, the guillotine of the armies of the Revolution, chastity belts, etc..."

Between the Boulevard Saint-Germain and the Rue Soufflot is the solemn and deserted Rue Saint-Jacques, lined with buildings that look like university barracks. When I stopped in front of the Panthéon, I tried to picture the astonishment of the visitors if their guide had addressed them after this style :

" Ladies and Gentlemen, this monument was built by Soufflot, a pastrycook, according to the Goncourt brothers, with money won in a lottery. It was originally the Church of St. Geneviève, but in 1791 the French Revolution extinguished the candles and dedicated it to the great men whom we generally honour after we have ridiculed them during their lifetime. Napoleon, of course, removed the Republican sign, which was replaced by an actor from the Odéon in 1830. Napoleon III relit the candles, but in 1885 the

church was finally deconsecrated and Victor Hugo's coffin was on exhibition in front of the bronze doors which since then have only been opened to give passage to the biers of the elder sons of a grateful Motherland.

I think that there are in the funereal vaults of the Panthéon some forty or so dead : Jean-Jacques Rousseau, sorrowful and bitter; Monsieur de Voltaire, whose smile could never have been as hideous as de Musset claimed; Lazare Carnot, wearing his general's greatcoat and his cocked hat with the Republican plumes; his great-grandson, Sadi-Carnot, in the black frock-coat of the President of the Republic, with the wide silk ribbon

The Panthéon.

of the Legion of Honour across his shirt-front; Victor Hugo, like some doyen of French Poetry; Marcelin Berthelot, thoughtful as an alchemist; Emile Zola; citizen Jean Jaurès, with his coat pockets stuffed with political tracts, and two or three others as well."

" You know those, but what of the others ? "

" Rémy de Gourmont devotes an article to them. It appears that Napoléon reserved the Madeleine for the glories of the army and the Panthéon for civilians; ' but,' he said, ' after the military, Napoleon only respected one kind of men—administrators; so much so, that his Panthéon became the refuge of the former Prefects and defunct Senators. The list of great men that he interred there is comic : it includes Resnier, Petiet, Béguinot, Durrazo, Saint-Christian, Mather, Cabanis, Winther, Sers, Galles, Champmol, Songis, Hain, Viry, La Paigne, Demenier, etc., almost all of them senators. Add to this list three foreign cardinals :

Mareri, Ferskine, Caprara, and a former notary, le Sieur Bevière...
These worthies are still in the Panthéon, alongside Voltaire, who must
be having a good laugh, and Victor Hugo, who is probably highly
indignant...' "

The most respectful of visitors would do as Voltaire did, in the burial
crypt over which Puvis de Chavannes has painted, in madonna blue, a
fresco showing St. Geneviève praying for the little town that was to
become Paris and that was already threatened by the barbarians !...

The letters patent for the university were conferred on the Latin
Quarter by Philip Augustus in the year 1200. Other districts may boast
the Louvre or the Elysée, the Stock Exchange, High Finance, or Fashion,
the Ministries or the populous suburbs, or trade, but here, since the
13th century, have been the Four Faculties.

The hotel rooms are let out to students; text-books and exercise books can
be seen even on the marble wash-stands and the Louis-Philippe armchairs.
When I was the age of these young tenants and we arranged to meet at the
Panthéon, it meant the *Taverne* of that name at the foot of the Rue Soufflot.
Every café then had its own character and its own devotees.   At the
Soufflot there was Raoul Ponchon; at the *Vachette*, Jean Moréas, Maurice
Maindron, and the poets of the Romantic school; but the *Taverne du Pan-
théon* belonged to the students from the south and to young writers.

> Each street has the name of a doctor or a sage,
> Of a great historian or an old humanist,
> Of a learned physicist or a naturalist...
> Here byways and houses looked old and heavy with history and the past :
> Michelet and Renan taught here ;
> Here too Pasteur, black skull-cap on head,
> In his laboratory from break of day
> Pored over the unseen, intense and swarming,
> Prodigious life contained in a drop of blood...
> I returned...
> Under the moonlit roofs of the Faculties and St. Geneviève,
> Of the College of France and a host of other Schools—
> The piles of books—a great enchanted people—were dreaming in their palaces...
> Above the domes
> The night sky shivered with those distant circles of light
> That are to Light's splendour as a far echo to a sound...

From these libraries arose
The light and the Poesy that were Greece...
The moon of Abelard and of François Villon
Was Phoebus too, whose chaste rays were
Still silvery, secret, vaporous, and magical
Like the crystal of purest water in the depths of an antique glass.
Over this quarter sleepy as an old professor,
As an historian or as a printer,
The stars appeared like golden asterisks
On a page eternal.
Oh, pensive and beautiful night.

There must still be living in the departments of the Lot, of the Lot-et-Garonne, the Gers and the Tarn, solicitors, doctors and barristers who wasted at the *Taverne* hours that should have been spent on the *Pandectes* or at the Faculty of Medicine.

We used to see there, too, youths who perhaps became ministers in one of those Balkan and semi-oriental kingdoms that I can never place on the map.

At nightfall, coming from the Rue des Ecoles, the Rue Monge, and the Rue Gay-Lussac, young women who had tended sheep in Normandy, or been milliners in Toulouse, or who deserved a prize for remaining virtuous for twenty years in Brittany, all left their lodgings and made for the *Taverne*.

God knows what has now become of them—if they are still alive ! One feels like murmuring the lovely " Ballad of the Ladies of Long Ago" that François Villon wrote in this quarter, one evening in the 15th century :

" *But where are the snows of yester-year ?* "

Doubtless the students no longer frequent the cafés of the Boulevard Saint-Michel as they used to in the time of Louis-Philippe or under the Second

Empire, when Henri Murger sang of Bohemian life, or when, under the presidency of Monsieur Armand Fallières, a small black coffee cost two sous and one could, with 25 centimes—the price of a bock—stay in the brasserie until midnight. Life is no longer free and easy, drinks are expensive and young people have other cares. The newspapers announced recently that the *Taverne* was to be closed. Like the church of Sainte-Geneviève, it had already been almost deconsecrated and having changed its name, was called *Capoulade*.

I did not want to sit at one of the tables outside, recognising nothing around me and comparing myself to an Atlante who had escaped when the kingdom of Atlantide was engulfed. So I crossed the street and had a drink at the old *Mahieu* from where one can see the delightful Gare de Sceaux. No traffic congests it; it hardly ever sees trunks, and tickets are only taken for the not too distant villages. One only goes to Arcueil-Cachan, Bourg-la-Reine, Fontenay-aux-Roses, or Sceaux, and it seems to have been built especially for the couples who go to have lunch at the famous haunt called " Robinson's Tree."

One would like to inscribe around its clock-face those two lines of La Fontaine :

> " *Lovers, happy lovers, where would you roam ?*
> *Perchance to not far distant banks !* "

The Luxembourg is only a few steps away. This garden, which stretches from the Odéon to the Observatory, is the enchanted park, the paradise, of the Latin Quarter.

A thousand images could be conjured up in the place where I came to sit down: I had no need to wander in those avenues laid out by Marie de Médicis around the palace built in 1629 by Salomon de Brosse... Here was this fat Florentine banker's wife who became Queen of France, ungainly, appearing even stouter in her stiff brocades, decked out in all her wonderful jewelry which she loved so much; I saw her disappearing behind the trees, with her train, like a Carnival Queen at Mid-Lent, while the procession disbanded in the Place du Panthéon. Her château was in turn the property of the House of Peers, the Duke of Orléans, the Directors, and it served as a prison under the Terror. I imagine a gala night after the 9th of Thermidor. Barras is entertaining! I hear the violins of the fête and see the dazzling beauty of Madame Tallien, leading the elegant Directory Ball.

The good old days! Ultra-severe historians call them corrupt! They have the charm of a beautiful afternoon in which the tempest that raged in the morning is still remembered. Revolution has no longer the strength

The Luxemburg Palace.

The Rue Lhomond.

to guillotine and the well-powdered heads that did not roll into Sanson's basket have learnt to smile again. Could one find a more pleasant spot than this palace in this garden? The fragrance of roses drifts through the open windows and mingles with the perfume of the young women, in garments as scanty as those worn by goddesses of Opera, waltzing in the arms of *Muscadins* and *Incroyables*.

Footmen pass to and fro, offering sherbet, orangeade and liqueurs... Among those nymphs, whose figures are barely veiled by puffed muslin and whose bare feet are revealed through antique buskins, there stands—a little to one side—the grave, serious and beautiful Juliette Récamier. And I perceive a brunette, as amber in colouring as a Créole, to whom Madame Tallien introduces a young general whose long, straight hair sweeps the gold braid of his coat collar. It is Bonaparte, seeing Josephine for the first time!

And now I see Murger's *Bohême*, students going to Michelet's lectures, studious youths and young ladies of easy virtue—Rodolphe and Mimi...

Many phantoms come your way when you can dream on, seated outside an old café in the Latin Quarter.

Charming Decamerons take place under the trees of the Luxembourg on fine afternoons in spring or summer. All the young men and girls seated on the benches or the garden chairs have books in their hands, a sight not found in other public gardens, and the statues of queens and princesses have heard as many poems as declarations of love.

> *There we passed in idleness our days*
> *That should to studies and the law have been devoted.*
> *O baskets of flowers, balusters and fountains,*
> *Stone nymphs with festooned roses...*
> *The trees disclose a palace, an old castle,*
> *Like a scene in a fairy play.*
> *Near us—on the bench—the book, and the white lilac*
> *Wreathing the hat of the girl we have just met.*
> *Then, in the sleepy, enchanted afternoon,*
> *Under the leafy arches of the tall green chestnuts*
> *Our dreams, the doves, our amours and fine verses...*
> *A lost Eldorado, a garden of Armida, a bower in*
> *The midst of Paris, the Luxem-*
> *bourg is the island*
> *We shall never discover again,*
> *Once the light of youth has ceased*
> *to guide our steps...*

Garden of queens and poets ! Here are the statues of Anne of Brittany, Anne of Beaujeu, Anne of Provence, and Madame George Sand who lived in the Rue Racine in 1862.

Passing beside the iron railings in the Rue de Médicis, we can see the bust of Théodore de Banville. The sculptor has represented him as a personage of antiquity, with a wisp of drapery over his naked shoulder—he who felt the cold so much !

A great winged female figure

holds out a palm to Leconte de Lisle who was librarian to the Senate.

There are other poets, and we must not forget Paul Verlaine who drank so many absinthes in all the cafés of the Latin Quarter where he was a familiar figure with his Inverness cape, his hospital muffler and his big stick. Field marshals, great philanthropists, inventors and statesmen would be out of place here, but the poets are in their element, as are the children playing in the avenues. These youngsters are not quite like other Parisian children.

Those who are taken, for instance, to the Parc Monceau, have an air of affluence. Nurses, dressed like English evangelists or deaconnesses, scold them severely but respectfully. The little girls already have dresses from good houses; the little boys are probably not very different from those to be seen in London. They all play without taking off their gloves, under the eye of Guy de Maupassant, whose statue is perfectly in keeping there. The children to be seen in the Luxembourg Gardens are not quite the same. To begin with, most of them have a young mother or a grandmother who embroiders, sews and chatters while they are at play.

The parents of the children of the Parc Monceau might be heroes from Maupassant; they are reminiscent of the classic background of Fortune : the town house, the butler, the bank, the board of directors, the car, the big dinners redolent of truffles and Chambertin—all that dazzled a provincial lady reading, about the year 1890, a novel by the author of *Bel-Ami*.

The fathers of those who are taken to the Luxembourg seem to belong to that indigent and worthy nobility of Science and the University. We imagine that they do not eat meat in the evening for reasons of health, or rather, economy; that they are preparing a final edition of Virgil or Rabelais. Or else they are to be found in a laboratory in the Rue de l'Estrapade or the Jardin des Plantes, inoculating guinea-pigs, rats or monkeys, studying cancerous cells or standing, masked, in white gown and rubber gloves, over an operating table. We see them, now and then, after a lecture, a consultation, or a medical visit and they are infinitely likable. All of them are at heart complete idealists, even those who believe that truth is contained within the field of a microscope or the glass of a test tube. They are also men for whom money is not everything.

The little boys who play in the Luxembourg Gardens have something provincial about them. They will become doctors, engineers or lawyers.

Perhaps some of them will pass through the Garden of their boyhood in the evening of their days. It will be winter. They will be going to a meeting of the Senate, reflecting how swiftly life passes and that it was only yesterday... There were sunshine and flowers, for the days that have fled are always sunny and flowery... They used to study Law or Letters. On this deserted bench they will recapture the vision of a young couple, recall a bright face framed by fair hair, a simple little frock, a pretty smile—and an old bore. Then—with heavy steps, they will go to the Palace to preside over a Commission, discovering in the deserted Garden all the melancholy of ruined Edens, lost Paradises, murmuring the verses of Paul Verlaine—if they can still remember them—

> " *In the old park, solitary and frozen,*
> *Two phantoms have evoked the past.*"

LÉO LARGUIER,
of the *Académie Goncourt*.

Montparnasse

VAN DONGEN. — *Van Dongen as Neptune.*

MONTPAR-

nasse has had its day. It lasted no longer than fifteen years, but that was enough to secure for this quarter a world-wide renown. Its popularity was at its height between the two wars. The occupation of Paris by the German army very largely—though not entirely—destroyed its special charm. Montparnasse has preserved its unique character and I think it would take very little for it to rise like a new phoenix from its ashes. Meanwhile let us have a look at the Montparnasse of today. I was present at its birth, its coming-of-age, its glory and its decline, and now when I pass down its streets, a thousand memories are awakened and follow behind me. I will repeat to you what these ghosts of the past whisper in my ear.

The quarter of Montparnasse lies astride the 6th and 14th *arrondissements*. It extends to the Parc Montsouris and to Montrouge, but the cemetery in the Boulevard Edgar-Quinet forms a more natural boundary. At the opposite end Montparnasse is lost in the neighbourhood of Saint-Germain-des-Prés, in the existentialists' cellars and the poets' cafés. The western boundary is the Gare Montparnasse, the Avenue du Maine and the rue de la Gaîté; the eastern, the Luxembourg, the Avenue de l'Observatoire, with the *Closerie des Lilas* marking the end of the Latin Quarter.

The Boulevard Montparnasse crosses it from west to east. It is at once its backbone and the very heart of its life—along with the little streets which, to right and to left, extend its radius.

To visit the quarter we will begin at the Gare Montparnasse — or rather the Place de Rennes — which nowadays offers no picturesque features (except possibly a very busy Dupont Café). It is surrounded by hôtels, cafés, and restaurants, frequented for the most part by visitors; but even before the heyday of Montparnasse, many artists were to be seen there, especially at the Café de Versailles.

MONTPARNASSE

La Rotonde

A.S. 1949

Let us take the Boulevard Montparnasse stretching in front of us as far as the eye can reach. Here we see the characteristics of the district: large cafés, a few restaurants, dance halls and bars, bookshops selling works of art, reproductions of modern paintings, and reviews. The outfitters display the boldest fashions. There are also a few antique shops, sellers of paint and artists' materials, a florist's, but, paradoxically enough, not many big art dealers.

The stage is still set as in the great days of old; the actors and the extras of the past have gone, but nothing is to prevent others from taking their place.

But let us proceed. On our left, at the end of a *cul-de-sac*, is the Théâtre de Poche, a minute theatre seating only sixty people. The audience is so close to the stage that one has the impression of being indiscreet and catching the actors unawares in their more private moments. Plays of outstanding merit have been produced on this miniature stage. More recently the Théâtre de la Huchette and the Théâtre du Petit Musc have done even better. A little farther on, on the same side of the street, we discover the Foyer des Artistes at No. 89, where artists can get meals at a very modest price; its friendly atmosphere is particularly appreciated by those who come from afar. Every effort is made to make their life more pleasant. Meetings and lectures are organised and, once a year, a large fancy-dress ball sets the whole district in an uproar. One has the impression of returning, for one night, to the good old days. Matisse himself, in the course of one of the last festivities, was not above presiding over a competition for the most beautiful model. The Foyer des Artistes is the link between what was, and what perhaps will be, one day in the future.

And now we come to the only public monument in Montparnasse, the old church of Notre-Dame-des-Champs, around which, at night, countless visitors' cars used to be crowded in the great days of the past.

Opposite is a florist's, its façade entirely of glass, like an enormous greenhouse full of the rarest and most varied flowers. Regardless of the vicissitudes of Montparnasse, it continues to decorate the whole of Paris.

Now we have practically arrived at the Vavin crossroads, the heart of Montparnasse, which was once the crossroads of the civilised world. It is there that we find a group of colossal, cosmopolitan cafés—the Coupole, the Dôme and the Rotonde. They still exist, but it would only be by chance that we should see a celebrated artist there now.

You can dine at the Coupole and you can even dance there. The Dôme and the Rotonde are also very popular; in the evening the number of cars lined up there is considerable, but it is not quite the same as in the old days.

It is at this point that the associations and the ghosts of former days join in from all sides to bring back to your mind a vision of what Montparnasse once was.

Do you wish us to go back to the time when Montparnasse was hardly ever mentioned, a district without the least spectacular attraction ? Charles-Louis Philippe wrote *Bubu de Montparnasse*, and Bruant sang of the dissolute people who hung round the station and beside the cemetery wall. There were already a few painters in the district, —they were by no means lacking in talent. But they were not talked about—although Whistler was living in the Rue d'Assas and Jongkind in the Boulevard Montparnasse, in the house now occupied by the new *Jockey Club*. The Académie Colla Rossi and the Académie Delécluze were attracting foreign pupils. Christian Krogh, the father of Per Krogh, was gathering Norwegian artists around him. There was a farm in the Rue Campagne-Première, and all along the Boulevard from the station to the Bastille, there jogged a little single-decked tramway, painted red and drawn by two ponies.

The house that bears the number 9 in the Rue Campagne-Première—a curious, ramshackle building, partly constructed of materials from the débris of the 1889 Exhibition was then—and still is—a painter's abode. It housed a number of artists who played an important part in the evolution of painting, and in particular those who gave new impetus to the *Salon des Indépendants*, shortly after 1900 : painters such as Charles Guérin, Jules Flandrin, Othon Friesz, Marval, etc. Luc-Albert Moreau lived there for a short time before settling down in the Rue du Cherche-Midi.

The Montparnasse that we knew before the first World War had already its own characteristics and there was clear indication that it had a future. Many artists from Montmartre had crossed the bridges. Although the Rotonde was still only an ordinary bar, it was already renowned for its automatic slot-machines, ranged round the counter. Blaise Cendrars, who had not yet lost his arm in the war nor won his

A Studio at the Grande Chaumière.

Military Medal and the nickname " *N'a q'un bras* " was already quite a hand at this kind of game. Lenin and Trotsky were sometimes to be seen taking coffee there, while Modigliani, who had left Montmartre, would welcome Utrillo with shouts of joy when the latter came to visit him. Riotous evenings ensued, each of the two painters presenting the other as the best drinker, and after various adventures they usually ended at the police-station.

The Dôme, a quiet little café, was the meeting-place of German artists, and it was from there that the delegation set out to meet Pascin at the Gare de l'Est when he arrived in Paris from Munich in 1907. Archipenko gave wild parties in his studio. Canudo, with an ivy-leaf in his button-hole, was a loyal habitué. When Van Dongen returned from his first visit to Egypt, it was in Montparnasse that he settled, in a strange studio built of reinforced concrete. For a party held there on March 24, 1914, he distempered the floor and ceiling red and green; he received his guests, stripped to the waist and with his beard adorned with little knots of blue and pink ribbon. The same night, Brunelleschi held a party reminiscent of the Comedia dell'Arte in his house in the Rue Boissonade. There was soon established a two-way traffic between the two parties, which became a pretext for countless adventures, to the considerable discomfiture of jealous guests. On the other hand, Douanier Rousseau—even before 1909—was holding intimate receptions of a delightful and charming character in his studio in the Rue Perrel.

We recall these facts to show that even at this time Montparnasse was asserting its personality. On the 14th July 1914, a large ball lit by Chinese lanterns was organised at the Vavin crossroads. Many artists —painters and poets—were present. The festivities were riotous, but a few weeks later came the collapse. War was declared. On this occasion, however, nothing was destroyed. As soon as peace returned, Montparnasse began to live again, more intensively than ever. It was going to have its day.

The Vavin crossroads then became the crossroads of the artistic world. Montparnasse was a new Mecca for the artists of both continents, who, in studio and in ghetto, dreamt of coming to Paris, of breathing the air of freedom and of finding kindred spirits while contemplating the old masters in the French museums. They discovered a new meaning in painting as they became impregnated with the soft light of the Ile-de-France caressing the noble vistas of the Seine riverside, from the Louvre to Notre-Dame. From the impact of the meeting of great foreign artists such as Picasso, Chagall, Zadkine, Van Dongen, Foujita, with great French artists such as Matisse, Rouault, Derain, Vlaminck, Dunoyer de Segonzac, Utrillo, etc... was born the movement that brought French prestige to such a height, and I am perhaps the first to have dubbed it " the Parisian School." Montparnasse was the crucible of so many living forces, and it was that which gave this district—only too often thought merely a pleasure ground—its title of nobility.

Moreover, Montparnasse still continued to develop. This is how it happened.

One December afternoon in the year 1923, the Rotonde, now enlarged, was solemnly inaugurated, as if it were a monument.

Mr. Gustave Kahn, poet and art critic, made a speech. The guests were invited to eat and drink free of charge, and they were expected to look at the paintings. This ceremony had considerably more import-

The Vavin crossroads on July 14th, 1924.

ance than was realised at the time. It was not only the new Rotonde that was being opened, but the new Montparnasse.

The new landlord had done a good job. His bar had become a Gallery of the Fine Arts; there were paintings on all the floors and even on the staircases—more numerous than in a picture-dealer's. The Rotonde swallowed up the adjoining shops. A grill-room, a restaurant and a jazz-band were started on the first floor. There was dancing; there were draught screens, cloak rooms, expensive drinks, small tables, customers in evening dress, fashionable society. It was almost the equal of the Place Pigalle.

The Dôme had a fresh start too. It was renovated, and it reopened its doors to reveal rooms newly-decorated with flowered wall-paper—and nothing else. The Dôme has never slavishly followed the fashion of other cafés, and this quasi-nudity has never struck anyone as unseemly. Some time afterwards the Dôme was again enlarged, and took in the adjoining building to install a bar with red leather fittings and chromium chairs. Then came another great event, the opening of a third large café, one evening in December 1927, which was followed by a night of glazed frost that can still be remembered. The Coupole was decorated by local artists, and its bar soon became a very brilliant spot with barman Bob, who remains one of the last witnesses of those heroic times.

The Coupole, the Dôme and the Rotonde were the wildest expression of Montparnasse. What a fair-ground! Motor-coaches brought the tourists there. Montparnasse was a word that was bandied in all languages—to the same extent as the Moulin-Rouge or the Folies-Bergères. A white coffee was enough to keep you warm in winter. Whole tribes assembled around a table: cropped heads and pink heads; frizzy shocks of hair, mufflers, sweaters, old cloaks, cowboy hats and coloured shirts open wide at the neck, heavily made-up faces, savagely red and ochre and yellow, bare arms, hair cut short at the nape of the neck, silk stockings or heavy woollen sports ones, with daringly short skirts. There were all kinds—corpulent bespectacled clowns, lean rakes, impecunious professors, and revolutionary chemists; a strange, preposterous assembly. They all swarmed there, gossiping and chattering to the accompanying clatter of saucers and spoons, the clink of glasses on the tables, the calls to waiters, the purring hubbub of conversation. Painting was talked of, and there were dealings in curios. Sometimes fights occurred in this ghetto, made up of all the ghettoes in the world, in this *Cour des Miracles*.

This aggressive picturesqueness, however, did not last very long. Montparnasse became a fashionable haunt. Soon a clientele from the

" smart districts " was to be seen there, especially in the evenings, which marred the original picturesqueness.

A magnificent prosperity now reigned in Montparnasse. The verandahs of the famous cafés were filled with boys and girls in easy circumstances, often extravagantly dressed. There was dancing at the Coupole and the Rotonde, and fashionable ladies came there for tea. Montparnasse became an object of middle-class outings; on Saturday evenings shop-girls and clerks joined the noisy throng. Montparnasse was in a fair way to dethrone Montmartre. The artists were kings. Wealth flowed into the studios, and painters and sculptors, taken aback by unaccustomed riches, spent money recklessly. Derain drove several large sports cars, and Foujita went about in a car lined with grey

On the Terrace of the Dome.

doeskin, driven by a chauffeur in white livery. He naturally had his town house, and Braque designed him a country house. Utrillo bought a château near Lyons, and others had their yachts. Every Tuesday, Van Dongen invited the whole of Paris to his large villa in the Rue Juliette-Lambert, and every Saturday Pascin took scores of people, whom he did not always know, to drink at his expense in the night clubs of the Place Pigalle. Not a week, hardly a day passed, without a dance or a fancy-dress ball in a studio, at *Bullier's*, at the *Maison Watteau* or at the *Moulin de la Galette* where the whole of Montparnasse went up to the " Ball of the Far West, " to Douanier Rousseau's ball, the ball of the Chienlit and many others. The most insignificant " varnishing day, " the award of the slightest decoration, served as a pretext for banquets that went on until dawn. At daybreak it was not unusual to see Derain, Pascin or Foujita pay the bill of all those present. At the negro dance-hall in the Rue Blomet, Madeleine Anspach gave an *Ubu* ball which is still talked about.

The Bal Bullier.

And then came the crash. A financial crisis in America was followed by an upheaval in the world of painting in Paris. Pictures were not sold. To add to this, everyone was nervously exhausted, frayed beyond measure by the ceaseless festivities of many years. Pascin committed suicide, as did Madeleine Anspach. Foujita secretly left for Japan to escape from the tax collectors. Several heroes of that great bacchanalia went to prison; lean days followed the feast. " The hangover after the party," wrote Basler.

We shall still find traces of that former prosperity as we continue on our way

UTRILLO. — *The old Jockey Café*
(from the Caillaux collection).

along the Boulevard Montparnasse. After leaving the Vavin cross-roads we pass the restaurant " *Au Bon Coin*," which used to be called " *Chez Baty* " (nothing to do with Gaston Baty), whose cellar was famous. We have drunk many a bottle there with two regular customers— Guillaume Apollinaire and André Billy.

Now we have arrived in front of the house that bears the number 127. A plaque recalls the fact that the great Jongkind lived there, and the ground-floor is occupied by the " *Jockey* " cabaret. But here there is a point to be noticed.

The first *Jockey*, of illustrious memory, was not here, but a little farther on, at the corner of the Rue Campagne-Première, in premises that then were occupied by another cabaret, the *Caméléon*, founded in 1921 by the sculptor Levet, in the tradition of the old-time literary cafés. Expropriated by the *Jockey*, the *Caméléon* was revivified by the poet Mercereau and settled down at the other end of the Rue Campagne-Première, at the corner of the Boulevard Raspail. Poetry and literary evenings were held there, lectures also. Art was taken seriously and those who came respected the place. Ernest Prévot found the right word when he bestowed on the *Caméléon* the title of " the Sorbonne of Montparnasse." This serious-minded cabaret did not, however, last very long.

The success of the *Jockey* was, on the other hand, dazzling. What was the *Jockey*? When Bob, who is today barman of the Lido, directed it, it was an establishment that gave people who had not been far afield a fairly good impression of a Texas bar or of some place in one of those great ports where the heroes of Pierre Mac Orlan or René Bizet used to meet.

It was very much the bar of the adventure novel : that atmosphere was created—as to the rest...

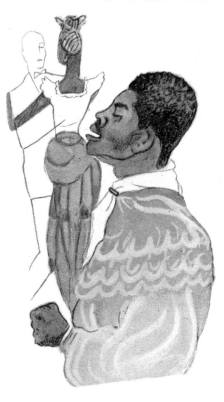

I remember it. The exterior was somewhat sinister, with doors and shutters all closed. You entered. In an instant you were pitched into a complete uproar. A cowboy hammered away at a piano, there were Hawaiians with banjoes and couples trying to dance in the scrimmage, people squeezed against the tables and others looking for seats, shouting and clouds of smoke in a makeshift setting with decorations from films such as *Dr. Caligari* and *Raskolnikof*, bursting with colour. The walls were covered with large multi-coloured posters such as one sees anywhere, but stuck on crosswise, overlapping one another—at all angles— on the walls and ceiling. Others were suspended like banners from the cross-beams, and large white placards were hung in this

The Boule Blanche.

dazzling blaze of light like flags, often bearing facetious injunctions in bold handwriting, in untranslatable English.

Near the door was a wooden bar where you drank standing up, balancing your glass. On the tables were paper table-cloths, and you were lucky if you could sit on half a chair. That was the way to make a success of an establishment. Those who came were people of quality. It was a public resembling no other, where everything was mixed and con-fused—expressions, gestures, attitudes, heavily made-up faces, cropped hair, light beige coats, spectacles, Pascin's round hat and Kisling's velvet jacket, the white-coated barman, lovely girls with bare arms and backs, who danced tightly clasping their partners, while other couples hopped about; there were the posters and the placards, the white-capped negro cook who appeared at the top of the staircase. There was

The Rue de la Gaîté.

atmosphere... Such was the *Jockey* in its early days, and Kiki with her barrack-room songs was the animating spirit. But it did not last long.

The *Jockey* had set the tone. The night life of Montparnasse was becoming organised. The Rue Delambre, the " basement of Parnasse " became at dawn a happy meeting-ground between the flower of Montparnasse and the journalists from the right bank. All-night bars were opening up everywhere. The *Select* was crowded, especially in the morning. Opposite, the very popular *Kosmos* was the chauffeurs' meeting-place. Henri opened the *Jungle* on the spot where the present-day Jockey stands. At Nº 60 Boulevard Edgar-Quinet, the *Monocle* welcomed the ladies who only require the company of their own sex to have a good time—and it still does. Opposite was an establishment that has since been closed by law—like all of its kind—and which attracted the whole of Paris. The success of the *Bal Nègre* in the Rue Blomet was responsible for the establishment of the *Boule Blanche* at Montparnasse—which is still in vogue even today—and where beautiful " *doudous* " in local costume danced the quadrilles of the Antilles. The Stavisky affair gave the name of "*La Villa*" to another establishment that can still be found at the Vavin crossroads.

Venus, at 129 Boulevard Montparnasse, offers a show in which, as at Montmartre, the principal attraction is a parade of nude women. There is a sprinkling of restaurants and bars of all kinds in this area—the *Poisson d'Or* in the Rue Vavin, the *Schubert* in the Boulevard Montparnasse, or *Jimmy's* in the Rue Huygens.

Continuing along the Boulevard, we reach the cross-roads that marks the end of Montparnasse. Marshal Ney on his pedestal brandishes his sabre and the *Bal Bullier*, of illustrious memory, where there has been no dancing for some time, withdraws into itself and its past associations — as does the *Closerie des Lilas*, that once had world-wide fame and is now only a café like so many others.

The *Closerie des Lilas* really belongs more to the Latin Quarter than to Montparnasse. It is, if you like, the frontier post between the two districts. Originally it was Montparnasse that appeared to be the suburb Then the rôles changed, and the Latin Quarter became the suburb. The *Closerie des Lilas* lost all its brilliance after Paul Fort ceased to hold there his Tuesday meetings which attracted both poets and writers before the first World War.

Paul Fort was the chosen prince of poets and Han Ryner the prince of story-tellers. This launched the War of the Two Banks, the left against the right, the *Closerie des Lilas* against the *Napolitain*. After the 1914-1918 War, the Tuesday meetings ceased, but literary banquets were held at the *Closerie* where poets were fêted. The death-blow to these reunions was struck by a surrealist offensive, in the course of a banquet given in honour of Saint-Pol-Roux the Magnificent. The surrealists claimed to be communists and partisans of Abd-el-Krim, who was at that time fighting against the French troops in Morocco. There was a thorough riot, Rachilde was insulted and more than a thousand francs' worth of crockery (francs of those days) was broken. After that there were no more banquets at the *Closerie*, which relapsed into a humdrum existence.

On arriving at this cross-roads we have a choice. Either we can take the Boulevard de l'Observatoire as far as the Place Denfert-Rochereau —near to which, in the Rue Boulard, lived André Lhote —and then go up to the Parc Montsouris where Foujita and Derain had houses, and where Braque still has one; Despiau also lived near by. We could also make for the Porte de Versailles, and the Square Desnouettes, where Antoine Villard collects the finest Douanier Rousseaus, and the Rue Vercingétorix where Gauguin, as well as many others, lived; or the Rue d'Alésia, also rich in painters; but this whole area is really

The " Quat'z Arts " at the Coupole.

on the outskirts of Montparnasse. On the other hand, if we wish to stay in the heart of the district, let us take the Boulevard Edgar Quinet. We pass alongside the cemetery and reach the Rue de la Gaîté.

The Rue de la Gaîté has not been unjustly named " Rue de la Joie " by the local inhabitants. It was always a street of pleasure-gardens, cabarets and places of amusement. The tradition is not completely dead; the cinemas, the bars, the luminous signs, the gramophones and the mechanical pianos maintain, to the best of their ability, the atmosphere of a perpetual fairground, peculiar to this street. In 1819, when Seveste built the Théâtre Montparnasse, the Gaîté was lined with acacias and presented an attractively rural appearance. The inexpensive Argenteuil wine persuaded the workmen and their families to go there for a little relaxation on Sundays and Mondays after the week's work.

Seveste's theatre was an additional attraction. At first its clientele consisted entirely of local people. Its shows were lavish. Two

The old Bobino.

melodramas and a revue were often presented on the same night. The curtain rose at six o'clock and finally came down after midnight. In the middle of the room was a large stove, on which the spectators heated up their dinners. Whole families ate the classic cabbage soup during the interval. No-one dreamt that a century later Gaston Baty would make this theatre the rendezvous of Parisian society, of the smart set, artists and poets, and that first-class plays would be put on there.

The " Rue de la Joie " offered many other amusements during the 19th century; there were cafés-concerts, dances and restaurants. The dance halls, from that of the *Eléphant* to that of the *Veau qui tette*, were ill-frequented. In 1833 the *Mille Colonnes* was opened and had an immediate brilliant success. A restaurant was added later. The *Ecole des Arts Décoratifs* held a fancy-dress ball there in 1901, which was discussed long afterwards. Later it became a cinema, and today it is a music-hall, the *Bobino*.

There was also the Gaîté-Montparnasse, that Agnès Capri transformed to produce shows of a higher standard. The Casino Montparnasse has kept its popular character, although many other places of amusement have been turned into cinemas, for cinemas are in favour in the Rue de la Gaîté. Little shops selling special dishes are still to found there. In the evening, cars are lined up along the whole length of the pavement; cafés and bars are overflowing with customers. With its noise and light, the Rue de la Gaîté is still the Rue de la Joie.

Today the stars of the Théâtre Montparnasse have cars, and they do not linger in the Rue de la Joie. One sometimes sees the artists of the Bobino having supper in the *Iles Marquises*, an old-established restaurant, famous for its oysters and its *Muscadet* wine. It now has an elegant clientele, but we knew it when it stayed open all night, and was frequented by doubtful characters, although it was next door to a police station.

At the top of the Rue de la Gaîté we find the Avenue du Maine, which—if we turn right—leads us back to the station and the Place de Rennes, from where we set out on this tour of the district. But there are still other discoveries in store.

Although less spectacular, the life of Montparnasse still goes on, and artists have their place in it. The art schools are always thronged with French and foreign pupils. Every day, towards the end of the afternoon, the sketching classes attract a very varied crowd, in which professionals and amateurs come together. Every Monday morning, in the Rue de la Grande-Chaumière, there is held the market of models which is not without its picturesque side.

In this street is the most important of the private art schools, Colla Rossi, linked with the Grande Chaumière. Othon Friesz taught there till his death. There, too, are pupils of Yves Brayer, Picart le Doux, Mazo, MacAvoy and Zadkine. Those of André Lhote have for a long time occupied the Rue d'Odessa, while Despierre teaches in the Rue du Départ, in a studio which is a kind of offshoot of Marc Vaux's " Foyer des Artistes."

There are in the district a number of studios that have been occupied by distinguished artists; those who live there today will perhaps follow in the footsteps of these great masters. We have already spoken of the famous building that bears the number 9 in the Rue Campagne Première, where so many painters have lived and are still living. No. 3 Rue

Joseph Bara is a house that has known even more famous occupants. Kisling lived there, also Per Krog, who settled there after the First World War without knowing that it was the same studio that Pascin had occupied before going to America. It was there that Zborowski was living when he had Soutine and Modigliani to stay—the latter even painted large figures on the doors. André Salmon lived opposite, —so that he had only to cross the street when he wanted to see his friends. The caretaker, Madame Salomon, was a difficult but colourful woman; she added to the character of the house.

If the clientele of the Coupole and the Rotonde, like the Dôme Bar, is nowadays more well-to-do—meaning fashionable rather than artistic— the old Dôme is at times the refuge of all kind of Bohemians, old and new. Kiki is often to be seen there in argumentative groups where young models are found side by side with old ones. *Le Marronnier* is also a meeting-ground for old cronies; so too are the little cafés and restaurants such as *d'Allan*, situated between the Dôme and the Coupole. There is also *Patrick*. It is in such places—and especially the Foyer des Artistes—that one finds the characteristic elements that preserve the spirit of Montparnasse and which, when the time comes, will revive the life of bygone days.

André WARNOD.

THE OPÉRA AND THE CENTER

E·M·PÉROT

RENOIR. — *La Loge*.

OUVRE, CI-

té, Marais—there is only one way of considering those districts and only one way of describing them. But this vast area, comprising the Opera, Réaumur-Sébastopol, the Rue des Petits-Champs and the initial slopes of Montmartre, is contained within arbitrary lines of demarcation, which will, however, stand closer inspection. And there are a hundred ways of seeing, savouring and describing it—this long rectangle that is on the one hand bordered by two highways of quite recent origin but of very disparate character; and on the other hand is furrowed with a complex network of old streets, for the most part winding and narrow and often ill-adapted to the intensity of modern life. How is it possible to present it, such as it is, as a unity to the foreigner, to the provincial, to the tourist, to the business man and to a varied host of Parisians, all of whom have their own way of looking at it?

If the geographical centre of Paris is the Palais-Royal, the real nerve centre of all the city's activity is certainly in the Grands Boulevards between the Opera and the Richelieu-Drouot cross-roads. And that was the case more than a hundred years ago when this area was still on the outskirts of the city. As far back as 1830, people were already calling it "The Heart of Paris," and were saying that the boulevards were the High Road of the capital.

We have to delve into the past if we are really to portray this *pays parisien* which, in its broad outlines, includes almost exactly the entire 2nd and 9th *arrondissements*, together with a part of the 10th, and which seems at first sight to be a vast conglomeration of impersonal masonry, without a green space, without a single great monument hallowed by the centuries or steeped in history and legend; where even the churches have a drab and commonplace appearance.

In the light of history, this great urban block, seeming only to have a purely functional character, begins to take a new shape in the visitor's

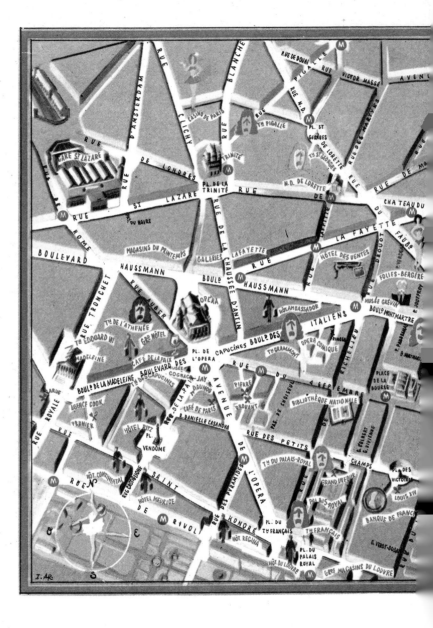

le CENTRE

mind. Although the existing evidences of a past are less apparent than elsewhere, they are nevertheless more numerous than one realises. They betoken an intriguing, animated life that fully justifies its permanent reputation as the centre of Paris.

It is unnecessary to go back to the Middle Ages, except possibly to recall the fact that the "Court of Miracles," that den of truculent beggars and rogues, was on the site of the present No. 100 Rue Réaumur, behind which there is still a cluster of old streets with topsy-turvy little houses propped up with wooden struts and a multiplicity of plaster bandages. We can imagine the town expanding on all sides very early on, invading the countryside and overwhelming the fields with residential buildings. As there were few religious houses to protect the open spaces, the land was soon split up into building plots, thus laying the foundations of the future blocks of flats. Soon innumerable luxurious mansions covered a large area, completely changing its face. This happened in the Rue de Richelieu, for instance; in 1684 Germain Brice stated that it was one of the finest streets in Paris, as regards length and frontage. By the death of Louis XIV, the districts of St. Honoré and Gaillon were filled with princely residences. Up to the 18th century, building continued, with a number of well-to-do private houses, large and small, semi-rural, semi-urban, right up to Percherons, the first village on the way out of Paris. It was regrettable that the delightful mansion in the Rue Chantereine (Rue des Victoires), where Josephine and Bonaparte lived and where the 18th Brumaire was organised, was destroyed in 1857. Regrettable too, nearer our own time, was the demolition, stone by stone, of the charming Pavillon de Hanovre built by the Duc de Richelieu at the far end of the large garden of the Hôtel d'Antin, to be replaced by the horrible Berlitz Palace. It was a pity that this pleasing rotunda and this great balconied *salon* could not remain to recall to Parisians and their foreign friends that in this place once stood a provincial mall with leafy shades, instead of the former ramparts.

By the eve of the Revolution, what we now call the Richelieu-Drouot cross-roads still had the appearance of a garden on the outskirts of the country. Every corner of it was adorned with a cluster of greenery; quiet avenues of evergreen shrubs led up to it, and from the terraces could be seen, beyond the stream that flowed down from Ménilmontant, the windmill-crowned heights of Montmartre.

The Restoration found the same setting, with the emphasis on luxury. Carriages and horsemen presented a gay picture. Soon came the romantic period: fashionable establishments increased in number, and the district became the dandies' freehold. On the other hand, the Chaussée-d'Antin and its surroundings again changed in character. Instead of the hide-outs, pleasure resorts and summer houses of the ladies of the Opera and their nobleman friends—which had replaced the baser type of amusement places, such as Ramponneau's—there arose more substantial buildings or opulent blocks of flats inhabited by financiers, bankers and business men. A little farther east rose in its turn the enclave of Notre-Dame-de-Lorette, and young ladies of easy virtue with gay charming manners were the first occupants of apartments—at a purely nominal rent—designed originally for respectable middle-class tenants; ever since, they have taken their title (Lorettes) from the name of this district.

It was the dawn of the era of the Boulevard. Its characteristic traits, that were to focus the attention of the whole world on Paris, were developed in the course of three periods of history—the reign of Louis-Philippe, the Second Empire, and the Third Republic until about the year 1900. Cafés and restaurants in these parts were to leave resounding names, as famous in history as the most celebrated victories. Dreamlike memories still surround the *Tortoni*—the steps leading up to it, the large, mirrored first-floor room—and the *Café de Paris*, the haunt of the most refined epicures. And every street corner had its claim to fame; it became the stopping-place in turn of cabriolets, gigs, barouches, and even the first motor-cars. The rakes, the rips, the jades,

the queans—in a word, the fashionable set from all over Europe—flocked there. There was also the *Café de Foy*, the *Maison Dorée*, the *Café Riche*, without mentioning the *Café de Madrid* where Baudelaire, Banville, Villiers de l'Isle Adam and others were to be seen, and, later, Gambetta, Vallès, Rochefort. The history of the *Café Anglais* at first highly respectable, even strait-laced, and later losing caste through its wild revelries (though its "Large No. 16," the most famous of all *cabinets particuliers*, remained the symbol of all the best parties of all times)—would merit an entire chapter to itself. It witnessed a procession of the most varied celebrities of Parisian life from Cora Pearl to Edward VII, then Prince of Wales.

But strangely enough, behind this tumultuous and hectic firework display, the Parisian continued to live a private life of his own, which found its most complete and typical expression in this enclosed and reserved territory. His family would have thought it a fall from grace to leave for other quarters—except for one day in the year, or even less, and for a visit to the country once in a lifetime. Thus the Parisian became identified as the Man of the Boulevards: the spirit of the Boulevards, through the mouthpiece of a few outstanding journalists and talented actors, became the personification of the French genius. But he was by no means the first of his line. His ancestors numbered among them the *Constitutionnel*; then Girardin's *Presse*; the Théâtre des Italiens in the Salle Ventadour which, after housing the Opéra Comique, is today a branch of the Bank of France, and the Opera which even after

a succession of fires, still remained faithful to this atmosphere that suited
it so well. There came a time when a single word from the editorial
office of the *Figaro*, the *Evènement* or the *Gaulois* could make or unmake
a reputation, and even sway national opinion; or when in the theatre
world of the boulevards—it might have been either the Variétés or the
Vaudeville or the Gymnase (famed for its theatre companies)—a gag was
enough to establish the renown of its author for many a long day. Today, except for the *Figaro* that has migrated to the Champs-Elysées, the
newspapers still abound over a widely extended area of this quarter.
But their only concern nowadays is to give information vaguely tinged
with politics. And as for the theatres, although they are still there—
apart from the Vaudeville which has gone for ever—they have for a
long time been bereft of repertory as well as troupes, and epoch-making
plays couched in the idiom of the day are no longer seen on their boards.

The Interior of a Café in 1830.

JEAN BÉRAUD. — *Glope, the confectioner's* (in the Carnavalet Museum).

None the less we must still acclaim here the great figures of the past—
Scribe, the younger Dumas, Augier, Labiche, Sardou, Meilhac and
Halévy, Donnay, Capus, Feydeau, de Flers and Caillavet.

While we are thus weeping at the bier of Thalia, let us spare a tear for
some of the Café-Concerts such as the *Olympia, Parisiana* and the *Petit
Casino*; they all had their charm and they inevitably perished when the
cinema unwound its spools, the first coils of which were seen that
memorable evening of the 28th of December 1895, at the *Grand Café*.
It was in the very heart of the Boulevard, which thus found itself in the
position of having nursed in its bosom the moving-picture viper, whose
insidious vigour was to prove fatal to its most famous institutions.
The heavy, white block of the Paramount is now enthroned on the site
of the Vaudeville that saw the triumph of Réjane.

But this is not all that the Boulevards of olden times remember. At
the end of the last century the Boulevard and its surroundings contained a
whole intellectual climate, the elements of which are now scattered to
the four corners of the city. Thus, the first galleries of the great art

dealers were set up there long before those of the Rue de la Boëtie, and connoisseurs roamed the Rue Lafitte to see the Durand-Ruels, the Bernheims, the Cailleux, the Sagots and the Vollards.

It was equally natural that the Boulevards should harbour bookshops that were veritable " literary salons " such as those of Rey and Floury, worthy descendants of the *Librairie Nouvelle* that was set up just over a century ago—in 1849—at the corner of the Rue Grammont, and was the resort of Maxime du Camp, Barbey d'Aurevilly, Baudelaire and Murger, without mentioning Céleste Mogador and others of her kind. For one of the characteristic features of the Boulevard was always a fondness for women and a willingness to welcome them without fear of scandal. Perhaps it was in this respect that it was so completely Parisian. Yes, I know—this liberal welcome was often extended to the extreme limits permitted by convention. Yet, even supposing that venal usages were admitted here to such a degree as to be reproved by morality, was it not the natural thing—in this spot where intellectual inspiration existed to an extent that we shall never know again, that Eros, the most smiling of all philosophers, should have been peripatetic ? And since it is better not to leave this matter in a falsely prudish light, we must acknowledge that the ladies of the promenade at the *Folies-Bergères*, and at the *Olympia* of former days, the sprightly descendants of the light-hearted Lorettes, did as much, whatever one may think of it, to establish the reputation of this " Centre of Paris " as all that I have just recalled to mind.

Now I notice that I have not mentioned the Jockey Club whose members from 1834 onwards carried their anglomania the whole length of the boulevards, to the corners of the Rues du Helder, Scribe and Drouot, into more and more luxurious premises; nor that former Hotel de Montholon, at 23 Boulevard Poissonnière, built by Soufflot, where fashionable ladies of the Third Republic held literary *salons*. I have not even attempted to bring to life again Murger, Berlioz, Hugo, Dumas, Déjazet, Halévy, Doré, About, Sarcey, Géricault, Horace Vernet, George Sand, Chopin (I mention names at random, probably forgetting others equally eminent), all of whom lived in this area. Illustrious personages, whose souls must now be experiencing eternal peace in a paradise bathed in " *Parisine*," that must contain a phantom vehicle they did not all know in their days on earth, but that men of my generation lament—the last brown omnibus of the *Madeleine-Bastille* route, with its upper deck pitched

between earth and heaven.

But with all these excursions into the kingdom of the dead I am liable to give the impression that the part of Paris about which I am writing in this volume, is nothing more than a necropolis. The reverse is true, for the Place de l'Opéra is probably the most important traffic centre in Paris. What was once a somewhat closed-in region has become an open zone. The pulse of the capital beats here, and in all the nearby streets, in the most vital manner imaginable, and with spectacular intensity, even in its most complex bottlenecks. Trade is represented in its most varied and active forms. Only the types of attractions and the psychology of pleasure have changed in accordance with the times in which we live. By extending our investigations to the farthest limits, it is now the time to show how the many contradictory features of the past and present are blended here in such a surprising manner as to amaze and intrigue the foreign tourist least aware of the *nuances* of the Parisian atmosphere.

We could not do better than begin our walk by way of that wonderful Place des Victoires which, in its original state, must have been a match for its Parisian sisters, the Place Vendôme and the Place des Vosges. There is a marvellous nobility in its circular arrangement of uniform façades with their regular Ionic pillars, two stories high, their bases supported by large arcades surmounted by mascarons and crowned with wide mansard roofs. It was begun in 1685 from designs by Jules Hardouin-Mansart. But great architecture has rarely been so badly treated. Only by a close study of the whole is it possible to rediscover the original unity and grandeur that have been wantonly destroyed by advertisement hoardings, false fronts, additions, mutilations of all kinds, and demolitions to make openings on to Haussmann-like highways.

Behind this circus, opposite Notre-Dame-des-Victoires, the Place des

Petits-Pères is no more than an irregular enlargement of streets, without a definite plan, with a variegated tangle of 18th century houses, some of which are by no means so ugly when one succeeds in isolating them from their trappings and imagining them stripped of their unseemly daubings. The Place Gaillon near the Avenue de l'Opéra is scarcely larger, but it has on one side a harmonious group of buildings with an elegant fountain in the centre.

There is nothing to say about the Place de la Bourse, a vast open space for parking various means of transport, but the Place de l'Opéra must hold our attention for a moment. It is a typical example of the Haussmann conception of a turntable for urban traffic: a cross-roads open on all sides, in place of the enclosed and monumental square of former times. It must, however, be recognised that here a fairly successful attempt has been made to give symmetry to the incoming streets, by the grouping of façades, as well as by the contrast between the bulk of the enormous building that dominates the whole area and the well-balanced view that faces it. It is undeniable that the Place de l'Opéra, in the midst of its ceaseless hum of activity, stands out as by far the most harmonious of all the squares of modern Paris. All the principal arteries of this central part of Paris converge here, although it is not in the middle but in one corner of the area we are now covering. First of all, there are the *Grands Boulevards*, whose past we have discussed at length,

The Place Gaillon.

The Place des Victoires.

and whose ancient, noble quarters still survive here and there in the midst of a diversity that is, in spite of everything, fascinating. . They make a wide and gentle sweep eastwards, somewhat reminiscent of the Seine. With their rows of trees, they are always varied and pleasing to look at. Certainly they no longer present an atmosphere of originality but, from the Porte St. Denis to the Madeleine, they reveal a subtle variety of changing characteristics in such a way as to constitute one of the most pleasing walks in Paris. With a pell-mell of shops of all kinds and of all grades, large cafés with orchestras, or milk bars that were fashionable fifteen years ago, they pass imperceptibly from the *petit bourgeois*, or almost plebian, to the luxury atmosphere of the Opera or the Madeleine. At the end of their path they are weighed down by solid blocks of masonry—the principal offices of the large banks, gigantic cinemas, immense cosmopolitan hotels—one, at least, of which can be considered as a kind of historical monument, almost ancestral, which since its foundation has astonished generations by its magnificence. In fact, the *Grand Hotel*, a contemporary of the Opera, also decorated by Garnier, was from the first renowned for the number of its rooms, its general spaciousness, and its dining room in the form of a rotunda marked out with columns. The Boulevard Haussmann rushes headlong into the great boulevards and tries to imitate them—with scant success. But at least it boasts two large departmental stores, tempting labyrinths for people of limited means in search of the " *chic parisien* ".

The broad, straight Avenue de l'Opéra seems squat in spite of its length. It spurns large cafés with terraces. On the other hand, it contains a series of shops of old and solid repute; some grew up with it, others are immigrants from the Palais-Royal or even the Boulevard Sébastopol, but they all confer a well-to-do character upon the avenue. The Rue du 4-Septembre and the Rue Lafayette, on the other hand, are noisily commonplace and full of bustling monotony. They stretch out straight ahead, their shop-windows crammed with a jumble of articles. Even the temples lining the way, whether they house a church or the Stock Exchange, do not stay their course. But if the Rue Lafayette has no real character, neighbouring streets have certain intrinsic qualities worthy of note. The Rue du 4-Septembre seems to be the heir of the Rue du Sentier, in that it has become a specialist in the cloth trade. As for the Rue Réaumur, it attracts attention because of a strange perversity: in some respects it seems the least Parisian of streets, and might equally well be in London or Berlin. The Rue du Faubourg Montmartre, with a medley of local shops congesting the sweep of its course—shirtmakers, drapers with shop-windows full of lingerie, petticoats, ties, scarves—not to mention perfumery and chemists' shops—is a perfect reflection of the tastes and needs of the local inhabitants who, for professional reasons, generally like extremes, both in form and colour. It still represents a picture of the Paris that reached its peak about the year 1900. We have just mentioned the Rue du Sentier, which is equally famed as the former home of personalities of note and as that of the wholesale cloth trade, which flourished there to such an extent that the general appellation "Sentier" evokes the idea of fabrics in the minds of Parisians. Another road, much farther to the north, is also devoted exclusively to a single trade: the Rue de Paradis, where crockery, china, glassware and pottery hold sway.

One strange thing: if you consider the boundaries that I indicated at the beginning of this chapter, you will notice that it is within this area that all the "passages" of Paris with all their varied aspects are to be found, apart from the two "galleries" in the Champs-Elysées. Most of them were built a little more than a hundred years ago, and they were especially popular between the end of the First Empire and the Restoration. This identity of period gives them a certain similarity of style—arcades, rounded windows, rather heavy Egypto-Roman decorations,

CLAUDE MONET. — *The Gare St. Lazare.*

bas-reliefs representing large allegorical figures. They are not without charm to-day. And now they are the domain of shoe-blacks, perfumery stores, music dealers, sellers of picture postcards and Parisian fancy goods or of rubber goods, sandwiches, florists, jobbing tailors. With their serried rows of shops and projecting signs, their shallow windows, gimcrack booths, flooded in limelight or bathed in a grey, aquarium-like daylight, they have all acquired a strong family likeness.

One famous haunt has disappeared: the *Passage de l'Opéra.* This arcade contained everything a man needed in life—shirtmakers, shoe-makers, restaurants, hotels (with rooms by the day, the night... the half-hour !). At the far end was the Théâtre Moderne, minute, shabby, and musty. Who would have dreamt that this had once been one of the most famous and brilliant " couloirs " of Parisian life, where well-to-do dandies came to wait for the former Opera Queens ?

The oldest of the existing passages is the " Panoramas." It was opened in 1800. In 1807 it was one of the first highways to be lit by gas. It is composed of a maze of galleries with endless ramifications, threading their way alongside the block of houses that lines the Rue Vivienne. It is perhaps the passage with the most aristocratic trade, meaning by that the most long-standing. A bookseller who caters for great booklovers decorates his front window with an octavo bound in red full Morocco. Two engravers display escutcheons of all the armorial bearings of France. Crossing the Boulevard Montmartre, we enter the Passage Jouffroy. It is still the most lively of all. Less "classy" than the Panoramas, its trade represents the flourishing middle classes. In an almost motionless atmosphere, hairdressers's shops and restaurants emit their respective odours which are undisturbed by our passing. In the evening, this passage is brilliantly lit with electric arc-lamps which give it a heady festival atmosphere.

Then from the Rue Grange-Batelière to the Faubourg Montmartre runs the Verdeau Passage, disorderly and regular at the same time. One could enumerate a host of others—the Choiseul Passage where Lemerre, the publisher of the *Symbolistes*, seems to be hidden away; the Passage du Havre, where an artist used to execute astonishing pictures in hair, naive, but charmingly romantic; the Passage des Princes, formerly Mirès, where Poulet-Malaissis, the publisher of "*Les Fleurs du Mal*" set up a bookshop as luxurious as a palace. In addition, there is the Passage du Caire which goes down from the Rue d'Aboukir to the Rue St. Denis, bristling with signs like a Chinese street, and fluttering with a thousand coloured specks. This long, straight alley harbours only sign-writers and poster artists, publicity printers and sellers of labels and placards. Higher up, beyond the *Grands Boulevards*, there is the same impression of excessive colours—even clearer, fresher and smarter— that seem to tremble at the slightest breath of wind. This is the Brady Passage, entirely given up to feminine garments—ready-made frocks, lingerie, etc., light and pretty, in little shops no bigger than a cardboard box, where one can hardly move.

There are also passages as silent at cemeteries, were the slightest footfall resounds. Two such are to be found near the Place des Vic-

toires from whence we started this tour. One is the Vivienne Gallery,
formerly one of the most frequented. It is decorated with the Colbert
arms, but no shops enliven it. The other is the Vero-Dodat Gallery,
renowned for the beauty of a sausage-maker, to whom it owes its name.
It still fascinates us by its succession of uniform shop-windows in the
purest Restoration style: mahogany panels and glass-work surrounded
by copper tubes, joined by small colums of the same metal. It is one of
the most delightful commercial decorations in Paris.

Moreover, the need for open spaces on the fringe of the general stream
of activity is such that we also see in this area a series of private ways and
secluded courts that are really a form of open air passage. Of this type
we can mention the Cour-des-Petites-Ecuries—a kind of dead limb of the
street of the same name, but inhabited by artisans; the Bergère and the
Rougemont *cités*; the Violet Passage, clean and peaceful, that has fortunately kept the atmosphere of the *petite bourgeoisie* of the time of Louis-
Philippe, etc. One might add that the tradition is not lost, since even
today the Rue Edouard VII continues the species in the modern style.

Now for the public buildings. The first to mention is the Opera.
Agreement on its aesthetic qualities is far from unanimous. While it
cannot be considered as a work of art, it is too often disparaged on
account of its heaviness and its composite style. It must not be forgotten
that it was designed in 1861, i.e., at the most pompous stage of the Second
Empire, by a first-class architect who knew his job—Charles Garnier.
At that time all architectural tradition in France had been lost—we shall

see that later in regard to the churches. But it was a brilliant epoch, and the master of the country's destiny thought on a grand and lavish scale. Garnier's genius lay in giving balanced proportions to the " gigantic "—the Opera was until recently the largest theatre in the world. His was the task of uniting the most richly varied elements into a single harmony and, finally to discover a style that was decorative but really imposing, without at the same time overriding all kinds of practical considerations. Regarded in this light, the Opera is the most truly representative example of the style of the Second Empire. Can we imagine it otherwise than it is, with its 210 ft. depth of stage counterbalanced by the splendour of its blue and pink marble columns and its golden bronze, by the magnificent spaciousness of its staircase designed for great displays of elegance, its purple hangings and the sparkle of its monumental lustre? And then it offers one of the marvels of modern statuary—in its detail at least: Carpeaux's *Danse*.

DEGAS. — *A Ballet Rehearsal.*

JEAN BÉRAUD. — *In the wings at the Opera.*

Not far from it, one might almost say in its shadow, hiding away and stupidly turning its back on the boulevards, the Opéra-Comique merely gives the effect of a large provincial theatre. We will surely be forgiven for not mentioning all the other places of amusement. But we must keep a place for the Théâtre des Variétés—the oldest in Paris—because of its delightful façade, reminiscent of the boulevards of past days; and the Théâtre Pigalle, the youngest of Paris theatres (except the Palais de Chaillot), representing a modern type of decoration very different from the traditional, with its bright red woodwork and nickel tubing, but which seems to have aged more in twenty years than its older rivals— for instance the Gymnase (formerly the Théâtre Madame) or the Athénée, so redolent of the " Gay Nineties."

Let us pass from the profane to the sacred. It would, alas, be better to pass by in silence. For none of these 19th century churches deserves anything other than regrets for the lost art of building. This is equally true of Notre-Dame-Bonne-Nouvelle, the shop-girls' sanctuary, Notre-

Dame-de-Lorette, dull and paltry, and the Trinité which is nothing more than a pretentious edifice in the Italian Renaissance style. Even Notre-Dame-des-Victoires, older, and for the most past in the "Jesuit" style, was already the precursor of this decadence. It is better known as a place of pilgrimage than as a successful example of religious architecture.

A reference must finally be made—we cannot do more—to a few buildings at which every art lover ought at least to have a glance: the Hôtel de Lulli at the corner of the Rue des Petits-Champs and the Rue Sainte-Anne, the Hôtel Titon, 58, Boulevard Poissonnière, a fine example of the pleasing severity of Louis XVI classicism, the remarkable Hôtel de Bourienne in the Rue d'Hauteville, which is, with the British Embassy, the sole example of the architecture of the Consular period. It has the merit of having preserved, almost intact, its composite ornamentation, marrying the grace of the late 18th century to an expression of the growing taste for Graeco-Pompeian antiquity—not to mention the influence of the style that was in vogue on Napoleon's return from Egypt. Finally, there are the three small "*hotels*" in the Rue de la Tour-des-Dames, with their associations with Mlles. Mars, Duchesnois and de Talma. One could then proceed to discover other interesting relics, unhappily much spoilt, in the Rue du Sentier or the Rue Drouot, (the Hôtel Aguado, now the town-hall of the 9th *arrondissement*). Whatever happens, time must be spared for a visit to the *Bibliothèque Nationale*. Not only is it renowned for its magnificent collection of books and its wealth of manuscripts, medals and prints, but its buildings include some of the best preserved fragments of the former Palais Mazarine, such as the noble brick and stone façade of the Hôtel Tubeuf, and the sumptuous Mazarine Gallery that the Cardinal built to house his art collections. Part of the Court of Honour is not without a certain fascinating grandeur. And this *mélange* that remains so alive bears the mark of the greatest French architects—Le Muet, Mansart, Robert de Cotte. After so many regrets and disappointments, we will end our walk musing on this grand finale—what more could we ask ?

Such is this kernel of Paris, so full of contrasts and contradictions (many of these streets so animated during the week are as dead as provincial towns on Sundays). It merits a more attentive, a more "psychological" visit than many others, if its secret charms are to be discovered. Otherwise it just looks like a vast warehouse "for wholesale and retail goods," or a large railway junction for provincial or foreign tourists. It is the latter characteristic that leaves the most lasting impression. "Everything for the tourist" might be the motto of the 9th *arrondissement* which, in its own way, represents the very essence of the purest "Parisianism." For here the visitor is king. To convince himself of this, he has only to cast a glance at the terrace of the Café de la Paix on a fine summer's day. One could think that it was a beach, offering samples of every type of nationality in their distinctive clothes. The waiters there are accustomed to all kinds of accents and one feels that these travellers, whether they are there for the day, the week or the month, derive a wonderful bliss from being at the very heart of Paris, just to watch Parisians pass by "in their every-day clothes" and to see an endless procession of traffic streaming past. Large motor-coaches from all corners of Europe cross the wide open space, brilliant with sparkling colours and nickel, like great yachts crammed with cruising spectators, trying to follow their guide's explanations of the rapidly changing scene. The cruisers berth at the tourist agencies in the Rue Scribe, the Place de la Madeleine and the Avenue de l'Opéra. On one side of the Opera is the parking place for

The Square Louvois.

expensive hire-cars. There, too, are the sellers of the plans of Paris and the series of coloured picture postcards that unfurl to ground-level like great plumes; they look like birds that have borrowed their variegated feathers from the eye-catching shop-windows, which are plastered with a medley of bright colours invitingly announcing "tours" of "Paris by night," Versailles, Fontainebleau, the Battlefields, or "really Parisian" shows. It is there that the Brussels household, the inhabitant of Kansas city or the Londoner will book their seats for the Folies-Bergères, the Casino de Paris, or the Concert Mayol, which all happen to be in this area. I hope I shall not be expected to devote to this type of theatrical production the pages that it merits. It is mainly composed of *tableaux vivants* decorated with gilt, and lavish materials, plumes and waving feathers capped by heady displays of naked women. Parisians have known that kind of thing from their adolescent days (and only generally regain their taste for it in ripe old age). Our guests could not imagine a stay in Paris without a visit to one of these establishments, especially the first, which has become a sort of national institution. My description could then teach them nothing.

In contrast to this dynamic display of undress, it is pleasing to notice how many other *tableaux vivants*—this time static—with remarkable illusionary effects, drawing their inspiration from history or present-day realities and always decently clothed (in a delightful 1890 setting, with columns, loggias and cariatides enriched by complicated gilding) still have an equally faithful clientele. As you will guess, I am referring to the Musée Grévin.

I can only advise the foreigner who wants to know this quarter better to abandon his super motor-coach, avoiding those Babylonian air-conditioned cinemas, the like of which he will find in every capital of the world, including his own country—and yield to the pleasures of an idle stroll. There is no better place for the supreme art of living *à la Parisienne*. The only way of really becoming a Parisian is to become a saunterer. The only way of appreciating the distinctive features of ech street is to do a little "window-shopping." I would also advise the visitor to stop in front of the little booths and the tables selling nicknacks that now seem to have a permanent home on the *Grands Boulevards*. He will be thrilled with a thousand ingenious inventions. He will marvel at the glibness of the cheap-jacks. In four lessons—meaning

The Bourse.

by that, four halts—he will learn more of the genius of the French language than in all the manuals of conversation. He will receive an initiation into the rich, spirited and colourful language of the street that will enable him to be understood anywhere.

However, if he wants to press his investigations even farther into the daily life of Paris, I then advise him to try and make the acquaintance of an old Parisian. They still exist, and always have time to spare. This gentleman—who, after all, is only cantankerous in the Métro—will do his utmost to show the foreigner the sights in a friendly spirit, since he is proud to know of their existence. He will take him to that remarkable music-dealer in the Rue du Croissant where the salesmen know by heart (words and music, couplets and refrains) all the popular songs that have stirred hearts at street corners. Then he will introduce him to the secrets of the Hôtel des Ventes in the Rue Drouot, where marvellous bric-à-brac is mysteriously dispersed (the game takes some time to learn), in rooms sometimes hung with dull sacking and sometimes with Turkey-red cotton. If it is during the *Tour de France*, he will stop with him in the Rue du Faubourg Montmartre to look at the dramatic telegrams and exciting results of the bicycle race, pasted up on the windows for the benefit of an amazing conglomeration of humanity that only lives for the next episode of this modern "*chanson de geste*" that rolls over hill and vale.

Finally, at the close of the day, he will reveal his yearning for the time when, here, at nightfall, the façades used to gleam in the light of a myriad luminous signs as if each evening they were decking themselves out in their scintillating array of diamonds and carbuncles to appear worthy of the capital. And I know that, to make amends for this lament, he would at the same time show the visitor one last picture, one of the most engaging in the city : framed in the rectilinear axis of the Rue Lafitte, as though seen through a strange pair of opera-glasses, the white and almost unearthly vision of the *Sacré-Cœur*, fading into a sky of changing colour, in a sort of haze of human breath, sometimes to reappear, glistening in the intense blue of a magic and peaceful moonlight.

Louis CHÉRONNET.

UNDER THE SIGN OF SAINT MARTIN

QUIZET. — *The Saint Martin Canal.*

DD TOGE-

ther two large railway stations, six
theatres, two hospitals, two triumphal
arches, a town-hall of noble bearing—
that could well play the part of a castle—
two wide, distinguished-looking avenues—the Boulevard de Strasbourg
and the Boulevard Magenta—a unique
water-course, the Canal Saint-Martin
in its liveliest part, belonging to it
by right, and a symbolic portion of
the statue of the Republic—and you
have the 10th *arrondissement*, offering
itself to map-readers and walkers and
even to historians, as a little independent state, quiet and intimate,
within the heart of Paris.

Situated between the city wall of Charles V and that of the Fermiers
Généraux, this quarter has very well-defined frontiers that appear to
be entirely natural: in other words it would be impossible to imagine
them otherwise. They form a neat enclosure: the main boulevards to
the south, the outer boulevards to the north, the Rue du Faubourg-
Poissonnière to the west and the Rue du Faubourg-du-Temple to the east.
These last two streets, alive and humming, by themselves form precise
boundaries and are a sure guarantee against any quibbling. We are
dealing then, with a district that has been given its own distinctive appearance, and the dotted line that surrounds it on the maps for convenience
seems to have been prescribed by the configuration of the ground and
the force of circumstances rather than the will of man. Finally—and it
is this that gives the comforting effect of a domain, of a kind of family
estate or patrimony—practically all this district covers land that formerly
belonged either to the abbey of St. Lawrence or the priory of St. Lazare.
We must note the latter, before going any farther, not only because it
constitutes one of the most pathetic sites in Paris, as Léon Daudet used
to say, but because it was once a central point.

There was, almost at the top of the Faubourg St. Denis, an old leper-
house founded in the time of the Crusades by the Hospitallers of St. La-

zarus (the leper of the Scriptures) that drew its revenues from the Fair of the same name. In 1632 the monks of the leper-house united with those of the Mission Congregation, founded by St. Vincent-de-Paul, who became director of this domain, died and was buried there, and remained there in a silver shrine until 1823. On the eve of their solemn entry into Paris, the kings and queens of France stayed at this monastery and received the oath of the authorities at the *Logis du Roi*, a building that had been set apart for that purpose. It was there also that they passed their last night, in the coffin, before being taken, according to custom, to the vaults of St. Denis. Under Louis XV, St. Lazare served as a penitentiary for priests and the sons of noble families; then, in 1793, at the time of the revolution, it became an ordinary prison. André Chénier was imprisoned within its walls, and there he wrote the *"Jeune Captive."* Among its other notable inmates was Hubert Robert, denounced by David, and who has left us the most striking pictures of the transporting of prisoners from St. Pélagie to St. Lazare, such as Marie-Louise de Laval, Duchess of Montmorency, the last abbess of Montmartre, who, though deaf, was nevertheless accused by Fouquier-Tinville of a secret conspiracy. From the time of the "Consulat", the house of St. Lazare—on which Eugène Süe later enlarged in his " Mysteries of Paris "—was transformed into a women's prison and remained such until 1935. Nowadays, in this rather hidden and romantic quarter of courts and passages, of demolitions and small hotels embedded in the walls of buildings like shrapnel, it is a nursing-home, reached by way of the Rue de la Ferme St. Lazare : a nursing-home with modern improvements, freed from its past history, in a setting of brick, in sober

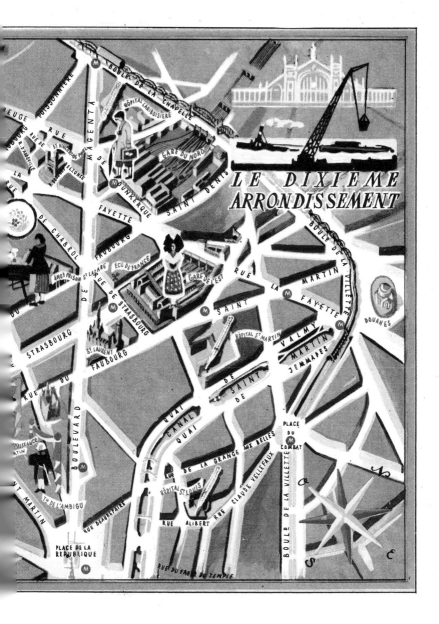

LE DIXIEME
ARRONDISSEMENT

lines, standing beside an imposing building of the Electricity Company. However, it is still partly reserved for patients who are under police surveillance.

At the very centre of the district, where the Boulevard Magenta and the Boulevard de Strasbourg intersect, lies huddled the tiny church of St. Lawrence, rich, but modest and delicate; by this church our little village is linked to the remote past of the capital.   An abbey in the 5th

André Chénier in the St. Lazare prison.

century (it is mentioned by Gregory of Tours), pillaged by the Normans in 911, a parish church in 1180, dedicated by a bishop in 1429, enlarged in 1548, restored in 1595, and again in the 17th century, the temple of Hymen and Fidelity under the Revolution, the Temple of Age in 1795, restored to the faithful and its patron saint by the Concordat, endowed with a flamboyant porch in 1866, at the time of the construction of the Boulevard of Strasbourg—this church, lost in its surroundings, is infinitely dainty, clothed in gracious humility.   It remains, despite its commercial environment, the place where the spirit breathes, the symbol of piety and hope, the hallowed spot around which this dense area slowly developed.

Between the church and the monastery of St. Lazare, was held in former times the famous St. Lawrence's Fair which lasted three months, from June to September, by special authorisation of the king, dated 1344. For Parisians greedy for new and varied shows, it existed for nearly four centuries, in a suburb that in earlier days was somewhat remote. But noble lords were not above applauding, in the company of beggars, marionette displays, tight-rope walkers, clowns and trainers of various kinds of animals. All this greatly displeased the French Comedians, hostile to travelling troupes. The St.Lawrence Fair, however, had its day and it was a long one. It also had its chroniclers and poets, for the site was good and far-famed, and seemed to bring good fortune to the players. Even in the 18th century a real theatre braved public opinion and set up there, daring to take the name of the " Opéra-Comique ", and the Comédie Italienne gave performances there that were greatly appreciated in 1716. The Fair finally disappeared in 1775. Today the stalls and boxes, the stage, the pleasure gardens and galleries of this vast open-air theatre, where the prestige of the *Circenses* was so long tested and maintained, have been replaced by the station yard of the Gare de l'Est, formerly the Gare de Strasbourg, built according to Duquesney's plans by the engineer Sermet and opened in 1850.

The past has left no traces here; the railway scene and its new poetry, its movements, its signals, its energy, its necessities also, have absorbed everything. More than any others, the Gare de l'Est is for the Parisian the station of mobilisation and wars, significant, patriotic, leading to Alsace—the station from which red-trousered soldiers set off in 1914 in the middle of a delirious crowd that shouted incessantly for a whole day "To Berlin". But it is also, by its position and its role, the station of invasion and exile.

Between the Gare de l'Est and the Gare du Nord, those two hives of industry, milling with travellers, the perpetual animation is further swollen by the crowds and traffic of the Rue Lafayette, the Boulevard Magenta, the St. Quentin market and the Lariboisière hospital. The district is at one and the same time both restful and noisy, impulsive and circumspect. One of the most illustrious of its adopted sons, Léon-Paul Fargue, who lived in the Rue du Faubourg St. Martin and later in the Rue de Château-Landon, used to say in a friendly way: "Oh, those bagpipe noises that pierce the air from the locomotives of the East and North stations. They may take us a few miserable yards nearer Switzerland or

The Gare de l'Est.

Germany, but they soon bring us back to the strong, familiar smells of the Rue d'Alsace or the Rue Louis-Blanc. Old quarter dear to us with the magic of the voices we love... "

It only takes a few minutes to go from one station to the other, especially by the stairways of the Rue d'Alsace, and yet the Gare du Nord, whose official address is 18 Rue de Dunkerque, still in the ancient St. Lawrence enclosure, is distinctly different from the Gare de l'Est. It has a more sombre appearance; it has no courtyard, it rises out of the very fabric of the town like a bank or a theatre. The travellers are different too. The extremes come from Sweden or the Baltic countries. They are blond, slow-moving and silent. Those of the eastern railway network—beyond Alsace and Switzerland—represent Central Europe, and show more emotion. Two worlds, each with a different spirit. The Gare du Nord with its lovely interior, its delicate girders and its Pullmans, is the work of Hittorf, who was also the architect of the neighbouring church of St. Vincent de Paul, in the Place Lafayette—still within the St. Lawrence-St. Lazare enclosure from which we cannot escape.

In the time of the " Father of the Poor "—a remarkable film has sketched his life for the whole world to see—there was a pleasant summer-house and legend has it that " Monsieur Vincent " often stopped there " to meditate and to devote himself to his duties and his good works." One can easily conjure up this picture today, in the calm seclusion of the streets adjoining the church of St. Vincent, built on the site of the summer-house—the Rue Belzunce, the Rue Bossuet, the Rue Fénelon—abruptly withdrawn from the bustle of the neighbourhood, little disturbed by traffic, away from the hubbub and the placards — almost provincial, in fact. One would love to have a retreat here, an ivory tower, an island of stone in the midst of the uproar of Paris and the whistling of locomotives which, far from destroying its character, would season it. But the briefest stroll will subtly lead us back to the stir and

commotion, and we find ourselves once again in front of the courtyard of the Gare de l'Est, from which the Boulevard de Strasbourg with its buses, its shop-fronts, its balconies, its slate roofs, leads towards the Boulevard de Sébastopol, the Seine and the Latin Quarter, towards youth and fame—almost as the crow flies.

Starting from the centre of the quarter, if we cross the ancient Roman road which has become the Faubourg St. Martin and make our way eastward by the Rue Terrage or the Rue des Récollets we discover, with delight, and not without a certain element of surprise, a new feature of this dis-

The " Foire aux Jambons ".

trict and one that is little known, but nonetheless a masterpiece,—the St. Martin canal, a miracle, a poem which, from the Rue du Faubourg du Temple to the Stalingrad Métro station (formerly Jaurès) hallows and enlivens the 10th *arrondissement.* Let us first of all give some precise details. To the eye of man, the St. Martin canal flows exclusively through the territory of this district; it is, in a way, its river and its pride. At the Place Jules Ferry, on the edge of the 11th *arrondissement,* between the bust of Frédérick Lemaître and the statue of the "grisette" of 1830, it lives and moves in another and secret world, underneath the Boulevard Richard Lenoir, where the Ham Fair is held in fine weather. Near the Gare du Nord it emerges into the Villette basin, but between these two poles, between the quays of Valmy and Jemmapes, it triumphs and scintillates, visited at times by unexpected birds, adorned here and there with barges which, in the eyes of the local inhabitants, resemble the finest Marquet paintings. The decision to create it was embodied in a law of Floréal 29, year X (May 9th, 1802), in an age of victories and young generals. This law ordained that a navigation canal was to be opened up below the Arsenal bastion extending at far as St. Denis and ultimately Pontoise, by way of the Villette basin, then barely finished. Its purpose was to cut short the loops of the Seine and save boats the ten miles of river through Paris. The work was begun in May 1822, under the direction of the engineer Devilliers, and cost the municipality of Paris fifteen million francs. In point of fact, the canal stopped at St. Denis and was opened on November 4th, 1825. Such is its administrative history.

But it has another history, more real and more concrete, with no bearing on dates : one that for Parisians is lasting, that consoles lonely people or happy couples who go there to whisper softly and sweetly or meditate in a vague, brotherly way. It is a history that is found in some romances, in certain films, in poetic literature. Aristide Bruant, Fargue, Eugène Dabit, Mac Orlan, Francis Carco, and others, never tire of saying how much they appreciate the charms of this melodious corner, a little Dutch, a little suburban, that goes right to the heart. At one time there was even talk of founding a society of the "Friends of St. Martin's Canal" or at least holding a lunch on the spot in spring-time, with invitations for Maurice Ravel, Dignimont, Poiret and Maurice Chevalier to attend this touching ceremony, as all of them are a little intrigued by the charm and the delightful discovery of this corner of Paris, so expressive and downright, and yet possessed of a thousand musical tones.

Since the appearance of Dabit's " *Hotel du Nord* ", the district has its place on the literary map. But its fame also resounds in other directions. Scores of articles that appear in the Avenue Matignon, the Faubourg St. Honoré or the Place Vendôme in the form of luxury-goods—ladies' handbags, scent-bottles, or gloves—are raw material here, hand-worked or mass-produced : wholesale goods from horny hands. The walls are lined with series of superfluous posters, advertising glass-ware for

The " *Chope des Singes* " (caricature).

perfumery stores, castings for construction work, the National Federation of Chemical Industries, the master boot-makers of the Seine, skins and hides. These details are not, however, immediately perceptible. They have their place on the walls and they play their part in the life of the modern industrial city, but their tone is less pleasant than the signs of the small cafés and modest shops. While Paris, at this particular spot in its kingdom, seems more spacious, purer, perhaps a little inscrutable, one is at first charmed by something aery, delicate and out-of-date, where the names of artists and cities are jumbled in our imagination : Poulbot, Verhaeren, Dantzig, Leningrad... We notice, as we stroll along how the language is enriched by new words, sometimes heard, sometimes rediscovered in the memory : words for the lock-chambers, the lock walls, the " college, " the sluice gates, the life-saving posts. All along, as far as the bend between the Rue des Récollets and the Rue de la Grange-aux-Belles, the gay and artless waters of the canal are bedecked with little gardens where spindle trees grow on leafy banks, like a Dufy drawing. Little girls are at play as the barges pass by, while kitchen smells entwine with an air played on the accordion. The swirling waters of the rapids and the lapping of the calmer waters of the canal mingle with the outpouring from workshops and schools, the muffled sounds from the café terraces, the tread of horses' hoofs, the secrets of the sky, the rhythmic life of the locks, a few shouts, a few indefinite or sustained inflections—all that Ravel called " the violins of Paris." An industrial scene—a scene of art, painters, capstans—all " a delightful jumble," as Paul Valéry used to say. Poetic and untidy France... Here on fine mornings is a fragrance, an indescribable feeling, a tone that suggests something between the Lake poets and the works of Simenon, something subtly thought out and decisive, answering the most peremptory demands of the senses. Movable gangways and arched bridges in the Japanese style join the two banks in an elegant play of metal-work. A crowd assembles to watch the passing of a boat, spotlessly clean, laden with a family, or empty and indolent. We unconsciously read the names on these carefree craft : Danube, White Queen, Montluçon, Dolly or Parisienne. The barges exchange impressions, reminiscences, talk shop—not without a certain fleeting, melancholy pungency for those who catch an echo of their conversations.

It is at the Jules-Ferry-Faubourg-du-Temple crossroads, a noisy

The Saint Martin Canal.

corner filled with shops and cafés, that the canal suddenly emerges, and drunkenly pours itself out. It has just spent two hours in darkness and rejoices to bring its dark, silvery shoulders to light, into the busy sunshine. Up to the Rue de la Grange-aux-Belles it traverses a contented, even enthusiastic zone, lined with shrubs, long narrow walks, benches, poets, bushes, old men smoking pipes and spirited youngsters. Then brusquely its character changes and it becomes a dark stream, stripped of its trees and its romance, as stern as a canal in a great city or a vast plain. From the Rue Terrage to the Villette basin its general appearance is severe, its outline is that of an engraving, or indeed a wash drawing. It is an ill-famed spot, empty and terrifying, but not without grandeur. Chirico and the abstract painters would like this sombre and somewhat uncompromising part of the district, and would probably prefer it to the other which is nearer to the delights of the dance, the open-air chip shops and the pleasure of idle musings under the inviting shade of gentle trees. It is also at the point where it curves eastward, right on the corner formed by the Quai de Jemmapes and the Rue de la Grange-aux-Belles, that the canal, formerly a deserted highway, has its darkest associations; for it was here, two hundred years ago, that the gallows of Montfaucon, designed for sixty convicts, was erected.

Facing the canal, at the end of the Avenue Richerand—from the name of the author of " Popular Errors concerning Medicine "—there rises, noble and smiling, in dull grey stone, relieved by the soft pink of the brickwork, like a baronial hall in this little kingdom, the St. Louis hospital with its fine skyline. We will not be surprised at the beauties of this building, despite its purpose, when we learn that it is the work of Claude Vellefaux, the architect of the Place des Vosges, one of the wonders of Paris. The hospital dates from 1619, and was from the outset reserved for sufferers from plague or skin diseases. That is why it received the name of St. Louis, in memory of Louis IX who died at Carthage as a result of contracting the plague in Palestine. During the Restoration, the hospital was even, for a time, the rendezvous of those Parisians who did not care for mass excursions and strolls with the crowd, but the Prefect of the Seine at that time, Mr. de Chabrol de Volvic, had installed in a hangar at St. Louis the first gas generator and this sensational attraction was worth the journey ! Until then, the capital had been lit only by lanterns and the night air reeked of lamp oil. It was difficult to resist the pleasure of going to see the new white lighting, clean, preternatural, and the miraculous way in which it was produced.

The only people nowadays who go to St. Louis are the sick, those who tend and those who visit them—an assuredly hygienic precaution due to the contagious nature of some skin diseases. But it is a loss—for the old-world charm of the hospital courts, the lawns, the general proportions, the sense of balance and an aspect of old France that is happy and wise, with a few rare colours mellowed by time, the elegance of dormer-windows, in a word, a harmony that is barely visible but nevertheless present, give a subtle contentment that is not found everywhere. The hospital is provided with a library with beautiful wood-carving and a museum full of warm and gilded nooks, pleasant in its proportions and its *cachet*, though its contents are horrible. On leaving this superb building—where windows, vaulting, the play of light and shade, recall the dramas of history and princely receptions which might well have taken place in this setting that seems really designed for aristocratic functions—on passing through the Alfred Fournier gate, one catches a glimpse of the canal like a sheet of water, appearing as an emblem of beauty.

So many features of this district bear the name of St. Martin : the canal, a boulevard, a church, a *faubourg*, and a gateway. The latter, after having frequently changed its place since its humble origin, was

The Great Courtyard of the St. Louis Hospital.

finally erected on its present site, and adorned with carved stonework, in 1674, by Pierre Bullet, in honour of Louis XIV's victories and the annexation of Franche-Comté. The allies took it over in 1814 and, three times, revolutionaries established a resistance stand there: in 1830, 1848, and 1871. This spot, which is a kind of entrenched camp of the republican population, boasts three celebrated theatres, all of them in different ways having had their glorious days: the *Ambigu*, the *Porte St.-Martin*, and the original *Sarah-Bernhardt* theatre, now the *Renaissance*. The Rue de Bondy had its places of amusement too: the *Comte* theatre, the *Vauxhall*, and the *Variétés Amusantes*. None of these now exists. The dust of oblivion that covers the past of every city and of every sensitive spot get thicker and thicker. In this sort of little dramatic principality of the Porte St.-Martin that learnt to love so many actors, that has seen so many cabs pass, heard so many sighs, smelt so many flowers, that has been present at the triumph of Sarah Bernhardt, then of Lucien Guitry, lived through that extraordinary dress-rehearsal of *Cyrano de Bergerac* (December 28, 1897) yes, in this living canvas that might have been, once upon a day, by Watteau, who still remembers the splendour of yore, the dramas of love and those of the stage? Who now knows that the popular Béranger, Frédérick Lemaître and Paul de Kock, inhabited this romantic and hallowed region—revolutionary, joyous and reminiscent of Victor Hugo in turn, and that Lisette, the real Lisette, had her famous garret in this block of theatres?

In the same atmosphere—still of theatres, but theatres that have been engulfed by the necessities of mass-production, from bicycle accessories to shell-fish—starting at the Porte St.Martin and as a continuation of the street of the same name, begins the *faubourg*, which has the honour of harbouring the local town-hall. The latter adds nothing to the monumental splendour of Paris, and no-one would dream of making an artistic pilgrimage here. But the building, spacious and substantial, is not without refinement and attraction, and readily takes on the air of a palace. Not without reason, for it was the only town-hall opened by a President of the Republic: Félix Faure, in 1896. It possesses a grand staircase like the one at the opera, and some stately rooms, and holds dances every Sunday for the local inhabitants. On its present site there was formerly a river that flowed into the Seine by way of the Opéra and the Champs-Elysées. And now, coming from the Place de la République, we have—still under the protection of this majestic town-hall—the Rue du Château-d'Eau, with its own topical sign: the Labour Exchange, teeming with syndicates and trades' unions. And this highway has further information to supply for those who like to pin-point things and ideas: the headquarters of the Federation of Retail Traders of France, the General Warehouse of the Tobacconists and also the Porte St-Martin market, an abundant emporium, its walls tattooed with a courteous invitation for customers to visit them, inscribed in enormous letters by the management itself. It is pleasant and cordial, and gives a clear indication that whereas, elsewhere, you may find luxury or amusement, here the main concern is hard work and material necessities.

On the western side, in a quadrilateral formed by the Boulevard St-Denis, the Rue de Chabrol, the Boulevard de Strasbourg and the Faubourg Poissonnière, the 10th *arrondissement,* which occupies an area of 572 acres and is one of the most populous in Paris, shares in the intense bustle of the capital. It seethes and brims over with life and the activity of making its contribution to wholesale trade. There are more theatres: the *Antoine* theatre, which saw the birth of a new form of art, the old-time *Eldorado* and *Scala*, the *Gymnase*, the *Concert Mayol*, with lasting memories of Gémier, Dranem, Henri Bataille, Polin and of Maurice Chevalier's *début*. Everywhere are shops, bars, hotels and offices, packed tightly together like the compartments of a railway coach. We are far from the family life of the northern end of the quarter, round the Métro station Louis Blanc, far from the gentle calm of St. Vincent de Paul or the intimate poesy of the canal, that little private river where the windows of the quays seem to fall into the water like petals. Here are one-way streets, traffic congestion, impersonal crowds; it is the domain of commercial enterprises, with managers and clerks whose private lives are lived elsewhere; wholesale furriers in the Rue de Hauteville; porcelain manufacturers in the Rue de Paradis—so named to counterbalance the name of a neighbouring thoroughfare formerly called "Hell Street"; drapers in the Rue des Petites-Ecuries; insurance firms; transport firms, experts... Advertising is ubiquitous, and one wonders what would be the appearance of the buildings if they were suddenly, by some magic operation, stripped of their signs, their marble plaques and their large lettering on the balconies. This eloquence is at least indicative of craftsmanship— and it spells business : glass-ware, wool, cloth, curtains, silk, cork, hide, embroidery, export trade; it signifies efforts and results. You feel some-

The old Scala.

what alone in the midst of this wealth, which seems to spring forth from
every side—especially if you are just on a stroll. But at the same time
you have the feeling of being in a great city and reading its thoughts and
actions. It ends by giving you a stimulus. And suddenly the scene
changes, and without warning you find yourself in the Faubourg St-Denis
— an immediate feast for the eyes.

You must see this street on a week-day, at about eleven in the morning,
in brilliant sunshine and—according to the season—with its piles of
sausages and eggs, shell-fish or tomatoes, oranges, chickens, leeks, flowers,
cheeses, all against a background of chemists, butchers, and taverns.
It has a vast, moving gaiety. Amid the jumble of produce and the babel
of voices, buses hoot, and housewives who never go shopping without
having the local gossip on the tips of their tongues—in the
form of a tirade—offer lively challenges to each other, over the costers'
barrows. The windows are open on all sides and silhouettes are out-
lined—faces, busts, heads, as on the side of a steamer. This *faubourg*,

The Old Clothes' Market.

The Porte St. Denis.

so vital, vibrant and colourful, descends from La Chapelle on an invisible
sledge and shoots like a torrent under the Porte St-Denis. It is wildly
cheerful and is guaranteed to give a shock to tourists fresh from any
other district.

Then one understands and is glad that the popular zest, the open-air
trading, the spirit of revolt, history, ceremonial, associations of the past,
all meet there on grand occasions and that a monument proclaims it.
The Porte St-Denis, that served in olden days for triumphal entries, also
led to the burial-place of kings. Paris offered this arch to its population
and to posterity in homage to the conquests of 1672 and Louis XIV's
crossing of the Rhine.

Let us come back to a general view of the quarter and its four so different
parts : the small provincial atmosphere around St-Vincent-de-Paul and
the bustle of the two stations close by; seclusion and escape by the
canal and the hospital; the uproar in the lively sector of the two gateways. In the Rue Louis-Blanc, beside the Gare du Nord, the Rue de
l'Aqueduc and all along the outer boulevards, in the humdrum rhythm
of districts deprived of monuments, large cafés and elegant strollers,
live the peaceful little households that have never been to the Opera
or the Longchamp races, let alone Copenhagen or Bucharest, as the locomotives that whistle beneath their windows invite them to do, recalling

the stage-coaches, horses and postilions of former days. Three great arteries are absorbed by trade and export and deafened by the telephone — the Boulevard de Strasbourg, the Boulevard Magenta and the Rue Lafayette--somewhat lacking in personality and reminiscent of the practical, bustling, spacious Paris of Baron Haussmann, just like the station approaches of the Gare du Nord. On either side of these airy, commodious highways, where cars have it all their own way, it appears that the local population takes refuge and shuts itself away, playing an unobtrusive part—at least to outward appearances. There are no grand receptions, no fashionable crazes; its poetry is bitter and caustic, the beauties are rare. The word "work" takes precedence over all others and the preoccupations of daily life are in the foreground. That is why the couplets of Parisian songs appeal, in a kindly, friendly way to the youthful imagination of this area, as they do to even duller districts. Nevertheless, the 10th *arrondissement* has its little secrets and they count in its history. First of all, it possesses a number of famous passages, known only to ramblers of a discerning nature: the Brady passage, a surprising succession of stalls of leather goods for small purses and modest pretensions. For "lost illusions" there is the Passage du Désir, that takes its name from the misleading sign of an old lodging house not far from a former Franciscan monastery; then there is the Passage de l'Industrie, a tool market and a permanent exhibition of mechanical instruments— the handy-man's paradise; the Passage of the St-Martin's market, the Passage des Récollets, that of the Petites-Ecuries, and some streets that are only long passages, such as the Rue Taylor, the Rue Bouchardon, the Cité Riverin. They all make one think of a rather unkind and sad remark of Jules Romains: "The passage shelters and cloaks them (the passers-by) in an almost domestic gentleness; it is as if the street were withdrawn and the interior constantly being opened up to us."

Our quarter, like its neighbours, has not failed to assign a place on its records to illustrious names and outstanding events. The "Chaussée de la Nouvelle France," today the Faubourg Poissonnière, owes its name to the fact that it led to the former fish-market. Here were the old barracks of the Gardes Françaises in 1772, the canteen of which was none other than the room of Sergeant Bernadotte. Lower down stood the *Alcazar d'Eté*, where the singer Thérésa, a popular idol, created "La Femme à barbe" before a delirious and insatiable crowd. Cherubini and

Corot both died in this same street, and the capitulation of Paris was signed nearby in 1814, in the house of Marshall de Marmont. Formerly one could make the discovery of the famous and delightful " *Concert Parisien* " where Yvette Guilbert began her career. Voltaire had an office in the Rue du Faubourg St-Denis, and Ninon de Lenclos a house not far from the building where Félix Faure, a local boy, first saw the light of day. In the Place de la République on the spot now occupied by the most important and most complex Métro station in Paris, Alexandre Dumas wanted to found yet another theatre. Close by, in the time of Napoleon III, was the *Salle Barthélémy*, where inquisitive folk went to see the dancing of the daughters of the executioner Sanson, of the illustrious family of licensed guillotiners. Those two names, Dumas and Sanson, did not fall by accident in our quarter. You will often see, on an inviting seat beside the canal or in the calm of the St-Vincent-de-Paul district, a youngster immersed in a book and quite indifferent to the rest of the world. He has probably just become acquainted with the novel about his district, the private diary of his own quarter. What is related by Dumas and Balzac, Marivaux and Flaubert, Paul de Kock and Simenon, Zola and Dabit, has existed, if only in a fragmentary form, in the Faubourg Poissonnière or the Rue de Bondy, or the Rue d'Enghien : the Rue d'Enghien, to be exact, because there modern reporters have taken the place of the journalists of old France. There have not always been all those wireless sets, sports articles, batteries of kitchen ware and prefabricated clothes around St. Lawrence's church. It has a past : a past that is not so striking or vivid as in other parts of Paris (never sufficiently explored) and that is dealt with in a more flattering way by the story-tellers—but for all that, a past. Somewhere mention has been made of extremely beautiful aquatic fêtes held in the Villette basin in the time of the First Empire. It is then that the young reader seems content to realise that the dismal surroundings in which he works, hopes and suffers, are not without hidden treasure, not without that innate depth of riches that gives the streets a little soul and life, and a certain comforting quality. There were certainly, once upon a time, stately homes in the region of the Portes St-Denis and St-Martin, the Rue de Hauteville and the Rue de Lancry; their place has been taken by cinemas, banks, and those compendious buildings housing printing-presses, commission agents and families that are constantly on the move. New songs are sung. Present-day life is exacting : it levels out, it marshals, it is intent on the happiness of all.   There are, however, some signs of the past remaining, and those signs give more body to the quarter where we live, more background to its salient features—the stations, the hospitals, the passages and the canal—when one belongs to the 10th *arrondissement*, that little village inside Paris, whose spirit is earnest and whose people are loyal.

André BEUCLER.

THE DOMAIN OF THE PARISIAN

E. M. PÉROY

CHRISTIAN BÉRARD. — *La Parisienne*.

ARIS HAS

to be seen in perspective if we are really to appreciate it and to understand why we appreciate it. The Parisian never loves Paris so dearly as when he is in exile. How could he be expected to experience wonderment at the Cour du Louvre that he passes every day or the Place de la Concorde that he has seen darken in the evening light a thousand times? It is not surprising that it was a foreigner who wrote these lines:

"There is Paris—magnificent in itself; and in Paris there is *l'article de Paris*; there is woman and fashion—the Parisienne! It is the ballet in your opera. It is the fountain in the park. When you think about it, it takes quite a number of days to visit your great *salons* that have launched upon the world, like a lasso, that pervasive and hackneyed word—but always precious!—that something whose value is as gold. I mean charm!"

There Edgar Wallace has given us the key-word—Charm! That explains the prestige and attraction of Paris. That sums up its art of giving pleasure and enjoyment. That word, so much the right one, contains everything—the delicacy of the sky, the grouping of public monuments, the gentle patter over stones, the nobility of that princely captive of a river, the elegance of the passing ladies, the luxury of the shops, the harmony of what has been and what is to come, the prettiness of the gardens and, above all, what Paul Valéry called "the most intense power of expression combined with the most intense power of absorption."

Amid the world's hubbub each city has its speciality. London has its shipping, Amsterdam its precious stones, Budapest traffics in *tzigane* melancholy, Paris deals in charm. São Paolo suggests coffee, Cordova leather, Hamburg furs, Paris—smart women.

And that is the cause of its charm. It is because Paris has worked for centuries to enhance feminine seduction that it distils charm as a bee makes honey. But Paris also owes this speciality to its climate, to the

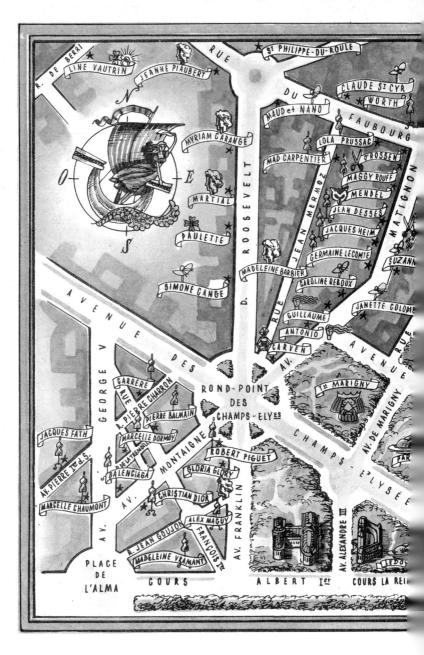

Le DOMAINE de la PARISIENNE

character of its people and to the spirit of emulation of its women. The whole of France shares in it, from the weavers of Picardy to the needle-women of Lorraine, from the jet-cutters of Aude to the Breton lace-makers. The whole town collaborates, from the hill of " Ménilmuche " with its host of fairy-like working girls, to Passy with its well-to-do customers. It is work all day long, from dawn when the belated reveller crosses the path of the window-cleaner, to dusk when the sparkling festoons of the night-signs hang from the balcony of heaven. But it is evident that one district of Paris is more obviously devoted to that func-tion. It is there that we see this charm displayed in its most lavish and extravagant form.

Hither the Parisienne hastens immediately upon her return to the capital in October, glutted with sunshine and eager to feel the friendly tread of " her " asphalt under feet that are tired of walking on lawns or sand. Once again she is in search of her dressmaker, her shoemaker, her hairdresser and all the others who conspire to transform her from a temporary wilding into a beautiful slave of high society, captive for a glamorous winter season.

But the Paris of the Parisienne is also the Paris of the Lady from Abroad who dreams of perfecting her eloquent beauty here. A handsome car awaits her outside the Ritz. Delightedly she yields to the temptations that the streets of Paris offer. She has already been transformed by a fur coat whose magnificence in no way spoils her figure, already she wears an austere little hat, all feathers and tulle, she is already sprayed with the latest fashionable scent. To these allurements she adds the ease of a much-travelled woman, and like a human ship she billows along the glittering docks that sparkle with vanities. The demon of covetous-ness rustles in her sails.

Where exactly do we encounter this Parisienne and this Lady from Abroad ? In the Rue de la Paix, that universally magic address ? In the Faubourg St-Honoré, a stream whose source is in the pleasures of life ? In the Avenue Matignon, a drawing-room open to the sky ? The ans-wer is—in all these streets. But can we fix the boundaries of this town within the town ? It is difficult, and moreover its centre changes. It follows the whim of the western districts. While the Place Vendôme was for a long time, if one might so express it, the navel of French Ele-gance, it appears that now the Rond-Point des Champs-Elysées occupies

that role. The migration continues. Yesterday the Avenue Matignon was annexed. Now the flood swells to the avenues radiating from the Place de l'Alma. Now it is the ascent of the Champs-Elysées, although the Rue de la Paix has not been deserted, and these two extremities are linked by the Rue St-Honoré and the Faubourg St-Honoré. The town extends outwards in accordance with natural laws; for over a century its confines have been the eastern ramparts —the heights of Belleville, Charonne, the Buttes-Chaumont, while westward it stretches out into the featureless plain beyond Chaillot.

The Paris of the Parisienne has followed this movement especially because it has brought with it a worthy setting. Little by little it has come to occupy the old mansions that have been deserted by an aristocracy that had not the means to keep them up. There is nothing surprising in the fact that luxury shops now line Le Nôtre's Champs-Elysées and have spread towards the Etoile that was originally planned by Colbert. This is a recent annexation. Eugène Marsan remembers having been able to count on the fingers of one hand the number of shops in the Champs-Elysées.

" Even I, who am by no means a Methusaleh, and barely the senior of Paul Morand, " he wrote in 1931, " knew, when I was a little boy, the tobacconist, the English chemist, the coach-builder, the florist. In the Rue du Faubourg St-Honoré the shops were a little more numerous, but for the most part modest and mysterious, serving a few faithful customers, almost their own friends."

Since the Paris of the Parisienne has opened its own opera in this district, as a pendant to the other and more famous one—the Théâtre des Champs-Elysées—luxury trade has gained ground. Guerlain perfumes the Champs-Elysées; Christian Dior in the Avenue Montaigne, Madeleine Vramant in the Cours Albert I, and Jacques Fath in the Avenue Pierre Ier-de-Serbie, mark the farthest points of the invasion. The whole of this Paris is born to animation. Sleeping Beauty's castle is transformed into the Palace of the Arabian Nights.

I picture the impatience of the young foreigner who does not want to get lost while exploring the Paris that interests her. " That's all very well, Mr. Roundabout," she says, " but it is a little vague. You surely have a plan, like the other authors of this book."

Let us then settle it for today. I say " for today " and not for tomorrow, because I should not in the least be surprised if a dressmaker set up tomorrow in the Avenue du Bois or if the Avenue Henri Martin one day saw jewellers competing there. I will draw my imaginary line. Starting from the Place de l'Alma, it runs the length of the Avenue George V, crosses the Champs-Elysées, and joins the Faubourg St-Honoré by way of the Rue de Berri. It then follows the Faubourg as far as the Rue Royale, proceeds in the direction of the Madeleine and the boulevards as far as the Place Vendôme, via the Rue de la Paix. It then takes the Rue de Castiglione to the Rue de Rivoli, thence to the Place de la Concorde and back to the Alma by way of the Cours la Reine and the Cours Albert Ier.

Enclosed within this area is the fictitious city of pleasant creations, of refined discoveries and individual genius consecrated to making life more beautiful. Within this framework of streets, competition and co-operation mingle paradoxically to create a thousand and one trifles that make up the sum total of constantly-changing fashion. Here, better than elsewhere, man finds the means of embellishing the object of his love—an exquisite token of civilisation.

And does it not all begin with the artificial ? Artificial—the gossamer lingerie, which we owe to the patience of those who work regardless of time, for those whose only master is time! Artificial, those wreathes, those feathers, those bouquets and lace! Artificial, too, are those real jewels in their delicate settings and those fantasy jewels— delightful when they are false real and not real false! Artificial, too, are those hair styles built up by famous hairdressers on the basis of artificial waves! Artificial, the shoes—shells abandoned by the tide of coquetry on the strand of carpets of real wool! So too with the fan, the screen, the umbrella that is only really elegant when it is not raining, the scent—that invisible ambassador of seduction; the hand-bag—repository of woman's secrets and her portable banker; the gloves, the muff, the handkerchief, the scarf, the mantilla, the ruffle. Artificial, all that swarming, proliferating, seeding, blossoming life of the streets; of this corner of the town where for ten centuries all the most independent and most idle, the most specious in taste and the freest in manners have intrigued in a thousand tender relations!

Four thousand invisible hands toil ceaselessly for this unending gala, not only in the dressmaker's palaces but in the old decayed dwellings of the less glamorous districts. The second *arrondissement*, among others, is full of small workshops from whence issues at midday a swarm of smiling young sempstresses.

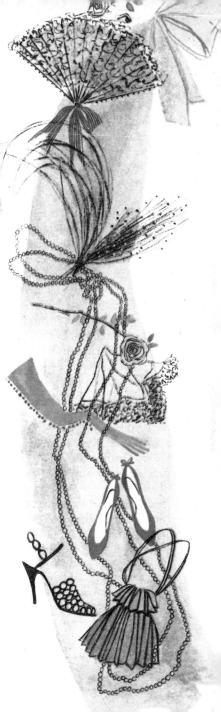

The clothiers are established in the Rue du Sentier. Hosiery occupies the Rue St-Martin.

But once again I am straying. I beg your pardon, Madam. You have chosen me as your pilot. Where are you, in point of fact? On the threshold of the Ritz, facing the Place Vendôme, with its tiles burnished by the sun to the colour of old gold, so admirably in keeping with the genius of Mansart?

Very well. You couldn't do better! Do you know that Chopin died at No. 12 and that this column with its festoons of trophies was overthrown by the 1871 revolutionaries? You are not interested? Of more concern to you is the princely woodwork with which Boucheron has covered his walls, and even more delightful are the jewels he displays, all resembling family heirlooms in the jewel-case of Paris. And now come the famous dressmakers—Bruyère who clothes high-born Parisians, Schiaparelli whose shop-window, framed in gilt and bamboo, conceals, amidst other dangerously seductive toys, perfumes with such insolent names as *Shocking* and *Zut*! And still more jewels! Now it is Van Cleef and Arpels, who make precious stones cunningly vibrate on supple metal stalks. Then comes Lucien Lelong, who, once a dressmaker of note, now only deals in high-class perfumery. How grateful I am for your attention! It is a rare pleasure to watch a woman in the excitement of making her choice. You have to be as quick as lightning to catch at a glance the ill-restrained feverishness of her gestures and her little pouts, such as even love could not inspire.

But perhaps you are already a little tired? Elizabeth Arden's rooms, decorated by Vertes and Drian, offer you their restful couches. It is really a sort of accelerated cure that you can take there, a nervous and muscular relaxation in which various beauty

treatments play their part—you can make your choice at pleasure—and also the atmosphere of warmth, the soft, gentle lighting and the velvet silence that prevails in the midst of all the activity.

No? Too many things to see? Well, since you wish it, we will be on our way. The Rue de la Paix opens up in front of us. In spite of the westward thrust of the city, the street remains just as Napoleon III wished it to be. Certainly, Worth, Guerlain and Caroline Reboux, who supplied the Empress, and whose descendants continue to work for the prestige of Paris, have moved their household gods elsewhere. But if Doucet is no longer at No. 21 nor Deuillet at No. 24, Paquin stays on at No. 3 and Grès has come to No. 1 to rejuvenate the street with her youthful genius. Paquin has always clothed civilised affluence to the accompaniment of the wild odour of musk, the animal violence of fur and barbarous jewels. How exquisitely you, too, would tame that animal voluptuousness and that mineral extravagance! But at Grès you will find a different atmosphere, a kind of antique grandeur, a purity that is the result of a diversity of causes and that aims at nothing less than perfection. Mme Grès is the youngest woman in France to hold the Legion of Honour, civil division, and that distinction bears witness to the importance that is accorded to her artistry. Alone in her little studio, looking on to the crossroads of world elegance, burning with inspiration and endowed with an incredible capacity for work, this great little lady pins together with adroit fingers, like the pecks of a beak, the newest reflection of the world's desire. All the dresses are her own creation. She tries them out on a mannequin worn out with fatigue. The workshops then make a scrupulous copy of the model. On the same side of the street are two famous jewellers—Mellerio-dits-Meller, who supplied the Queen of Spain's jewels, and Cartier with branches in London, New York, and India. Close by, in the Rue des Capucines, is a famous dressmaker-perfumer, Nina Ricci.

You don't know where to look? For the coquette, the Rue de la Paix is Joy Street, the wonder of wonders, the inimitable jewel of Paris. Leather-goods shops, shoemakers, stationers selling notepaper for the loveliest of love letters, shirtmakers for Maharajahs, antique shops and illustrous silk-mercers. Here is Ducharne; a little farther on is Bucol; and then Staron. The Rue de la Paix is full of life; princesses pass down it, as well as gossipping shop-girls. Their laughter goes right to my heart. I admire the fact that their hands, so red with cold, can be the hands of magicians. Their coquetry seems to me a little short of heroic. For it is heroic to dress and make up with scrupulous care in the darkness of early morning, when a suburban train awaits you with its crowd of sleepy workmen. It is heroic to succeed in making a pet of a hat, in your rare moments of leisure, from a piece of felt that has already done service for two winters.

But we have no time for these reflections. Let us recross the Place Vendôme and take the Rue Castiglione, where books, ties, and Parisian goods are sold. We reach the Rue St-Honoré, and there the sinuous flow of elegance begins that does not display its full splendour until the street changes into the Rue du Faubourg St-Honoré. But what joy to choose a perfect pair of shoes from Bunting's shop-window, a sports frock from Véra Boréa, a pleasing scarf from a shelf in Calixte's, or a fox stole that lies curled behind the glass of " La Reine d'Angleterre !" Dear old street, slumbering for so long between parks and gardens, you have kept as relics your old-fashioned houses into which one would hardly be surprised to see a heroine of Beaumarchais enter. " Here luxury becomes poetry and the superfluous becomes the beautiful," wrote Jean-Louis Vaudoyer.

At the crossroads of the Rue Royale we have reached the milliners' domain. Le Monnier, Jane Blanchot, Legroux, Rose Valois, Sygur and many another are here or in the neighbourhood. We will enter, if you wish, one of those nurseries hung with mirrors, where the latest creations wait to be adopted—shapes without form or body. While customers get irritated thinking they are neglect-

ed, the saleswomen come and go, as in a ballet, descending the spiral staircase, vanishing into cupboards, arising from a stream of ribbons or a shrubbery of feathers, reappearing to adorn, with a fragile wonder, the head of an impatient lady who was on the point of leaving.

The *patronne* darts from one to another of her regular customers, shapes a straw base over one knee, indents a felt with a powerful thumb, and gives poise to a hat in obedience to some mysterious impulse. She hustles her assistants and apprentices, becomes agitated and nervy and then

suddenly quietens in the ritual act of creation. She has just caught a glimpse of your face, the face of a foreigner, in the mirror, and it has inspired her. An original creation will come to life on your harrased head. You will, of course, be respectful and a little excited. The creative genius busies herself with ribbons, flowers, feathers, linings, pins, like a sleep-walker in the vortex of invention. Her task finished, she returns to the whirl of activities and issues instructions—and imprecations— leaving her masterpiece to an assistant, who replaces each pin by a light stitch.

You leave the shop rather bewildered and breathless but full of good spirits for the rest of the day. And you find you are in the Faubourg St-Honoré.

Yes, this time it really is the Faubourg. There is no mistaking it. Fashion reigns—and has done for a long time. It has won its title to nobility. But first of all let us make a detour by way of the Rue Royale, which is sewn to the Place de la Concorde by Cleopatra's Needle. It is assuredly a royal highway. That was the opinion of Léon-Paul Fargue, "It is impossible to say which of the famous saleswomen in this street is queen—they all are. But all these queens obey one supreme king— Love with a capital L. It is for that insufferable archer that they scheme colours and concoct those marvels that make Parisian women resemble birds or moths. They do not fail to reach men's hearts. The little god keeps them docile, optimistic, generous..."

Here is Molyneux, the most Parisian of dressmakers, of perfumers— of Englishmen. He has British phlegm but is French in spirit. He loves—with equal fidelity—bridge, Louis XV furniture, opium cigarettes,

French cooking, clear Touraine skies and the mists of his native Ireland. His success is due to this multiplicity. In Molyneux' conception of elegance there is nothing of the narrowness of the Victorian era, although there is an impression of dignity in even the most fantastic of his dresses.

Then comes Creed, the tailor. Opposite is Charles Montaigne, another tailor who combines with his own severe technique the softer lines of Madeleine Vionnet, whose pupil he was. Then there is Christofle, the jeweller No. 1 and Lachaume, the florist No. 1, where window-shoppers such as we can enjoy ourselves, admiring the well-arranged tables of the former and the clustered orchids of the latter. When we know each other better, I will ask Lachaume to make you up one of those copious bouquets, the secret of which he knows so well.

But let us leave the Rue Royale. We could stay there all day. Beauty is well represented and luxury abounds. We will resume our way along the Faubourg, for good this time. It was only in 1765 that a royal decree authorised building on the strip of drained land joining the Porte St-Honoré to the mansion erected in 1718 by the Comte d'Evreux, which Louis XV had recently acquired and which was to become the Elysée. Wishing to turn the whole district into a Vanity Fair, the king presented it to Mme de Pompadour. On her death it passed to her brother, the Comte de Vindière whom the people immediately called " the Comte d'Avant-Hier " (the day before yesterday). This induced him to change his name to that of the Marquis of Marigny, which lent itself less to punning. There only remains an avenue of abundant chestnut trees and a theatre, as a twofold symbol of the magnificent success of La Pompadour's family.

This was the time when the newly-rich financiers dared to compete in their luxury with the debt-ridden aristocracy. The nabob Beaujon settled in the Elysée Bourbon. In a house nearby, the illustrious cook Carême, who became Marquis of Brunay, displayed his pomp. Louis Chevalier had three identical mansions built, one of which is occupied today by the Inter-Allied Club.

There was also life on a grand scale at the Hôtel de Pontalba, built by Visconti and later purchased by the Rothschilds. So pleasure had its sway in the Faubourg St-Honoré. At the present time it serves for the pleasure of all those, from all parts of the world, who want to " live in beauty." It must, without a doubt, be haunted by the wild ghosts of the Princess Borghese (who lived on the site where since 1814 the British Embassy has stood) and the Duc de Choiseul-Praslin, who lived at the Hôtel Sebastiani near by and whose love drove him to crime.

" All that is probably very exciting, but I live in the present," protests the eager young woman I am piloting.

It is not entirely possible here, my dear friend, past and present are so closely linked. Certainly present reality is adorned with the newest and most intriguing creations. When you go into Houbigant's to try the latest perfume, how can you forget that he sent aromatic pastilles to St. Helena for Napoleon to burn ? Consider what Yvonne de Brémond d'Ars inscribed on the concave window of her curiosity shop : " The window seems to open on to a corner of the past."

Let us go into Hermès, the saddler, where you can dream of buying

a brand new valise for air travel, and tell me whether Constantin Guys could not still find there all the refined details of a dandy's *equipage*. While choosing the latest type of gloves, you seem, in these surroundings, to be on the point of embarking on the great adventure, as in the olden days. The heavy metal-rimmed helms, the storm-lanterns, the enamel-ware that famous captains used under canvas, the saddles that were once used for the harnessing of parade horses, all jumbled up with the latest trinkets amid the strong smell of leather, here give elegance an epic quality.

Ever since 1860, the three Henrys who succeeded each other under the sign of "A la Pensée" have sold luxurious trifles to the last of the queens and the latest of social successes. Molinard, who distills his own perfumes at Grasse, has celebrated the centenary of his firm; Delion, the hatter, also.

Other tradesmen and other creative artists of the Faubourg St-Honoré may be less distinguished, but they have adapted and submitted themselves to the aristocratic rigour of a tradition whereby every shop window represents the most far-sighted fairyland. Jeanne Lanvin understood that. She conquered the Faubourg, beginning as a milliner's apprentice in an attic and leaving to her daughter, the Comtesse de Polignac, the entire house, which she won over floor by floor, and where titled heiresses now buy their clothes. Then she acquired the house opposite that now represents the height of masculine elegance. This artisan of genius, who was also a very great lady, used to say : " The secret of success ? It is assuredly to work hard, to work as much as one can; and it also means not wanting to do everything. Allow a mere woman to make this comparison—a general ought not to sweep the barrack square."

This very legitimate pride is similar to that of Jean-Charles Worth, the great ancestor of dressmaking, whose portrait in cloak and fur cap, just as he used to arrive at his business on horseback every morning a century ago, still adorns the great staircase of the house in the Faubourg where his descendants carry on the business he created.

"I am a great artist," he used to say. "I have Delacroix' sense of colour, and I compose. A costume is a picture. Art is a god, and the *bourgeois* exist only to take our orders."

Worth was right—and not only as far as he was concerned. All the business people who have shops here are artists. The milliners Agnès, Maud and Nano, Claude St. Cyr, are artists; so too is the dressmaker Jacques Griffe, the latest comer, but one who has already made his mark. Artists too, are the tailor O'Rossen and the shoemaker, Casale; Jad, who turns the ridiculous umbrella into an object of art, is also an artist. Artists in living materials are Jeanne Piaubert, who models delicate busts, and Helena Rubenstein who remakes faces. Marcin the jeweller and Marin the goldsmith are artists. Line Vautrin, who has revived the art of fancy jewelry, is an artist, and so is Lola Prussac, who has launched a new style of elegance in sportswear. All the hairdressers of the quarter are artists. It is this dignity that gives real value to their calling.

They do so much more than simply work for feminine coquetry. There is a valuable lesson to be learnt from a minute examination of all those little theatres whose curtains rise on to the Faubourg St-Honoré. Paul Morand recently asked whether we live in a great era or an inferior one. We are too much inside it to give an adequate answer. We have a way of regarding certain flashy indications of the contemporary spirit as exact manifestations of present-day taste, even though they are likely to be forgotten in fifty years time. The clearest answer is here.

For those who are trying to see the matter in a detached way, I advise them to attribute more importance to the style of Parisian shops than to certain present-day manifestations of snobbery. What is permanent in any period is what has pleased it and what has been the object of its love. Now Paris is, of all cities, the most sensitive to art, and very naturally the creative trends are popularised. Applied to business houses, this means that they cannot allow themselves to be completely disinterested in pure art. There is always a certain risk in launching unusual novelties. The cabinet-maker, the potter, the weaver, the dressmaker, all of whom have behind them workshops and factories, are not free to adopt new ventures. They must produce. They must sell.

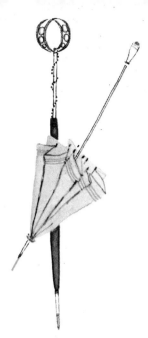

They must please not the tastes of tomorrow but of today—if they are to keep their workers employed. Applied art, then, especially when it aims at making woman more alluring, must be based on the artistic sentiment of the day.

It is also important to understand exactly what one means by a great epoch. " Under a regime that makes everything on a small scale, little dishes, little flats, little newspapers, little books attract you," wrote Balzac, and it is a fact that nothing big remains either in architecture, decorative arts or fashion from the time when that giant brooded over the human comedy. The cluttering up of interiors, the absurdities in dress, the insignificance of neo-gothic architecture, the baroque exuberance of jewelry—all were so many signs of an inferior age. The shops where the celebrities and dandies lingered must have indicated the same tendency.

Just before the last war, after the post-romantic freedom of the " modern style " had been followed by a period of deliberate coldness—with interiors like barns or factories, excessively simplified fashions, abstract painting, architecture obsessed by a mechanical utilitarianism—a reaction in favour of an intellectual and emotional romanticism had just set in. It claimed to discover charm in a mysteriously picturesque ugliness. Antiquaries pillaged the street markets. Surrealist painters drew their inspiration from Italian still-life tricks. Rococo hangings, crinolines and bustles made an odd reappearance within the white walls of immense modern blocks of flats which went out of fashion immediately they had been built. By about 1938, all the shops of the Parisienne excelled themselves in this strange Byzantinism of taste.

What lesson is to be drawn from these modern tendencies ? It seems at first sight as if the perverse pleasure that the smart set took in pressing the claims of contortions in stucco has taken a downward path—even to the extent of the shop windows of the large stores. Eminent antiquaries are returning to the purity of style of the early Renaissance and the end of the 17th century. Interior decorators produce furniture with great nobility of line, and without systematically excluding ornamentation. Jewellers, glovers, makers of leather-goods, create seductive articles that derive their charm more from their precious materials and their rare colouring than from over-elaborate designs. Feminine fashions revert to a hard sobriety that represents neither the superficial sentimentality of false rococo nor the deliberate poverty of the *robe-chemise*. A thousand and one other signs that a quick eye notices in the course of a day's walk in the living museum that is Paris, seem to indicate that we are witnessing the birth of a new style and that we are on the threshold of a new great era.

A plaintive little voice pulls me up in the middle of these reflections. " It is all very well for you to play the philosopher, but you have left me at the corner of the Avenue Matignon. Moreover, you have not solved my particular problems."

The Avenue Matignon, a recent conquest of the world of elegance, owes something to Watteau, the Russian ballet and Van Dongen. With its " folies " amid the remains of greenery, and its window displays, influenced by the Parisian school, behind their railings or beside porches planned for horse and carriage; with its princely halls and subtle perfumes escaping from windows looking out from fashion houses, or from ladies who hurry by on their way to a fitting; with its ribbons, its trinkets, its scent-bottles—this is a highway that, more noticeably than any other, gives foreigners the sense of bewilderment so often produced by Paris. Her grace makes them fail to appreciate her strength; her exquisite care for form blinds them to the profound resonance of her message.

The Avenue Matignon contributes to the world's happiness—but after the manner of Rameau's music. We will not call it " superficial "— everything here has been taken over by fashion, the last gateway opening out upon dreamland and poetry. What were once baronial halls now vie with each other in their shop signs. Dressmaker-perfumers are represented by Germaine Lecomte and Jacques Heim—their shop-windows appearing like two silky eyes beneath eyebrows of ivy. Then there is Marcel Rochas who is on the way to becoming the leading merchant of frivolities in the world—trifles for Titania or a fairy princess: perfumed gloves and boxes of black Chantilly, handbags and precious stones, all kinds of *objets de maintenance* as they used to be called. Then there is Jean Dessès, who has settled in the pompous Hôtel d'Eiffel—the "man of the tower" who exhibits his ball-dresses like a scene from a ballet. And the latest comer to the street is Maggy Rouff, who shares with the furrier Mendel the historic home of La Vaupalière, and is thus a neighbour of Max Leroy.

Are you looking for another new hat? You need a dozen in Paris. You will find, almost next door to each other, Janette Colombier and

CONSTANTIN GUYS. — *Fashionable ladies out driving.*

Suzanne Talbot. Moreover, the Avenue Matignon contains the oldest-established of Paris milliners, Caroline Reboux, and the most recent, Jean Barthet. In the next parallel street, Rue Jean Mermoz, we find Gilbert Orcel, another talented milliner, and in the Rue du Cirque, the parallel street on the opposite side, is Mad Carpentier, an inspired dress-maker.

Are you looking for a hairdresser's? Since you are now approaching the Rond-Point des Champs-Elysées, you can take your choice from three, who for some years have been rivals in the lordly art of transforming women's faces—Fernand Aubry, Guillaume, and Antonio. How many hours have been spent there by the most brilliant and the most independent creatures in the world; white-robed and in silent submission, amid the angels of the drying machine and the seraphims of the permanent wave— finding new life in these half-way houses between society drawing-rooms and operating theatres?

We pass the celebrated terraces where smart crowds gather in spring-time in the shade of the flowering chestnut-trees, and reach the Rond-Point des Champs-Elysées, which is the boundary between the delight-fully antiquated part of the avenue—whose leafy bowers frame majestic architectural lines—and that teeming artery of modern life that is surmount-ed, as by the saddle of a sacred elephant, by the Arc de Triomphe de l'Etoile.

This is the domain of two dressmakers, Robert Piguet and Carven. The first of these, Swiss in origin and a member of a family of bankers, was driven by an irresistible urge to take up the art of dress-making. The second, a small energetic Parisienne, has a gift for publicity in addition to her professional talent. Whether she is launch-ing a new perfume or powder, a lip-stick or a new dress design, she immediately organises a party to focus the attention of the pleasure promotors on her invention. Her mannequins have sensational adven-tures. Her travels—she is an indefatigable globe-trotter—are always accompanied by spectacular happenings.

Carven belongs to that growing aristocracy of young dressmakers, all of whom are in the front rank, and that is governed by a triumvirate —Jacques Fath, Pierre Balmain and Christian Dior. They, too, are all within the area covered by our walk : the first in the Avenue Pierre Ier-de-Serbie, the second in the Rue Fran-çois Ier, and the last-named in the Avenue Montaigne.

Jacques Fath has won his place by dint of apparent unconcern. Never-theless this handsome, smiling, shrewd young man thinks only of his work. The moment the time comes to create

his "collection," he takes off his coat, shuts himself up in his studio and goes into a trance. To keep going he eats porridge like his small son. He lives like this for a month, shut away among beautiful, semi-naked, girls whom he transforms into queens. Cloth manufacturers, furriers, embroiderers and all kinds of assistants are the only people who have access to this den, which at times resounds with bursts of sonorous laughter. At the end of this captivity, at H hour, the young magician entertains the whole of Paris in his garden, which is decked out for the occasion as for a *fête galante*. Whilst he amuses himself he draws up a balance sheet that beats those of all his rivals.

Pierre Balmain goes big-game hunting with maharajahs, disguises himself as a cowboy in the Far West and is on familiar terms with Hollywood magnates. He comes back to Paris and then tours the world again, but this time by way of a hundred and one drawing-rooms. You meet him in every kind of *milieu* and at all festivals. He is equally the friend of Odette Swann and of the Duchess of Guermantes—and he is dressmaker to both of them.

Finally, Christian Dior is the star of Parisian dressmakers. His lightning rise to fame created quite a flutter. It must be added that this timid showman has real genius. Paris quickly discovered this; and what Paris discovers is soon known to the whole world. There is not a woman who is not enraptured by Dior's dress designs. There is a "Dior rush"; it is the age of Dior.

You now know, little lady, almost as well as I do, who are the rulers of Paris fashion. If you are not exhausted—and I am sure you are—we might now walk down the Avenue Franklin D. Roosevelt that contains so many beauty parlours. They answer to such names as Myriam Garange, Madeleine Barbier, Martial or Gloria Glory. You will also find there two more milliners—and by no means the least famous—Simone Cange and Paulette. Then we will take the Avenue George-V to visit two dressmakers "in the international class," as they say of boxers and dancers—Marcelle Chaumont, the favourite pupil of the celebrated Madeleine Vionnet, and Balenciaga, the invisible man whom everybody admires but nobody knows.

What romances could we not write, now that we know each other better, around a simple rose of Judith Barbier, a Knizé glove, a handbag by Violette Cornille, a jewel by Sterlé or a perfume of Caron! In what a flirtatious network of departures, returns, promises, betrayals, petty coquetry and grand passion, are all these seductions presented to us! It is the very life of woman herself, her private and her public life; it is her intimacy, her grace, her tenderness, her perfidy, that is offered to us in these few acres of Paris, like a long confession accompanied by rustling silk and tinkling metal.

" And this woman, the Parisienne, is she so extraordinary, to have aroused all that ? "

" Extraordinary ?   She is and she isn't ! "

I sense my companion's impatience with her guide.

" Explain yourself, " she says.

Can it be explained ?   Can charm be shelled like a nut ?   No, the

Parisienne is certainly no more beautiful than any other woman. Nor is she more trivial, despite all that has been said against her. But she is *chic* by nature, just as some people have large noses or eyes like a cat. It is a matter of inheritance, of tradition.   To this emulation is grafted.   Her attractive coquetry, her fascinating unruliness, her transient beauty, captivate us in a different way from the ice-cold perfection of the sporting woman who seems to be made for the stadium, or the ceremonious affectation of the enamelled queens of the international night-clubs.   In addition, the Parisienne knows how to be gay.   Her natural mental impulses combine mischievousness and unconcern.   How right she is ! Quibbling about the colour of the horizon never keeps the storm away.

Parisian women know how to have friendships with men without any element of misunderstanding to embarrass the relationship. Learning at an early age the art of being a confidante, and sharing in the pleasures of concerts and museums, they know how to listen with exemplary consideration. To indulgence and understanding, the Parisienne adds a charming willingness to help us solve our problems.

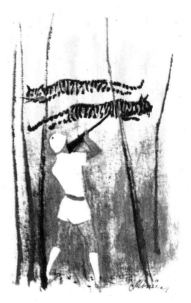

But her rôle is not limited to that of a listener. She takes an active part. With what art, with what diversity of inspiration, with what simple grace she fills in the gaps in the conversation ! Here her charm results from the manysidedness of her character. It is extraordinary how monotonous men are, compared with these lively companions, who act a part, certainly; but one in which they believe. There are also the great ladies—born gossips—who can tell you in ten minutes all the tittletattle of Paris; and the coquettes—born nurses who, despite their appearance, astonish us, by always having the necessary remedy to hand.

Such, I believe are the reasons for the pre-eminence of the Parisienne —and not her beauty. She is neither slave nor concubine. She reigns. She shares in life. She is *within* it. It is that which makes her the excellent promoter of the luxury in which Paris excels, and in the creation of which she takes her part. It is her taste that makes the choice; her critical sense that discards; her mind that settles. No success is gained in Paris without the guarantee of the Parisienne. The customers of the Rue de la Paix and the Faubourg St-Honoré may be wealthy foreigners who are the life-blood of Paris's luxury trade, but is it the Parisienne who samples, decides, and launches. She is first the guinea-pig, and then the carrier pigeon. It is she that people imitate. It is she that maintains the Parisian tradition of always marrying the beautiful with the useful.

That is what I wanted to say to my young foreign friend. But alas, those are the things that one feels but for which one cannot find words. We were silent. Pretty, attractive, perfumed women, ravishingly dressed, their faces intent on " making a hit," were passing by.

" They are amazing," my companion said softly.

Amazing ! That is it; that sums it up. Moreover it was getting late. We were reaching the last stage of our trip. The spring evening was framed in the revolving door. A Paris evening. Springtime in Paris. It was as if the city had just loomed up out of a picture, with the Seine running crosswise and the Arc de Triomphe in front, the whole clad in flowering chestnut-trees. That explains what I have written above. I would like, with this fleeting picture, to close these pages that I began with the words of a celebrated Englishman, if it were not that I had in mind the opinion of a South American. "A strange city," wrote Ventura Garcia Calderon, " that has no common measure with others. The half smile that rectifies any excess, an immediate liking for everything that is fine and new, a politeness bred of indulgence. A people brought up in a palace, whose feet never slip on waxed floors."

Lucien FRANÇOIS.

THE
BALLADE
OF THE
CHAMPS
~ELYSÉES

F·M·PÉROT

BRENET. — *The July the Fourteenth Review*

OES THE

sun suddenly shine? Then from the Place de l'Etoile to the Place de la Concorde the chestnut blossom is bright with colour; in thirteen turns of the handle, the waiters draw the awnings down over the café terraces, the sunshades keep the Neapolitan ice cream cool. Notwithstanding the policemen who, brandishing their white batons, strive to direct it, the stream of traffic at high tide overflows on to the pavement. It is like a mechanised ballet, which the actors—you and I—desert during the intervals, to enjoy a drink of anisette or peppermint. Not a leaf is missing on the plane trees in this open-air studio set. Tourists in motor coaches arrive on time from Copenhagen, Amsterdam, Antwerp. They all seem ready for this ballad in triple time—with a pause at the Arc de Triomphe, one at the Obelisk, and one in between at the Rond-Point, where fountains play, operated by an electric system. There is no doubt about it, Springtime in Paris begins its tour of the town with the Champs-Elysées.

Close to the Figaro building, the smell of lead comes through the windows of the basement printing presses. I listen to the clicking of the linotypes, the thud of the galley on the marble slab, and I recompose in my own way the chronicle of the Champs-Elysées. Though phaetons, pony carts and carriages may have gone, there are still hackneys stationed there, with their axles and spokes painted to look like lottery wheels. Why hail a cabman whose mind is at peace beneath his bowler hat? I do not need to jolt along in a carriage in order to conjure up visions and memories. The Champs-Elysées still tempts one to wander on foot, just as in the days when Guy de Maupassant used to listen to the sparrows serenading in the leaves, and watch the children bent on building sand castles.

For twenty francs youngsters can still climb on to a donkey resembling the one in the Countess de Ségur's tales, and for ten francs they can

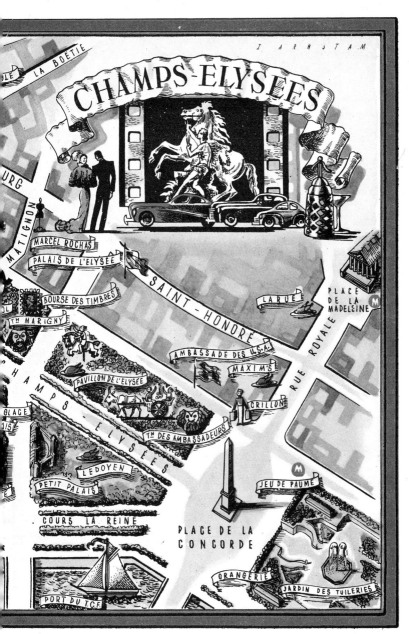

jump into a little goat cart, as if they were gaily off on a holiday. All the trappings are still there : the swings for carefree children; the "*Vrai Guignol fondé en* 1881" (the genuine Punch and Judy show, founded in 1881), the merry-go-rounds that revolve to the sound of sentimental songs without words. At the sight of so many bags of sweets, hoops, coloured marbles and paper windmills, little girls and boys can dream that one night they will fly towards paradise in one of those kiosks, borne by a thousand and one red balloons.

The landscape gardener who, as early as 1667, drafted the layout of the Champs-Elysées with a single stroke of his pencil, was indeed far-sighted. Tracing this alley through the fallow land, he thought only of the beauty of the view, and we can now share his delight. He was called Le Nôtre. In this very spot, in 1713, a nobleman, who was also a producer, asserted his taste for outdoor opera; I am thinking of the Duc d'Antin, who turned the French guards into woodcutters and to the sound of the drum had elms planted in rows of five. Later, a general, Baron Thiébaut, described his emotion at the "death of a doe that, hunted by the Comte d'Artois in the Bois de Boulogne, crossed the Champs-Elysées, and, followed by the whole pack of hounds, the huntsmen, and the ladies' coaches, was brought to bay in the Rue Royale." Today the *chasseur* at Maxim's welcomes another kind of game, and Josephine, the mad woman of the Concorde contents herself with petting a stray cat. Amidst the groves, where the lamp globes look like immense aniseed balls, only a Paris historian can remember that on the 2nd of December, 1804, a body was discovered in the underbrush. At daybreak it was identified as that of Lebon, the inventor of gas-lighting.

No doubt it is between the two Marly horses that we should begin our stroll, as in the days when Lord Pembroke used to canter with the Duke of Ayen? Personally I prefer to wander at random towards the Cours-la-Reine, created by Marie de Médicis. These avenues have long ceased to be the pretext for rendezvous in coaches and torchlight walks. I loiter, however,. among the iron chairs, arranged to form a setting for some " Lesson of Love in a Park," subject for the Sunday artists who, at the first sign of spring, begin to dream of the opening of the Autumn Salon. Here the

The Place de la Concorde.

band-stand awaits the season for brass-band concerts, and over there the ghost of Lavedan, who wrote so wittily about Parisian society, watches for the return of the Tziganes with their walrus-like moustaches. At a slight distance from the Grand and the Petit Palais, the bronze figure of Clemenceau seems to be striding off its rock : his great-coat buttoned in haste, his muffler blowing in the wind, remind us of " *Père la Victoire*," and of the models of French riflemen as depicted in catalogues. Failing an invitation to accompany him, I will go and cool down on the seats of of the Palais de Glace, where Toulouse-Lautrec sketched Mlle. Liane de Lancy, the " Professional Beauty." The skating rink is open to amateurs, who are " requested to go up to the cloak-room to change their shoes." Couples interweave their initials on the ice, twirling round on the rink, and the glass of the mirrors throws back their reflection.

Along the Avenue Gabriel, beyond the public conveniences—which are tended by an old dowager with as much care as an historical monument —hose pipes lie around like serpents, and the lawns are bright with clumps of geraniums. Perched on their iron railing, the two cocks of the Elysée look as if they were about to fly off towards the Palace lawns. From the Théâtre des Ambassadeurs — where Bernstein's play *La Soif* grips the audience—to the Marigny theatre, where Jean-Louis Barrault is producing a new version of Molière's *Fourberies de Scapin*, the trees grow so densely, their branches are so entwined, that the theatres are like open-air stages, where the curtain seems to be not of iron, but of leaves. Since 1875, the stamp market has been attracting philatelists around the Marigny. It looks like a family reunion, where Aunt Jemina

is selling "D-day trophies at sale price" in order to buy Cousin Joe's air-mail stamps. If there are really eight hundred thousand philatelists in Paris, we shudder to think that they might all meet at the same time. But they must have a means of identification, and are wise enough to make dates in order to discover the forged Pétain stamp that was used in the Resistance Movement or to take a trip round the world, without moving, by turning the leaves of an album. The stamp dealers' stalls extend as far as the Avenue Gabriel, while the purchasers invade the benches of the Avenue Matignon where, equipped with brief cases, boards, magnifying glasses and tweezers, they exchange their vignettes, with the usual thrill experienced by collectors : beware of obliterations and perforations !

Nothing remains of the Mabille Dance Hall, which shocked Monsieur Taine so very much when he ventured amidst the revellers. The Allée des Veuves is today the Avenue Montaigne, and Céleste Mogador, Rigolboche, and

Chicard can no more be seen hopping and side-stepping like so many Jacks-in-the-box. Nor could La Païva, were she alive, hear the strains of the quadrille in her garden, which the Goncourts compared to a garden in Pompeii. But on the gate she would still find the initials of her second husband, Count Henckel von Donnersmarck; she (or her ghost) would also find her mansion still as it was, with its sculptures by Carrier-Belleuse and the ceiling by Baudry : it is now a club. This mansion is the only one that remains to remind us of the days when Princess Mathilde entertained in the Rue de Berry, when the Duc de Morny lived in the " Niche à Fidèle " and when Cora Pearl lodged in the Rue de Ponthieu. The Duc d'Uzès' garden has disappeared ; the estates of the Duc de Massa and the Marquis de Casariera have been broken up. In the course of thirty years, the Avenue des Champs-Elysées, with its sites between the Etoile and the Rond-Point reserved for banks, fashion houses and motor-car showrooms, has become, and remains, a permanent film festival and *café chantant* show.

Apart from Fouquet's, where, as Léon-Paul Fargue rightly said, you feel as though you were an honoured guest, most of these cafés are more like stations into which tankloads of lemonade are poured—or like open-air waiting rooms, from which travellers hope to catch a glimpse of the sea. There are, in all, about thirty of these liners moored to the Champs-Elysées with, besides, flotillas of bars anchored in the side streets; and whether they bear the flag of the *Colisée*, the *Marignan*, the *Select* or the *George V*, all the films we shall never see are constantly beings plotted there— films that would amaze us if they were produced, instead of being idle projects that never materialise. How many producers have we met

The Café des Ambassadeurs.

who live alternately on forgotten promises and the hopes that have been given to them between two coffees; how many distributors who are counting on the returns from a film that is "dubbed" in an out-of-the-way dialect? There is talk of a Prince, prepared to show esteem for an acrobat; of a pretty lady who is always ready to convert an Emir. In the course of these parleys the accomplices, who are themselves mere ciphers, throw millions up into the air, but never a franc falls back upon the table. The go-betweens disappear with pasty faces, cross the street to avoid a disappointing encounter, and notice with secret distress that all the banks are closed.

However, films are shot — but otherwise and elsewhere — for instance, in the François Ier studio. Fifty film companies are set up in the Champs-Elysées: about forty of them can be counted between the Avenue George V and the Rond-Point, about ten between the Etoile and the *Select*. Critics pay a daily visit to the dark room for the previews which take place in succession in the twenty-six cinemas of the district. Curiously enough, the film titles often contradict or complement each other—sometimes one sees advertised simultaneously: "Holiday" and "It always rains on Sunday," or else: "I marry my Wife" and "The Bride is Crazy." The pictures unwind across the screen almost as continuously as on 42nd Street in New York. Whether it be technicolour films such as "Deadly Sin," or the American style floor shows at the *Lido*, the Avenue des Champs-Elysées gives us a continuous performance both indoors and out. The show goes on either behind the closed doors of a full-house or in the open air. That is how the man-in-the-street can unexpectedly

witness a parade of mannequins leaving the fashion houses, or enjoy a musical saw recital, given surreptitiously behind the policeman's back, or, again, the performance of a one-man band, with rattles on his head, a drum on his back, drum sticks on his arms, bells on his feet and an accordion in his hands. With its arcades such as the *Galerie de la Boëtie*, reminiscent of the skyscrapers on Broadway (men take their hats off in the lift when ladies are present !);

that of the *Biarritz*, where Mimi Pinson awaits the foreigner at the door of a dance hall; that of the *Lido*, where Felix Odzinski cuts out silhouettes in an atmosphere laden with the aroma of coffee trickling through percolators, mingled with the fragrance of perfumery; the *Galerie des Portiques*, where a white wooden jockey gallops on a green wooden horse; and that of the *Tyrol*, guarded by the Cerberus from a dog show—the Champs-Elysées is a real *Passage des Panoramas*.

News bulletins, short wave transmissions, foreign relations department—these are three major sections of the broadcasting service installed in the Maurice Bourdet Centre. There we can meet representatives of the B.B.C. and the Swiss Broadcasting Company, also French favourites such as Pierre Mac Orlan, who comes from Saint-Cyr-sur-Morin to record the accordion tunes he loves, and Bourvil, who tries to speak English by reading a text written in phonetic signs, hoping that listeners from New York will tune in. The aerial erected close to the building is so light that it looks as if it might float away on the waves. The Washington Studio is set apart for variety programmes. The Duplex broadcasts permit listeners to admire a virtuoso of the harmonica playing in London, and an instant after to hear a volley of applause from an English audience which has been listening in to a nightingale singing in Paris. The *Impromptu des Champs-Elysées* is presented here twice monthly, on Sundays. This title might well inspire a cantata for which the poet and composer would engage the mermaids of the Place de la Concorde that Fantômas made to sing, a choir formed by the statues of the eight prize-winning

Sports in the Champs-Elysées.

towns of France, the woman trumpet player whose chariot appears ready to
fly off from the corner of the Grand Palais, and the musicians sculptured
by Bourdelle on his bas-relief of the Théâtre des Champs-Elysées. All
we would have to do then would be to mobilise Rude's *Marseillaise*
for the National Anthem—but Hector Berlioz has already orchestrated it.

It was in 1836 that the Obelisk in the Place de la Concorde and the Arc
de Triomphe on the Place de l'Etoile were inaugurated. Sure of its
fame—thanks to the tomb of the Unknown Soldier, whose desire to remain
incognito is respected by no one, and whose sleep is perpetually disturbed
by brass bands and the tramp of marching men—the Arc de Triomphe
welcomes the admirers who approach it by twelve avenues, from all
the points of the compass. We do not need to follow the guide; we
simply take the lift in order to visit the exhibition inside the Arch, and
there we can reconstruct the history of the monument, built in accordance
with Chalgrin's plans. Looking at the photographs, lithographs
and cheap coloured prints, we seem to be reliving an earlier existence. We

can watch the watering-carts drive by, in the days when the Arc was still outside the walls of Paris and the two gate-houses of the Etoile Barrier marked the entrance to the town. We can see the return of the Emperor's Ashes, as described by Victor Hugo in *Choses Vues*. We can be present at the sixteenth celebration of the July festival, amidst luminous fountains ; at the anniversary of the proclamation of the Republic in 1851 (the Champs-Elysées was then decorated with statues representing Joan of Arc, Jeanne Hachette. Jean Goujon,

An English Bivouac in 1815.

Richelieu, Condé, Jean-Bart, Jacquard, Papin, Corneille, Molière, Poussin, Molé, Duguay-Trouin, Turenne, Kléber and Ney); or at the procession of Napoleon III and the Empress Eugénie which marched by under three hundred and fifty four archways, the alignment of which was broken by twenty six porticos lit by coloured glass lamps, framing the eagle that soared above a celestial sphere at the Rond-Point des Champs-Elysées.

From the top of the Arc de Triomphe, we can look out upon the sky-line just as we might look round our own garden. For a moment, we can even imagine that the wonders of Paris are ours. Like a moving staircase, the Avenue carries away yesterday's memories, both the good and the bad. It also carries away today's passer-by—the " rubber-neck" who has just feasted his eyes on the latest picture of the big city. The great parade continues, and I recall the lines of that beautiful poem by Blaise Cendrars, in which, as early as 1916, he imagined Victory Day on the Champs-Elysées :

" *The sun will come out early like the candy-man on feast days,*
It will be spring in the Bois de Boulogne and at Meudon,
The cars will all be perfumed and the horses will feed on daisies.
At the windows the little war orphans will be wearing fine
                                        patriotic dresses ;
From the chestnut trees on the boulevards the photographers will aim
                                        their cameras,
Groups will form round the cameraman who will swallow the
                        pageant better than a snake-swallower can ;
In the afternoon
The wounded will hang their medals on the Arc de Triomphe and
                        will return to their homes without limping,
Then,
At nightfall
The Place de l'Etoile will rise to Heaven."

Paul GILSON.

THE INVALIDES
AND THE CHAMPS DE MARS

E·M·PEROT

DELAUNAY. — *The Eiffel Tower.*

T IS AN eastern proverb that says "Paradise lies in the shadow of the sword." If that is true, then the district of the Invalides must be a veritable paradise, since it contains the "military monuments" of Paris, grouped—intentionally? fortituously? — as in a kind of fortified area. A bird's eye view of this quarter gives the impression of a Roman camp, with its regular streets, its strictly laid-out squares, its parade and manœuvre grounds. The very word "quarter," when one thinks of it, has an army connotation. In France, when speaking of an infantry barracks, one reserves the term *quarter* for the cavalry and artillery. The Invalides quarter is then the military quarter, par excellence, the one in which the life of civilians counts for little and is subordinated to the domination of the military.

The district is shaped like a fan, the handle being formed by the junction of the Boulevard Pasteur and the Avenue de Breteuil. Were it not for the fact that its hard outline is softened by the Seine, one would have the feeling of captivity that barracks always give to those who inhabit them—fortunately to a lesser extent than prisons. Even the garden of the Champ-de-Mars, with the military ring of its name, never seems quite like a real garden.

Moreover, it is dwarfed by the great hollow pyramid of the Eiffel Tower; a series of giant ladders for spiders with a craze for climbing. For a long time the aesthetic value of the Eiffel Tower has been in dispute; the vestiges of a romantic tradition regarded this preposterous legacy of a former World Exhibition as a "blot on the face of Paris." Irate and well-meaning artists have voted its annihilation, without giving a thought as to what would happen to this monstrous heap of scrap-iron if their anger triumphed. The Great Wheel that formerly stood beside the Eiffel Tower was the mystic O beside the sacred I, turning without respite close to the perfect static, the metallic constant. The wheel has.

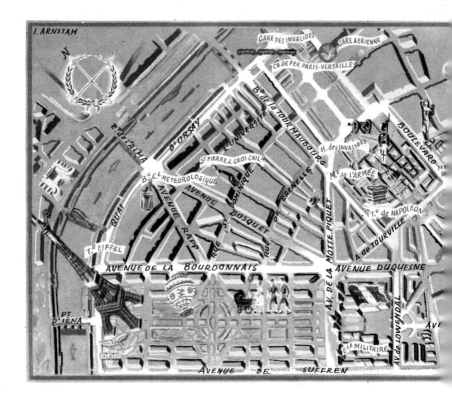

disappeared; the static—rebelling against the wrath of the aesthethes—asserts its indestructible right to survive, thanks to Mr. Eiffel's ingenious framework, and provides a pleasant balcony for foreigners and provincials who want to combine dizziness with a " monumental " view of Paris.

The Eiffel Tower serves no other purpose than this slightly nauseating view. On its first platform you can have dinner; on the higher levels you are nourished only by air, space and wind. A motor-car manufacturer, wise to the employment of unexpected forms of publicity, used it for a time to announce to the world the excellence of his vehicles. We are now told that it promotes the diffusion of sound-waves; for my part, I always see it as the lost peak of an immense helmet, a crest forged

for a giant's casque, like those that figured in English novels of the romantic period: an object too cumbersome to find a place in the *Musée de l'Armée* and consequently relegated to the garden.

If you like figures, the books will tell you that the Eiffel Tower weighs ten thousand tons, that its metal parts are rivetted together with two and a half million bolts, and that the Tower was "opened" by King Edward VII of England who, when he first mounted the three platforms, was still Prince of Wales.

However peaceful the uses that have been made of it by motor-dealers, wireless broadcasters, tired and breathless visitors, the Eiffel Tower has nevertheless a bellicose mien, with its blustering air of wanting to cleave the sky, its lance-like arrogance and its sword-like imperturbability. It would be out of place in any other quarter. Here it has all the space it needs to plant its four elephantine iron feet, under which stream, from the multicoloured coaches, scores of height-hungry visitors; orientals of tobacco hue mingling with Scandinavians the colour of honey or snow.

In the shadow of this gigantic sword pointed heaven-wards, are grouped in warlike array, under the baton of an invisible Field-Marshal, the military monuments of Paris. But not all, since the Boulevard des Invalides does not succeed in arresting their eastward thrust. Multiplying in proportion as red-tape hampers the progress of armies and the functioning of modern societies, the "services" are escaping from their "reserved quarter," where they were intended to be cloistered. They overflow into the Faubourg St-Germain, invading the fine old mansions that have known no swords other than those used for court or ceremonial purposes.

The Invalides quarter is a region consecrated to arms. Consecrated in the first place, as everyone may see, by the very names of its avenues. These are noisy with crests and banners, accompanied by muffled cannons or the blare of trumpets—Saxe, Duquesne, Villars, Breteuil,

Ségur, Joffre, Suffren, Tourville, Galliéni, Rapp, La Bourdonnais, Cambronne, Dupleix, linking soldiers and sailors, generals of the old régime and generals of the Revolution, marshals of the Empire and modern celebrities, with good-natured eclecticism. One pictures these warriors busily recounting their former battles to each other, in conversation beside the trim lawns of the Champ-de-Mars which seem made for the purpose, and where it would be unseemly even for the children not to leave aside their frivolous dolls and toy buckets, to play at soldiers.

Everything here conspires to create and foster a warlike aspect: the snarling old cannons on the terrace of the Invalides, the dormer windows opening like slits in armour, the bugle-calls wafted from the Babylone and Fontenoy barracks nearby, the very air we breathe in these spacious avenues, from the far end of which we always expect to catch a glimpse of a squadron of hussars approaching on prancing white horses, to the shrill sound of trumpets.

Because of its military calling, this quarter gains what other districts lack—space, which seems to be the most valuable asset of a city. Here, as at Versailles, the sense of space, so noble and majestic, was the creation of the monarchy. It was Louis XIV who one day had the charitable idea of founding a hostel for soldiers wounded in his campaigns; but it was Robert de Cotte, Hardouin-Mansart, and Liberal Bruant who conceived the idea of making this utilitarian creation a thing of beauty and a joy to the eyes and the imagination. Modern utilitarianism, accustomed to adapting everything to suit its own convenience, has found it necessary to sink its trains and its railway station below the ground level of the Esplanade which was designed by the great rococo architect. The empty space takes on an extraordinary nobility and an impressive eloquence. In an over-populated city, an undeveloped area is in itself a luxury, a prodigality. It seems as if space has been wasted throughout this quarter with a kind of aristocratic generosity, of royal munificence. One is always astonished when some exhibition or fair has the audacity to plant its palings and its tents on the Esplanade of the Invalides, which ought to be reserved—apart from great national funerals—for those nocturnal cavalcades of armoured and prancing ghosts to whom Detaille, a second-rate painter but a master of costume, gave free rein in his pictures.

JEAN BÉRAUD
At the Foot of the Tower.

The Champ-de-Mars is less intimidating and has a popular appeal. It gladly welcomed the crowds that came for the great revolutionary ceremonies, when the Federation was celebrating an illusory fraternity, or glorifying a " Supreme Being " whose cult was set up in the open air so that it might more easily be expelled from the churches. It was there that the executioner beheaded a mayor of Paris, and that Napoleon distributed the eagles to his victorious regiments, and the Legion of Honour to his moustached grenadiers. There the crowds flocked to see the departure of the primitive, beribboned balloons, and watch the bold wind-navigators waving their three-cornered hats and their handkerchiefs Horse-races were held there for the amusement of the nobility prior to the organising of race-courses for the excitement of Sunday crowds.   And then all kinds of exhibitions, bearing the greatest variety of titles, erected their cast-iron or pasteboard edifices, their booths, their Aztec palaces, and their nougat stalls.   The military avocation of this quarter, and the great designs of royal town-planners, have suffered somewhat from the glaring indiscrimination of these modern sanctuaries, built to the glory of trade and industry.

Depending on whether we approach the Invalides from the front, coming from the Seine and crossing the Esplanade, or from the back by way of the Avenue de Tourville and the Place Vauban, we are impressed either by the barrack-like character of the building or by its consecrated aspect.   We will enter by one approach or the other, according to whether we feel inclined to pay our respects to the Emperor's remains and the faded flags, or to study the picturesque blend of museum and guard-room which constitutes the ancient hostel for Louis XIV's disabled ex-servicemen.   The Governor's garden and the little low houses that border the Boulevard des Invalides have kept alive the memory of heroic cripples, smoking their clay pipes in the sun, their three-cornered hats over their eyes and their blue greatcoats negligently undone.

Today there are no longer any *invalides* in the mansion built for them: not even that legendary personage whom generations of peasants, convinc-

ed of his existence, have enquired about from generations of bantering guardians —the soldier with the wooden head. There are no wooden heads except those of the figures in the Musée de l'Armée, dressed as Gallic warriors, or crusading knights, musketeers, French Guards, soldiers of the Year II of the Revolution, veterans and foot-soldiers. Nothing is more attractive than a silent conversation with these picturesque heroes, scattered throughout the rooms of the most unobtrusive and solitary of all Paris museums.

It seems wrong that this should be,

The Invalides.

because there is not another museum in Europe that equals it in richness and variety. In fact, you can find here all the most ingenious inventions contrived by men to massacre each other in the most rapid and effective manner. Museums of arms always furnish one salutary lesson to visitors: they demonstrate that the nations have, in building their engines of destruction, expended a wealth of skill, science, talent and even refine-ment almost equal to that which goes into the finest works of art. For, indeed, these swords, pistols, carbines, daggers, blunderbusses, falconets and claymores, set out in an orderly manner in glass-cases, are real works of art. They are surrounded by a host of associations, and the historical rooms in the museum appear to the dumbfounded visitor as a kind of immense panorama, recording by means of objects and actions, with the stiffness of cheap coloured prints, the heroic deeds of former days. There he makes the acquaintance of arms, vaguely guessing their names and uses, alongside costumes scarcely powdered with dust or eaten by insects, that tell of forgotten campaigns, of pyramids forty centuries old, of Muscovites steppes and Tonkin ricefields.

A strange silence reigns in these rooms. When the Sunday strollers and their weary children have left the museum and the church, the Invalides resumes its true rôle of a vast tomb, a cemetery of persons and things, a clamorous crypt filled with arms and men-at-arms. The air pervading the shredded banners beneath the vaulting of the church of St. Louis, and the grave where sleep side by side the " Eagle " in his red granite sarcophagus and the "Eaglet" in his bronze coffin, is the same as that sur-rounding the equestrian figures in the museum and the glass-cases full of swords. It is a sort of spectral wind, a funeral breath, intermingled with the muffled sounds that emerge from the lips of trumpets and the mouths of the cannon.

To house these departed spirits—the successors of the *invalides* of former times—Jules Hardouin-Mansart built the gold and jade cupola, crowning the simple, majestic, classical building of Libéral Bruant. It tones so well with the Parisian sky. Here the word " classical " assumes its noblest and most complete sense : it means, in fact, balance and energy, economy and power, beauty and restraint. The balance of solid masses, the pliancy and lightness of volume, the clear-cut perfection of form, here effect a kind of miracle. Matter is spiritualised and spirit is clothed in corporeal form; the genius of the architect has rarely achieved so exquisite and so complete a miracle.

Napoleon's Tomb.

" I wish my body to be laid to rest on the banks of the Seine, among the French people whom I loved so well, " wrote Napoleon, in his last will and testament. He wished to be buried in an ordinary cemetery, so that he might feel he was still mingling with the people whose enthusiasm and adoration had sustained and stimulated him throughout the length of his reign. Even if it is not quite in conformity with his wishes, the tomb at the Invalides is at least becoming to the great Emperor who was for so many years the arbiter of the world's destiny. It is a simple tomb, without ornament, majestic, massive, impressive by reason of the clearness of its lines and the grave beauty of its purple marble. And just as the loyal generals of the Napoleonic era—Duroc, Oudinot, Jourdan, Moncey, Bertrand—thronged round him on the battlefield, so now in ghostly array they escort his familiar silhouette, wearing the grey redingote and the black hat with the upturned brim that one cannot look at, in the Musée de l'Armée, without being moved.

The École Militaire.

The Ecole Militaire embodies the same aesthetic principles as the Invalides. There was not only the question of housing the stalwarts who had been wounded in the service of the King, but there was also the necessity of preparing "cadres" of officers worthy of commanding regiments. Mme. de Pompadour, who is known to have been the originator of the boldest and most intelligent projects of Louis XV's reign, suggested to the financier Pâris-Duverney that the foundation of a college for future officers was desirable, just as in the seminaries ecclesiastical science was instilled into future priests. And since the nobility of the provinces had so often impoverished itself in order to serve the nation, it was agreed that five hundred young men of reduced circumstances should be housed and instructed there "in the arts of Bellona," as the saying went in those days.

If the ghosts are friendly to you and not too shy, as you stroll through the courtyards and passages, you may perhaps overtake a furtive youthful phantom, in his blue uniform, his wig tied with a ribbon at the nape of his neck, a sword at his side, and books under his arm. Look carefully, and you may see an ardent and ambitious youth glide past, with fiery eyes—it is the ghost of young Napoleon Bonaparte, who, before going to Brienne, learnt here the secrets of strategy and of the government of peoples.

The Hôtel des Invalides no longer fulfils its original purpose, but the

The Courtyard of the Ecole Militaire.

Ecole Militaire still performs the same functions. The instruction given nowadays turns out soldiers of a type never dreamt of at the time when the young Corsican was receiving his initiation of fervour and contempt within these walls. Who ever supposed at that time—not so far distant from our own days, after all—that flying machines would convey the armies of one continent to another, that guns would be self-propelled and that cavalrymen would be enclosed in chariots of iron and fire ? The art of war has today become so complicated in its technique that it requires as intense a study of mathematics as do the chemical and engineering professions.

I said that this quarter was exclusively military. It is true that one comes across more equestrian statues than horse-drawn cabs, and that the children playing in the Champ-de-Mars are the possible future conscripts. But what could be more *bourgeois*, more civilian than the streets that make up the district called the *Gros Caillou* (Great pebble) ? Why the *Gros Caillou* ? Ask the geologists, as historians competent to delve into the strata of old Paris, why this erratic block fell into the midst of these martial buildings. The *Caillou* was certainly there well before the founding of the nursery for young officers or the asylum for disabled soldiers; but even the inhabitants of the district, who ought to know all these things, have never been able to tell me anything about the pebble in question. The Gros Caillou numbers a few antique mansions—in the midst of some cheap, noisy and cheerful houses—that are rather like the extreme ends of feelers stretched out by the Faubourg St-Germain from the other side of the frontier separating the civilian world from the military: noble, classical or rococo edifices, such as the Hôtel de Behague, which conceals a most picturesque Moorish theatre behind its Louis XV façade.

For those who are tired of the warlike display of the Invalides district, there is a wonderful refuge. A few steps from the little low houses where grenadiers were reminded of their battles through the twinges of their wounds in damp weather, and still overlooked by the matchless cupola of Hardouin-Mansart, are the quiet and lovely gardens of the Hôtel Biron, peopled with marble figures. What a marvellous age it was when the best architects of the day built this abode for the convenience of a wealthy barber! Simple and perfect, with an amazing nobility of line, as rhythmic in form as a Mozart *andante*, this building has known all the vicissitudes that befall houses as well as human beings.

I do not know whether the wig-maker Peyrenc, for whom Aubert and Gabriel expended so much genius and good taste, ruined himself in wild parties, or whether he grew weary of a perfection that was too refined and too restrained. But, in short, it was a great soldier and a great nobleman who succeeded him—Maréchal de Biron. And this little palace, delighted at belonging to this new master, graced itself, for posterity, with the name of "Hôtel Biron." Then the Revolution swept away the aristocrats like dead leaves and sent them in cartloads to the guillotine. When calm reigned again,

The Gros-Caillou.

the Papal Nuncio, Cardinal Caprara settled in Abraham Peyrenc's "folly," and held his diplomatic banquets here. But even diplomats change, and the Emperor of Russia substituted his coat-of-arms for that of the Holy Father. The garden that had known the presence of unobtrusive monsignors was filled with cossacks and foot-soldiers. In the course of less than a year came the war that was to drag the French Army across the icy stretches of the Beresina and through the flames of burning Mos-

The Hôtel Biron.

cow. The Russians became unpopular in Paris and as soon as the last attachés were packed into their coaches, the embassy closed its doors.

Despite the uproar caused by the riotous and pathetic marble figures with which Rodin filled this palace—which would have been much more suitable to receive the works of Houdon, Pajou, or Pigalle —you can still experience in the avenues the silence that descended after the flight of the Muscovites. When life was resumed in the little palace, it was to the murmur of prayers and the peaceful rhythm of liturgical chants. Mother Sophie Barrat brought her nuns of the Sacred Heart here. Their bare cells were installed in the apartments of the Duchess of Maine, who was the *locum tenens* between the time of the wealthy wig-maker and the Duke of Biron. A neo-gothic chapel was joined to the little rococo palace to supply the spiritual needs of the community; Rodin was later to make it his studio, after the stormy times of the *Séparation* when a police commissioner in scarf and silk hat was sent to inform the pious women that their order constituted a hotbed of subversion, endangering the democratic and secular Republic.

That was how it came about one day that, in those shady groves where saintly souls were preparing for Paradise, the *Gateway to Hell*, its panels swarming with tortured forms, made its appearance. Rodin, with his great beard, his smock flecked with marble dust, his mallet and chisel, set up his studio here. An art such as his needed space.

The fact that the Musée Rodin succeeded the Hôtel Biron seems to us not a little sacrilegious. Not so much because the sculptor bought church property at a time, when it was up for auction, and planted his dramatic nudes in the nuns' oratory, but rather because the character of his art does not in the least accord with the house that he filled with his pale and gleaming marble blocks. The latter appear at greater advantage under their glass casing at Meudon than here, where a less resonant genius would have harmonised better with the architecture of the miniature palace and the design of the little park.

Raise your eyes: Mansart's dome glitters in the setting sun and Gabriel's façade is the colour of rose. These two classical masterpieces are in calm and noble colloquy, and I am struck with the thought that their destinies are similar, for they both shelter two immeasurable geniuses— Napoleon and Rodin. The former wanted to break the world and re-mould it between his powerful hands. Now he sleeps, the prisoner of the purple monolith under his crown of battle-worn flags, the sleep of St. Helena. The other, out of brute stone, forged a whole world of happy or suffering beings and, one may say, took in hand a programme comparable to Balzac's when he constructed the *Comédie Humaine*. Would it be disrespectful to say that Rodin found his St. Helena in the Hôtel Biron ?

The Hôtel Biron is full of admirable fragments ; the *Gateway to Hell* abounds with examples, and the modelling of a shoulder or a thigh is fraught with genius. Then one imagines what they might have been, the one for the other, had they lived at the same epoch — the Emperor whose bones rest beneath the cupola, the artist whose soul remains linked to the statues scattered throughout the Hôtel, the chapel and the garden. It is not difficult to imagine Rodin as the portraitist of the Napoleonic era: and what art would have gained if the one had found a model commensurate with his genius, and if the other had possessed an interpreter worthy of his work and his spirit.

Marcel BRION.

CHAILLOT, PASSY
AUTEUIL

BERTHE MORISOT. — *The Auteuil Viaduct.*

N THE 16th

arrondissement few traces remain of a past whose very drama lies in its lingering death. But sufficient remains for it not to have completely lost *atmosphere*. How many times have I stopped in one of those out of the way streets, in front of a carriage gateway or an old wall, behind which one divines the presence of an old house with an old-fashioned garden that seems deserted but is not quite so in reality, where families or bachelors —as described in the novels of the *régionaliste* writers—persistently continue to live their gentle, leisurely lives. These strange, old-world beings, ignorant of the aeroplane, the wireless and even the telephone, have never ventured beyond a certain circle round their dwelling; they have, for the most part, remained out of sight, and I am quite sure that to their presence is due the quality of the air that we still breathe there, indefinably tranquil and delicate and so refreshing, coming as a sudden contrast after the vain and furious agitation of the great traffic centres.

What first strikes one in the " Sixteenth," even from a glance at an ordinary map, at any plan of Paris, is the unusual importance of the open spaces that surround it. Except on the north, where its boundaries are the Avenue Marceau and the Avenue de la Grande Armée, and on the south where it is bordered by a short stretch of Boulogne, it has no built-up town areas as frontiers. It is in fact like an autonomous town in the midst of a vast countryside. On the one side is the Seine, at one of its widest stretches and over a length of two and three quarter miles; on the other side is a two and a half mile stretch of the Bois de Boulogne (one of the finest parks in the world). It is clear that no other district of Paris enjoys such advantages, if only from the point of view of health, for the air its inhabitants breathe is continuously ventilated, refreshed and purified by the breezes that have passed over the river or the Bois. I say nothing of the pleasures they derive from its situation: as strollers they have

CHAILLOT
PASSY
AUTEUIL

only to take a few steps to find themselves in the middle of a real forest, where in certain spots they can enjoy the comforting illusion of the most complete solitude; or simply as spectators, if they live on the quay-side, for they have only to open their windows to contemplate one of the noblest landscapes of stone and water in the world. One never wearies of the beauty of the Seine.

This topographical situation, absolutely unique, is one of the factors that, I think, gives the Sixteenth a character of unity, more authentic and distinct than the diversity it derives from its past— when its districts (now merged into one) were still in process of formation; when, for instance, the hill of Chaillot, as well as Passy or La Muette, had its own life, and if I may so express it, its own *style*. I am not overlooking the fact that it would be pleasant to describe, as so many geographical "personalities," some fragment of old Auteuil, contrasting it with that magnificent hill of Chaillot, where the newly-made cutting of the Tro-cadero has revealed its stirring and majestic altitude. But within the limits of this short study I cannot dwell at length on these subtle differ-ences; I prefer to emphasise the resemblances or likenesses, since they arise from the even more important fact that resemblances exist between the inhabitants. The man of the Sixteenth, whether he lives in the Avenue de Tokio or the Rue de Perchamps, the Chaussée de La Muette or the Place de l'Etoile, is recognised by a certain air of satisfaction and secret pride, as if he were aware of the privilege that Fate had bestow-ed on him in allowing him to live there. And this feeling creates yet another, even more subtle, which in its turn influences the general aspect of the place and effaces local differences. If Balzac were still living, what an amusing and piquant monograph could he not write under the title of " The Physiology of the Man of the Sixteenth!" He would reveal him in his heroic role as the supporter of traditions, contrasting his sense of leisure with the restless racket of modern life; he would depict his proprietary dignity when he entertains the inhabitants of other districts in his own private park, the Bois de Boulogne. He would quote with a smile some of his favourite expressions, the drollery of which he no longer realises—as, for instance, " I am going up to town " when he makes his way to the Madeleine or Montparnasse, for it is a recognised fact that the Sixteenth is not quite Paris; it is already the country.

How can we help recalling the time—certainly long ago, but still

very vivid in the minds of those who study it, when the whole of this western portion of Paris was nothing more than a great forest ?   Little by little this forest was peopled with the villages of Auteuil, Chaillot and Passy.   One can think of the numerous green islets that have remained (parks, estates, orchards, hamlets, villas and wasteland) as touching remnants of that primitive woodland.

It is nevertheless undeniable that the Sixteenth, whose "style" is so markedly individualistic, compared with other districts, is, for all that, not homogeneous. Auteuil is not quite the same as Passy. When going from Chaillot to the Porte Dauphine, one has certainly the feeling of passing through different *strata*. But the boundaries of those four "sectors" are not clearly defined. There are contested territories and "no man's land." Auteuil only becomes definitely Auteuil below the Rue de l'Assomption. A little of the spirit of Passy invades it—unless one prefers to put it the other way round and say that the essence of Auteuil extends as far as La Muette. I am willing to add that, in some portions of those districts that have no official names, there

reigns a certain spirit, style or essence—call it what you
will—that has nothing to do with administrative descriptions, but which an experienced eye recognises. Thus,
around the Avenue du Bois stretches an irregular quadrilateral whose luxurious appearance seems to have nothing
in common with the maze of little streets in the neighbourhood of the Rue Raynouard and the Rue de Boulainvilliers.
But, even there, nothing is sharply defined or clear-cut.
The most sumptuous highways have streets with modest
little shops or even tumbledown buildings as their immediate neighbours. Therein lies the undoubted charm of
this quarter—its phantasy and its freedom. I have often
heard it said—and it is moreover my own opinion—that
in archaic, traditional Spain, the true democratic spirit
reigns : not in institutions but in manners. A well-bred
familiarity unites the nobleman to the proletarian. Well,
it is the same for Auteuil; at least for its buildings. Poky
little 18th century houses jostle attractively with palaces
and edifices that are proud of their modernity. I recall
having seen, not so long ago, vegetable gardens, stables
and poultry-yards in the Rue Raynouard or in some *cul-*

The Trocadéro.

de-sac on the way down to the Seine. It took a long time to lay waste these summer resorts with their trees and birds. The Rue de l'Assomption still remembers the time (not so long ago) when the convent of the ladies of the same name was situated in the midst of an immense garden. Providentially, the park stretching between the Rue Mirabeau and the Avenue de Versailles belongs to the Institution St. Périne, and it is accordingly protected. Clinics and welfare establishments always have round them a certain amount of breathing room which they fill with lawns and copses. In this case we must even be grateful for the waste lands, for the inertia and negligence that lets them grow up here and there is after all better than the anonymous and implacable will of bureaucracy which would automatically transform them into "plots to let." Yes, the more I think of it, the more striking I find this phenomenon of reciprocal endosmosis which means that, from one end to another of this charming little town that constitutes the Sixteenth *arrondissement*, each of the numerous " districts " of which it is composed can be rediscovered in the most unexpected places. Thus, a humble little greengrocer's in the Rue Chardon-Lagache has its double in the Rue Duret, or some wealthy and rather forbidding house in the Rue Pergolèse will reappear with the same aloofness at a corner of the Rue Jouvenet. And so on. But I ought to add that Chaillot somehow eludes those analogies—doubtless because of its geographical position. It stretches down to the Seine with such magnificent grace ! And the transformation of the Trocadéro has accentuated its glamour. It must be admitted—and the people of the Sixteenth are not a little proud of it, with good reason—that the breach made in that absurd public building (so ingeniously rebuilt) opens up one of the finest views imaginable over the whole of Paris. And the gardens that have grown so quickly, so well-wooded and well-designed, carpeting the slope down to the river's edge—as well as the basins of water in tiers, with their fountains—all this constitutes a scene of infinite harmony. Not even the double stream of mammas

taking their children for a walk, and of foreign tourists who flock there to admire the wonderful view, can ruin it—this wide open space, without limit or encumbrance, stretching endlessly before us. One would think that it gathered to itself the whole of the hill. But the slope does, in fact, reach much farther, even as far as the Place des Etats-Unis.

If the Sixteenth is the poorest of all the *arrondissements* of the capital in ancient monuments, the reason for that is identical with the cause of its charm. If neither churches, town-halls nor palaces with gardens are built, that does not mean that History has no claim here. Great men, as well as simple citizens, want a place to rest from their labours and they inevitably leave memories behind in the spots they choose for their relaxation.

The Palais de Chaillot.

It was only from the 17th century onwards that the fashionable world
began to resort there. It is said that Louis XIII often came to Auteuil
to go nesting for blackbirds, to bathe, to hunt wolves, and to dine with
friends. Louis XV also had a hunting box at Auteuil where, as at Passy,
there were thermal springs, and later on Marie-Antoinette used to go
there to visit her sister-in-law, Mme. Elisabeth.

But what obviously interests us more is that Molière, Racine and Boileau—all united by the warmest friendship—lived in this village, and that
they took every opportunity of coming here to work and to muse at
leisure in their country house; they were jovial fellows and loved to
get together in a tavern, although since those days they are always
represented in more solemn guise with the ceremonial and academic wig.
They were often found in company with La Fontaine at the *Auberge du
Mouton Blanc.* I myself have frequently dined at this inn in company with
Delage, the composer, and a few friends, and although, as one may be sure,
the surroundings were very different, it was not without emotion that I
took my place in the back parlour where Molière had read the *Misanthrope*
to his friends immediately after he had written it—an episode reproduced
in a large picture that hangs on the wall. The house of the great comedian
stood there, at the corner of the Rue d'Auteuil and the Avenue Théophile-
Gautier where I resided; Racine's house was opposite, and a few steps
away, Boileau's. I lived for many long years in this corner of the world

and I do not know how many times my footsteps have traversed this ground so often trodden by theirs. And whatever else I may have had on my mind at the time, I do not think I can ever have passed that way without thinking of them, of their private lives, their ideas and their interests. In their day, numerous vines brightened the hillsides on which their houses stood and whose sweet wine they tasted. There they entertained Ninon de Lenclos and La Champmeslé. They produced comedies. The river coach, starting from the Louvre, took them there. Boileau entertained prelates and important noblemen, writers and artists. How can one remain unmoved by what, for so many people, are only side lines of history ? How could one fail to see in the meeting of this authentic " great four " the origins of the literary fame of the Sixteenth ? And it was, in fact, thanks to these four poets that the popularity of Auteuil began, so to speak. For after them came a whole procession of celebrities —from Mme de Helvétius and Mme de Boufflers to Villemessant and Masset, Hubert Robert and Gavarni. Lauzan and the Prince de Ligne were seen there, and Bonaparte, who, it is said, liked the place very much; also Cabanis and Condorcet. And nearer our own time, the famous Goncourt brothers who, in their mansion in the Boulevard Montmorency, installed all the marvels of their art collection, as well as the no less famous " attic," overlooking a garden, that was the resort of the young writers of the day—" a few square yards to yourself which nature covers with foliage and flowers for the special and intimate delight of an old Parisian " as they used to say, those artists—those inventors of artistic writing. Were they not thus expressing the dreams of so many town-dwellers weary of the feverish life of great cities ? Is it not just that which makes them the spiritual heirs of the Racines and the Molières, those other devotees of Auteuil ?

As to Passy, it was more especially the holiday resort of the wealthy class, of the farmer-generals, who, from the beginning of the 18th century, set up their " *folies* " there. That word, so expressive in its derivative sense, was formerly spelt " feuillues," in allusion to the parks, paths and clumps of trees that surrounded these refuges for furtive love-affairs. The Château de La Muette, a residence of the kings of France, where magnificent festivals were held, was the first of a host of town houses. Boulainvilliers and La Popelinière were the most notorious of the great financiers. And the Princesse de Lamballe lived at the Château de Passy, which later became the famous nursing-home of Dr. Blanche, where Gérard de Nerval was a patient and which bordered on the Rue Berton, in one wall of which was the secret door used by Balzac when fleeing his creditors.

For we are now in that little corner of the world, the most pathetic spot in the whole of the Sixteenth, whose appearance has not, thank God, changed very much. A second-rate lodging, and a terraced garden, long and narrow. There, the master, entering by the Rue Raynouard (then the Rue du Roc) descended one floor to reach his apartment, which was faked as in a detective film.

When he was afraid of being harassed by some sleuth-hound and bearded in his den, he raised a trap-door and made away by the Rue Berton. How many times have I stopped there, in front of that mysterious little door, a few paces from the milestone that formerly marked the boundary between the two domains of Auteuil and Passy, gripped by a kind of inexplicable agony, as if at any moment I expected to see him suddenly appear, with his large head and colossal figure, running like a delinquent or a thief—he who had brought millions to so many people and would even have helped them to gain more, but whose contemporaries understood neither his genius nor his greatness !

That poor Maison Balzac, where there was little in the way of furniture during his lifetime and where nothing remains today! But no matter; as it stands in its bareness, it is a fitting symbol of the fate of the great novelist. It has nothing to mar it and, looking as if it had just been emptied by distraint, it is more moving then if it were cluttered up with the costly curios with which sucessful authors surround themselves like trophies.

Balzac was poor, and could not be other than poor; and when, to conform to the wishes of Mme Hanska—who found the romantic and uncouth lodging atrocious—he left it to settle down elsewhere, he died a few months later. . .

All these people belong to the past and, in spite of everything, are remote from us. While on the other hand our contemporaries, even those whom death has taken away—if only our heart remains faithful to them and if only our mind is interested in them—stay near us in a sense; it often happens, when we recall them to mind, that we ask ourselves whether they are just momentarily absent, as was the case when we used to call on them unexpectedly and find them out.

In this way the Sixteenth is, for me, the place of ideal encounters. Thus the Rue du Ranelagh is always associated with memories of Elémir Bourges, the delightful poet of *La Nef;* he lived at No. 51, on the top floor, and from his window he could see the large garden—which is still there. He loved and was loved by young people.

Not far from there, in the Hameau Boulainvilliers—where the poet Fernand Gregh now resides—lived Pierre Louys, in a little villa covered over with greenery. I wonder why—since he always used to turned night into day. As Henri Bataille wrote, in his portrait of him in the admirable album entitled *Têtes et Pensées*, there was "a gentle secret about that man." But we shall probably never know what this secret was.

A striking contrast to Bourges and Louys was René Boylesve—who lived near them in the Rue des Vignes at Auteuil. He had everything he could wish for—a magnificent house (the former Hôtel Mors, which contained a theatre, and a very fine one at that), a charming wife, substantial fortune, considerable talent and the friendship of most of his colleagues. But I have rarely seen so sad a man. Who would not be happy today with that garden? When it was broken up, Boylesve devoted a novel to the subject: *Souvenirs d'un jardin détruit*. He could only see the part of which he was defrauded.

The Avenue Kléber has certainly not much character, and in vain would one search there for the picturesque element to be found in the southern part of Auteuil. The same is true for the Rue Boissière and the Rue de Villejust (the present Rue Paul-Valéry). But these three commonplace highways are sacred spots for me, places "where the spirit breathes." For in these streets there lived, for many years, O.W. Milosz, Henri de Régnier, and Paul Valéry. Heaven knows how different they were, but these three great poets had in common their cheerfulness, their good-humour, and their generosity—and what wit! The Lithuanian, the Norman and the Languedocian, how Parisian, how brilliant they were! Milosz, the greatest of all, was possessed of an irresistible dynamism and an extraordinary vitality. That was how he was able to bear the unjust neglect of his genius for so many years with the same smiling indifference as the other two accepted their fame. I can reconstruct in my imagination our long walks in Paris, for he was an indefatigable walker and an astonishing discover of the comic and the pathetic at every turn of the road.

And I can still see the apartments of Régnier and Valéry: in his Venetian salon, the author of *Tel qu'en songe*, with his monocle, his Gallic moustache, his grand manner, as of a tired and blasé nobleman, his jokes with double meanings and his treasury of humorous

The Rue des Vignes.

Auteuil.

anecdotes; in his study, brimming over with books and papers, Valéry with his everlasting cigarette, his agitation, his inexhaustible train of ideas, his paradoxes, and that unrestrained schoolboy roguishness which, up to his last days, so delighted his friends.

Milosz, Régnier, Valéry—73 Avenue Kléber, 24 Rue Boissière, 40 Rue de Villejust. Look at the little triangle marked out in the middle of Chaillot by these three points on a map of Paris. You will agree that a hill such as this is indeed the equal of all those that antiquity venerated—a holy hill. And now other memories come back to my mind, recollections of other remarkable beings I have known, all of whom inhabited the Sixteenth. One might almost think that no other fatherland was possible for scholars and thinkers.

There was Anatole France at the famous Villa Saïd, visited by all who had a name in the intellectual world; there was Paul Adam in his apartment on the Quai de Passy; the Comtesse de Noailles who died in the house in the Rue Scheffer where she had spent nearly all her life. There was also, still among the poets, Guillaume Apollinaire, the leading figure in the school, whose fame does not diminish and who always awaited us with his sovereign joviality in his lodging in the Rue Gros. And, among the painters, there is Jacques-Emile Blanche, bitter and malicious, mundane and solitary, full of talent and of doubts about himself.

Finally, in the Boulevard Beauséjour, Paul Marguerite, that laborious disciple of Flaubert and Zola, who always found time to entertain, and who did so with infinite good grace and with tasteful display. All those of whom I have spoken are still so vividly present that I find them endowed with much more life and reality than many an insignificant person I meet at any time of day, and who gives me the impression of being a mere supernumerary in the great comedy of daily life.

When I left my house, it was for boulevards lined with chestnut-trees or plane-trees, or else for a tangle of little provincial streets where one sensed the presence of modest and upright middle-class folk, following the rules of conduct of their ancestral traditions. The famous 25 tram, that had recently been electrified, still linked Auteuil with the learned and ecclesiastical St. Sulpice district, and I do not think I am mistaken in asserting that, thanks to this antiquated vehicle, some circulation of mental effluvia was maintained between these two poles of the Parisian scene. Yes, the more I think of it, the more I believe that one of the most authentic charms of the quarter was derived from this analogy. One might say that the slow and peaceful soul of St. Sulpice had come to rest in Auteuil and Passy, to continue the tradition of a certain conception of life—that of the average Frenchman of former times—which has often been laughed at, and which we are gradually beginning to regret more and more, as we experience more and more deeply the febrile excitement which has replaced it...

Undoubtedly present-day life, a little absurd in its futile agitation, no longer has time for those fine discussions, those long strolls, those encounters, that gave so much value to life of former days. And who knows whether it is not with the unconscious thought of recapturing it to some degree in this quarter, the last retreat of careless ease, that so many celebrities have taken refuge here : the great Colette, after a number of earlier moves to escape from the gardens of the Boulevard Lannes, that she depicted in such a moving manner; Rosemonde Gérard with her son Maurice Rostand; Georges Lecomte; Claude Farrère; Louis Jouvet; Makhali-Phal who conjured up for us the world of the Far East; the subtle Max Dairaux; Georges Boskoff, Chopin's spiritual son; and finally Marcelle Castelier, the author of the excellent symphonic novel *Leur Solitude*, and so many others as well.

Dear friends, who live only for thought, for ideals and for poetry, how well they realise that they could not really be happy for long in any place other than Auteuil or Passy. They would miss something; some indefinable air that one breathes nowhere else. They certainly suffer from the changes that the quarter has undergone. Each blow from the pickaxe on an old building resounds in their hearts, and wounds them. They cling with renewed fervour and eagerness to the charm and sweetness of living that still remains in the Sixteenth. They form, so to speak without knowing it, a sort of little secret society, which makes them more or less at one with every inhabitant of the quarter who is sufficiently sensitive to experience a little pride in living there. And in their rare moments of leisure they go to the Bois de Boulogne—which, after all, is their personal garden. Basically the Bois de Boulogne—despite its well-groomed, civilised and familiar appearance—is, and always has been, the ancient forest of the far-distant ages, that has now at last been protected and saved. It is posed there like a guardian and like a symbol. It represents their love of nature. It is their bulwark againts the invading onslaught of the suburbs. It offers to citizens from far and near the possibility of finding in the course of a day's journey the equivalent of what they would seek at Saint-Cloud or Saint-Germain, at Sèvres or Versailles. Dear Bois de Boulogne, the greenwood of the sixteenth *arrondissement*, if you had not existed they would have had to invent you, they would have

The Rue de Boulainvilliers.

created you out of nothing. And when they go to the Bois de Boulogne, they take the ferry-boat and go—

to the Island...

The Island ! Their isle ! For there are many islands in Paris, and I should not be the one to underrate the Ile de la Cité, which is the heart of the civilised world, but the Sixteenth has only one island—the Ile du Bois ! And those who savour its charm know very well that, at certain hours, one is sure to find there what man has always sought in islands since the foundation of the world—the peace of Solitude.

Francis de MIOMANDRE.

THE BOIS DE
BOULOGNE AND
NEUILLY

E·M·PEROT

CHAPELAIN-MIDY. — *The Bois de Boulogne.*

IVING WITH

the Bois de Boulogne as my neighbour, all I can see from my windows is this forest, which extends to the left as far as the Porte Maillot and the Porte Dauphine, and to the right as far as the banks of the Seine. Each capital has its forests. London cherishes Hyde Park and Regent's Park—these are real parks and not woods. Brussels and Buenos Aires, copying Paris, keep their original forests. But the Bois de Boulogne is just the *Bois*, unique, inimitable, just as Rome was The City and the Thames is The River.

Our Bois has a complex character. In parts it is a real forest and nearly wild. In springtime, a carpet of wood violets, cowslips and primroses covers the rich ground. But the streams and the lakes are artificial. The bridges that bestride them have an unreal and romantic air. The ducks and swans seem to be functionaries of the town. They even have holidays, when they disappear, while their lakes and ponds are drained, exposing the concrete foundations. Then the water returns and with it the swans and ducks. The Bois has its secret paths where loving couples embrace with impunity, but it also has its wide roads, its bridle paths, its public walks, its restaurants, its cemetery. So this forest is a town without ceasing to be a forest.

At the beginning it was but a forest. The Bois was then called " Forêt de Rouvray," which was another way of saying "oak-grove." In 1256, Isabelle of France, sister of Saint Louis, who was later beatified, cleared the land which is today a training ground, and built there the Abbey of Longchamp, which no longer exists. The name of Boulogne only came into the picture in 1319, when a group of devout people, who had been on a pilgrimage to Boulogne-sur-Mer, asked permission to build a church, identical to the one they had just seen, and to call the parish Boulogne-sur-Seine. And so the forest was baptized like a Christian. Being close to the capital, it gradually became enriched with

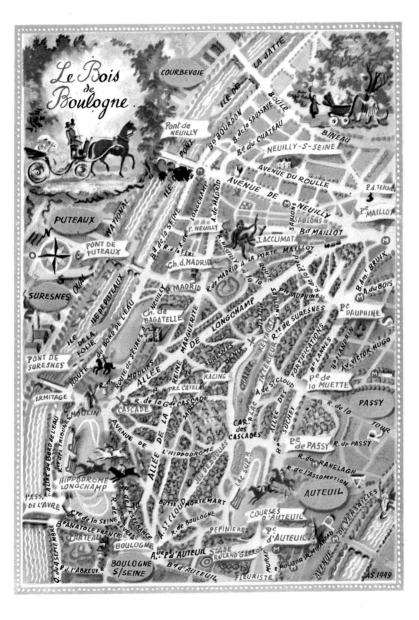

Le Bois
de
Boulogne

COURBEVOIE

LA JATTE

ILE DE

Pont de
NEUILLY

Bd BOURDON

Bd de la SAUSSAYE

Bd du CHATEAU

BINEAU

NEUILLY-S-SEINE

AVENUE DU ROULLE

P. d. TERNE

AVENUE DE NEUILLY

PUTEAUX

NATIONAL

Bd de la SEINE

A. de MADRID

P. NEUILLY

R. d. la FERI

R. NEUILLY A LA PORTE MAILLOT

SABLONS

Bd MAILLOT

P. MAILLOT

J. ACCLIMAT

B. Am. BRUIX

A. du BOIS

PONT DE
PUTEAUX

Ch. d. MADRID

MADRID

R. de MADRID à la

ROUTE

P. Dauphine

Pe
DAUPHINE

SURESNES

QUAI

ILE DE LA
FOLIE

ILE DE PUTEAUX

Ch. de
BAGATELLE

REINE MARGUERITE

LONGCHAMP

R. te de Suresnes

B. LANNES

B. FLANDRIN

Av. VICTOR-HUGO

PONT DE
SURESNES

ROUTE du BORD DE L'EAU

ROUTE de Sèvres

MOULINS

ALLÉE

DE LA

DENIS

SURESNES

FORTIFICATIONS

Pe de
la MUETTE

ERMITAGE

R. d.

PRÉ CATELAN

RACING

A. de St-CLOUD

ALLÉE DES

R. de la

PASSY

CASCADE

R. de la Gde CASCADE

SAINS

CARR.
des
CASCADES

Bd SUCHET

Pe de PASSY

R. de PASSY

TOUR

ALLÉE DU BORD DE L'EAU

R. des TRIBUNES

MOULIN

AVENUE DE

ALLÉE DE L'HIPPODROME

RUE DE BOULLIAS

LAC SUP.

Pe de RANELAGH

R. de l'ASSOMPTION

AUTEUIL

HIPPODROME
LONGCHAMP

R. de la

R. de

PASS. LA
DE L'AVRE

R. de l'ESPÉRANCE

Ste de la SEINE

R. de Sèvres

BUTTE
ST-CLOUD MORTEMART

A. ST-CLOUD

R. de BOULOGNE

COURSES
D'AUTEUIL

Q. du 4 SEPTEMBRE

Bd ANATOLE-FRANCE

R. d. l'ABREUV.

CHATEAU

BOULOGNE

PÉPINIÈRE

Pe
d'AUTEUIL

A. de Pe d'AUTEUIL

STADE
ROLAND-GARROS

Bd AUTEUIL

MURAT

R. MOLITOR R. MIRABEAU

AVENUE DE VERSAILLES

BOULOGNE
S/SEINE

FLEURISTE

AS. 1949

historical memories. Olivier le Daim hunted there, and Louis XI used to visit him. In 1528, Francis I called on great artists such as Philibert Delorme, Primaticcio, Della Robbia, to build for him a château in the Bois, decorated with multicoloured earthenware, a country house which the Parisians sarcastically called " Château de Madrid " because the King was as invisible there as when he was a captive. Sully persuaded Henry IV to set up a silk-worm nursery there; Sully put silk-worms everywhere. However, Marguerite de Valois, to whom the King had given the " Château de Madrid," got rid of the silk-worms and opened up the beautiful avenues of the Reine Marguerite, which enabled her to go on pilgrimage to the tomb of Saint Isabella at Longchamp. Later on the Château was destroyed and a restaurant, the hiding place of lovers and duellists, was established in the outbuildings.

The first horse-race took place in 1651, in the Bois de Boulogne : Madrid to La Muette and back. It was the forerunner of Auteuil and Longchamp race courses. Yet in the eighteenth century it was not horse-racing that drew the court and townsfolk to the Bois. It had become the fashion, throughout Holy Week, to go to the Abbey of Long-champ to attend *Tenebrae*. A great singer who had taken vows attracted the whole of Paris. The church authorities were disquieted, and Christophe de Beaumont forbade entrance to the Abbey. But in vain. It had become a habit. Horsemen and carriages continued to go to Longchamp, and drive round the Abbey, no longer only at Easter-time but all the year round. And so the Bois became fashionable.

The eighteenth century was, in that part of the Bois that borders Neuilly, the time of the " Follies ". The wide Royal Road taken by the carriages on their way from the Louvre to Saint-Germain or Versailles passed by Neuilly. The royal princes, the noblemen and the financiers who drove there discovered on the way delightful spots, groves that looked like parks and a river lined with poplars and willows. Many of them thought it would be ideal to have a small house there; some turned their dreams into stone and cement, garden paths and flowerbeds.

The Comte d'Artois, after a wager with his sister-in-law, Marie-Antoinette, built the " Folie d'Artois," now the Bagatelle, in 74 days : *Parva sed apta* read the inscription engraved over the front, and the Bagatelle is still a delightful resort. After many misadventures it became the property of Lord Hertford in 1832, then of Richard Wallace, his illegitimate son—hence the name of one of the Boulevards that skirt the Bois. It now belongs to the City of Paris, which is responsible for the upkeep of the beautiful gardens and the famous rosery. There are few places close to the City that have as many charms as this park, which is a masterpiece in landscape gardening. Nothing is missing : there are trees, rocks, artificial ponds covered with water-lilies, a large formal rose garden, beds of tulips, forget-me-nots, irises, hyacinths, wide marble steps and fountains. On weekdays visitors are rare, and the fortunate neighbours enjoy the "Folly " of the Comte d'Artois all to themselves.

Belanger, the architect who planned the Bagatelle, also designed for the financier Baudard de Vaudesir, Baron de Saint-James, another " Folly " which still stands today in the Avenue de Madrid; it has both peristyle and pediment, and rough-cast walls of a golden yellow hue. Part of its vast garden has been broken up ; but the Rock, famous in the 18th century, can still be seen—a mass of stone brought there at great cost to satisfy the taste for pre-romantic gardens that prevailed in those days ; it led Baudard de Saint-James to be nicknamed "Man of the Rock." Lucien Bonaparte lived at the Folie Saint-James ; so did Laure d'Abrantès whom Napoleon called " governor" and who became in her old age a source of inspiration for Balzac. Chateaubriand, Madame Récamier and Thiers also strolled in its gardens.

There are other châteaux in the Bois : that of Longchamp, a very unpretentious mansion where lived the Baron Haussmann, Chauchard, and later François Coty—the perfume manufacturer and " *Ami du peuple* " (friend of the people) as was called the newspaper he edited; that of La Muette, the work of Gabriel (but this château was pulled down and in its place a large modern house was erected by Henri de Rothschild), was inhabited by Erard, the great piano maker, then by the Comte de

The Château de Madrid.

The Day of the Longchamp Races.

Franqueville whose name was given to a neighbouring street. Another street nearby is called André Pascal: this was the pseudonym of the dramatic author, Baron Henri.

However, besides these beautiful private houses, the Bois was rich in places where people could meet for pleasure and amusement. It has its century-old restaurants: Armenonville, the Pavillon Dauphine (in olden days the Pavillon Chinois), the Pré Catelan—whose centenary will be celebrated in 1956. No one will ever describe better than Proust the Allée des Acacias, the Sentier de la Vertu, the Tir aux Pigeons and what the Bois was like in the old coaching days. We can no longer pass by these bridle paths without unconsciously searching for Odette Swann, neither can we look at the very artificial islands on the greater lake without conjuring up that unhappy day when Marcel Proust had an appointment there with Mademoiselle de Stermaria, to which he was greatly looking forward, but which was cancelled at the last moment.

Napoleon III, who had lived in London during his exile, and who who loved English parks, did a great deal towards giving the Bois its

Bagatelle.

present-day appearance. It is to him that we owe that maze of paths, the waterfall, and the Jardin d'Acclimatation. The miniature train that runs from Porte Maillot to this dormant Zoo remains in the memory of all Parisian children. In days gone by otters and lions used to wake me up every morning. Since the second World War, there are only two mournful bears, a few birds, monkeys, and merry-go-rounds with multi-coloured cars awaiting the children who come on Sundays. The great menagerie of the Second Empire is now but a sleeping beauty. However under its foliage it is still a beauty.

Through five gates—Sablons, Neuilly, Saint James, Madrid and Bagatelle—the Bois opens up the route from Paris to Neuilly-sur-Seine. Originally there was a fishing harbour and a ferry at the spot where today stands the Pont de Neuilly. Later, in the plain that separated Neuilly from Paris—which was not as large a city it is as today—the villages of Villiers and Ternes came into being. For a long time they formed the rural district of Neuilly. The village of Neuilly, after remaining undeveloped, expanded rapidly when it became possible to cross the Seine by way of a wooden bridge destroyed in 1780, and by a stone bridge built by Perronet. The district near the bridge has witnessed many tragic events. Henry IV was nearly killed there. Pascal also barely escaped death there. The Duc d'Orléans, son of Louis-Philippe, perished nearby. In 1727 the village of Neuilly numbered eight hundred and eighty eight inhabitants; in 1827 seven thousand six hundred and fifty four; in 1949 approximately sixty thousand.

At the beginning of the 19th century, the principal local industry was laundering. Jacques Dulud, laundryman to the Emperor, lived in Neuilly. One day he ran out of felt for his pressing irons, and one of Napoleon's valets gave him an old felt hat of His Majesty's. He was a fervent Bona-partist, and kept this relic instead of cutting it up. It has been preserved as a family heirloom, and each year a *"dîner du chapeau"* is given to celebrate its passing from branch to branch of the family.

In 1825 the Sablonville area was parcelled out; till then it had been used for drying the laundry. A new Neuilly then developed in the neighbourhood of what is today the Porte Maillot. From then on, the whole history of Neuilly concerns the closing of the gap of waste land between Sablonville and the village of the Pont de Neuilly.

Gradually houses began to line the two large avenues. The Town Hall, which for a long time stood on the bridge side of Neuilly, became too far from the centre for the liking of the people of the plain, and in 1836 it was rebuilt in the middle of Sablonville. The bridge area complained. In 1885 the Neuilly Town Hall at last found its real place in the very centre of the built-up area. It is the present day Town Hall, majestic, opulent, of a rather too conventional style, but worthy in size of a large city.

Meanwhile, the Château de Neuilly was also making history. Murat had, with a great flourish, enlarged a country house which was built for the Count d'Argenson in the 18th century. Later, Pauline Borghese led a life of pleasure and dissipation in this new castle. In the person of Louis-Philippe, Neuilly at last found a citizen after its own heart, a respectable family-man and a Bourgeois King. The deep respect shown

The Pavillon d'Armenonville.

GREVENBROECK. — *The Château de la Muette.*

by this town for the junior branch of the House of France is perpetuated in the street names: Rue d'Orléans, Rue Louis-Philippe, Rue de Chartres, which have not been changed (neither, in fact, has the Rue Borghese). However, in 1848 looters from the outskirts of Paris set fire to the castle. One wing alone remained and when the rubble had been cleared, Louis-Napoleon divided up the park. The Boulevard du Château, the Boulevard de la Saussaye, the Boulevard d'Inkermann, the Boulevard d'Argenson, the Boulevard Victor-Hugo were opened up—that chess board of wide avenues with trees on either side, bordered with gardens that extend beyond the church of Saint-Pierre.

Neuilly today has ceased to thrive on its châteaux and laundries. Its major industry is that of children. Great numbers are born there —even greater numbers than can be answered for by the inhabitants. The purity of the air, and the beauty of the parks have caused maternity

homes to multiply in the district. Still greater numbers of children are educated there, for Neuilly is a town of schools. Not only is there a great grammar-school, the Lycée Pasteur, but also the Sainte-Croix Institution; and for girls, Sainte-Marie (one of the Institutions of the Seine where studies are extremely thorough); also Sainte-Geneviève and many other smaller ones. There are proportionally more large families in Neuilly than in any other town in France. That is because children are happier here than in Paris. Besides, the private gardens, the vicinity of the Bois and the wide shady avenues make life healthier in this area. Nursing homes and surgical clinics have, like the schools, chosen Neuilly, where convalescents can take exercise in spacious gardens and where patients find it easier to breathe. The fine American Hospital, with its fair-haired nurses, is located in one of the outer districts.

It stands to reason that Neuilly has commercial activities in which all trades take part; along the Avenue de Neuilly there is a free market which is unusual, for even luxury goods are sold there at the mercy of the elements. We can see in the Neuilly market not only greengrocers, fruiterers, egg and cheese stalls, butchers and fishmongers, but booths where textiles, earthenware, glass-ware and antiques are sold—real bazaars. Many Parisians come there from long distances to market and the place is extraordinarily lively. In olden days, the Neuilly Fair or "Foire de la Saint-Jean" was held on this avenue, as a result of a decree of 1815, with its merry-go go-rounds, its lotteries and its shooting galleries, but it disappeared in 1937, to the great satisfaction of the "Nullileans", whom it deafened without making them any richer. The Neuilly shops have a character of their own. Some of the luxurious shop windows could certainly be Parisian, but in many others we find that conglomeration of objects typical of the haberdasheries, chemists and stationers' shops of a small provincial town.

Political life here is quiet and moderate. After having been Orleanist and Bonapartist, Neuilly became, under Gambetta, truly Republican and Radical, as befitted a small town of small French bourgeois in 1880. The two first Moderates who became members of the Municipal Council, caused a sensation. Today, the development of wealthier quarters has caused the majority to lean more to the Right. However, political activity continues to be very mild. Local groups are traditional rather than professional. They have very odd names such as Philotechnique or the Cyclotourist Society. The great number of booksellers in

the district reveals the presence of cultivated people interested in art and history.

Many artists and writers have settled in Neuilly, which they find quieter than Paris. Baudelaire was for a time a citizen of Neuilly; the mayor Ancelle was also his tutor. It is quite surprising that Ancelle should have a street dedicated to him, but not Baudelaire. Théophile Gautier, the poet with a red waistcoat who, in his youth, was the terror of the bourgeois, came to live there amongst them. Anatole France was married there to Valérie Guérin de Sauville; his father, François-Noel Thibault, the old bookseller, known as " Le Père France," settled in the district when he sold the " Librairie de France," his shop on the Quai Voltaire; he died and was buried in Neuilly, Anatole France joined his parents in the family vault, in the small overcrowded cemetery which, for a long time, has ceased to admit any more deceased. Robert de Montesquiou lived there in the lovely *Pavillon des Muses*, unfortunately destroyed in 1937; it was situated at number 95, Boulevard Maillot. Gyp  owned a property in the neighbourhood, on the corner of the Rue de Chézy and the Boulevard Bineau where his son, the famous surgeon Thierry de Martel, was brought up. Maurice Barrès also resided there, in a white house surrounded by a small garden on the boulevard which today bears his name. Some of the Nullileans remember having seen him strolling under the chestnut trees with the Abbé Bremond and Father Tyrell, the Jesuist modernist. The Tharaud brothers lived in Neuilly before choosing Versailles for their abode; so did La Varende. Montherlant, when a child, played in the Passage Saint-Ferdinand. Dancers and exiled kings loved the district. The last Queen of Naples, and more recently King Carol of Roumania, stayed there; Isadora Duncan's studio was in the Rue Chauvau, and the Dolly Sisters had a small house nestling amidst flowers. We can understand why those artists who were able to, chose Neuilly for their work or retirement rather than other places. They were close enough to Paris not to miss any tempting occasion or gathering of friends, but far enough for the return

Longchamp Race Course.

to Neuilly, on a summer night, to seem delightful. From my very Nullilean window all I can see is an ocean of green leaves, and above them in an infinitude of blue, some little fleecy white clouds that Sisley or Pissaro might have painted.

No distractions reach us tonight from the Town, which is under the spell of the summer festivals. Birds are singing in the chestnut trees; beneath them a horseman rides by; a young girl takes her dog for a walk; a woman pushes her baby in a pram; a young man on a bicycle rides past with one hand on the handle-bars, the other round his girl friend's waist. We might be in the neighbourhood of some quiet seaside resort, when on Sundays, the countless families who at supper-time come out of the small pine-grove that surrounds the lake of Saint-James, walk home with a peaceful provincial step, slowly and quietly. Such is Neuilly-sur-Seine.

André Maurois
of the *Académie Française.*

THE
PLAINE MONCEAU

E-M. PÉROT

D. BOUCHÈNE. — *The Parc Monceau.*

ET ME AD-
mit that, had I been asked ten or fifteen years ago, to write about the Monceau plain in a book dedicated to Paris, I might have been reluctant to do so. And yet, this district is very familiar to me. I spent the whole of my childhood there, and a considerable part of my youth; it was very nearly my birthplace. But as soon as I was free to do so, I left it, with no intention of returning. It was a district which seemed to me to be lacking in features as well as in character. It was rather as a provincial returning to his native town that I used to visit my mother and father, when they were still alive, in our house in the Avenue de Villiers beyond the Place Péreire, just before reaching the fortifications.

Today when I visit those of my friends and relations who live in the Monceau plain, I sometimes feel a kind of longing which might almost be a longing for a paradise lost. I have ceased to consider this district, where I lived as a little boy, as being either beautiful or unattractive. Elsewhere I love and seek for the past of Paris; here it is my own past that I seek for and love; here that past awaits me. It looks out for me; and sitting on the terrace of a very commonplace café on the Place Péreire, after a morning prowl in the neighbourhood, I have the feeling of being in the heart of a cemetery: all the shadows I have awakened are there around me in such numbers, thronging so closely together, that I hesitate to count them.

Apart from slight alterations, nothing has greatly changed. Generally speaking, the scene has remained as it was. Had that most attractive circular garden not been laid out in the centre of the Place Péreire, it would still be just as it was at the beginning of the century; that is to say, as un-Parisian as possible, reminding us of the peaceful greyness of a small country town off the beaten track. The railway cutting for the *Petite Ceinture* is still there. Few trains run today; they are like the small country locals by which villagers reach their county town. The

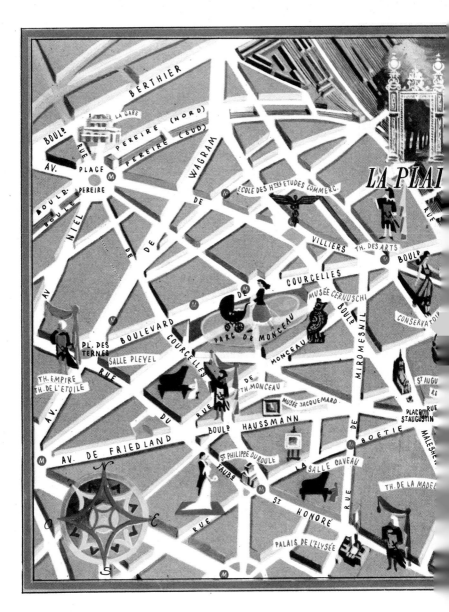

little white station—a touching sight, like an antique trinket, or a child's toy—is still there, inviting the local inhabitants to "go down to Paris."

" Go down to Paris " was the stock phrase at home. In the days when the Métro did not exist, in the days of the slow horse-drawn coaches, there was only this *Petite Ceinture* railway line to bring the half-citizens, as we then were, rapidly into the centre of the town. We only felt Parisian when the convoy of antiquated double-deck railway-carriages had emerged from the Europe tunnel. The Place de Rome, the Terminus Hôtel, the cafés and restaurants in the Rue Saint-Lazare were for us the threshold of the civilized world.

All around the Place Péreire I can recognize the same shops, most of them still faithful to the same trades : the dairy where *cœurs de Fontaine-bleau* were so rightly famous; Christine the pastrycook; the two cafés (the " Dessirier " and the " Café Blanc "); the hairdresser's; the chemist with his large coloured pear-shaped jars. On both corners of the Avenue de Villiers on the Paris side, a grocer and a glass-works still face each other. But a florist has taken the place of the stationer where I used to buy my copybooks from a one-eyed, fuzzy-haired, bearded old woman; opposite the Métro exit an astounding bar, the last word in fashion, has taken the place of the pork-butcher's where, at all seasons, a large bouquet of roses, made of lard, ornamented his shop window. These immaculate white roses would have faded from my memory long ago if they were not still kept fresh in my mind by their association with a beautiful plump fresh-complexioned butcher's wife who was the living image of Titian's *Flora*.

Nearly everywhere throughout the district

I have found in the course of my pilgrimage that same constancy of setting. A few large modern blocks of flats have appeared since those I saw rise up in days gone by; either on the land owned by the Gas Company (in the Rue de Courcelles) or in place of Marie Bashkirtseff's mansion (Rue Ampère), or again on certain plots of waste land and private gardens sacrificed to speculative builders.

The district of the Monceau plain continues, and in some ways seems fated to be, a district of private houses.

Nearly all these private houses are quite small. Their narrow fronts, bracketed together, give the impression of a display of samples. They are individualistic and extremely diverse: a number of them imitate, more or less faithfully, more or less successfully, French, Gothic or Italian Renaissance style. Others try to imitate Norman chalets or Moorish pavilions. Some are decorated with mosaics or oriental earthenware. Stained glass abounds in the windows and wrought-iron work on the doors. Quite often these picturesque façades conceal small gardens, which, surrounded by the small gardens of the neighbouring houses, together make a sort of interior park, shady and full of blossom, where blackbirds used to respond to the musical notes of the pianos.

In some streets there is a practically continuous succession of these small private houses, that conjures up over half-a-century of Parisian life; a life nearly as distant from ours as that led by Madame de Sévigné's contemporaries in their private houses of the Marais district.

The vogue for the Monceau plain was brought about by the artists who adopted it before the end of the last century, tempted to do so by its tranquillity; and tempted also by the fact that there they could purchase land cheaply, and so, in houses built to their taste and in accordance with their desires, they could feel at home whilst among their friends. This vogue came about shortly after the 1870 war, and reached its peak between about 1890 and 1900. It almost entirely ceased during the First World War. Today all the artists who inhabited these private houses are dead, and, with very few exceptions, have not been replaced by other artists. Material difficulties of present-day life, hard or impossible to solve, have resulted in most of these artists' families leaving the district in the course of the last few years. Companies, offices, government departments have taken their place—or consulates and other public services. Others are now " studios " where dancing, music and other accomplishments are taught; others again have become " beauty parlours." This host of changes has profoundly altered the unity and harmony of the Monceau plain. Its general appearance has remained the same : only this morning I recognised its features. But alas ! henceforth I am afraid they have lost all personal expression.

Painters predominated among the artists who lived in

the Monceau plain in my childhood and early manhood : a type of painter which is still perhaps in existence but which is now generally speaking superseded; no longer appreciated by, or even known to, the public. The painters in those days were "society painters" and, if not men-about-town themselves, they were at least appreciated and praised by "society people." They were in no way innovators, nor, on the other hand, were they academic. Their object was to be appreciated by a wealthy, cosmopolitan and fashionable clientele. Nearly all of them had been awarded decorations, and could more or less qualify as members of the Institute. The great event of the year was the *Salon*—or rather the *Salons* —that of the Champs-Elysées (the official one) and that of the Champs-de-Mars (the dissident one). The whole of the Monceau plain was in a state of effervescence and frantically at work for varnishing day, when an unbridled fever spread without restraint from house to house.

I can still see myself in some of these houses to which as a special favour, I occasionally accompanied my parents. They would go there as neighbours and often as friends—invited to ritual receptions where the pictures that were to dazzle the crowds in the two "*palais*" (long since razed to the ground) were presented.

The honoured guests at these parties were welcomed in vast studios that covered the whole of the top floor of these small houses. The most fascinating of these studios was that of the Hungarian painter, Munkacsy, in the Avenue de Villiers, facing the Monge school (today the Lycée Carnot). It appears that Liszt greatly appreciated Munkacsy's huge canvases, bold and vigorous in execution. The artist was short, stout and nimble, but dreaded climbing ladders. He had, therefore, in order to avoid perilous acrobatics, opened in the floor of his studio a long slit through which, by an ingenious mechanism, his gigantic canvas could be raised from, or lowered to, the room beneath, according to which part of the picture he wanted to work on. This contrivance seemed wonderful to me, for I could imagine that I was at the theatre !

Most of these painters "specialised;" they were past masters in one subject or in one style, to which they limited themselves. Every spring one went to the Rue Alphonse de Neuville to admire the shepherds with their flocks, painted by Gaston Guignard; and to the Avenue Gourgaud to admire Taulow's rushing waters. In the Boulevard Berthier, where there were houses full of painters, Cazin's sand dunes

by moonlight awaited admiration; so did Duez' beach scenes, the
flourishing beauties of the day by Bodini, the ploughmen and reapers
painted by Lhermite, Rochegrosse's *Chevaliers aux fleurs*, etc. The Rue
Ampère and its surroundings belonged to the traditionalist portrait painters—to Flameng and Roybet. All these names—I could extend the list
indefinitely—are more or less forgotten today. But who knows whether
posterity will not one day "discover" pictures bearing these signatures,
which will become well-known, not so much for their artistic value as for
their documentary interest?

A few steps away from the café where I am writing this, lived two
painters whom I knew well, and whom I liked and admired very much:
Albert Besnard and Cappiello. For many years I was welcomed with
affection in that house in the Rue Guillaume Tell that my father had built

for Besnard. I had free access to the *grand atelier du fond*. I witnessed the birth of many a wonderful painting shimmering with light and diversified with rainbow colours. I feel sure that one day they will find their place in the museums from which they have so unjustly and ungratefully been excluded.

Cappiello lived in the narrow and dismal Rue Le Châtelier nearby. How many times has he kept me company on the terrace of the Café Dessirier ! Will he not suddenly appear round the corner of the avenue, slim and elegant, like the Harlequins that play around in his pictures, with his quick gestures and his amazingly mobile face and features ? He will sit down beside me and start to tell me one of his stories, always a little difficult to follow but always devoid of malice or spite.

In those days there were as many actors and singers as there were painters in the Monceau plain. They also had a fondness for private houses. The most famous of all was unquestionably Sarah Bernhardt. The house where she lived so long, and where she died, can still be seen in that part of the Boulevard Péreire where the railway cutting has retained grassy banks and where the acacias smell sweetly in spring. On my way to and from the *Lycée* I sometimes chanced on the strange carriage that bore Sarah to her theatre. This carriage was a combination of cab and victoria.

Behind the coachman and liveried footmen one could just see a gilded old idol, lost in veils and furs, nestling in the shell of the cab. Sarah, then at the peak of her legendary fame, used to respond graciously to the constant greetings of the passers-by, who were moved beyond words. In her principality of Monceau Sarah was treated as a queen or as a fairy godmother. Most of the time one faithful admirer or another would take post before her house. When Sarah was away on tour I was once, while still a child, taken into her house by her old friend, the painter Georges Clairin, who was also a friend of my mother's. I have faint recollections of a vast studio, encumbered, and choked with a litter of woodwork, palm trees and animal pelts. A mysterious light, submarine in effect, displayed a welter of bric-à-brac such as antique seats, divans, ewers, trinket boxes, chests, bronze pieces, musical instruments, enamels, lanterns, perfume-burners etc. It all seemed to have arrived there like an alluvial deposit. One had the impression of being in a gigantic shrine. However, all these ill-assorted relics, whilst being a demonstration of Sarah's bad taste, revealed at the same time her genius which loathed disorder and never gave way to the hazards of improvisation. Even in her lack of taste Sarah was sure of herself, after the manner of a great artist and of a perfect craftsman. Like Poussin, she could have said "I have neglected nothing."

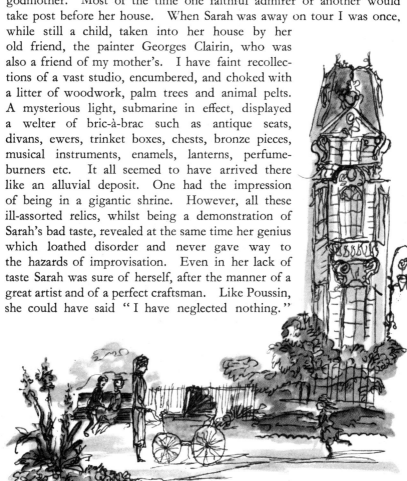

The Comédie Française was also represented in the Monceau plain by Julia Bartet ("the Divine"), by Suzanne Reichemberg ("the *Petite Doyenne*"), by Raphael Duflos and Coquelin junior; the Opéra by Rose Caron, Bréval, Litvinne, Jane Hatto, Cléo de Mérode, and by the tenor Alvarez. Jeanne Granier, Marguerite Ugalde, Paulette Darty, Manon Loti, Otero, Liane de Pougy also lived there. At the time of the Flower Show these ladies could be seen driving to the Bois in barouches decked with garlands and bouquets.

What a very "small town" appearance Paris had in those days. There was not a motor-car in the streets; only horsemen and bicyclists and those light cabs with flap-seats and no taximeters, whose drivers charged one franc fifty "for the run" (whatever the distance) and two francs "for the hour." When these cabs came from the station, some poor devil would

The Interior of a Town House about 1860.

JONGKIND. — *The Monceau Toll-Gate.*

nearly always run behind to unload the luggage on arrival. Street lamps were still lit by gas and the lamp-lighters wore great blue smocks with small crimson collars. The postmen brought the mail—four times a day—in stiff leather boxes rather like small coffins. To water the roads, jointed pipes were used mounted on minute wheels. Spare horses, followed by thousands of sparrows, were stationed at the bottom of the Rue du Rocher and of the Rue Monceau. Sick people were nursed and operated on at home and not in nursing homes, and when the case was serious, or the patient well-known, a thick bedding of straw was laid in the street in front of the house to muffle the sound of wheels. Hot baths were still brought to the house. What has become of those quaint, hand-drawn vehicles where the hot water barrel was topped with the bath tub and flanked with half a dozen copper pails ? And what has become of the wooden boards of the sandwich men ? What has happened to the grubby little round of felt with which the unfortunate old Brichanteau used to wander from café to café, making it into Louis XI's cap, Basile's or Napoleon's hat ?

I have taken to the road again, in the district where this morning I am the only idler. Before " going down to Paris " again I want to continue and end my pilgrimage by going first to the fortifications, then to the Parc Monceau.

These fortifications, which were razed at the beginning of the century, used to rise like an insurmountable barrier between the Monceau plain on the one hand, and Levallois-Perret and Neuilly on the other. They were quite close to our house and it was on their *glacis* that, as a child, I used to play while the maid kept an eye on me—more or less. She was very vexed at having to go there, considering—justifiably—that the place was vulgar and ill-frequented. As for me, I thoroughly enjoyed it and delighted in racing along the path above the moat, in company with perky little urchins, and in digging deep caves out of which my brother and I had to be dragged by force, covered in dust and with bleeding knees. Another great pleasure was to throw stones at the boys of the "Zone" who used to play outside the walls of Paris. There was also a game which was not quite as innocent, and in which I took part only as a spectator. One of my rough little friends would hide in a corner at the top of the fortifications. He would then let a rope down, to the end of which an accomplice at the foot of the wall would surreptitiously tie some foodstuff—chicken or rabbit—that was liable to town dues on entering Paris. When I reached college age, the fortifications passed out of my life.

Where they used to stand, there now extends a district of new houses that might be aeroliths. Because of its massive proportions and its particularly " twentieth century " style of architecture, this district belongs neither to the antiquated Monceau plain, nor to wooded Neuilly, nor to industrial Levallois.

This long stretch of blocks of flats is dated by the names of the streets. There are, on the one hand, reminders of the heroism of the " Great War "—the Boulevards of Dixmude, Yser, Douaumont, Fort de Vaux; on the other hand a bold miscellany of writers, musicians and artists, most of whom died in the decade between 1915 and 1925—from Ferdinand Brunetière to Jean Moréas, from Catulle Mendès to Paul Adam, from Gervex to Odilon Redon, from Claude Debussy to Albert Samain. The most " consequential " street was given the name of Stéphane Mallarmé.

It is too soon for these houses to have given the district a character. The fundamental and organic fault to be found with it is that it grew up too rapidly, although this happened in two phases. Everywhere else Paris gradually caught up with and annexed villages in her slow process of development. Beyond the walls that were called the " Fermiers

Généraux" the capital expanded by absorbing La Chapelle, La Villette, Belleville, Grenelle, Auteuil, Passy, Chaillot, Roule etc. But between the hamlets of Ternes and Batignolles, the Monceau plain was a vast hunting ground, with fields and vineyards sparsely dotted over it. It extended, with scarcely an inhabitant, as far as the village of Villiers, which was then the end of the world.

This district would therefore be devoid of ancient remains if the Duke of Orleans had not taken it into his head to create out of nothing a park in the English style, on the outskirts of the plain; this park was later reduced in size and disfigured, but it nevertheless links the Paris of today with the Paris of former days.

And here I approach that gloomy Rue de Prony, at the end of which there appears, as isolated and venerable as a relic of the past, the Rotunda (or Pavilion) of Chartres. It is older than the Parc Monceau, for it was one of the gates of Paris that was erected by the architect Ledoux in the " Fermiers Généraux " wall.

As to the park itself, it is the work of a charming amateur and not of a professional—Louis Carrogis, very much a plebeian, who had come from the Ariège to play his part in Paris. He succeeded in doing so by becoming, under the name of Carmontelle, the official entertainer of the Duke of Orleans—" Fat Philip " or " Gros Père. " During his twenty three years of court life, he wrote for the court hundreds of proverbs, and sketched hundreds of portraits. Both the proverbs and the portraits were delightfully spirited, skilful and elegant. The easy-going nonchalance they express leaves us the most accurate picture of the fashionable world of that period and gives their author a definite place among the " petits maîtres. "

When the Duke of Orleans died in 1783 Carmontelle stayed on in the service of his late master's son, Philippe-Egalité, and it was for the latter that the old " entertainer, " then in his seventies, designed in the new style—that is to say in the English style—the park that we have just reached.

Alas ! nearly all the novelties with which Carmontelle so abundantly decorated the *Folie de Chartres* have now disappeared. Where is the maze with its echoes, the Chinese village with its pagoda, the Dutch village with its windmill, the Swiss farm, the remains of the Temple of Mars, the hill planted with vines and topped by a minaret ? Where are the gardens of yellow flowers, of blue flowers, the marshes full of water lilies ? Where are the ruins of the Gothic castle, whose arches concealed a voluptuous oriental lounge ? Of all these charming and picturesque fancies there only remain the Egyptian pyramid, a grotto, and a small-scale naval spectacle.

It would be idle to regret it : notwithstanding these few relics, the *Folie de Chartres* exists no more. Its eighteenth century fragrance has vanished for ever. Now one breathes only the rather thick and heavy perfume of the Second Empire. In point of fact, the Parc Monceau dates from 1861, when it was entirely redesigned by Alphand. Such as it is, it has its style, its charm—an opulent style, a fulsome charm, that conjure up the days of crinolines and wide-brimmed straw hats. The Parc conjures up, for ageing survivors of the nineties, the heroines, of the younger Dumas, of Bourget and Guy de Maupassant; furtive

The Folie-Monceau.

rendezvous under the trees, "the first kiss through the veil" before the clandestine and conclusive visit to the "bachelor's rooms"—close at hand. Also those fine wholesome nannies, shining like pumpkins in their vast braided mantles, their refined lace bonnets whose pins with large golden knobs secured wide crimson, emerald green or tartan ribbons billowing to the ground.

This Second Empire and Third Republic stamp is still more apparent in the private houses that surround the park. Here they are certainly not small private houses, and they were not artists, writers or actors who dwelt in these ostentatious dwellings that look like castles or palaces. Now they have for the most part been given over to commercial firms, high finance, chocolate kings, wine magnates—and successful foreigners. The latter have given their names to the museums—as for instance the Cernuschi and Camondo collections—all that remains to remind us of the Chinese village and the eighteenth century of old Carmontelle.

And we would like at this point, before laying down our pen, to express a wish. Since Carmontelle is the only ghost of the past who can be expressly located in this district, would it not be a friendly and worthy gesture to dedicate to him some small memorial in this park? On the day of its unveiling one of his delightful *Proverbes* might be performed close by, for they were written by their author to be acted in the open air—*La Maison des Boulevards, Les Enfants Désobéissants, La Sortie des Orangers,* or *Le Moment de la Promenade.*

Jean-Louis VAUDOYER,
of the Académie Française.

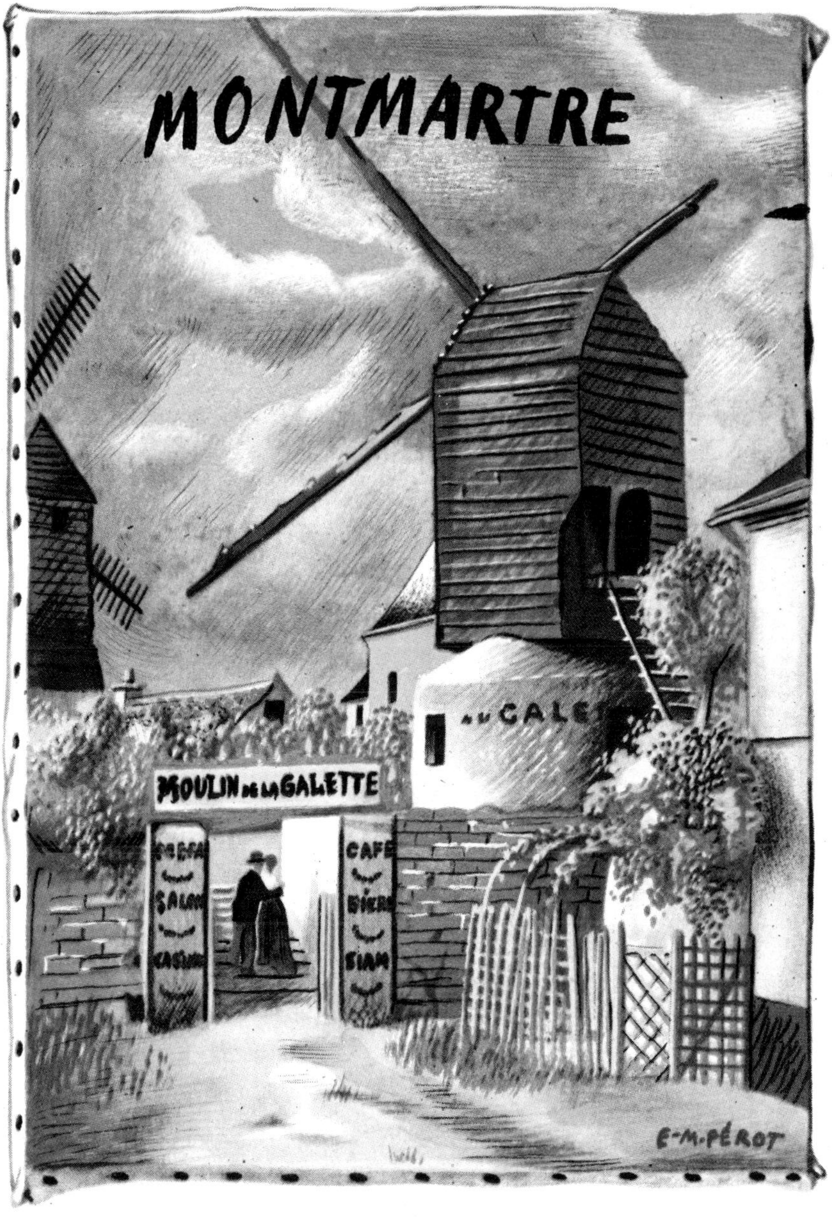
MONTMARTRE
MOULIN de la GALETTE
CAFÉ
SIAM
E-M-PÉROT

UTRILLO. — *Montmartre.*

OWN THE

course of the years, a regular lamentation has been heard, a note of bitter sadness that tinges every conversation on the subject—Montmartre is dying, Montmartre is dead. " Ah, if only you had known the real Montmartre, " the veterans say, " that of Degas, of Toulouse-Lautrec and of Renoir. " The succeeding generation sighs, a little contemptuously... " Yes, the Montmartre of La Goulue, of Grille d'Egout, and Valentin le Désossé. " The greatest period, however, was immediately after Impressionism, before 1914 : Frédé, the Lapin Agile, Dorgelès, Carco, Mac Orlan, the counterfeiters and the *fauves*, the *bateau-lavoir*, Picasso and Max Jacob. Then the alternate choirs, very far away, begin to wail : " the black habits, the Abbey, the Black Cat, oh ! the Black Cat of the black habits " and the doggerel and " he who won the Golden Fleece, " Rodolphe Salis, and Aristide Bruant... " Parce Domine " and " Saint-Lazare. "

In reality, Montmartre is still the same object of curiosity, sentimental, both retrograde and ahead of the times, and with only slight changes of setting—so slight !—almost impervious to changing fashions : a magnificent and squalid repository wherein to weep over the memories of youth, since it is admitted that everyone—even those who vegetate in the remotest provinces—everyone took " three short turns, " at least on the northern or southern flank of the hill, long ago or recently, for better or worse, to exercise their memories.

Montmartre, established firmly within its frontiers, does not change. It has its smell of trees and thin smoke, its neighbourly familiarity, almost Mediterranean, and its well defined standards of conduct in its various quarters.

For Montmartre is a town, although it is generally agreed to call it a village by reason of the central hamlet, intellectual and village-like, that dominates and crowns the hill.

Walk in Montmartre without taking any notice of explanatory guides. But pay attention to the frontiers ! They are more definitive than any illusory iron curtain.

Montmartre is not large, but like all labyrinths you have only to go down the same street in a different direction to discover an entirely different aspect. These melancholy gardens with gaps in the wall revealing clusters of nettles, brambles and rubble composed of regular pyramids of rusty tins, mattress springs and waste paper like letters on a battlefield, these are not like the waste land that is to be found in all large cities—there still remain some clumps of lilac and, here and there, like a gay reveller, a hardy cherry-tree spreads out its pink and white decorations on a rather crumpled lawn, between a rabbit hutch and a cage containing a bird already full of reason and wit, such as a magpie or an oriole, or one of those species of river quail that seem to thrive only in *concierges'* lodges. Between narrow streets, a park as sumptuous as a forest is enclosed within propped-up walls, with small hotels, little houses and hovels side by side. Such are the immediate surroundings of the hamlet of Montmartre.

Montmartre is bounded on the west by a cemetery, like a stagnant pond of memory, under the Caulaincourt bridge. The Rue Caulaincourt and the Rue Custine, defended by staircases like counterscarps, form, with the Boulevard Barbès, the north-eastern boundary of Montmartre. The south is vaguely bordered by an illuminated front of night-clubs, restaurants and cafés with their regular customers and their swindlers, and, right in the centre,

MONTMARTRE

a lighted shop—" Chemist open all night "—with white-coated assistants and the smell of ether —a first-aid post for attacks of the " blues," the suicides that did not come off, the over-lively arguments and brawls. Nearby, the most celebrated cabaret in Montmartre still bases its shows on sexual inversion; it is the classic example of sham.

In the morning, the south of Montmartre comes under the spell of springtime and, from the Rue des Abbesses to the Rue Chaptal, it resumes its original

character. We realise that this pleasure district possesses all the family graces of upper Montmartre—its ingenuity, its careless imitation of a provincial town, its market with barrows lining the pavement of the Rue Lepic, its well watered terraces; its loafers, sleek of hair and blue of chin under their bizarre felt hats; ladies in négligé, shopping bag in hand; and that lesson of optimism and laziness that is provided by the first buds of the forlorn-looking trees extending from the Place d'Anvers to the Place Clichy, on that charming, but ill-famed stretch of boulevard that has inspired so many songs.

During those four years of night that weighed on the world, Mont-

TOULOUSE-LAUTREC. — *Bruant.*

martre, as a prisoner of the invading power, resigned herself very un-willingly to the heavy-handed gallantry of the conqueror. The black-out was more sinister here than elsewhere, with scattered strains of music rising apparently from the cellars and that mixed rabble of guides and girls, captives of their own debauched destiny.

During the war, the satire of the Montmartre *chansonniers* was subdued. They took little heed of the invader. There was talk of a few occasional pin-pricks that were paid for by the closing of a cabaret. Oléo's sponta-neous interjections to the audience from her window at the Théâtre de Dix-Heures deserve mention in despatches. That mischievious imp, with her mop of black hair like a seventeenth century wig, a broad smile revealing her sparkling teeth, was unable to resist the pleasure of making an unequivocal remark to some late-comers to the boxes, in the year 1943: " It's not easy to get through—as at Stalingrad." The next day the gentlemen from the Kommandatura invaded the little theatre, revolver in hand, and left the director, Raoul Arnaud, half dead on the floor. The Théâtre de Dix-Heures has witnessed the début of such rising stars as Pierre Destailles, Jacques Morel and Grello. Raoul Arnaud has a way of ferreting out youthful talent.

The Lune Rousse is, if I may dare make so bold a comparison, the Comédie-Française of musical cabarets. Well-established artists have given lavishly of their best. It is a worthy gesture, since the stars of satire, like those of song, do not often resist the allure of the higher salaries offered by the fashionable and exclusive cabarets.

The Deux-Anes goes in for comic songs and revues, with an acid and bantering tone that is not the least of its charms.

The Montmartre of Gay Paris has taken some time to resume its neon-signs and to light up the doors of its night-clubs again. But it is all there now—the machine for raising the visitors' emotions is functioning anew, with its style, its art, the courtesy of its head waiters, the dignity of its courtesans and the set standards of its habitués.

The Tabarin is an exception. It is a very resplendent show with popular appeal, based on compositions in colour, precious materials and tissues, live, naked caryatids, as beautiful as the very image of nudity; frenzied dance numbers, but as well-regulated as a parade; delicate eroticism presented with lightning speed and snatched away—such as quickens desire. This Ali Baba's treasure offers its splendours to the gaze of thousands of bewildered tourists who swarm out of motor-coaches led by stern guides for whom " Paris tonight " is no joke but a night march with carefully planned halts and a rapid succession of shows.

If you do not number among those who enjoy gregarious pleasures, you will like to enter the ranks of the aristocrats of the night hours for whom " supper in Montmartre " has a traditional connotation of good tone, freedom without licence, mild intoxication, dances, floor-shows and a rather crazy atmosphere among good friends. Then reserve your table at Chez Florence because you cannot get in there without booking. One meets and greets acquaintances there and it is less a cabaret of habitués than a sort of open club which royal personages sometimes care to grace with their presence, unmasked and undisguised, with the full knowledge and tactful assent of an audience that is too well drilled in the proper respect due to princes to regard them as strange animals.

Chez Florence, founded about 1928 by a Negress singer of the "Blue Bird" troupe, was immediately adopted by the élite—which is always somewhat clannish in its amusements. In the course of twenty years it has maintained its prestige as a distinguished night-club with a drawing-room atmosphere.

In a totally different style, "Eve" seasons with a gently erotic flavour an evening party where an excellent swing orchestra, combined with laughter and animation, will enable you to forget yesterday and not brood over tomorrow.

The night-clubs offer floor shows and expensive champagne, but the ordinary little man in Montmartre goes on living his humdrum life. Some people refer to the "wings" of Montmartre, meaning thereby the *cafés-tabacs*, the small restaurants and bars, that are quiet during the day-time, and wake up to a strange night life, which appears "shady" only to passing visitors. They are what they are, with their hubbub of conversation, political and professional, and the regular noises of card-players. Obviously there are the "pimps"—there is no hesitation here in calling a spade a spade. And there is the drug traffic, there are the smash-and-grab merchants and the slashers. After all, it takes all sorts to make a world. But there are also the employees of the night-clubs, the artists and the musicians, those who are out on the spree and those who are out to line their pockets with the odd coppers, and even worthy middle-class folk who find it impossible to go to bed before the tenth glass of beer and the tenth game of cards.

Night clubs come and go, but the *cafés-tabac* remain; restaurants also take their tone from the whim of the moment. Montmartre retains a few little outposts with dwindling garrisons. And there the brightly-lit front of Clichy-Rochechouart ends.

Though the names of the night clubs have changed, though the Abbaye de Thélème has, in losing its sign, also lost its former reputation for luxury and tradition, and the Moulin-Rouge has become a cinema, still the successors of the Abbaye are on the look-out for new forms of attraction, and the Moulin-Rouge has still the same outward appearance, like those venerable relics of the " nineties "—Le Ciel and l'Enfer with their sorry-looking paste-board decorations " paved with good intentions, " for over half a century. The Moulin-Rouge, despite its lethargic slumber between 1910 and 1920, maintained its place in the world's esteem. In 1913, I was present at a duel in its gardens that had an unexpectedly absurd ending. After ten bouts, one of the contestants

thought he heard the order " stop. " He put up his sword and at once received from his opponent a thrust that pierced his forearm and biceps. At that moment, a worthy musician who was leaving a rehearsal at the Moulin, touched my shoulder and said, " What tricks they get up to at the cinema nowadays. " That goes back to the days of duels, top-hats and the last ladies to be sumptuously entertained; days that have gone for ever and are now practically legendary.

After the first war, between

1926 and 1928, the fashion for men of letters to meet late at night in restaurants came to an end. The Brasserie Hans in the Place St. Georges, that Georges Feydeau, Capus, Gomez Carrillo, etc, made their resort before the war, had disappeared, and a whole group of writers met in a very strange spot that was called La Potinière, between the Place Blanche and the Rue Coustou. The lady at the desk wore a monocle and the pianist, called Wolf, played whatever was asked of him. Diners were requested to bring their own good humour and to provide their own turns. In that heavy, smoky atmosphere and in a lingering odour of fried potatoes, could be seen

A poster by Chéret.

Carco, André Derain, Michel Georges-Michel, André Warnod, as well as *comédiennes* and *chansonniers*. La Goulue, down on her uppers, came there to scrounge at about two in the morning and to swill a jug of red wine. Henri Béraud made his appearance about 3 a.m. There was already pandemonium in that haven of grace, and *chansonniers* such as Noël-Noël did not have to be asked twice to provide something from their repertoire, while the intervals were filled in with old military and medical student airs that became " bluer " with the approach of dawn. The public knew how to create an atmosphere, of which the least that can be said is that at times it suggested the din of a sergeants' mess when someone has made a wager, or a Flemish Fair when a prize fighter has made his appearance. As an excellent waiter, who loved this restaurant, artlessly expressed it : " People don't know how to enjoy themselves like that nowadays. "

But to end this idle chatter : the stories, anecdotes and dramas in this one little corner of Montmartre that lies between Pigalle and Clichy would be sufficient to fill a library. The walks are not always peopled with ghosts of the past. Nothing is less ghost-like than this quarter, that is at the same time so old and so young, popular without being vulgar, full of mysteries, yet crystal-clear, and whose diversity of attractions produce an atmosphere that is still appreciated even by those who no longer want to be attracted.

The Rue Lepic, which is the extension of the Rue Blanche, and rises and twists round the side of the hill to reach the Moulin de la Galette, has twenty different facets at the same time of the year, and even on the same day. It rises late—not until the sausage-makers have put in their shop-windows the bait for rapid lunches. A perfect angelus sounds in the dairies (for the custom of early morning delivery has gone) and white doors standing wide open exude the powerful scent of many cheeses. Then the procession of barrows begins its upward march. The stage is set. The coffee percolators emit their jets of steam. Bar-tenders, like jugglers, in blue overalls and rolled-up sleeves, arrange rows of

The " Ciel " and the " Enfer ".

The Moulin Rouge.

glasses on the counter and fill them with white wine. It might be a scene in the Halles—but no, this is definitely Montmartre. It is the summit—there is no need to go any further—it has its own atmosphere.

At midday the call of the *apéritif* or the *Vittel-menthe* assembles the local inhabitants. Those who have to mingle in the world of foreigners will be going down to the cafés of the Place Blanche.

Here the Rue Lepic recognises its own people; they are, as they say, " good types." In summer, most of them calmly walk about in their shirt sleeves; the tradespeople sit down to table in their professional clothes. They have no time to waste, preferring to hurry back to work and return to the café later for a white wine or a *pastis*. The sun beats down with full force on this charming street. The talk runs on sport; the lottery booths are within spraying distance of a soda-syphon and tickets are taken at the last moment. The water in the gutter bubbles merrily like a cascade; the café awnings, slanting and narrow, create coloured shadows reminiscent of seaside beaches and watering places. The little barrows have put out to sea, rolling like barques towards the plains of the city. The Rue Lepic, with no buses and no noisy traffic, is about to have lunch in peace. It is the hour when the cats make discreet visits from one house to another, when the free dogs of the free commune of Montmartre wander off to important functions, watering the lamp-posts and keeping guard lest any mongrel should breach the frontiers of the proud and independent Rue Lepic, the country of unleashed hounds and masters indifferent to police regulations.

Towards evening the street becomes active, gossipy and domestic. Little groups assemble on the door-steps. It is five o'clock. Some well-dressed women have a few secrets to confide to their concierges. There are some last shopping errands to be done; "Whatever made me forget the lights for the cat, the wine and the *cotelette pannée* for last thing at night?" "I've not overlooked anything? No." And, weighed down with her household cares, the gallant lady goes off to earn her bread and butter in the neighbourhood of the Galleries or the Gare St. Lazare, or perhaps to some confidential rendez-vous in a quiet little flat.

None the less, the street remains peaceful and honest, immutable, with that un-ruffled tranquillity that braves wars, revolutions and even changing fashions—because it appears insignificant but is in reality as enduring as human nature.

A wedding party goes down the Rue Lepic. It follows the family tradition; tables are booked on the

DEGAS. — *L'Absinthe.*

first floor of a restaurant which, for more than a century, has commemorated first communions and marriages far more indelibly than the preceding religious ceremonies. Do not expect anything picturesque : here is the expression of a great, tradition—popular, lusty but charming — which, in its costumes, songs, jokes, dances and nice collective inebriation, assures the prosperity of these temples of wine and wit that defy fashion, scepticism and even the ancestral faith.

Walk up the street on the right-hard side. One café seems to be reserved for men in their forties, all serious in mien and similar in appearance. You overhear scraps of conversation in this vein :

TOULOUSE-LAUTREC
Valentin Le Désossé and La Goulue.

" Old chap, I began as a lift-boy in 1926 at the Carlton in Cannes. "

" No bluffing, old man. You were a page-boy. "

" Lift-boy, I say ! "

" I was there as a clerk, same as my boss. "

" And I'm telling you—I made 250 francs a day. "

" Then you were working in a sweatshop. I was making 450 a day in 1926—it was the regular rate. "

So do these worthies who have been page-boys, porters, head waiters of night clubs, tell their tales of the heroic days when a five franc note was real money, and when countries with a high rate of exchange did not hesitate to abuse that financial superiority and crush the proletariat of the palaces with their largesse.

At night the Rue Lepic is silent; a few American cars like gleaming shadows go up the street during the dog-days towards the Place du

411

GEORGES MICHEL. — *The Windmills of Montmartre*.

Tertre. Then the cats take over the street, on the ground level.

We will come back tomorrow when it is daylight. Not by the road we have just taken. Every winding road should be explored, in Montmartre more than anywhere else.

We will take the Métro to Pigalle station. The moving staircase rattles away, turning two steps at a time at the end of its course. A landing, a second moving staircase, and we are out in that charming *Place* that, in bygone days, was the terminus of the strange, creaking omnibuses, just in front of the Café des Omnibus (strange coincidence !) where the " models' market " surrounded the fountain. Nowadays the *Place* is clear, except for an excess of street hoardings. A queer café houses the " musicians' market. " Every evening they come there in the hope of filling in, or getting an odd engagement.

The Cirque Médrano, rich in artistic associations with Degas and Toulouse-Lautrec, looks, with its familiar architecture, like a veritable circus museum. It has not changed since the time when, under the Second Empire, it formed one of the boundary marks of Paris. Montmartre was at that time a pleasant suburb outside the walls, a suburb that had jealously kept its village-like appearance—although joined to the great city—with its windmills and lanes, its background of farms without crops or cattle, its diminishing orchards, operetta vineyards and cottages for two. Montmartre was annexed by Paris in 1860 and submitted to the invasion of the artists with the gentle, mischievous smile of a village servant girl. The advance guard of the painters, and the sculptors who needed roomy studios, invaded the Rue Berthe, the Rue Gabrielle, the Rue des Martyrs and the Rue des Abbesses, before daring to attack the heights where useless windmills turned, without wheat or flour, and on whose sails a miller had been crucified in 1814.

By way of the Rue Dancourt we reach the attractive little Théâtre de l'Atelier, which is neither provincial nor suburban. At the far end of a pleasing square, it represents the last architectural relic of the theatre of melodrama outside the city boundary, where the same little audience used to come to applaud the heroes, hiss the villains, and fall in love with the young heroines. It needed a man who was crazy about the stage, like Dullin, to rediscover that passionate, popular love of fiction, of the sonorous verb and the illusions without which it is impossible to live. A theatre beyond the city walls, beyond compare, the theatre of Montmartre.

From that charming square we will set out on a devious course through streets that have not changed—the Rue Berthe, the Rue Gabrielle—

RENOIR. — *The Moulin de la Galette.*

craning our necks at those flights of steps whose summit is lost in the skies. To climb them is a matter of breath and youth. By way of the Rue Durantin we will rejoin the Rue Lepic in the loop that it forms there.

And here is the Moulin de la Galette, so dear to the author of " La Bonne Vie " (Galtier-Boissière) which maintains all the traditions of dance and love with or without " the little blue flower."

The Place du Tertre used to look rather bogus with its three rustic cabarets for tourists, its sunshades, its tribe of street musicians, singers, tragedians, acrobats, jugglers and fire-swallowers. Today, unshakeable in its traditions, the Place du Tertre is like a toy : every house is ornamented with painted cross-beams or cottage rough-cast. Each one is a tavern trying to outbid its neighbour. " La Mère Catherine, " of ancient renown, has not changed its appearance nor its style—representing hutments and turrets in a garden no bigger than your hand. Rivals appear—the pastry-cook Patachou, who has become a caterer and cabaret-keeper, sees the arrival of sumptuous American cars and of a select public. At the same time, on the Place du Tertre, other silent and powerful vehicles bring their contingents of tourists who like a pleasantly dusty and open-air atmosphere with service that is leisurely but hardly noiseless. In summer it appears as if an operetta, always the same— " Le banquet au village "— is played there every evening; and it must be admitted that—in spite of the ingenious artifices of the setting, the twenty restaurants side by side and the other attractions—this new, attractively painted face of Montmartre does not lack a certain naïve charm, both refreshing and amusing, under the beach parasols, the vast sky and the misty horizons transforming the confused murmur that rises from the city into the semblance of a stretch of sea front.

It is not our task to write a monograph on the Sacré-Cœur. It is better viewed from afar than close to; seen from Paris, it is a crest. Seen from nearby, it is artificial, bastioned with booths selling rosaries and souvenirs, traversed by pilgrims who seem to be borne on the wind. Posed up there like a giant architect's design, it gives the impression that it will never be finished.

St. Pierre, the village church over which the shadow of the basilica passes each day at sunrise, has other attractions for sensitive hearts, and the prayers that are uttered here ought, by their rarity, to have more value.

The Lapin Agile.

The cemetery, charming in its old age, gives death a noble and complacent countenance. It has lost its wrought-iron work, and while its wall has long since crumbled in ruins, it still has its sunshine and its dead.

We must hurry on. There would be so many things to say, if they had not already been said by Carco, Mac Orlan and so many others who loved this village. Dorgelès has devoted a book to the *Château des Brouillards* —so rich in legend. Renoir, an impenitent Montmartrian, lived and painted there.

The Rue St. Vincent has preserved its character as a country lane, with little cottages and rustic villas where painters live. Naly, the illustrator, brings together there the " Friends of Montmartre," among whom are celebrities from every country in the world. The originator of the Marshall Plan is one of the most enthusiastic members.

Yes, the St. Vincent cemetery still has its large trees, and the Rue des Saules has the *Lapin Agile*, a cabaret that has perhaps become more commonplace than it used to be. But souvenirs still embellish its walls, and though there is a terrace and a setting that has not changed, yet Frédé and his nice little donkey are missing.

Now we have reached the Rue Caulaincourt, flanked with flights of stairs that tower above the quarter of the *Grandes Carrières*; the Rue Caulaincourt, domain of the smiling, tubby André Warnod who, though Parisian and man of the boulevards, refuses ever to leave the Montmartre that he has written about for so many years. Here is Manière, a restaurant frequented by all the artistic and literary world; on the same side of the street is the Restaurant des Arts, the meeting-place of film stars and producers, when the Pathé studios in the Rue Francœur are working.

The Rue Caulaincourt goes down to Paris in a gentle, sloping curve. Marcel Aymé, who loves its light and its trees, has sung its fame. Auguste Renoir's studio was there between the years 1905 and 1915. A little farther on is the gay, bright and somewhat Bohemian studio where Gabrielle used to joke with the landlord and with Pierre Renoir, as handsome as a hero of tragedy.

The Rue Caulaincourt goes down towards Paris. And at the Place Clichy we have left Montmartre behind. You are at once aware that you have crossed those invisible frontiers that keep one of the most vital quarters of Paris from dying.

Pierre LESTRINGUEZ.

FROM BELLEVILLE TO GRENELLE

DOUANIER-ROUSSEAU. — *The Parc Montsouris.*

UESTION

the children in the schools of Belleville, and you will discover that many of them have never seen the Seine and that their only knowledge of the Place de la Concorde is the picture in their school-books.

This astonishing observation was made by a schoolmaster, and it has a counterpart in the profound significance of the couplets that Aristide Bruant used to bawl at the end of last century :

" This is the real way
To be a good citizen—
Grow up without a care
In Belleville, in Belleville ;
Shout " long live freedom "
With a merry, jovial heart
And you have all you want
In Ménilmontant, in Ménilmontant."

The " strategical " replanning of Paris by Haussmann drove workmen and artisans out by their hundreds of thousands. This exodus has not completely effaced the characteristic features of the old centres of population, but it has buried them. Charonne, Belleville, La Villette, despite the unfortunate advance of early nineteenth century buildings that have loomed up without plan or grace on the green slopes of the old hillside, have managed to keep a smack of the soil. The new occupants have made adaptations after their own fashion. That inimitable accent that is called " Parisian " in the world at large, but which the real Parisian can localise without hesitation, still preserves, in its strength and substance, the imprint of the homely genius of the old-time vinedressers, the exiled artisans of the Marais and also of the " loafers of the purlieus," sprung from heaven knows where.

What unconscious affection is expressed in that phrase, repeated

a score of times in factory and workshop, " I'm from Ménilmuche "—proudly flung at a colleague who has his abode in some other part of Paris : that Paris so haughtily ignored because " we grow up without a care in Belleville. "

Old maps of Paris give us a picture of what these places were like : Belleville, Ménilmontant, Charonne, villages huddled around their church towers and nestling among the vineyards of the slopes of the most prominent of the hills that skirt the loop of the Seine. At their base was La Villette, whose population used to group round a communal winepress which every year produced a little white wine quite as famous as that of Montmartre or Argentueil. Between these villages and the city boundary there was open country. It was the domain of Popincourt, of which there now remains only a forlorn district. Up to the end of the 18th century, that part of the original marshes, having been a hunting-ground linked up with the rabbit warrens of Montreuil and Vincennes, remained a pleasure resort dotted with fine houses and large gardens filled with flowers. Their graceful titles are now meaningless : Folies Régnault, Roquette, Folie-Méricourt, your names sing out from the blue plaques at street corners, but where are your rustic graces ?

A few secluded pleasure resorts made a precarious living along the country roads. It was in one of these, in the Rue Haute-Borne, now the Rue Oberkampf, that Cartouche's career as a bandit was finally brought to an end by the treason of one of his own gang. He had elected to spend that particular night in a cabaret " At the sign of the Pistol. " Cartouche was repairing his breeches in a room where three of his companions were sleeping. The door was broken open by heavy shoulders even before the order of arrest had been given—" Surrender in the name of the king ! " The four bandits found themselves bound in their shirt-sleeves, before they had time to seize their pistols. Then a cruising cab conveyed them to their fate.

The construction of the boundary of the *Fermiers Généraux*, towards the end of the 18th century, cut the district off from the surrounding country. The gardens were divided up into building plots. The old roads that meandered between the mossy walls of the estates were bordered with proletarian houses and workshops, whose sombre lines were reflected in the waters of St. Martin's canal. Later, the broad avenues of the Second Empire gave Popincourt a little air and space at the expense of an urban beauty and picturesqueness that had never been its lot.

When the Place du Château-d'Eau—now the Place de la République—was built, it entailed the destruction of that portion of the Boulevard du Temple that Parisians called " the Boulevard of Crime." In the many theatres that abounded there, pantomime or lurid melodrama was played to an excited public which, while making fun of the show, enjoyed it none the less. The crowd trembled and wept over the loathsome machinations of the villain. The atmosphere of agony was accentuated

A Gay Party.

by " noises off." In a certain drama, the sound of a door being unlocked had to occur at a specified point. The stage manager in charge was following his copy of the play. He read " crack ! snap ! " (the noise of a lock) and mistook that for the text. From his post behind the scenes he declaimed the phrase in his most cavernous voice. That night the audience wept —but they were tears of laughter.

Every year, in the early hours of Ash Wednesday, a strange procession of horse-coaches, landaus, cabs and gigs used to pass slowly down the " Boulevard of Crime." They were full of masqueraders forming clamorous pyramids. All Paris was there. Those who were not taking part hired out their windows a month in advance to people who wanted to be present at the " *Descente de la Courtille.*" Sweets, balls of flour, plaster confetti, baked apples and raw vegetables were thrown from one carriage to another, and abusive remarks were exchanged. Those who were afraid that they would not be sufficiently

A Haven of Love.

well-equipped for this Homeric combat had taken the trouble to read, the previous evening, the "*Catéchisme poissard*" (the "*Billingsgate Catechism*") or even "*L'Art de s'engueuler en société*" (The art of backbiting in society).

All classes of society joined in the hullabaloo at the end of this democratic orgy, in which Lord Seymour, nicknamed "My lord Blackguard," took the lead. Renowned for his fortune and his originality, he had decided that the height of good form was to associate with the stevedores and counter-jumpers of La Courtille.

La Courtille was the present-day Faubourg du Temple and Rue de Belleville. Nowadays its noise and bustle ends when the cinemas close. The sombre buildings of the *faubourg* have taken the place of the groves were young girls once lost their virtue.

On the hillside Parisians used to come to eat gooseberries and to pick lilac. All that remains of the lilac now is the name of one of the approaches to Paris (Porte des Lilas) and a rather sordid district. Laden with their sprays of flowers and tired after their Sunday's recreation, they used to rest in the groves, eat rabbit and drink the local wine. Ramponneau had already begun to make his fortune by selling Paris claret at three and a half sous a pint.

Arthur and Malvina, Jeremy and Estelle—the shop-assistant and the dressmaker's apprentice — performed breathless dances at the *Tivoli Vauxhall, the Spirit of Salt, the Jumping Flea, the Turnip Field Dance Hall,* and *the Island of Love* (so named because the garden was surrounded by a muddy ditch). Drapers' assistants and young

Vidocq.

424

milliners joined in rowdy dances; legs were kicked high without ever suspecting that a new school was thus being formed, and that from these frenzied quadrilles professionals would produce the " can-can " with its figures that have now become classical. The party never failed to end with a final galop that a contemporary has described thus :

" Sometimes in the middle of this frenzy, scarves disappeared, blouses and skirts were torn. Woe betide anyone who tried to stop to straighten her dress, for the relentless galop swept over her like a whirlwind and crushed her under its feet. "

Among the good-natured clientele of the town there mingled those disquieting figures, the loafers of the purlieus. The police were somewhat loath to venture into the dance-halls they frequented. One ought to read an account of a raid made at *Chez Desnoyez* in the memoirs of that swaggering scoundrel, Vidocq.

It was the most ill-famed establishment in La Courtille. There frequently occurred skirmishes in which an enormous hairy rascal, nicknamed The Bear, especially appointed for this task, used to make a lively end of these affairs by picking up a combatant under each arm and throwing them out into the street. Vidocq himself was greeted that evening with cries of " Throw him out. " In spite of that, and the fact that he was escorted by only eight police inspectors, he had everybody, except the women, thrown out. He marked those he recognised with a chalk cross. They were one by one arrested by the police posted outside. Vidocq's regular customers generally wore caps and blouses so that he had no great difficulty in distinguishing them.

La Courtille had not a particularly good reputation with the respectable middle-class, who were far from enthusiastic about this form of entertainment. It was their habit to sing:

> *The vines that grow in La Courtille*
> *Are fine as maid or dame ;*
> *Fine looking but with small returns—*
> *To trust them is a shame.*

The Ménilmontant highway was also lined with pleasure resorts. But their " family " atmosphere was in marked contrast to that of La Courtille. Boys and girls used to dance respectably under the eyes of their parents, and many a wedding was planned to the strains of the hurdy-gurdy. At the *Bal des Barreaux Verts*, every cavalier was given, on entering, a rose with paper petals which he had to offer to the young lady he invited to dance. If he was accepted, the lady took it and pinned it on her blouse, to show that she was " booked. "

Between the wall of Paris and the village, the police patrolled. It was unwise to venture at night-time on to the waste land. Undesirables were out on the prowl, driven to crime as much by their evil genius as by the necessity of making money. The descendants of this class of society, now fortunately far less dangerous, still seem to find a particular attraction in the outer boulevards. Their characteristic type of elegance consists of a cap and bell-bottomed trousers.

At the Barrière du Combat, the present-day Place Fabien, these gentlemen found the means of satisfying their sanguinary tastes around a sandy

arena surmounted by a large amphitheatre. Bull-fights and dog-fights
were the order of the day. On holidays, to heighten the effect, the fights
continued to the kill, thus reviving the ferocity of the circus games of
the ancient world. Sometimes an extravagant element was mixed in
with the atrocities: as, for instance, an encounter staged between a donkey,
with a monkey attached to its back, and an Alsatian dog. It is astounding
to think that these horrors were tolerated as late as 1833.

It is hard to believe that the bleak setting of La Villette basin, with
its hunch-back footbridge reminiscent of Venice, its warehouses and
factory chimneys, was once the resort of smart skaters when the water
froze. We read in the *Ladies' Journal* of February, 1827: " During
one of the very cold days, a lady was seen skating on the Villette basin
with as much grace as boldness. If she wore pantaloons, they must
have been very short, because when the wind ruffled her dress, all that
we could see above the laced boots was a very shapely leg."

And about the same period, an obscure Academician has left us an
account of a visit to La Villette that a reader of the *Ladies' Journal* would
have taken to be a society gathering. M. de Jouy made his way to Mother
Radig's cabaret opposite the basin with its gallant winter visitors.

" Mother Radig, noticing me at a short distance from her, offered me
one of the jugs she had just filled. I refused as politely as possible.

" 'Well, you old dolt, if you don't want to drink, what do you come
here for ?'

" 'To see you,' I answered with a smile.

" 'Do you take me for a strange beast ?' said she, and with that she threw the wine she had offered me in my face. Her movement was hasty rather than well-aimed. The libation prepared in my honour completely drenched a coal-man, who made no allowances for the lady's intentions and abused her so violently that an exchange of insults was soon followed by an exchange of blows, so near to me that I considered it prudent to retire."

There was once such a den where carriers, dockers, haulers and boatmen—a race so well depicted by Bruant—ate, drank, and slept. They were perfectly at home in this forsaken corner, whither the Ancient Regime had formerly transferred the gallows of Montfaucon, and which then served as a garbage dump for the great city nearby. The manure was much sought after and used by astute manufacturers, who gave it the nice name of "powdered night-soil of Montfaucon." At La Villette it was possible in those days to forecast the weather simply by sniffing the air —it was an infallible way of discovering the direction of the wind.

The Buttes-Chaumont.

The Bassin de la Villette.

The slaughter-houses and the cattle market have driven away these evil smells. Thanks to them, a scrap of rustic picturesqueness still remains in these unlovely outskirts. On market days—Mondays and Thursdays—the district is peopled with men wearing smocks and carrying heavy sticks. They are not dangerous, and their large ruddy faces indicate that they are great meat-eaters. Under the heavy starched linen, wallets bulging with bank-notes are hidden—proclaiming their solvency. All around the cattle—whose weight they can judge at a glance—secret meetings are held. The proprietor only releases the tail when the deal is concluded. They then clap hands together and go and have a drink. At about half past twelve, the hour for soup, the eating-houses justly become gold-mines. The best grills in the world are eaten there, as thick as the buyers' wallets and as " tender as a baby's bottom. " Large buildings open on to the streets near the Avenue Jean Jaurès, bearing an enigmatic sign " Cloak Room." Men in smocks enter; gentlemen wearing well-cut suits come out and get into their Citroëns, or sometimes more luxurious cars. Cattle dealers go there to assume their business-man's attire once again before making their way to their offices and their telephones.

The dismal Rue de Crimée goes right up to the summit of Belleville

Saint-Germain de Charonne.

Hill, " once a fresh village, a little green corner, a vineyard **bordered**
with pleasure resorts." On its right, it leaves behind the verdant **chaos**
of the park of the Buttes-Chaumont so skilfully designed by Alphand

on the Carrières d'Amérique, driving out the loafers and tramps who had set up a *Cour des Miracles* there, and restoring to the district a few of the trees that the speculative builders had pitilessly felled. Who would believe nowadays that Rousseau had only to climb these slopes to indulge his passion for botany?

A hundred years ago, Belleville was a village where everyone had his little house, garden, courtyard and well. The peaceful life of its population of retired middle-class people, artists, and priests made a singular contrast to the perpetual saturnalia of La Courtille. It was in its heyday, and an echo of it is found in the novels of Paul de Kock. Every year, the ceremony of the *Couronnement de la Rosière* (Crowning of the Virgin) took place. Paris was far away. Bold spirits who believed in progress talked of building a funicular railway. But nobody took it seriously. At the summit of the hill, the Chappe telegraph wires sent out messages that—so well-informed people said—went as fast as lightning. The trees of the park of Lepeletier had not all fallen. It needed a debate on the town council and a prefectorial decree to save the last one, which now stands behind an iron railing, like a strange animal, on the pavement of the Rue de Belleville. The water-tower that has replaced the telegraph-station is the proud crowning piece of 19th century ugliness—a tradition which our own century gaily carries on.

To discover the remaining traces of that peaceful era requires careful seeking. A few little strips of garden, a small house, tumbledown but with a harmonious front. Why bother to pick them out? Tomorrow these frail remains will have disappeared, crushed by the solid onslaught of bricks and cement, that in turn will have to be torn down sooner or later when the statisticians disclose, too late, that the lack of green space is closely bound up with the increase in tuberculosis.

This spot has been the scene of two Parisian tragedies. Eternal cities have the sad privilege of frequently undergoing this kind of anguish. In 1814 the troops of Marmont covered themselves in glory before being overwhelmed by Blucher's army corps. This *combat d'honneur* with the foreigner came to an end with the capitulation of La Villette, painful but inevitable. It was not the same in 1871. Civil wars mean extermination. The last of these took place there, with fierce fighting in both camps. Belleville witnessed the shooting of hostages, in the Rue Haxo: summary executions of men whose only crime was that of having horny

hands. By the Mur des Fédérés at the far end of the cemetery of Père Lachaise the last of the Communards perished, without the satisfaction of dying with their boots on.

On the southern side of the hill the clock tower of St. Germain-de-Charonne rises on the right-hand side of the Rue St-Blaise. A little country cemetery still surrounds it—a setting unique in Paris. The old families of Charonne still have the right of burial there. The porch joining the church to the presbytery opens on to an avenue of grave-stones of recent date. But farther on, to the left, under the large trees whose roots are imperceptibly causing havoc to the deserted tombs, stands the statue of a strange man, in 18th century dress, wearing a three-cornered hat. On the pedestal, which is surrounded by a grill with curious masonic emblems, it is possible to decipher the epitaph, engraved in bronze letters : "Here lies Bègue (alias Magloire) house-painter, poet, philosopher and secretary to M. de Robespierre, 1793." We know very little about the man in whose honour this costly mausoleum was raised.

In this old parish, the vast property of the Folie Régnault overlooked Paris. When the Jesuits acquired it in the 17th century, they gave it the name of Mont Louis and made it their last resting place. It was later re-named after the most famous of them, Père Lachaise, who was father confessor to Louis XIV. Rambuteau, prefect under Louis XVIII, wanted to make it an immense burial ground, whilst preserving its garden-like appearance. It is now full to overflowing. The pilgrimage to the tombs of Abelard and Heloise, Racine, Molière, La Fontaine, Boileau, exiled to these parts by an administration that is solicitous of literary piety, is a moving experience. But what abusive widow, inspired by a simple-minded frankness that is unusual among the writers of epitaphs, has engraved on a tombstone :

C.L.M.N.
Divisional Inspector
Wait a long time for me.

Philippe LEFRANÇOIS.

OOKING

at the 13th *arrondissement* in detail, we find that, of all the districts in Paris, it is the one that has longest maintained its suburban appearance, in the manners, the language, and clothing of its inhabitants.

The Bièvre, the only river that flows into the Seine in the very heart of Paris, runs through this district and has inspired many poets. Its course, as it flows through the City, is not the usual path of a river.

After it has, from its very source, brightened up a charming countryside, it disappears underground at the Poterne des Peupliers, to reappear only at very rare intervals from its underground bed till it reaches the Seine. Less than a hundred years ago, the entire stream was in the open air and Balzac was able to describe its deep valley, " with rural factories and patches of greensward here and there, irrigated by its tawny waters."

When it enters the 13th *arrondissement*, its subterranean course meets with a natural obstacle and works its way around it—La Butte aux Cailles (The Quail mound)—one of the numerous hills of Paris and not the least important of them. This hill was famed as particularly rich in game. It was only a few years ago that the shooting lodge on its slope, where Napoleon I used to rest after shooting quail, crumbled to the ground from old age—hence the name. Until about the end of the 19th century, green fields could still be seen on its summit where stood a large windmill. The fields were watered by the Bièvre and covered with ice in wintertime. Then, in this suburb, that was once the village of Petit-Gentilly, skating took the place of hunting. People came there from all over Paris. Of this attraction, nothing is left but the name of a street—the unending Rue de la Glacière—and a Métro station.

It was a poor district, dotted here and there with

squalid houses that extended as far as the former fortifications. Victor Hugo, who lived at Gentilly, is said to have studied there the characters of his major novel "*Les Misérables.*" Leather-work was the traditional craft. For centuries, tanners, makers of wash-leather, curriers and dressers have been steeping leather in the Bièvre, whose murky waters, so they said,

The Valley of the Bièvre.

had amazing preservative qualities.

The Halle aux Cuirs (Hide-market) remains the distinctive sign of this district.

These workmen certainly held very different opinions from those of the people in the fashionable districts. During the 1848 revolution they entered the pages of history because of the massacre of General Bréa, who was sent to them with a flag of truce. Today there is nothing like the great reception room—"Le Grand Salon"—where the curriers used to dance barefooted on Sundays, and where Bréa was killed.

The old houses of the Bièvre valley, and the valley itself, have dis-

appeared with the levelling of the district. They have been buried beneath heaps of garbage and tins; new brick houses for large families have been built on this fresh soil. The district however, while modernised, still kept its distinctive character in places.

The area is a quaint one even in its religions. At the corner of the Rue Wurtz and the Rue Vergniaud, the Antoinist temple can be seen : it is the

CHATELET
RUE
DE RIVOLI
LE DE LA CITÉ
BD ST MICHEL
BD ST GERMAIN
ILE ST LOUIS
B. HENRI IV
R. S. ANTOINE
St PAUL
PLACE DE LA BASTILLE
Hᵉᵉ AUX VINS
R. S. BERNARD Qᵘᵃⁱ
JARDIN des PLANTES
Hᵉˡ de la SALPETRIÈRE
R. Gay LUSSAC
R. ST JACQUES
R. CLAUDE BERNARD AV
BD du PORT-ROYAL
BD ST MARCEL
RUE de L'HOPITAL
GOBELINS
Hᵈᵉ de la PITIE
SALPÊTRÈ
GARE
BD ARAGO
R. de
R. de la GLACIÈRE
R. CROULEBARBE
GOBᵉ BD de
PLACE D'ITALIE
BD AUGUSTE BLANQUI
LA SANTE
LA BUTTE AUX CAILLES
AV. DES GOBELINS
RUE du CHEVALERET
RUE DU
RUE JEANNE D'ARC
RUE du DENTAIRE
PL. CHAT.
P. CHAT.
AV. D'ITALIE
RUE de GENTILLY
PL. NATIONALE
DES RENTIERS
R. DE TOLBIAC
Rᵈᵉ PATAY
R. RAGNAULT
MASSENA
ALÉSIA
RUE VERNIAUD
R. BARRAULT
STE ANNE
RUE DE BOBILLOT
TOLBIAC
R. DAMESME
R. de PHUEBERS
R. COLONIE
R. d. TAGE
PARC MONTSOURIS
R. RUNGIS
R. BOUSSINGAULT RUNGIS
POTERNE d. PEUPLIERS
BOULEVARD
BD JOURDAN
BD KELLERMAN
CITÉ UNIVERSᵉ
PTE GENTILLY
PTE D'ITALIE
A. de FONTAINEBL
KREMLIN BICETRE
RUE du FAUBᵍ
MARCHE
R. de MONTREUIL
ST ANTOINE
BD DIDEROT
DE LYON
R. du CHAROLAIS
AVENUE
N.D. BERCY
QUAI DE BERCY
ENTREPOTS BERCY
Pᵗᵉ TOLBIAC
GARE
R. WATT
IVRY-PORT
R. VICTOR H
Pᵗᵉ NATIONAL
QUAI

La Butte aux Cailles
ES OBELINS
Fᵍ Saint Antoine
Bois de Vincennes

sanctuary of a form of worship in which a workman was pope. Further down, in the Rue des Tanneries, was the Convent of the English Maidens, where prayers were made for the conversion of England.

Artists are at home here. They have chosen the most amusing streets to live in, such as the Rue Barrault that climbs the northern slope of the Butte. Edged by an iron railing, it overlooks small gardens and low houses in which sculptors and painters have made their studios.

It is by this street that we reach the Place Paul Verlaine, where the house of the Paris hangman used to stand. An artesian well has been bored on this village square, providing water for the swimming-pool of the Butte-aux-Cailles, where sporting contests take place. A maze of small, rather untidy streets, leads down from the Butte to the Rue Croulebarbe. This winding street follows the course of the Bièvre which flows beneath its cobbled way. Its name recalls a famous vineyard — the "Clos Croulebarbe" where a rather sour wine was grown, which the Parisians in those days enjoyed very much.

A few steps away is the Place d'Italie which, in the course of centuries, has changed its name several times: it was called the Barrière Mouffetard, then the Barrière de Fontainebleau, for it marked the bound-

ary of Paris. It is by way of this square that Napoleon re-entered his capital on his return from the Island of Elba.

Only a few years ago, we could see the last of the professional cut-throats walking freely about in this square, wearing peaked caps and high-waisted trousers buttoned up to their chests. There is a provincial air about the place, and it is still used as a fair ground. The Place d'Italie is circular and a number of avenues converge here.

One of these—the Avenue des Gobelins—gave its name to the district. It was called after the artists who began to make tapestries there. A number of streets in the neighbourhood bear the names of renowned painters—Rue Titien, Rue Edouard-Manet, Rue Watteau, Rue Philippe-de-Champaigne, Rue Primatice, Rue Rubens, Rue Le Brun.

The National Works of the Gobelins is without a doubt the oldest of French institutions.

The Rue Mouffetard.

Throughout five centuries, it has been continually enlarged but has kept the traditions that made its fame, and it has never moved from the spot where Jehan Gobelin, or Gobeleen—of Flemish descent—set up in the year 1450. Jehan Gobelin, then his sons and grandsons Gilles and Philibert, created on the banks of the Bièvre a manufacture of which the chroniclers tell us that

A Visit to the Gobelins.

" for fineness, for good dyeing and beautiful colour schemes of the silks and wools, it surpassed those of Flanders and England. " The river Bièvre, in whose waters the silks and wools were soaked, had the reputation of improving the quality of the dye; and thanks to the protection of a King who befriended the Arts—Francis I—the Gobelins acquired an immense reputation. In the course of centuries their manufacture suffered many vicissitudes. During the Revolution, the administration caused 296 models out of the 321 then existing to be destroyed, on the grounds that they depicted subjects " incompatible with Republican ideas." In 1871 the Commune, then masters of Paris, burnt down part of the buildings, as well as 114 catalogued pieces. If we enter the gardens, we are faced with an old-world landscape—a number of little plots cultivated by the artist-workers of the factory. In the middle of these gardens, flowing in the open air for some yards, the tawny waters of the Bièvre bring to mind this verse of the old Poet:

> *This drain of a river*
> *That passes behind you,*
> *Is but a stream that shrewdly takes*
> *Its name from Gobelin.*

At a short distance from the Gobelins, on the Boulevard de l'Hôpital, we find another, even larger state building, the history of which is linked to that of Paris—the Hospital of the Salpêtrière.

Originally it was a saltpetre powder magazine, which under Louis XIV was converted into a home for beggars, for the aged, and for mentally afflicted men and women. There was soon added to this a " prison for incorrigible and undisciplined women and girls."

Throughout the 18th century, this prison-hospital met with a variety of fates. Under the supervision of Madame de Moysan, who used to give balls there, it was one of the gayest places in the world, a little too much so, in fact, for the gaiety degenerated into orgies. However,

this state of disorder did not last very long, and the Salpêtrière became once more what it had been previously. Under Louis XVI, the prison-hospital was assigned to women only. Up to seven thousand were crowded there, two thousand of whom were prostitutes. The raving mad women were put into bonds behind iron bars, through which their food and the straw for their beds were handed to them.

In another part of the building, other prisoners were detained, some of whom were celebrities, such as Mme de Lamothe who was involved in the Affair of the Queen's Necklace.

During the Revolution, the Salpêtrière was the scene of an historical event. In 1792 a crowd of armed men and women invaded the place, set the prostitutes free, and massacred 45 political prisoners, in the courtyard lined with houses that can still be seen today, and which has been named the Courtyard of the September massacres. It is also there that the famous revolutionary Amazon, Théroigne de Méricourt,

was detained and died insane.

If we leave the Salpêtrière by the Boulevard de l'Hôpital, bordered on one side by the Jardin des Plantes, and on the other side by the Gare l'Austerlitz, we soon reach the Seine it the spot where the old Bièvre unobtrusively joins the river. Here we cross the Seine by the Pont de Bercy and pass through a district, dedicated by tradition to wines, and formerly called the Faubourg de la Grande Pinte.

The district of Bercy ends at a short distance from the warehouses. Almost parallel is the long Rue de Charenton, which prides itself on having been the triumphant road by which General Bonaparte entered Paris after his second campaign in Italy. As the Rue de Charenton approaches the Bastille, its character changes. On reaching the Rue d'Aligre it enters the Faubourg Saint-Antoine.

When this Faubourg was mentioned to a Parisian of the last century, he would reply either with pride, or with a kind of respectful awe, that it was the district where all the Revolutions came into being. The Parisian of today will merely tell you that the Faubourg Saint-Antoine is dedicated to the peaceful industry of furniture manufacturing.

It was from here that in 1789, 1792, 1830, 1832, and 1848, yelling hordes emerged and overthrew the Old Regime, the Restoration, and then the July Monarchy. Other districts underwent revolutionary scenes; this district was the Revolution itself.

At the very entrance to the old Faubourg, the Place de la Bastille opens up, with its bronze column capped with the Genius of Liberty. Here once stood the old royal fortress—the Saint-Antoine Bastille, rightly or wrongly considered as a

symbol of tyranny. It was taken without effort by the rebels of the 14th of July, who set about pulling it down the very next day. The majority of these insurgents came from the Faubourg Saint-Antoine, armed with guns and strange weapons of all descriptions, which they had stolen from the gunsmiths.

The straw they brought with them, to set fire to the Bastille, had been taken from the " Hay and Straw Market " that used to be held on what is now known as the Place d'Aligre—a charming provincial oasis in the very heart of Paris, with its old-time inns to which men of letters used to resort.

The real leader of these rebels was Santerre, a stout man, very popular in the Faubourg. He owned the Hortensia beerhouse (now No. 11 Rue de Reuilly) where the Duke of Orleans used to come as a friend. The latter was the father of Louis-Philippe and next in succession to the throne after Louis XVI. It was to Santerre's beerhouse that the liberated prisoners of the Bastille were brought, with their chains and the keys of the fortress.

At the eastern end of the Faubourg is the present-day Place de la Nation, called under the Old Régime the Place du Trône, in memory of the throne that was erected there for Louis XIV and Marie-Thérèse at the time of their first entry into Paris in 1660. The leaders of the Revolution changed the name and called it the Place du Trône Renversé; they then erected the guillotine there, which worked unceasingly till the 9th Thermidor, the day of Robespierre's fall, when it was set up on the Place de la Révolution, now the Place de la Concorde.

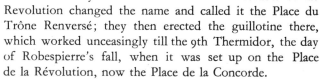

For a long time one wondered where the 1340 people who were executed on the Place du Trône had been buried. At last their grave was found in

the gardens of the Picpus Convent, then called the " Champ des Martyrs."
Later, in the enlarged cemetery, General La Fayette was buried.

Not far off, at No. 42 Rue Picpus, stood the convent of the Dames de
Sainte-Clothilde. It was, under the Old Regime, the starting point of
the solemn entry into Paris of the Ambassadors of the Catholic Powers.
These events were celebrated with great pomp and a military parade.
The convent became a prison under the Revolution—one of many in
the district. The most famous was, undoubtedly, the Mazas prison
of which there only remains the name in the square which opens from
Austerlitz bridge. It was close to the Seine, at the spot where the Rue

Traversière is today. In the Mazas prison celebrated
statesmen were detained, and this fact is recalled by many
19th century novels.

There are still traces of these political struggles in the
Faubourg Saint-Antoine of today. The district is one
of the most populous in Paris, and is inhabited by large
numbers of workmen and craftsmen : the traditional May
Day procession (the workers' festival), which gathers
together most of the trades unions of the Paris area,
marches from the Place de la Bastille to the Place de la
Nation.

The old Faubourg has other traditions, apart from its
political ones, which have survived until the present day; and we can
still see the Foire au Pain d'Epices (Ginger-bread fair) held in the month
of May, which spreads along the streets
near the Place de la Nation.

This famous fair, more than two
hundred years old was originally an
ordinary market, held during Holy
Week in the enclosure of the Royal
Abbey of Saint-Antoine-des-Champs.
There is nothing left of this Abbey—
which was founded in the 12th century
and gave its name to the Faubourg—
except for a few remains enclosed in
the Saint-Antoine hospital.

As for the Rue du Faubourg Saint-

Antoine, it is lined, from the Place de la Bastille onwards, with modern furniture stores that give one some idea of the pleasure that Parisians take in their homes. They make this very lively street one of the most unusual in Paris.

By the Rue du Faubourg Saint-Antoine and the Cours de Vincennes, we reach the Bois de Vincennes: this is for the east of Paris, what the Bois de Boulogne is for the west. The two forests were simultaneously included in the Capital when, a few years ago, the last fortifications were pulled down.

The Bois de Vincennes covers as large a space as its rival; it contains trees equally beautiful and just as large; it also has fine lakes and a race-course; it borders the Marne just as the other borders the Seine on one side. But, it is not as well cared for as the Bois de Boulogne; its roads and paths are not as tidy, nor as thickly strewn with sand; and it has not the same fashionable reputation. However, wide avenues run through it, and it attracts large crowds of visitors who enjoy it just for its simplicity

The Château de Vincennes.

and the beauty of its shady groves. It has two undeniable advantages over the Bois de Boulogne—its Château and its Zoo.

The first Château de Vincennes dated from the 12th century; Saint-Louis, who lived there, liked on fine Sundays after church to hold his Court of Justice in the forest; seated with his back to the finest oaktree, with his barons around him, he invited any of his subjects who might have a complaint to make, to approach without fear and state the facts. Without encumbering himself with clerks or long phrases, he administered justice as soon as he had heard what both parties had to say, and his verdict was carried out on the spot.

The successors of Saint-Louis continued to take an interest in the Bois de Vincennes. They planted trees and supervised their upkeep. A number of kings lived, and died, in the new castle, the foundation-stone of which was laid by Philippe de Valois. Charles V was born there and completed this fortress, called the *Château du Bois*; its walls were a hundred and seventy feet high; the surrounding moats forty feet deep and ninety feet wide.

Henry V, " Merry England's " ideal, Shakespeare's hero, Regent of France and King of England, died a natural death there in 1422, during the Hundred Years' War. Many of the acts signed during his reign were drawn up in the Château de Vincennes.

A century and a half later, Charles IX, the unfortunate King remembered for Saint Bartholemew's Eve, died there; as did Cardinal Mazarin in 1661. The latter had considerably embellished and enlarged the

Sunday at Vincennes.

living quarters of the castle.

Under Louis XV, the Bois de Vincennes was entirely replanted with oak-trees. A large number of the trees we see today date from the year 1730.

The castle ceased to be inhabited by the Court and became a State prison which witnessed tragic scenes, the most famous being the execution of the Duke of Enghien in 1804.

Throughout the 19th century it remained a political prison, while the forest became a meeting place for duellists. In 1833, the Comte Léon, Napoleon's illegitimate son, shot General Hesse, Wellington's aide-de-camp. In 1836 Emile de Girardin killed Armand Carrel there.

These are the memories that the crowds we see there every Sunday can conjure up, as they wander through the wood or rest on the spot where Saint-Louis used to administer justice, or while they visit the castle, or admire in the Zoo the wonderful collection of wild animals.

This Zoo has undoubtedly become the main attraction of the Bois. It was founded in 1934 and is today the most complete in the whole of Europe.

Amongst its six hundred mammals and its thousand birds, there are species that cannot be found in any other zoological gardens, not even in the superb American zoos such as that of Detroit.

The monkeys and tigers roam at liberty, in a setting that recalls their native forests;

and it has the distinctive feature—which it acquired not without considerable difficulty—of being able to exhibit animals all the year round, whatever the outside temperature may be.

This Zoo, then, is one of the finest in the world. It is placed on the very spot where, six hundred years ago, the Kings of France with their crossbows used to hunt deer, boar, stag and other wild animals, with which they had peopled the forest of Vincennes for their own pleasure.

Bernard NABONNE.

ITTLE

would one think that the three districts which later were to become the 15th *arrondissement*—Javel, Vaugirard and Grenelle—were born of two villages and a hamlet which barely a century ago were still outside Paris. The outer walls of Paris, then called the *Enceinte des Fermiers Généraux*, used to stand on the site where the elevated line of the Métro runs all long the Boulevard de Grenelle.

Let us turn our back to the Ile aux Cygnes and follow the Quai de Javel, where are situated the principal workshops of a large motor-car factory. The old hamlet of Javel dates back to the 13th century. It was then called Javet and the abbey of Sainte-Geneviève had a farm there. There was also a windmill called *Moulin de Javel*. The name was corrupted to Javelle before its spelling was simplified. In 1777 the factory of the Comte d'Artois was built there and that is where Javel water, so precious to washerwomen, was discovered and named.

Let us cast a glance at the Pont Mirabeau as we go by—not so much because its architect M. Résal, who built it between 1895 and 1896, adopted, for the first time, the process of compressed-air boxes for its foundation piers—as for the beautiful poem it inspired Guillaume Apollinaire to write some years later:

> *'Neath the Mirabeau bridge flows the Seine*
> *and our love,*
> *Can I fail to remember it ?*
> *Happiness ever came after a sigh. . .*

If we continue down the Rue de la Convention, nothing but high modern buildings devoid of character strike the eye. The Saint-Christophe church, however, that stands at the corner of the street of the same name, is quite interesting. It is a concrete construction built by C. H. Bernard between 1926 and 1934, and is a fine example of modern technique as applied to religious art. On the 25th of July of each year, the feast day of the great patron saint of travellers, the Archbishop of Paris gives his solemn blessing to motor-cars in this church. A little further, on the left-hand side we notice the characterless buildings of the Imprimerie Nationale (the National Printing Press), construction of which began in 1907, but which was only occupied in 1925. This printing works took the place of the Royal, then later of the Imperial, Press, which was first set up in the Louvre as early as 1640: then later in the Hôtel Penthièvre and later in the Hôtel Rohan.

Quite close by is the Boucicaut hospital, a reminder of the bounty of the lady who founded the Bon Marché stores. We can choose between the populous Rue Saint-Charles, the modern Avenue Félix-Faure, or, better still, the Rue de la Croix-Nivert, when we hasten towards the heart of the picturesque Grenelle district. The Rue de la Croix-Nivert owes its name to a cross that was erected at the point where that street joins up with the Rue Lecourbe, the ancient route to Brittany. It takes us to the junction of the Rue des Entrepreneurs and the Rue du Commerce, where, in the centre of the cross-roads, stands the church of Saint-Jean-Baptiste of Grenelle. This church, built between 1827 and 1832, would not be worthy of mention if Mademoiselle, daughter of the Duke of Berry, had not been present at the laying of the foundation stone by the Duchesse of Angoulême. A neighbouring street was given her name to commemorate this event. The Rue Saint-Charles was also christened at that time, in honour of King Charles X. We must not forget that by Royal Decree, dated 23rd October 1830, the independence of the village of Grenelle was proclaimed; it was then divorced from the village of Vaugirard and became a separate township. This state of affairs was only altered by the decree of 1859 which absorbed both communes into the city of Paris.

Less than a hundred years ago, this very lively district, while bearing no resemblance to the former vast warren (Garanella) from which its name is derived, was still called by the Parisians "The Grenelle Plain." In the 13th century the abbeys of Saint-Germain-des-Prés and Sainte-Geneviève shared it between them. On a map dated 1667 we can see that a Gothic castle stood on the present-day Place Cambronne. In 1580 Henry III built a hospital there for the plague-stricken, who were removed from Paris at the first sign of the disease. After the plague was over, two thousand beggars were housed there and fed by the King, who allowed them five pence a day; however, as they did not give up begging, they were turned out.

Many of the street-names recall the origins of the village of Grenelle. Fondary was mayor of Vaugirard-Grenelle from 1821 to 1830; Violet, Frémicourt, Letellier, Ginoux, and Tiphaine were architects or builders. All these streets, to which we must add, amongst others, the Rue de l'Eglise, the Rue du Théâtre and the Rue de Lourmel, which Francis Carco has described in a rather too sombre manner in his novel *Perversité*, are teeming with a population of workers, a colourful and lively people, including not a few North Africans who are mostly employed at the Javel factories. The army also brings a touch of khaki, brightened up by blue and yellow caps.

The Rue du Commerce is worth seeing between six and seven in the evening, when the lathes and machine-tools come to a standstill in the workshops. The pavements are alive with a good-natured crowd. The shop-windows, with their inviting displays, are ablaze with light and clamorous with noise: the pedlars cry their wares, and already through the doors of the dance-halls comes the sound of accordions. The inhabitant of Grenelle has a dignity of his own. He is jovial and fond of backchat; he is a "sportsman," too. How could he be otherwise, having as he does, at the corner of

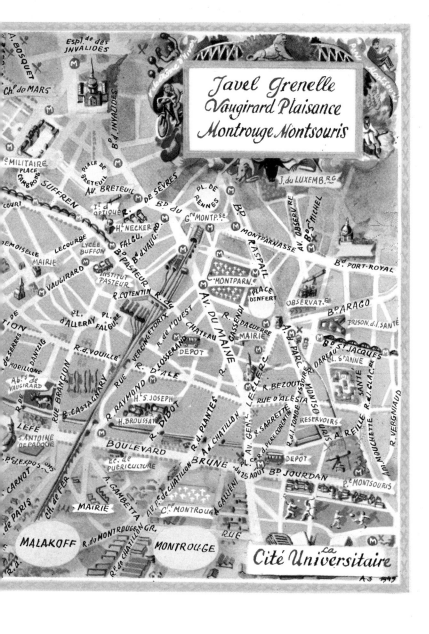

Javel Grenelle
Vaugirard Plaisance
Montrouge Montsouris

La Cité Universitaire

his Boulevard and the Rue Nelaton, the famous Vélodrome d'Hiver—commonly known as the Vel'd'Hiv or Palais des Sports, built in 1910? That is where the most important sporting events take place, from the six days' cycle race to boxing matches, all-in wrestling, skating and ice hockey. Sometimes, however, politics take the place of sport, and all parties in turn come to this spacious enclosure to vaunt their ideal system of government.

The aristocratic *Concours Hippique* (Horse Show) has chosen it in order to attract a larger audience to the noble sport of horsemanship, and the immense track on these occasions is covered with tan. On other days, as if by magic, it dons a coat of ice for skating and ice hockey.

Quite close by, on the Place Dupleix, which has existed since the 18th century—but whose present name only dates from 1815—stands a barracks in place of the former Hôtel de Craon which became later the Hôtel or Château de Grenelle. It was in this château that the chemist Chaptal installed a gun-powder factory that blew up on the 31st of August 1794. The explosion shook the whole of Paris, killing or wounding over twelve hundred people. As for the Métro station Dupleix, it is on the very site of the former Grenelle wall, which became famous for its sad associations with military executions.

The west side of the Avenue de Suffren is still part of the 15th *arrondissement*. Where we now find the " Swiss Village," with its knicknacks and second-hand-goods stores, there once stood the Great Wheel, a remainder of the World Exhibition of 1900, consisting of gondolas attached to a gigantic revolving wheel; it was demolished after the 1914-1918 war. The story is told of a couple who remained in a gondola that was at the highest point of the wheel when it stopped, and were compelled to spend an uncomfortable night a hundred and fifty feet from the ground, because their shouts and cries had not been heard. The Great Wheel was surrounded by gardens, where the duellists of the Third Republic used to settle their quarrels. Many duels were fought there, but fortunately with few deaths.

We now reach the Boulevard Pasteur and the Vaugirard district.

The old village of Vaugirard did not exist before the 13th century. The plain where it was built was called the Val Boitron, and the origin of this name has never been discovered. In 1258 the Abbot of Saint-Germain-des-Prés, Girard de Moret, built a rest-house for his monks

The Rue du Commerce.

and the Boitron vale then became the Val Girard. Houses clustered around this abbatial property, and a village came into being, which was fenced in by one of the successors of Girard de Moret, the Abbé Jean de Précy. Then a chapel was built. In 1343 the chaplain received the title of Parish Priest. However, it was not until 1790 that the Parish of Vaugirard was promoted to the rank of commune attached to the Sceaux district —and then only because the inhabitants protested, for the authorities had originally planned to include their territory in the commune of Issy.

The present Vaugirard district is divided in two by the street of the same name, which along its course through the 15th *arrondissement* has no other claim to fame than that of being part of one of the longest streets in Paris. If we leave it to our right to follow the Boulevard Pasteur, we come into the Rue du Docteur Roux. We can say nothing about the church of Saint - Jean - Baptiste - de - la - Salle that we meet on our way. It is an uninteresting building of the first decade of this century. But at number 29 stand the buildings of the Pasteur Institute, famous throughout the world. These buildings, together with the Institute of Biological Chemistry make up the greater part of the first Institut Pasteur, inaugurated in 1888 in the life-time of the great scientist, who, amongst other wonderful discoveries, invented antisepsis and asepsis and opened up new possibilities to surgery. There is a bust of Pasteur in front of the Institute and his tomb is in the crypt.

The street which makes M. Dutot, the 18th century economist, temporarily immortal, is the continuation of the Rue du Docteur Roux; it takes us to the Place and Rue d'Alleray, which prides itself on its post-office, a huge building which is of no interest whatever to art lovers. However, we must bear in mind that Sire Denis-François-Angrand d'Alleray, lord of Bazoches, Condé, Saint-Libière and other domains, was the last Lord of Vaugirard-lèz-Paris.

I do not consider it necessary to pass an opinion on the Vaugirard slaughter-house, in the nearby Rue des Morillons, where the Pound is also situated. Since 1898 it has been for the Left Bank what the Villette slaughter-house is for the Right Bank. The peculiarities of the district are the unsavoury smell of blood and the jovial faces of the slaughterers who cheer themselves up over a glass of wine at bar counters and at restaurants specialising in lamb trotters *à la sauce poulette*. Let us continue our stroll down the Rue des Morillons. Its name implies that vines grew there in far distant days, the *morillon* being a vine of the Pineau brand that used to be grown in the Paris area. After crossing the Rue Olivier-de-Serres and giving a thought to the founder of the Théâtre d'Agriculture des Champs, we will rest a while in a small shady square, at the junction of the Rue de Vaugirard, the Rue Desnouettes and the Rue Saint-Lambert. Here, a hundred years ago, stood a church called Saint-Lambert; it was demolished after the consecration of the new church in 1856. The land on which it was built was given to the Parish by the Abbé Groult d'Arcy, a Benedictine monk; he became Bishop of Nevers and died in 1847. A street was christened after him in recognition of this gift.

Barely fifty paces away is the Rue Blomet, which in 1672 was the road to Meudon. This peaceful street is lined with clinics, maternity homes and religious institutions. Tree-tops peep over the walls, nuns glide past, giving the place the serenity of a provincial town. However, when we leave to our left the *Mairie* of the 15th *arrondissement*, completed

The Boulevard de Grenelle.

in 1876, the street becomes narrow: we have now reached the centre of the former village of Vaugirard; here we discover a Negro night club, where West Indians in their native dress shake and sway. It met with such success that soon a second one was opened quite close by in the Rue des Volontaires, which the coloured folk enjoy just as much. And so we reach the Rue de Sèvres, where we find the Necker hospital—formerly the Monastery of Notre-Dame-de-Liesse, and the hospital for sick children which was in 1751 a school for impecunious young girls of noble descent. These are still in the 15th *arrondissement*.

There remains the southern part of the district—the former outer boulevards. At No. 28 Boulevard Victor we find the National Aeronautical School, a modern building, flanked at No. 30 by the Air Museum, where the heroic days of aviation are recalled by the *Demoiselle* (dragonfly) of Santos-Dumont (1908) and the original aeroplane—constructed by Deperdussin-Béchereau, whose pilot Prévost was, in 1912, the first to exceed the speed of two hundred kilometres an hour.

However, the main attraction of the district is the exhibition park at the Porte de Versailles where the Rue de Vaugirard ends. There, each year, in May or June is held the Foire de Paris which has gradually become

The "Six Days Cycle Race".

the most important trade fair in Europe, with its three hundred and twenty-three thousand square feet of exhibition halls and over one thousand five hundred square feet of open-air show grounds. The number of exhibitors has risen from five hundred in 1904 to approximately ten thousand in 1949. Not only do the French industries and the craftsmen present the latest techniques and national resources, but fourteen nations occupy four great halls there, and the Park is divided into eleven districts, like a real town, where it is possible to purchase clothes, furniture, food, houses, boats, motor-cars with trailers, and even a family tomb. Needless to say, food is not forgotten, and all the regions of France display their gastronomical specialities; a gargantuan Hall of Wines overlooks the panorama of the fair and reminds us, with its countless stands where wine is tasted free of charge, that French vinegrowers are the foremost in the world.

Before leaving the fifteenth *arrondissement*, let us have a look at the Vaugirard hospital for a moment; it was formerly a famous Jesuit college. It was there in 1944, during the Liberation of Paris, that the first French flag was hoisted.

By the Boulevard Lefebvre, we now make our way towards the

The Rue Linois.

Porte de Vanves and the Boulevard Brune, where the fourteenth *arrondissement* begins. To our right, the fortifications still stood until just after the First World War. Children could be seen rolling down their grassy slopes, and the inhabitants of this area used to improvise picnics while they watched the dwellers of the " Zone "—the dregs of the population—watering the vegetables they grew in the former moats of the fortifications. Today, there, as well as all around Paris, a succession of modern council flats, all very much alike, have taken their place. Let us point out in all this greyness, the attractive church of Saint Anthony of Padua, built between 1934 and 1936 by the architect Azema, with its fine brick and reinforced concrete tower, surrounded by the statues of Saint Francis, Saint Louis, Saint Claire and Saint Elizabeth of Hungary, ingeniously arranged.

Beyond the Porte de Châtillon, there is the Porte d'Orléans, with the avenue of the same name. In 1947 its name was changed, and it became the Avenue du Général Leclerc, for the second armoured division, under the command of that great soldier, entered Paris there on the 25th of August, 1944. This was formerly Montrouge ; some people say this name may be derived from *Mons Rubens*. Yet there are no mountains to be seen and the soil is not red, so we are more inclined to think that the godfather of this district was a Lord of Montlhéry, nicknamed *Guis le Rouge*.

The church of Saint-Pierre, at the corner of the Avenue du Maine, dates from the Second Empire. If we follow its iron railings to the left, we reach the bleak *Mairie* of the 14th *arrondissement*. Why was the Rue du Château, which faces it, called Rue du Château du Maine in olden times ? Because the son of Louis XIV and Madame de Montespan owned a house there, where he loved to play in his childhood.

If, on leaving Saint-Pierre de Montrouge, we take the Rue d'Alésia, we will soon find ourselves in the lively district of Plaisance, (pleasure). However, curiosities are few in this area, apart from two interesting modern churches—Notre-Dame du Rosaire, by Pierre Sardou in the Rue Raymond-Losserand, and Notre-Dame du Travail by Astruc in the Rue Vercingetorix. In the Rue Pierre Larousse, we must notice the Hôpital Broussais, where Verlaine was often a patient and where he wrote a number of poems.

Let us return to the axis of Saint-Pierre-de-Montrouge, and from there go straight ahead towards the Place Denfert-Rochereau, where the Lion de Belfort crouches. It is a reduced model of a bronze by Bartholdi, sculptured " to the glory of the defenders of the city and their leader, Colonel Denfert-Rochereau." It used to be called Place d'Enfer (Hell), as the street that climbed to the Observatoire was called the Rue d'Enfer (*Via infera*—lower street, as opposed to the Rue Saint-Jacques that climbed towards the Montagne Sainte-Geneviève). On either side of the square can be seen, facing each other, two pavilions, which remain as relics of the old barriers of Paris. By way of the pavilion on the right-hand side one descends into the Catacombs, old stone quarries that extend for nearly a hundred and twenty thousand square feet, and where the bones from the cemetery of the Innocents were transferred in 1786. It is the largest ossuary in the world, for, besides the bones from the cemetery of the Innocents, the bones from the Parisian cemeteries of Saint-Laurent, Saint-Jacques-du-Haut-Pas, Saint-Jean-de-la-Trinité, Saint-Leu, from the convent of the Carmelites, of Saint-Nicolas-des-Champs, Saint-Etienne-des-Grès and others were transferred there between 1787 and 1814. The remains of six millions Parisians have in this way been sheltered under the Montrouge plain, where they are displayed along the walls like gruesome trophies. At the entrance to this burial ground

The Rue Paturle.

a verse of Dellile has been engraved in the rock : " Halt, for here is the realm of death."

After climbing forty-four steps, one emerges from this gloomy empire into the Rue Rémy-Dumoncel, formerly Rue Dareau. From there, through the Rue d'Alembert, we reach the Rue de la Tombe-Issoire, legendary reminder of the giant Isoré, king of the Saracens, who besieged Paris in the reign of Charlemagne. If we believe the Chronicle of William of Orange, it is on this very spot that the medieval hero slew his assailant just as David felled Goliath.

Leave the Rue de la Tombe-Issoire at the turn of the Avenue Reille, and you will see in the distance, at the corner of the Montsouris Park, a redoubtable fortress with its high grassy slopes. Be reassured: it only harbours the water reservoir of the Vanne, a calmly flowing river, born in the neighbourhood of Sens and canalised in 1874 to provide spring water for the left bank of the capital. Its clear waters join those of the Lunain, dear to the poet Louis de Gonzague-Frick.

Turn your back to the sham fortress and let your eyes rest on the Montsouris Park. In 1860 this district was dependent on the Gentilly commune. It was called the *Mont-Souris* or *Moque-Souris*, the origin of the name being forgotten. Countless artists, painters, sculptors and architects have chosen to live in the neighbouring streets, the rue du Douanier and the Rue du Square Montsouris.

The Park was laid out under the Second Empire. It differs from the other parks in Paris, on account of a certain air of melancholy that lends it charm, reminiscent of the public gardens in London. Quite extensive, with its thirty-two acres, it is full of little hills with a waterfall and a lake. The Sceaux railway line cuts it in two from north to south, giving it a strange, romantic air, which is enhanced by an old building, the Meteorological Observatory. This is a replica of the Bardo Palace in Tunis, and as such was admired by the visitors to the 1867 exhibition. A modern meteorological tower has been erected in the vicinity. One can still see a milestone, twelve feet high—it was the old sighting mark of the Paris Observatory, set up in 1806—and also a pyramid to the memory of the members of the Flatters mission who were murdered by the Touaregs in 1881.

It is on week-days—other than Thursdays, when schools are closed— that the Montsouris Park is most attractive to lovers of peace and solitude.

The Parc Montsouris.

Noises are deadened by the mass of green leaves; even the rumble of the Métro is lost in its tunnel. Paris seems far away, and one can only hear the running of water and the song of the birds.

On leaving the Parc Montsouris by the Boulevard Jourdan, we at once see the buildings of the Cité Universitaire. It has developed considerably since the laying of the first stone in 1920, extending now for over eighty acres and for nearly a mile along the Boulevard Jourdan.

Construction was begun after the 1914-18 war, to provide much-needed accommodation for students. It originally comprised only the seven French Houses of the Deutsch de la Meurthe Foundation, the work of the architect L. Bechman; then later the House of the French Provinces was added. The centre house is topped with a bell tower. Space was not spared; ivy runs all over the walls, and the courtyards are brightened up with plots of lawn. It has doubtless been inspired by Oxford and other British universities, and, on the whole, the result is a happy one.

We can even go as far as to say that the International House, built by the generosity of Mr. John D. Rockefeller, Junior, and inaugurated in 1936, shows a certain grandeur in its style, being a *pastiche* of the second French Renaissance period. The French Houses are surrounded by sixteen foreign foundations, which give the Cité its international character. A number of countries wanted their students to stay in houses which would remind them of their homeland. That is why those of the Japanese and Indochinese students have roofs with upturned corners, like pagodas. Interior decoration for the first of these was done by Foujita. The Swiss architect Le Corbusier, entrusted with the blueprints for his compatriots' house, did not miss the opportunity of designing a building in the form of a square block, with innumerable windows, in accordance with his own aesthetic ideas. Even the Hellenic House, with its Ionian pediment, strives to give the impression that Greece has not surrendered its rôle as the mother of European civilisation.

As a whole, the Cité Universitaire, where the students can enjoy a park and many playing-fields, affords us a comforting feeling of orderliness, youth and mental and physical well-being.

In 1939 it had over two thousand four hundred rooms. It has its own central library, its theatre and its church. It is pleasing to think that, looking out over this green cloister, this source of inspiration—the Parc Montsouris—future artists and scientists can meditate in a peaceful and congenial atmosphere.

Yves GANDON.

THE QUAYS
AND THE BRIDGES

LET US AD-

mit that the adventure which inspired this journey was born in that fragrant city of wines, in the surroundings of the Quai de Bercy, near the Pont National, abounding in tank-waggons and drays which have almost become obsolete. On the right, going down the Seine, the Bercy warehouses open the gateway to Paris. It is a strange city, whose streets and courtyards are so many tributes paid to the vineyards—the vineyards of France —seen against a noble and melodious background of wine casks. From the Rue de Minervois to the Rue de Vouvray, the words Pommard, Sauterne, Bordeaux, Nuits, Romanée and many others, embellish the wine city with vintages whose names are familiar throughout Christendom. A race of cellarmen, arrayed in their professional aprons, surround themselves with the ancient and famous words of their calling. The cooper with the tools of his trade opens the gates · of a city, most moving with all its associations belonging to the great chronicles of history when they become public property. Between the Pont de Bercy and the Pont National, Paris offers a goblet of wine to the nymphs of the Seine, timidly hidden upstream, amongst the reeds of its banks. It has become difficult to conjure up their exact presence in this curious and well-preserved scene, where wines rest in their casks — replete as the well-known monks of the 16th and 17th centuries. All these casks, carefully stored in their appropriate cloisters, recall ancient ghosts, still lively enough to lead the traveller irresistibly towards the singers, viols, bagpipes and hurdy-gurdies of the Quai de la Rapée, in the days when the Picardy song-writer, Mr. Vadé, rhymed songs for Margot La Ravaudeuse or Madelon Friquet. The Quai de la Rapée is a continuation of the Quai de Bercy. Its fickle personality, slightly degraded by the reports left to us by the 18th century police, no longer offers the setting familiar to the Archers of the City of Paris, in the days when they carried halberds and

A View of Paris from the Pont-Neuf
(Carnavalet Museum).

wore star-studded shoulder belts. In those days the Port de la Rapée opened
out on to waste land, with piles of planks and boards here and there.
Though the plan of Paris is strictly defined, sentiment has not been disre-
garded and we cannot wander through the humblest or the most modern
parts of the city without coming across associations with its everyday
past.   This is why the Seine and its quays, with their long history, have
a pleasing way of linking the remote past with the most recent romantic
associations. It is scarcely possible to study Turgot's map without noticing
in this 18th century Paris—which temporarily comes to life again under
our eyes—the somewhat curious silhouettes of Restif and Vadé.   Farther
down the course of the Seine, we will later add to these the bearded face,
the flowing cravat and the tall hat that adorned Gérard de Nerval of
the Rue de la Vieille Lanterne.   One could give no better advice to anyone visiting Paris than to take with them a guide such as can be found
in the romantic world of the Quays of the Seine.   An old adventurer
on the quays of Paris set out from Bercy in about 1882, and eventually
reached Bagatelle in the course of 1936.   He had taken more than half

a century to achieve his aim, which was to settle as best he could in a tool-shed of the Department of Highways and Bridges. This shed, no longer in use, became his home. At nightfall, when the opportunity presented itself, he would relate the history of the bridges of Paris : that of Nini and the proud Chaloupeuse. The heroines of Jean Lorrain, those of the Grande Jatte, of the Point-du-Jour, and of Bagatelle, would appear at his diabolical command, as in " Sous les Ponts de Paris " set to music by Vincent Scotto, one of the delightful poets who sang of the streets, the bridges, and the hazel tinted quays.

Keeping to the itinerary of one of those amusing river steamers which until 1914 plied between the quays of the Seine, and which have reappeared today, and having passed beyond the Pont d'Austerlitz, so named after the battleground—formerly close to the station of the same name—the prow of the Ile Saint-Louis can be seen straddled by the Pont Sully. Access to this peaceful and distinguished island is simple enough; five bridges lead to its graceful and austere quays : the Quai de Bourbon, the Quai d'Anjou, the Quai de Béthune, and the Quai d'Orléans.

Artists and men of letters live there, occasionally in splendour, always sincerely enamoured of this Paris, which, in her eternal youthfulness, is still as enticing as one of the young girls we might meet in Dignimont's studio. A line of graceful trees, drooping over an almost deserted street, lend an air of dignity to the scene.

From the Pont de Saint-Louis-en-l'Ile one can see Notre-Dame de Paris : it is an austere sight and, moreover, a world-famous one; perhaps the most beautiful that Paris can offer. Here we will enter the Mother Island, on tiptoe; this Island shaped like a canal barge which, at the very dawn of French civilisation, germinated the seeds of the *Essais*, of Villon's *Testament*, the correspondence of Stendhal, the *Comédie Humaine*, and all the full-blooded and intellectual groups who enlivened the daily existence and traditions of the Nation. The Cité is of course under the august patronage of Notre-Dame.

The Palais de Justice, the Sainte-Chapelle and Notre-Dame are entrancing resorts, but their history is less intimate. One could scarcely find more impressive buildings than those which grace the Ile Saint-Louis, with its Hôtel d'Astry where Baudelaire once lived; the Hôtel de Pimodan, Daumier's house; the Hôtel de Boisgelin, and many other chapter headings in the history of Paris. However, the Cité, with its now imaginary

467

frescoes, is a unique starting poir.
for all the adventures of a great
spiritual pilgrimage. Eight
bridges give access to it—the
island willingly lets us into her
secret.   These bridges are : the
Pont Saint-Louis, the Pont d'Ar-
cole, the Pont-au-Double, the
Petit Pont, the Pont Notre-Dame,
the Pont-au-Change, the Pont
Saint-Michel, and the Pont-Neuf.
    The ancestor of the Petit Pont
was one of the first
bridges in Paris. It had
been destroyed many
times before it attained
its present form in 1853.
It is amongst the most
respectable of the big
family of Paris bridges;
however, the oldest of

them all is the Pont-Neuf. To tell its story would mean recalling every scene of popular life in Paris. A pleasant assembly of trim chambermaids, of dangerous footmen, of able coat-snatchers, of noisy and vain swashbucklers, of ladies of experience and of elegant youths, were the background of parading buffoons and clowns. When we speak of the Pont-Neuf we think of Jacques Callot, of Sébastien Leclerc, of Saint-Aubin and of Demachy. In this atmosphere of luxury were born all the romantic figures who were to inspire so many famous authors. The "Main de Gloire" galloped at dawn along the parapets of the Pont-Neuf, for, of all the bridges of Paris, the Pont-Neuf was always the only one on which no houses were built. Strollers were at leisure to gaze at the life on the river, which was far more active in the 18th century than today. The quays along the Seine in front of the Ile de la Cité are, as can be expected, rich in history. On the Right Bank there are two names worth remembering : the Quai de Gesvres and the Quai de la Mégisserie. The view from the Quai de la Mégisserie would enrapture even the most impassive of observers. The silhouette of the Conciergerie, along the Quai de l'Horloge, presents a striking picture—one of the most impressive, the most constant aspects of Paris, and the richest in voices of the past, achieving incomparable harmonies of matter and spirit.

These bridges, which link the Ile de la Cité to its four banks, hold within their compass the quintessence of the adventure of Paris. The Middle Ages, so dear to M. Héron de Villefosse and Pierre Champion, can never disappear from the mind's eye of a moderately well-educated person, a cultured man, attracted to, in fact captivated by, the hives of the old book dealers aligned along the ancient parapets. In my opinion, it is one of the most moving sights of Paris—this long row of pad-locked boxes where the good grain of literature mixes freely with the chaff. This "flea-market" of the book trade no longer offers really rare second-hand books. But students of both sexes still search there for a Quicherat bound in grey cloth, or a *Thesaurus Poeticus* by the same author. The men and women who are attracted to these gaping and worm-eaten boxes are fascinating types. Their faces are lit by the thrill of a literary discovery and sometimes of an amazing one. The hand of an old man, trembling slightly, finds there on occasion the sum total of the experience of a lifetime. The best people in Paris meet there, among the thousands of volumes framed by Notre-Dame and the Eiffel Tower which, with its figure like a saurian erect upon its hind legs, can, without a doubt, see as far as the estuary of the Seine, the Lieutenancy of Honfleur, Rouen, the Marais Vernier, and the ancient Mascaret. The bookseller on the quays represents one of the most authentic figures of everyday life in Paris. Seated on a camp-stool in front of the garlands of old prints which shield his book-chest, he seems to symbolise an invitation to a flight of fancy. One can associate him with those attractive ships in bottles which make up the colourful diversity of seaside book-shops. Perhaps one could unearth in these boxes the famous river steamer in a bottle, selected from among those that plied up the Seine more than thirty years ago. With their disappearance the Seine —supposing that she is a girl, as a recent and delightful song says—lost one of her most pleasing features.

Before going further down the river, one can stop awhile on the Quai de la Mégisserie. In the 15th century it was occupied by sellers of fish and poultry, and some traces of this activity still remain. It is there that one chooses pedigreed birds in the egg. All the aristocrats of the poultry farm can trace their origin to this quay. Some romantic-looking stores sell Chinese fish, ferrets, great horned owls, and other wily beasts of prey. Fine fishing-rods of English origin complete the collection.

Across the river is the Quai Conti where, opposite the Pont des Arts, the Institut and the Hôtel de la Monnaie can be seen. On the present site of the Institut rose the Tour de Nesle, patroness of cloak and dagger romances.

Beyond the Pont des Arts, the resort of those who aspire to glory, the Seine pursues its course among the most impressive reminders of the Paris of former days. Here we are in the enclosure of the Kings of France. It is like a film inspired by student life of the Latin Quarter followed by another film inspired by the Valois, whose life was by no

471

means lacking in picturesqueness, giving charm even to the daily habits of certain kings.

There is no need to describe the Louvre, for he who wants to walk along the bridges and quays will have other ideas than to look at an unhappy residence. The Louvre and its neighbour, the Church of Saint-Germain-l'Auxerrois, are inseparably linked together in responsibility for what is called the Saint Bartholemew Massacre. Legend has it that the elegant silhouette of Charles IX appeared in the embrasure of a window, and that this unhappy king was seen firing on the Huguenots who were being scandalously massacred by his captain of the Guards, M. de Cosseins. This tragic detail engraves the picture of this terrible night in the minds of school children and remains indelible even through adult life. Not a trace remains, and the Louvre as it stands today, much improved by Pierre Lescot and later by Jean Goujon, hardly recalls to mind the lugubrious ringing of the bells of Saint-Germain-l'Auxerrois. It is fitting that great historical homes should preserve in the dampness of their old walls the sounds of joyful violins, of cries of hatred, and the terrible lamentation of despair. Historical houses are always haunted to a certain extent: it would be astonishing if it were not so. But to penetrate, however little, into their secrets, one must have the key to dreams. The School of Palaeography possesses it, though its imaginative scope is somewhat limited.

On the Right Bank are the Louvre and the Tuileries, on the Left Bank is the Quai Voltaire with its famous antiquaries and booksellers. Between two rows of noteworthy buildings the Seine is full of tugboats from up-or downstream, their barges always at the quayside, near a sandpile where children play. Here and there poodles are preening themselves. The anglers of Paris are still with us, motionless and absorbed, deaf to all the noises which may upset the world but that in no way disturb the capture of little fresh-water urchins such as chub and gudgeon. The changing sights which the Seine offers are varied enough, but they belong to the landscape to be seen downstream, below the Pont de la Concorde. Upstream of these bridges, the quay of the Right Bank is the boundary of the stately Tuileries gardens, with lawns

and rose-beds extending smoothly to the Place de la Concorde—one of the loveliest spots in Paris and one whose essential character is contained in its name which has no need to be translated. The romantic quality of the landscape stems from the Quai Voltaire on the Left Bank. Musset lived at number 25; Baudelaire and Richard Wagner both lived in the Hôtel Voltaire. Finally, the Hôtel de Tessé was the home of Marshal Bugeaud in his last days.

Beyond the Pont Solférino, the quays of Paris are no longer those of the popular song, at least from dawn till dusk. From late afternoon onwards they are taken over by luxury cars. In the small hours they present quite a different picture: the lorries of the market gardeners, from Versailles and its surroundings, form an unbroken chain from the gardens and orchards of Seine-et-Oise to the pavilions of the " Halles Centrales." Until quite recently the night life of the Paris quays was still bound up with romanticism—and even occasionally with the fantastic social whirl of the city. All cities of the world have a night life, very similar in detail. Paris is not the only city where vagrants take up their abode along the quays or under the bridges, only to vanish in daytime.

The quays of Paris between the Pont Mirabeau, sung of by Guillaume Apollinaire, and the landscape of Billancourt, often served as shelter for inoffensive vagabonds from the banks of the Seine. A somewhat hazy world, of inveterate drunkards and girls who risk the hazards of the streets, used to resort there. Each of these types acquired habits and played several roles in a society of which, no doubt, traces still remain. The Pont de Passy and the Pont de Grenelle are the boundary of the long dismal Ile des Cygnes, where dogs are taken out for their " constitutional. " In the days of the " low dives " described by Eugène Süe, the Ile des Cygnes

sheltered that dangerous maniac, the Chourineur (the killer from the " Mysteries of Paris "). Certain islands of the Seine were dependencies of Paris and had names whose meanings were very precise. They undoubtedly suggested the rabble who seemed to find refuge on them. Nowadays, they merely afford strollers an excuse for harmless exploration. When we have left behind us on the Left Bank the dismal setting of the Javel factories and the Pont Mirabeau, we will, in crossing the Point-du-Jour, have reached the limit of the Seine's course through Paris. This definition is, however, arbitrary; for the Seine, in outlining its loop, comes back towards Paris and tries to encircle it, this time in the coil of a lasso which gathers to its quays the Bois de Boulogne and Levallois, the district famous for manufacturing so many desirable cars. Automobile chassis, without bodies, go down towards Suresnes, following the course of the Seine where the Isles are hitched on to one another like a string of barges, endowed with names, some of which have associations with the life of Paris. Jean Lorrain knew these Isles. Often he drew their contours and showed their human substance. This was no longer the time of the boatmen of the Grenouillère—contemporaries of Guy de Maupassant. This was no longer a sporting, merry Bohemia

that invaded the islands, perfumed by combined odours of sausage made with garlic, and of young Suresnes wine. The rabble of Paris haunted the dance-halls and roadside inns of the Grande Jatte near Levallois. Jean Lorrain, who wrote some fine songs about this deplorable company, often found his inspiration there in the voice of a frail singer somewhat past her prime.

One aspect of Paris cloaks the Isles like a dismal fog: it is the ugly side of life which goes on under cover, in fear of the police. Even the most exemplary of large cities are not immune to the curious psychological defects which serve as material for undoubted masterpieces—however worthless the subjects in themselves may be. Big cities such as London, Rome, Antwerp, and Paris represent an accumulation of unending exper-

iences. The quays of Paris, the bridges of Paris, and the acts they have inspired, go a long way towards building up the sum total of the experiences of a city whose emotional riches are never exhausted, even by the most adroit hunter of dreams and phantoms.

One can thus imagine an adventurer who has barely shaken off the dreams of adolescence, standing erect like a heron on one of the Isles, which in theory defend the first

bridge of Paris. One of this group of three islands is called the Ile d'Enfer. There are five of them in all. The Pont d'Alfort straddles the Ile de la Chaussée, which may be confused with the numerous waterways that branch off from the loop of the Port de Bonneuil. The navigator who undertakes this great tour of the islands of the suburbs and city of Paris is ageless. For him time means nothing. The departure for this great journey must be traced back to the first days of the existence of Lutèce, well before the birth of Saint Geneviève.

A light row-boat for one person, a rustic skiff—the forerunner of the dapper eights of the Lower Seine and a predecessor of the best planned ships—will be a precious asset in this expedition. The discovery of the last island of the suburbs, the Ile de la Loge, will coincide with the appearance, on the quays of the Seine, of de Maupassant, and later with that of Vlaminck and Derain. The navigator, having discovered the school of Chatou, may moor his boat in a film-like setting with a tug, its fog-horn silenced, moored at the end of a cable. Many centuries, even thousands of years, were doubtless necessary in order to create the atmosphere of this film. And the spool, momentarily immobilized, is ready to shoot new scenes of an unpredictable nature. On the Seine clusters of islands follow each other in succession. They conjure up pictures of rushes haunted by herons, storks, multicoloured kingfishers, otters and beavers; the scene will change into boathouses, cement quays, memories of famous painters, popular songs that lament the wretchedness of the people of the quays and of under the bridges.

Leaving aside the Ile Saint-Louis and the Ile de la Cité whose history constitutes the first chapter of the chronicle of Paris, here at the prow of the skiff, at the beginning of the elegant sweep of the Seine, are the Ile Saint-Germain, the Ile de Billancourt and the Ile Seguin, recalling memories of flower-decked inns, popular dances, fried fish and light white wines. Further on the Ile Folie, placed like a little pilot fish in front of the throat of a shark, baits the large Ile de Puteaux, separated by a narrow channel from the Ile du Pont (Pont de Neuilly). And then immediately after comes the Ile de la Grande Jatte, which was famous shortly before 1900 in the palmy days of the cycle tracks of the Seine, of Buffalo Stadium, of the racing districts, of *fours*, of *fives* and of tremendous shouts which ran around the tracks with their banked turns, cheering Jimmy Michaël, Zimmermann, Jacquelin, the two Lintons, Bourillon and their supporters and the fans of Choppy Warburton the trainer. In this procession, Tristan Bernard, Alfred Capus, Toulouse-Lautrec and Henri Desgranges also left their mark on this portrait of Paris lacking neither colour nor adventure.

Between two banks bordered by factories and quays suitable for car trials, one sees the Ile Robinson and the Ile des Ravageurs. The latter was for a long time the refuge of plunderers of wrecks. It played its part in the mysteries of Paris and brought fascinating documents in proof of the existence of pickpockets who enlivened Eugène Süe's novels and sometimes those of Alexandre Dumas. We will end this journey to the land of isles by those of Saint-Ouen and Saint-Denis. Near the latter, the loop breaks away from Paris. The water, reflecting week-end cottages, flows towards the estuary, and towards other tales.

I once had the opportunity, a long time ago, to sail down the Seine on a small cargo boat bound for Rouen. In those days, for me at least, the isles of Paris and its little known suburbs lost their insignificance, chiefly because of the names, charged with violent and suffering poetry, which made them known on the river chart. An island is always a little responsible for the flights of fancy of those who discover it. Paris was born of an island, from an egg in the form of a Cathedral, and grew along banks haunted by sailors and fishermen. As it spread, this incomparably fertile city encountered Villon. It continued to blossom in the shape of a heart. In tribute to the boatmen and duck-hunters who protected their fields or tended their flocks, their descendants designed a ship on the coat-of-arms of the city, an unsinkable ship, built on the model of the caravels which anchored along the banks of the new world.

This is no way of ending the story of the bridges and quays of Paris, by associating them with adventures on the high seas. However, the Port of Paris is gradually developing. Its marine sights are in no way comparable with those of the Thames but one may foresee an astounding future, when all that went before will merge into the splendid imagery of a world that is vanishing; a world which will, we hope, be preserved if only in libraries and museums.

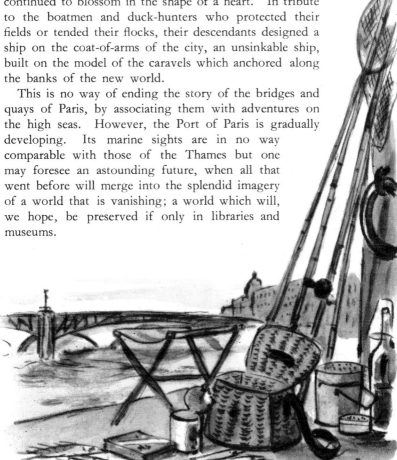

The song of the water, the wisdom of the water, the secrets of the water, are the undoubted evidence, for a very great city, of the quality of its past. All along the quays of Paris, one meets men who take pleasure in listening to the song of the water, even if they cannot drink it. There are still a few wise men left such as the many anglers who attune their inner rhythm, that of their blood stream, to the wisdom of the waters of the Seine. There are also those who collect poems about the city's river, and a diversity of engravings inspired by the ancient deeds of Paris society through the ages.

With these reflections, we conclude our journeys through Paris along the banks of the Seine. It is but the pastime of an idler, a "stroller on the two banks," as Guillaume Apollinaire wrote, at a time when he and I could see from our windows both the barges on the Seine and the ramblings of modish dogs on the Quai de Passy, behind the gasometers in the Rue de Ranelagh.

Pierre MAC ORLAN.

Paris, home of the epicure

E. M. PEROT

OTHON FRIESZ. — *Still Life (a fragment of a screen)* (from the Dubois-Pedron collection).

UST ASK

one of those great epicures, member or president of heaven knows how many dining clubs, which style of French cooking he likes best:

" Is it the Bordeaux, where Arcachon soles and Pauillac lamb are combined with butter from the Charentes and oysters from Marennes —all washed down with an exquisite wine ? Is it the cooking of Lyons ? Or that of Burgundy, with its *gougères*, its marbled ham, its stewed beef, its eggs *en meurette*, blended with Chambertin and Meursault ? Is it the cooking of the Nantes area ? or of Normandy, Savoy, Alsace or Lorraine ? Is it..."

The great epicure will raise his hand in a pontifical gesture to arrest your flood of questions. " It is Parisian cooking," he will reply—" all the others are too rich. " He will then fall into a profound reverie, while he savours the bouquet of a glass of old brandy.

Is it the vivacity and liveliness of Paris that inspires this amazing statement ? It may be. It is in fact true that there is a style of cooking peculiar to Paris, or rather a way of cooking in Paris that has nothing in common with provincial cooking, just as there are millions of provincials who have become Parisians. Most Parisian restaurants have a charming way of advertising their place of origin, just as Parisians cast a melancholy glance at the station where one morning they arrived from their province.

A meal does not take so long in Paris; the menu is not so plentiful, it usually has one course less than in the provinces. It is light, yet at the same time substantial, and above all it is larded less with fat than with conversation. It is Parisian conversation, that running commentary where talk flows freely on all and sundry, dominating the rhythm and details of a meal that is all the better for being light. It is also the chatter that gives Paris restaurants that kind of gay hum that strikes one on entering—and there are also the Parisian women.

They have good appetites, it is true; but they are elegant. We cannot imagine them wearing a flowery hat perched straight on their foreheads, facing a huge meal or the sort of dish a bricklayer eats. It is they who create the atmosphere and who turn the smallest of eating-houses—that they have made fashionable—into a gay spot, where the waitress wears silk stockings and has a permanent wave.

To this the provinces reply that in Paris the cooking is not bad, but the wines are poor. This is a matter to be considered and we shall come back to it later.

Truth to tell, the amusing side of Paris is its restaurants. They constitute, along with the stew perpetually simmering on the *concierge's* stove, the most typical and inimitable aspects of the capital. With tears in their eyes, old epicures still talk about "Voisin" at the corner of the Rue Cambon and the Rue Saint-Honoré, about "Paillard" at the corner of the boulevard and the Chaussée-d'Antin, with as much reverence as Balzac mentions the "Frères Provençaux," or Maupassant the "Tortoni" or the "Café Anglais." The large Paris restaurants are unique in the world, and the chef's white cap has conquered the globe: it triumphs in basement kitchens as well as in ocean liners. Large dinner parties used to be given in private houses with a number of courses, and sherbets between each course—the masterpieces of the hostess, who added to them a set piece—a brilliant conversationalist, preferably an Academician, who held the floor alone, and left the other guests to the pleasures of the table. But today there are no more pompous dinner parties in evening dress. Parisians have now adopted the habit of meeting in restaurants, four or usually six at a time. The cook has to go to the cinema some time. Everything, I repeat, has changed; so let us go to the restaurant.

The typically Parisian restaurant, which has become fashionable since the First World War, is the "bistro." This is a slang word that is perhaps derived from " bistre " (sepia) the usual colour of their walls. The bistro, with its curved and shining counter behind which the proprietor serves drinks and pours out wine; the bistro where the meals are cooked by the proprietor's wife; the bistro with its marble-topped tables, with a single waitress whom the *habitués* call by her Christian name; the bistro where one can only get two or three courses and good ordinary wine, where the telephone is in the broom cupboard; the bistro with its floor strewn with sawdust; the bistro where the proprietor stretches out a damp hand over the counter to greet you and treats you to a drink on New Year's Day; the bistro with its ham and sausages hanging from the ceiling, its iron tables outside enclosed by spindly trees in boxes on the pavement. The more remote it is, the better—in some little street whose name you can never remember and where you know nobody but where everybody goes, and that is mentioned in the smartest circles and in the bars of the Champs-Elysées, in a nonchalant way—" I know of a little place where we could go..."

Customers arrive, prices go up,

the *habitués* stop coming, the proprietor engages a cook, then a chef; he paints the walls and modernises his restaurant, he no longer appears in his shirt-sleeves but in a suit. The bistro has become ugly, it has lost its character and, with it, its charm. We must find another one. Thank goodness there are plenty.

One of the most typical is the " Louis XIV " in the Place des Victoires. It is quiet and charming; on the first floor there is a long, low room where, on the 28th of each month, the " Lunch of the 28th " takes place, uniting artists and scholars, most of them famous. Roast chicken and fried potatoes, that is Paris, but the stuffed veal suggests that the cook comes from Corrèze. You will say that it would be delightful to live in the fine houses of the Place des Victoires, and the charm of this bistro is doubled by its antique setting. There is also the " Boule d'Or " in the Place d'Aligre, on the site of the old coaching inn of the Lyons mail. The cobbled courtyard can still be seen, but the stables are now garages. You do not know the Place d'Aligre ? It is a small, circular place where polonia trees grow, and in spring their mauve clusters brighten it up. A small " flea market " is held there daily. It is situated beyond the Faubourg Saint-Antoine and was the old Haymarket in the time of the Revolution, and from there the people set out to storm the Bastille. The proprietor makes hot *foie gras* pies, sole cooked in champagne and a number of other amazing dishes, of which he serves large helpings. He is modest about his talent; but *Tout Paris* has discovered it and invaded it, after the manner of privateers who have captured a man-of-war. The local inhabitants watch with interest these newcomers with their American cars lined up all round the square, who will one day leave just as they came—if the cooking or the cook loses caste. One could almost believe that distance attracts the epicures, just as it has attracted them to distant Villette behind the railings of the market, from where the lowing of the cattle and the bleating of lambs can be heard. The wholesale butchers in their long dark-blue overalls, their wallets bursting with money, come there to swallow solid food—Chateaubriand steaks the size of a " Who's Who," and *pommes édredons* (eiderdown potatoes) puffed out and the colour of gold. One must be fond of under-done meat, and one must also have a car, for the never-ending Avenue Jean Jaurès is very dull. However, these restaurants at La Villette are renowned for the quality and abundance of their menus. The grilled

pigs' trotters, the kidneys, the meat of all kinds you get in those two restaurants, the "Cochon d'Or" and the "Dagorno," are still unequalled. It was in this last restaurant that between the two wars the journal *Crapouillot* gave noisy and gay dinner parties, where so many painters and writers—now famous—used to meet.

On the other side of the market, in the Rue de Flandre, one or two restaurants such as "L'Amiral" and the "Tête de Bœuf" also do honour to meat. Let us cross Paris as far as the church of Auteuil, where, opposite the band-stand, there is the "Clocher du Village." It is a simple and charming little restaurant with the additional attractive feature that the walls are hung with water-colours painted by the proprietor. On summer evenings that old village square, where Molière, Racine, and Boileau used to drink at the "Moulin Blanc" in the Rue d'Auteuil, is still reminiscent of a small provincial town. Not far from there, in the Rue Chardon-Lagache, a minute Italian restaurant, the " San Francisco," offers—at a ransom price—" Lasagne " with parmesan, smooth and melting, served by the proprietor himself, who has a face like a tenor from the Scala of Milan.

But for old Parisians the best restaurants are at the Halles. They follow the rhythm of life of this amazing market, for they open at dawn and close in the afternoon. During the night the pavilions are filled with the produce brought in by the market-gardeners and others—vegetables, flowers, poultry, butter, oysters, with sliced bullocks and whole lambs hung up behind the railings. It is difficult to get around in the Halles when they are filled up with these night workers, full of the riotous good humour that wealth and abundance always bring with them. All around the market, in the Rue Rambuteau, the Rue Pierre-Lescot, the Rue Vauvilliers, the Rue Berger, the Rue des Halles, the Rue de la Réale, restaurants open up, while working clothes are to be seen in front of the counters where white wine flows, or round the tables where onion soup holds sway with pork trotters and pickled pork. A

few night prowlers arrive from Montmartre and Montparnasse. Their dinner jackets and evening dresses jostle against the blood-stained overalls of the butchers who, without turning their heads, watch them in the long mirror behind the counter and, as in *La Vie Parisienne*, the sweeper stops, stares and exclaims " Oy ! you lucky devils ! "

Towards the end of the morning the Halles grow quieter, and one can have lunch peacefully in one of those excellent restaurants, quite unpretentious to look at, but where everything that is served is amazingly fresh. " Le Grand Comptoir " in the

Rue Pierre-Lescot, " Le Soleil d'Or " opposite the church of St. Eustache, " La Médaille " in the Rue Rambuteau, " Le Pied de Mouton " in
the Rue Vauvilliers, and " Monteil " in the Rue de la Réale, are outstanding for the warm welcome one finds there, the good humour of the
waiters in their shirt-sleeves and blue aprons, and the quality of the
cooking. Here is real Parisian cooking, simple and well done, without
complicated sauces and without any other flavour than that imparted
by the ability of the cook. This is the realm of the Coquille St. Jacques,
of grilled sardines, or pork sausages and the *entrecôte marchand de vins.*

The cheeses are always perfect and the wine is fresh and pleasant to
drink. The meal is served on marble-topped tables, service is rapid and
the atmosphere is one of good cheer. One cannot have supper there,
for the proprietor and the waiters are up at dawn; but there are two
restaurants open at night at the Halles. One is small, ancient and attractive—" La Grille " in the Rue Montorgueil, which cannot have changed
in the slightest over the last hundred years; the other is one of the best
restaurants in Paris, if not the smartest—the famous " Escargot
d'Or " in the Rue Montorgueil. It would be out of place in this
workaday district, were it not to a certain extent the façade of the Temple
of Trade, of Craftmanship and of Industry. People go there to enjoy
simple but skilful cooking, of an authentic quality, served by waiters
in white aprons and black coats, just as in the old days. The setting
is that of the Second Empire or the beginning of the Third Republic. We

can quite imagine Monsieur Perrichon dining there with his wife and daughter, also Gambetta and Clemenceau arguing together there after having taken their article to the Rue du Croissant quite close by. Little talking is heard, no ladies of fashion nor bar-loungers come there; it is frequented only by wealthy sedate people, who know how to appreciate a *sauce hollandaise*, or kidneys with juniper berries. One does not look at one's neighbour, one does not go there to be looked at. But it is good to be there and everything is perfect.

Let us cross the Pont-Neuf quite close by. There is the " Vert Galant " restaurant in the Ile de la Cité, which is opulent and excellent, and beside it there is the small restaurant " Paul," quite a picturesque place which has two entrances, the one on the Quai des Orfèvres, the other on the Place Dauphine. It is a charming little bistro, quiet and in keeping with the little square itself. Behind us is the Ile Saint-Louis, with " Le Bossu " on the Quai Bourbon—the chef is excellent, and the superb and smiling lady who owns the restaurant adds to its value. The clock of the church of Saint-Gervais chimes the passing hours. No gourmet would dream of coming or leaving Le Bossu without leaning on the parapet of the island, over that lovely quay, alongside which stand those beautiful houses, inhabited in bygone days by presidents of Parliament.

By crossing the Seine at the Pont de la Tournelle, we arrive at the " Tour d'Argent," as well known throughout the world as " Maxim's " or " Larue." At night, at the very top of the building, one can see from afar the blaze of light from its great windows through which the diners can admire the sunset behind Notre-Dame and the barges on the Seine. Its main clientele consists of rich foreigners, who are given the number of the " Canard au sang," the age of the old brandy worth its weight in gold, also the inventory of the cellar where the most famous vintages are kept. It is quite the opposite of the sedate " Escargot " hidden in the cabbage leaves of the Halles. As we go down the quay, we find " Mag-

deleine " whose blonde proprietress came from the " Le Soleil d'Or "
at the Halles—and this needs no comment. The restaurant is decorated
with photographs of renowned actors and actresses and wrestling champions. It takes all kinds to make a world ! A few steps further on we
find " La Bouteille d'Or, " one of the oldest restaurants in Paris; it seems
to have come straight out of an etching of the time of the Revolution.
Its *fricassé de poulet* is not to be overlooked. The vagrants from the
Place Maubert nearby warm themselves in the sun along the quay, a
bottle of red wine at their side, apparently without envying the diners
at the " Tour d'Argent " or at " Magdeleine." As we continue down
the quay, we pass in front of the " Rôtisserie Périgourdine," an immense
temple of truffles and *foie gras* without much atmosphere, and we reach
" Lapérouse "—the famous restaurant with low ceilings and pretty
window-frames—the ideal setting for a gallant 18th century etching.
It is charming and sedate, of good taste, smart without ostentation;
the cooking and the wines are as fine as the setting; the view across the
tip of the Ile de la Cité and the Quai des Orfèvres is enchanting.

At the beginning of the Boulevard Saint-Germain there are the restaurants of the Halle aux Vins (wine market), where the food is good but
the wine still better. " Ducottet," " Marius," and " Le Coq au Vin " are
the best. Towards the other
end of the Boulevard is the
Saint-Germain-des-Prés
district, enlivened in the
day-time by the students of
the Beaux-Arts, the young
writers of the " Flore " and
the " Deux-Magots," the
agitated youth of the night-
clubs installed in cellars, and
at night by Americans who
all hope to meet Jean-Paul
Sartre. There are number-
less bistros and restaurants
of all kinds. The best are
" Allard " in the Rue de
l'Eperon; " La Reine Christ-

ine " in the Rue Christine; " Le Catalan "—Picasso's restaurant—he lives close by in a beautiful 17th century house in the Rue des Grands Augustins; " Le Relais de Porquerolles," a Provençal restaurant in the Rue de l'Eperon; " La Méditerranée " in the Place de l'Odéon—also Provençal: " La Chope " and " Maître Paul " in the Rue Monsieur-le-Prince. There are more modest restaurants, enlivened as much as the others by the international youth of Saint-Germain-des-Prés. " Les Gourmets " and " Les Canettes," both in the Rue des Canettes; the " Petit Saint-Benoît " in the Rue Jacob and " Michaud " at the corner of the Rue des Saint-Pères. The quietest and most peaceful of all is " Gafner " in the Rue Dauphine.

As we continue down the Boulevard Saint-Germain, we arrive in the stately Faubourg Saint-Germain. There, in that amazing quadrangle that goes from the Rue de Lille to the Rue de Varenne, a very attractive little restaurant called " Albert " welcomes in the evening the smartest of people; they are the inhabitants of the district, and at midday the civil servants of the neighbouring ministries. Also in the Faubourg Saint-Germain, at the end of the Avenue Bosquet there is a Burgundy restaurant well worth a visit, if only to taste the national burgundy *apéritif* called the " Cassegrain "—that is to say, a glass of Montrachet coloured by a drop of black currant liqueur from Dijon. It awakens the appetite for the good cooking of the owner: ham fritters, steak *à la mœlle*, sweetbreads with truffles—all that is worth considering, and in the cellar are remarkable wines. What is more, it is not too dear — if only it lasts !

Let us cross the Seine. At the corner of the Rue François 1er and the Rue Pierre-Charron, " Joseph " behind its windows hidden by leaves, conceals a small and very smart restaurant of excellent tone, quiet and cosy, where the cooking is refined and savoury. So many other restaurants in the Champs-Elysées are but gastronomical bazaars that it is better to pass these teeming avenues and to go and have dinner at " Guyot " in the Rue Médéric. It is a minute restaurant, very clean, and the lady who owns it cooks delightfully. Unless—if you are a horseman or a protector of horses—you go to " L'Etrier," in the Avenue de Villiers, the proprietor of which won the Grand Prix with his horse " Souverain." On the walls are photographs of the horse, on the sideboard stands the gold cup. All this does not prevent the cooking from being very good.

Finally, the Rue Royale is the street of the most famous restaurants. If Foyot has disappeared from the Rue de Tournon, if Voisin is no more in the Rue Cambon, if Paillard has vanished from the Chaussée-d'Antin, there still remain two world-famed haunts in the Rue Royale : " Maxim's " and " Larue." Maxim's has just celebrated its fiftieth anniversary. Under the chandeliers, the brass and mahogany are blended, as for the entrance to a luxurious Métro station. The whole world and the *Tout Paris* still come to dine and dance there and breathe an air of *Belle vie*, of that life in the nineteen hundreds when a louis was worth twenty francs and a dinner at Maxim's half that amount. Here we have champagne and the soufflé Rothschild, and there are more foreigners than Parisians. But it is gay, and we could not imagine Paris without " Maxim's." At the other end of the street " Larue " offers the luxury of its pink seats, its lace curtains, its quiet and flawless approach, its refined cooking and its cellar sparkling with precious wines. It is highly fashionable, with a slight touch of the old-fashioned lending it grace. On a fine summer's evening with the windows open, one really feels in Paris there, and in winter when the rain is falling outside, its quiet warmth is like a soft light shining through a beautiful lamp shade.

There are many restaurants in Paris but these are the most characteristic. However, " Pierre " on the Place Gaillon has a fountain; opposite it " Drouant " has the Goncourt Academy; the " Belle Aurore " in the Rue Gomboust has its numberless hors-d'œuvres and its setting of the 1789 Revolution. What shall we say about the " Café de Paris," which is just as it was

thirty years ago, minus the Tziganes, plus the Samba ? About the foreign restaurants, the Russian ones such as " Korniloff " and " Dominique "; Spanish ones like " Barcelona " where everybody sings, including the proprietor and the clients, to accompany the dancer and guitarist; the Italian ones such as " Ferrari " in the Avenue Rapp; the Greek, the Turk, the Hebrew ones like " Mammy " in the Avenue Montaigne ?

There are restaurants that appeared at the end of the war after leading an obscure life during the occupation : little places where one sings, such as the gay " Patachou " on the Butte Montmartre; old restaurants like " Prunier "; the grill-rooms of the smart hotels such as the Chatham or the Ritz; the bars in the Champs-Elysées or Montmartre where one can sometimes get quite a good supper; good, well-established restaurants, without glamour but faithful to the good traditions, around the Gare de l'Est; those of the Bois de Boulogne where one dines out under the trees; those of the Park Montsouris, the Buttes Chaumont, Neuilly— such as " La Truffe Noire," " Le Progrès " or " Jarasse." They are as full of variety and diversity as Paris itself. Paris alone offers the delightful choice of all those restaurants, so varied and so welcoming, and if in the end I had to choose one, I really think I would go to Renault near the Pont de Neuilly in one of the by-streets of Puteaux. Old Father Renault is a kind of Ragueneau of painting and his restaurant is crammed with pictures, including many fine ones. Painters receive the best of welcomes. Is not this restaurant the synthesis of cooking and the fine arts, those two passions of the Parisians ?...

Jean OBERLÉ.

THE NIGHTS OF PARIS

E·M·DEROT

BERROETTA. — *The Place de la Concorde at night.*

edge of the lake of Armenonville, in the Bois de Boulogne, six people are seated at sunset in front of a bottle of champagne. They want to spend their evening in the best possible way, in the most Parisian way. Where are they to go?

There are so many ways of passing an evening in Paris, with all the resources of pleasure that it offers, that a little indecision is understandable and it is worth while reflecting before making a choice.

The man who wants a "smart" party, a fashionable evening, proposes this standard programme—dinner at *Maxim's* or the *Tour d'Argent*, a visit to *Chez Florence* and onion soup at the Halles.

For three quarters of a century, Maxim's, with its old-world setting, its private rooms, its flawless service and its slow orchestra has been the rendezvous of the fashionable world. One dines there for little more than one pays at a modish little restaurant in the Champs-Elysées, but the presence of eminent Parisians and ladies in dresses by Fath, Dior and Piguet, against the setting of the wine-coloured walls, is a sight of which one never tires. The setting of the Tour d'Argent is different; it stands among the foundation stones of Paris. Seated in a glass-covered terrace you dine on *canard du chef*; the dish is served to you twice —first the legs, then the wings. The bird has its registered number and you have the pleasure of knowing that you are eating the 210,000th. Right before your eyes are the statue of St. Geneviève and the towers of Notre-Dame. One word of advice: if you are going to the Tour d'Argent by way of the quays, make a slight détour when you arrive at the Place St. Michel. Turn left by way of the little Rue de la Huchette, and you will see a view of Notre-Dame that no photographer has ever succeeded in snapping.

An evening party that begins at Maxim's generally continues at Chez Florence. In Montmartre, this cabaret holds the palm among people of good taste. On Fridays, evening dress is compulsory. The Princess of Greece has a table permanently reserved for her among the tables of honour on the right. Jacques Fath and his foreign clients are inveterate dancers there. The band of the American Negro, Arthur Briggs, is made up of Negroes and white men — a long-familiar practice in fashionable spots in Paris, but only recently common in similar resorts in America. After three or four hours there, watching the well-known and much-discussed celebrities of Parisian life, one is apt to become hungry. Then is the time to have onion soup in one of those little eating-houses of the Halles. Their permanent clientele varies according to the time of night; it consists of butchers, market-gardeners and retailers —christened respectively " the meat, " " the vegetables " and " the salad. " They come to eat and drink there from ten at night until dawn. Between them and the idle rich from Maxim's there is always an exchange of coarse language, bantering but never harsh, indicating an ephemeral but sincere *camaraderie*. On leaving the *Pied de Cochon* or the *Cigogne*, at about four in the morning, a glow of dawn is already spreading over a sleeping Paris.

" We might perhaps try and book a table at the *Grenouille*, " suggests another member of the party, " and then take the chance of getting into one of the *caves* of St-Germain-des-Prés. "

In the days before the war Roger, the landlord of the Grenouille, trained his customers to ask his permission before bringing a friend : the family circle was a very closed one. Today those old-time habitués, who were then poverty-stricken students, have become eminent members of the financial, political and literary world. But they have not forgotten La Grenouille, with its 15 tables one behind the other. The traditional dish in this minute restaurant is frogs' legs *à la Provençale*. You read the menu from an immense slate hung on the wall at the end

of the oblong room, by means of binoculars that are passed from table to table. With its multi-coloured and multiform objects hanging from the walls and the ceiling, the Grenouille is one of the sights of Paris, and he or she who leaves without his little green frog in terra-cotta, received in exchange for a copious kiss from the land-lord, misses one of the treats of Paris. But a disadvantage of the Grenouille is the number of inquisitive strangers who go there. There are other places, such as *Louisette la Basquaise*, on the Quai des Grands Augustins, or the *Echelle de Jacob*, the *Trois Assassins*, or the *Quatrième République*, which are equally attractive.

All these little restaurants have one thing in common—you must dine there early. While waiting for the time when the *caves* of St-Germain-des-Prés liven up, we can take a seat on the terrace of the *Café de Flore* or the *Deux-Magots*, opposite the church. There is an inevitable crowd of foreigners, and always the pale and gaunt intellectuals of the Latin Quarter as well, with the students of the Beaux-Arts who, when there is a dance transform themselves into redskins and afford the delighted passers-by a show worthy of the Montmartre *chansonniers*. The crowd at the Flore always hopes to see a celebrity, an existentialist or an anti-existentialist, and from nine in the morning until midnight the tables are hardly ever empty. The development of the *caves* can be explained by a phenomenon analogous —or rather parallel—to the Sartre vogue. The first of this kind was the *Lorientais*, in the Rue St. Jacques, where young people between the ages of 15 and 20 used to go to celebrate, in quasi-barbaric dances, the existentialist doctrine : " Life is action." It was soon followed by the *Tabou* in the Rue de l'Ancienne Comédie. But the young enthusiasts of Claude Luter and New Orleans jazz grew tired of seeing the inquisitive, the smart set, and the uninitiated flocking round them, and they migrated to the *St-Germain-des-Prés Club* at a stone's throw from the church of the same name. Then as the Paris crowds, always avid for new amusements, invaded these haunts, the young existentialists surrendered : or rather they compromised. They have opened, one after the other, the *Club du Vieux-Colombier*; the two *Roses Rouges*—the one in the Rue de Rennes, where you will find the Jacques brothers and the Compagnie Grenier-

Hussenot, made up entirely of men who mime and sing, and the other in the Rue de la Harpe which Negroes have chosen for their home and which celebrates in music the charms of Darkest Africa ; the *Caveau de la Huchette*, in the little street of the same name, and many others more or less secret and hidden—for a few weeks at least—until they in turn are overrun by the legions of the inquisitive. But if you want four hours to pass like a flash, with no dancing, but just drinking whisky in the tiniest little vault in Paris, then go to the *Quodlibet*, in the basement of the Hôtel St-Thomas d'Aquin, in the Rue du Pré-aux-Clercs. The director, Francis Claude, a former inspector of taxes and a graduate in philosophy, who preferred frivolous pastimes and the art of the *chansonnier* to his more respectable professions, will help you to pass away the time, in spite of the smoke, the lack of air and the crowds—characteristics that are common to all the *caves* in the quarter, and without which they would be almost entirely lacking in atmosphere.

" Does that tempt you ? " " Possibly. But couldn't we divide the evening in two and see Montparnasse ? " An evening in Montparnasse, in pre-war days or even earlier, in the grand old times of Jaurès and the socialists, meant the *Dôme*, the *Rotonde* and the *Closerie des Lilas*. But fashions have changed, and the Parisian intelligentsia seems to have deserted Montparnasse for Saint-Germain-des-Près. Montparnasse appears no longer to enjoy the exclusive patronage of the students of all nations who came to Paris to discover the free, creative atmosphere that was, once upon a time, the prerogative of the boulevard brasseries. But one can still spend a pleasant evening dining at *Dominique's*, the little Russian restaurant where

you are served with borsch, shashlik, blini with salmon or with cream, washed down with vodka; and then going on to *Schubert's*, *Jimmy's* or the *College Inn* (which has nothing English about it, except the name) where excellent bands play until 5 o'clock, when the last couple yields to fatigue and goes home.

"But Montmartre?" asks the fourth member of the party at Armenonville. "Has Montmartre gone into the land of the 'has beens'?"

Without Montmartre, and especially without Pigalle, Paris would so disappoint foreigners that it could not afford to let them fall into oblivion. No, the *Butte* still offers gaiety, laughter, song and good cheer. Before dinner we can take an apéritif in the *Jardin de Montmartre*, with the Sacré-Coeur behind us and the whole of Paris stretching out at our feet. *Barbe* or *Patachou* will welcome you with open arms—on condition, however, that you have booked your table a week in advance. In both of these restaurants it is the guests who sing and act and who laugh at each other's turns, behind the roguish, mocking eye of the hostess, who seems to tolerate your presence as if she were giving you a meal out of charity. The whole repertory of French drinking songs and students' and barrack-room ditties, bordering on the indelicate, are heard there, and the hostess declares that nothing is funnier than to make foreigners —who are completely lost in these surroundings—utter vulgarities without in the least understanding their meaning. The dessert is only served about midnight. If we have any strength left, we can go to the *Lapin Agile* to hear the *chansonniers*. At about six in the morning, the Place du Tertre empties and resumes its normal life, as the centre of the free commune of old Montmartre, and the local inhabitants have it to themselves.

"We can't do both," decides the fifth member of the party. "In a single evening, it's impossible to do the Butte and Pigalle. We must choose."

Pigalle is the triangle formed by the Place Clichy, the Place St.-Georges and Anvers Métro station. It is at Pigalle that the night-clubs are to be found—always the same and yet different. The Pigalle of the crooks, of the "guides" who offer to conduct strangers through the maze of streets towards a cabaret worthy of them, has never failed to be attractive, entrancing and even exhilarating. A haze of glory has always surrounded it—the ineffacable legend of "having a good time." We might go to *Liberty's*, in the Place Blanche, where Tonton, the *inverti*, makes his audience blush with his interpellations, but undoubtedly gives them their money's worth. Or more simply, to appreciate the popular atmosphere of the streets, we might have a snack in one of the large *brasseries* in the Boulevard Clichy or Rochechouart, at *Wepler* or *Graff's*, listening to a gypsy band, and end up at one of the nightclubs that the whole world talks about—*Scheherazade, Monseigneur* or *Casanova*—where the champagne is

very dear but where the violonist comes to play at your table to help you forget the fact, and where the red and gilt walls hung with rich, heavy fabrics, invite confidences. There is also—above all—the *Tabarin*, where unaccompanied gentlemen, on the elderly side, take their pleasure in watching the loveliest girls in Paris undress and dance on the stage.

" But none of you has yet mentioned the quarter that is at least as famous as Montmartre or Montparnasse—the Champs-Elysées. Quite a time ago, ten years or more, the Champs-Elysées was nothing more than a promenade for distinguished people. Gradually, large modern buildings were erected, and commerce invaded the avenue. Nowadays, though it is predominantly a business centre, it is also a place of

entertainment at night. Why not dine in that part of the Champs-Elysées that still keeps its cool greenery, at *Le Doyen* or the *Pavillon de l'Elysée*? A little spiral staircase takes you up to the first floor where, in a warmly decorated rotunda, you can dine and dance. Or why not try one of those Chinese restaurants which have infiltrated into the Rue Marbeuf and the Rue du Colisée area? After dinner, we can argue as to whether we prefer a bright little cabaret such as the *Night Club*, whose proprietor, the *chansonnier* Maurice Martelier, knows how to create a perfect atmosphere, or the *Villa d'Este* next door; a show on the grand scale such as the *Lido*, or a night club with a sophisticated band such as the *Club des Champs-Elysées* which always manages to put on a good show; the *Bœuf sur le Toit* which, having known great days before the war, now attempts by means of an entirely different type of entertainment, to become the *Tabou* of the Right Bank; *Carrère*, famed for its high-class teas, its fashion displays, its fine dinners and its *chansonniers*; the *Ambassadeurs* that, once a year, beats the great American revues and borrows their ideas of ice-skating shows; or last of all and pre-eminently, the *Vernet*, the domain of Jean Rigaux, the *chansonnier* who has strayed from Montmartre to the Champs-Elysées, and who will make you weep with laughter for two hours on end. An evening in the Champs-Elysées rarely ends up without a visit to the *Club de Paris* or the bar of the *Relais Plaza* where the club sandwich and the welsh rarebit are the traditional snacks of a clientele made up of tired revellers and actors who have finished their evening's work.

" What do you think ? What shall we decide on ? "

We have not yet spoken about the Paris of the boulevards with its crowded café terraces, all the way from the Opéra to the Porte St-Martin, where small orchestras play popular music; the Paris of the Bastille and the Rue de Lappe, the Paris of the mob, vulgar and good-natured, the Paris of the Arab, Chinese and Jewish quarters, the Paris of the islands—the Ile de la Cité and the Ile St. Louis—where barge-men's eating-houses would give us a surprise.

" Shall we toss up for it ? "

Our six people may perhaps succeed in deciding by this means, but we cannot

blame them if, when they meet again, on a beautiful June night, the burning question that ten thousand Parisians ask every evening is again raised—where are we going tonight?

Paris in June, the Paris of the " *Grande Saison* " offers the night-bird two or three special performances every evening. Using the pretext of aiding charity, and taking advantage of the long warm evenings when women are most beautiful, dresses most ethereal, and the flowers smell their sweetest, every device is adopted to bring them together in new settings under the symbols of Beauty and Elegance.

There are the traditional " Nights " that begin with the " Rose Fortnight " in June—and they all have their own theme; there is the Lace Night, the Ribbon Night, the Fan Night—pretexts for the dressmakers to vie with each other in taste and ingenuity in garnishing their customers' dresses with lace or ribbons—and for the Fan Night, trinkets that have long gone out of use in this over-mechanised age. There is the Diadem Night when jewels of fabulous worth adorn hair, necks and wrists. There are the Republican Nights when the gentlemen of the Civil Service leave their customary stiffness behind for a few hours; the Chancery Night, honoured by the presence of the President of the Republic; the Palais Royal Night when the Counsellors of State and their wives dance the lancers' quadrille; the Legion of Honour Night, the Navy Night.

Paris, with your Nights of a thousand facets, when amusement becomes a charity function, what poetry will ever be lyrical enough to express your great Nights that levy a tax on pleasure to solace the misfortunes of the disinherited? The Artists' Gala Night, when every star performs a circus turn; the Night of the Little White Beds organised at the Opera, for the benefit of the Paris hospitals, when artists come from all over the world for the celebrated procession over the " Silver Bridge." To go up the great staircase of the Opéra between the rows of Republican Guards in full-dress uniform, to have supper at the little tables in the foyer of the theatre, to stroll over the floor of the house listening to song and speech, to see all the beauty, elegance and wealth of Paris—all this leaves a memory worthy of the *Arabian Nights*.

It would need the talent and imagination of a Scheherazade to describe the Paris Nights—those of the University, of the Commercial High School, the Polytechnic, the Schools of Medicine and Pharmacy, the

Beaux-Arts, the famous Bal des Quat'z Arts, when half-naked boys and girls, picturesquely disguised and uttering savage cries stream across Paris from Montparnasse to the Etoile; the Sporting Nights—that of the Chantilly Stud Farm, the St. Cloud Golf Club; the musical nights in the open-air theatre of the Parc de Sceaux. And the nights of the Fourteenth of July, when there is dancing at every street corner and when the great singers go from one crossroads to another to " do a turn " to the delight of immense crowds, wild with joy at the fireworks and the carnival atmosphere of the great national festival ! Nights of winter and nights of summer, nights of the " *Grande Saison*," every-day nights and gala nights, unrestrained Bohemian nights with *verve*, talent, taste, wealth, wit and even genius uniting to afford a few hours of relaxation and escape from a hundrum existence. Paris, generous city, offers beauty and luxury even in her streets, and one wants to say with Taine : " Amusement is a French word and only finds its real meaning in Paris."

A.-M. Max.

★

THE PARIS THEATRES

ATHÉNÉE. Director : *Louis Jouvet*. Has introduced the work of Jean Giraudoux and Jules Romains to the public. Revives almost every year a play by a classical author, generally Molière. It has its own company and a new juvenile lead appears in each play. Scrupulous care is taken with regard to production and scenery.

AMBASSADEURS. Director: *Henri Bernstein*. Before the war this was Alice Cocéa's theatre. Its principal characteristic is its beautifully finished production. The most fashionable theatre in Paris. In addition to Bernstein's plays, its repertory includes adaptations of foreign plays as well as light comedy. No regular company, but excellent actors.

ANTOINE. Director : *Simone Berriau*. A theatre whose origin is due to a great actor, André Antoine, the founder of the " Free Theatre. " Has acquired new glamour since it began putting on Sartre's plays. Important revivals.

A.B.C. Director : *Mitty Goldin*. A large, popular theatre famed for its music-hall shows and topical revues, and presenting some of the leading singers and actors—Mistinguett, Yves Montand, etc.

ATELIER. Director : *André Barsacq*. Rose suddenly to fame under its former proprietor, Charles Dullin, who put on classical plays. Pre-eminently a literary theatre.

BOUFFES-PARISIENS. Director : *Willemetz*. Light, gay theatre. Operettas or light comedies, as " The J3," " Sébastien."

CAPUCINES. Director : *Raymond Massard.* Light revues. Polished production and luxurious settings.

CASINO DE PARIS. Great, spectacular revues. Dances, ballets. Always features a great star.

THÉATRE DES CHAMPS-ÉLYSÉES. Director : *Roger Eudes.* One of the largest and best-known theatres in Paris. Very good acoustics. Ballets, concerts and recitals are held there.

COMÉDIE DES CHAMPS-ÉLYSÉES. Directors : *Claude Sainval* and *Roland Piétri.* Never presents classical plays. Excellent modern repertory including Jean Anouilh, Philippe Hériat, etc. Little attention given to scenery, but generally presents good plays, well cast and performed by young actors.

STUDIO DES CHAMPS-ÉLYSÉES. Very small theatre. Rarely presents well-known French authors. Its plays are original, both from the point of view of subject and staging. Great success with the plays of Federico Garcia Lorca.

CHATELET. Director : *Maurice Lehman.* A theatre of great popular successes. Great attention given to production and scenery. Revolving stage. Operettas ("The White Horse Inn"). Children's plays ("Round the World in 80 Days "). Concerts on Saturdays and Sundays.

COMÉDIE FRANÇAISE.

Salle Richelieu. (Great National Theatre). Director : *Pierre-Aimé Touchard.* Has its own company. Presents only French classics. Considerable care expended on variety of scenery and perfection of costumes. Change of programme daily.

Salle Luxembourg. Same organisation as the Salle Richelieu, but specialises in modern plays that have been passed by a reading committee. Occasional revivals, after many years, of some " boulevard " plays that are considered worthy of ranking in the repertory of French classics.

ÉTOILE. Theatre of revues and music-hall. Always presents a great singer. A very popular theatre, possessing a promenade.

FOLIES-BERGÈRES. Director : *Jacques Derval.* Great spectacular revues, with infinite care given to production, scenery and costumes. Ballets.

GRAND GUIGNOL. An entertainment always consisting of four short plays—two comedies and two " blood-curdlers. " Realistic scenic effects.

GYMNASE. Theatre of the " boulevard " type. Had a great vogue before the war when Francen played dramatic comedies there. Nowadays revives Cocteau's plays.

HÉBERTOT. Director : *M. Hébertot.* High literary standard. Plays well-known authors (Cocteau, Montherlant, Steinbeck.) Launches juvenile leads (Gérard Philippe, Hélène Vercors). From time to time invites foreign companies. Generally considered to be in the vanguard of the artistic world.

LA BRUYÈRE. On the strength of " Branquignol," specialises in " crazy shows " and eccentric plays.

MADELEINE. Director : *André Brûlé.* Formerly belonged to Sacha Guitry. Light comedy and light plays in general, both French and foreign.

MARIGNY. Director : *Simone Volterra.* Let out to two principal companies, Jean-Louis Barrault and Roland Petit's ballets. Barrault's productions, though frequently open to discussion, often achieve undoubtedly fine results. Classical plays presented—Molière, Marivaux. Has recourse to the best artists in Paris for its stage décor, music and costumes. A regular company under the direction of Barrault and his wife, Madeleine Renaud, a great actress.

MATHURINS. Directors : *Jean Marchat* and *Marcel Herrand,* both actors and producers. Its plays are in the vanguard of the intellectual world.

MICHEL. Director : *Parysis.* Light plays.

MICHODIÈRE. Director : *Yvonne Printemps.* Interesting productions by Pierre Fresnay. Plays chosen to give alternative leads to Yvonne Printemps and Pierre Fresnay.

MOGADOR. Exclusively a theatre of great spectacular operettas.

MONTPARNASSE. Director : *Marguerite Jamois.* Before the war belonged to Gaston Baty who introduced a new type of stagecraft with striking lighting effects, steps leading into the auditorium, etc. Gave to this theatre a tone that Marguerite Jamois, who is also an actress, has sustained.

GAITÉ MONTPARNASSE. *Agnès Capri's* theatre. Let out to various companies.

GAITÉ LYRIQUE. Large spectacular operettas.

OPÉRA. State-aided theatre. Grand opera. Very renowned for its ballets. Great national lyrical theatre. First-class singers and orchestra.

OPÉRA-COMIQUE. State-aided theatre. Comic operas and ballets. Revivals of old ballets with new *décors*. Creation of new ballets.

PALAIS DE CHAILLOT. The largest theatre in Paris (2,700 seats). A people's theatre. Concerts, festivals, recitals, galas, classical matinées. Occasional performance, for a single evening, of new plays and operas.

NOCTAMBULES. Directors: *Pierre Leuris* and *Jean Claude.* The theatre of the Latin quarter. Small. Very varied repertory.

NOUVEAUTÉS. Director: *Benoit Léon Deutsch.* Light, witty comedies.

OEUVRE. Director: *Raymond Rouleau.* A theatre with its own public. Formerly belonged to the great actor Lugné-Poé. Intellectual plays—including Huxley and Priestley. Often present poets' successes such as those of Jules Supervielle. Poetry matinées. Very finished productions.

PALAIS-ROYAL. Specialises in "bedroom" plays. Very light vaudeville, often *risqué.* Has the reputation of being the prettiest theatre in Paris.

DE POCHE. Very small theatre. Very advanced plays, not seen anywhere else. Poetic dramas.

PORTE ST-MARTIN. Popular light comedy. Operettas.

POTINIÈRE. Director: *Martine de Breteuil.* Gay plays, French and foreign (Noel Coward).

RENAISSANCE. Director: *Jean Darcante*, a producer of note. The theatre is let to the Grenier-Hussenot company, specialising in a combination of farce and pantomine. Excellent stagecraft.

SAINT-GEORGES. Director: *Mary Morgan* (actress, and wife of the Mayor of Deauville). Very carefully chosen and elaborate plays.

VIEUX-COLOMBIER. Founder: *Jacques Copeau.* Director: *Émile Dars.* Has a school of dramatic art and presents its best pupils. Highly intellectual plays with a minimum of scenery. Plays by Thierry Maulnier, Marcel Aymé, T. S. Eliot, etc.

VERLAINE. Director: *Marie Valsamaki.* A little theatre. Very varied plays.

Printing completed
on July the 31st, 1950 by
Gaston Maillet and Co, printers,
Saint-Ouen (Seine)

IMPRESSION N⁰ 54 - DÉPOT LÉGAL - 3ᵉ TRIMESTRE 1950.